THE MYTH OF THE
AMERICAN SUPERHERO

THE MYTH OF THE AMERICAN SUPERHERO

John Shelton Lawrence
and
Robert Jewett

William B. Eerdmans Publishing Company
Grand Rapids, Michigan / Cambridge, U.K.

Wm. B. Eerdmans Publishing Co.
255 Jefferson Ave. S.E., Grand Rapids, Michigan 49503 /
P.O. Box 163, Cambridge CB3 9PU U.K.

Printed in the United States of America

06 05 04 03 02 01   7 6 5 4 3 2 1

Library of Congress Cataloging-in-Publication Data

Lawrence, John Shelton.
    The myth of the American superhero / John Shelton Lawrence and Robert Jewett.
        p.   cm.
    Includes bibliographical references and index.
    ISBN 0-8028-4911-3 (alk. paper)
    1. Popular culture — United States.   2. Heroes in mass media.
    3. Heroes — United States — Folklore.   4. National characteristics, American.
    5. United States — Civilization.   6. United States — Intellectual life.
    7. Heroes — Political aspects — United States.
    8. Political culture — United States.   I. Jewett, Robert.   II. Title.

E169.12 L36 2002
973 — dc21
2002023825

www.eerdmans.com

For
   Ellen, Eric, and Jennifer

Contents

I OVERTURE

1 The American Monomyth in a New Century

As the United States approached the year 2000, waves of anxiety and hope crested. The technologically informed had worries that decades of short-sighted computer programming would allow the Y2K bug to deliver lethal bites, inflicting random damage on our economy and essential services. Citizens had few hopes that government would provide wise policies, suspecting instead that its own aged, behemoth systems would themselves collapse. Believers who viewed the calendar through a millennial lens thought that the Rapture might finally be at hand. Titles such as *Revelations 2000: Your Guide to Biblical Prophecy for the New Millennium* and *Spiritual Survival During the Y2K Crisis* appeared in bookstores alongside Pat Robertson's *End of the Age* and Paul Meyer's *The Third Millennium*. The popular Rapture-based fantasies, launched in 1995 by Tim LaHaye and Jerry Jenkins' *Left Behind: A Novel of the Earth's Last Days,* dominated the religious best-seller lists and brought forth a series of successors, such as *Tribulation Force: The Continuing Drama of Those Left Behind.* By mid-2001, the number of *Left Behind* end-time products sold — including millennial materials for children — reached 39 million.[1] There seemed to be widespread solace in the idea that we were not writing — could not write — the script of our national destiny and that a divine hand would wipe clean the social slate, saving a righteous few who would no longer bear historical responsibility.

At this moment of despair came a stylish film that combined the themes of computer dystopia and messianic deliverance — in effect, a Rapture away from America's computer-designed hell. *The Matrix,*[2] released in mid-1999, gives us a vision of our planet as redesigned to serve the tyranny of machines directed by malevolent artificial intelligences. Humans think they can disable these solar-powered dictators by blasting the atmosphere into a sooty darkness. But the "Agents," as they are called, respond by tightening their control. Humans are imprisoned in power plants that extract their heat; the bodies of the dead are recycled to feed the barely living. Yet there is hope in this situation. A person named Thomas Anderson works at the Metacortex Corporation as a lowly programmer in a Dilbert-style cubicle. Because of the clever virtual reality created by "the Matrix," Thomas has been unaware of his subjugation and its resulting illusions. But he has shown a resisting spirit of freedom by computer hacking and selling secrets. And this leads to the call from an otherworldly figure named Morpheus, who believes that Thomas is "the One" who can liberate humanity. After a period of testing and a rebirth with powers that permit him to fight the Agents, the newly christened "Neo" (no longer the doubting Thomas) is joined by a beautiful, previously rebirthed young woman named Trinity, who becomes his partner in world redemption. In a final battle, where these two haul an arsenal of weapons into the Matrix headquarters, Neo and Trinity float, fly, fire their weapons, and deliver bone-smashing kicks. In one moment, Thomas-Neo dies, is resurrected by Trinity's virtuous kiss, and then fights with magical fury. He catches flying bullets and enters the body of one of the Agents, exploding him. Then, once he has defeated the last Agent, Neo ascends into the heavens.

The Matrix quickly became a cult film. It ran for months in theaters after reports of earning $50 million in its first weekend, then quickly migrated to VCR and DVD formats for private screenings. A *Matrix*-themed video game and film sequels were on the drawing boards within a few months of its initial

After saving humanity from the Matrix, Neo (Keanu Reeves) looks heavenward before flying into the sky.
Credit: *The Matrix* © Warner Brothers Studios, 1999.

triumph. The story became the locus for numerous fan commentaries and discussions that enthusiastically worked out parallels between the Bible's language and events and those of the film. Other fans developed online versions of *Matrix* stories that project its heroism into new situations.

Less surprising than the outsized success of this tale of apocalyptic redemption is its conformity to an American formula of the standard superheroic character. Like the violent film roles developed by Sylvester Stallone, Arnold Schwarzenegger, Chuck Norris, Clint Eastwood, and Steven Seagal, among others, Keanu Reeves's Neo and Carrie Moss's Trinity are lonely, selfless, sexless beings who rescue an impotent and terrorized community. Early in Neo's training for world liberation, he is required to ignore a pretty woman in a red dress. And in their gun-toting relationship, Trinity and Neo behave as chastely as do the terminal loners Dana Scully and Fox Mulder of *The X-Files*. Neo's passion, perhaps the first of his life, becomes his zeal for the mission of world rescue.

These motifs of superheroic redemptive violence become significant points of departure in tracking American mythology because their predictability opens the doors to our sensibilities. As John Cawelti persuasively suggests, "Strongly conventionalized narrative types . . . are so widely appealing because they enable people to re-enact and temporarily resolve widely shared psychic conflicts." Invention in the dramatic realm strives after a statement of unique personal vision, while conventions "assert an ongoing continuity of values. . . ."[3] Our concern lies with these ritualized mythic plots because they suggest important clues about the tensions, hopes, and despair concerning democracy within the current American consciousness.

The Classical Monomyth

But, the reader may wonder, are these stories of heroic violence unique to America? Why do we suggest that American culture has generated a novel pattern of narrative? Not initially convinced ourselves, we tested our intuition about the American patterns by turning to one of the major studies of world mythology, Joseph Campbell's *The Hero with a Thousand Faces*. There we find a provocative description of the archetypal plot for heroic action in traditional mythologies. The *classical monomyth*, as Campbell called it, offers this story pattern:

A hero ventures forth from the world of common day into a region of supernatural wonder: fabulous forces are there encountered and a decisive victory is won: the hero comes back from this mysterious adventure with the power to bestow boons on his fellow man.[4]

One can find examples of this plot in the stories of Prometheus stealing fire from the gods to benefit mankind, of Ulysses undergoing his adventurous journey, of Aeneas visiting the underworld to discover the destiny of the nation he would found, of St. George and the dragon, and of Hansel and Gretel. Campbell incorporates myths, legends, and the fairy tales of many cultures into this framework, suggesting that the archetype is molded according to rites of initiation, in which persons depart from their community, undergo trials, and later return to be integrated as mature adults who can serve in new ways. We see this training for permanent social responsibility as an important benchmark in assessing the American pattern in heroic mythmaking. Since this aspect of the classical plot is not typically present in the popular materials of contemporary America, many analysts of myth have concluded simply that we have become a postmythical culture. The psychoanalyst Rollo May even argued that some of our cultural distresses can be traced to the absence of any mythic system whatsoever.

We disagree. The widespread current enthusiasm for materials such as *The Matrix, Rambo, Touched by an Angel,* and the *Star Trek, Star Wars,* and *Left Behind* franchises indicates that Americans have not moved beyond mythical consciousness. Moreover the form of the classical monomyth, with its symbolic call for lifetime service to a community's institutions, allows us to highlight its absence in the distinctive pattern of what we call here the *American monomyth.* Although there are significant variations, the following archetypal plot formula may be seen in thousands of popular-culture artifacts:

> A community in a harmonious paradise is threatened by evil; normal institutions fail to contend with this threat; a selfless superhero emerges to renounce temptations and carry out the redemptive task; aided by fate, his decisive victory restores the community to its paradisiacal condition; the superhero then recedes into obscurity.

Whereas the classical monomyth seemed to reflect rites of initiation, the American monomyth derives from tales of redemption. It secularizes the Judaeo-Christian dramas of community redemption that have arisen on American soil, combining elements of the selfless servant who impassively gives his life for others and the zealous crusader who destroys evil. The supersaviors in pop culture function as replacements for the Christ figure,

The apocalyptic *Left Behind* book series, launched in 1995, has established new sales records with the release of each new title.
Credit: © Tyndale House Publishers, 1995.

whose credibility was eroded by scientific rationalism. But their superhuman abilities reflect a hope for divine, redemptive powers that science has never eradicated from the popular mind. Figures such as Neo in *The Matrix* seem explicitly designed to offer contemporary moviegoers this new Christ — one who has dropped the ineffectual baggage of the Sermon on the Mount. Instead, he and his shooting partner Trinity carry a duffel bag full of pistols, guns, and explosives needed to destroy the command center of political evil.

Such stories and their power to evoke admiration from laDrge audiences have led us to explore some paradoxes associated with these American superheroic fantasies. Why, for example, in an era of sexual liberation, do we still have heroes marked by sexual renunciation? And why, amid so many signs of secularization, do large audiences entertain so many fantasies of redemption by supernatural powers? And why, in a country trumpeting itself as the world's supreme democratic model, do we so often relish depictions of impotent democratic institutions that can be rescued only by extralegal superheroes? Are these stories safety valves for the stresses of democracy, or do they represent a yearning for something other than democracy? And why do women and people of color, who have made significant strides in civil rights, continue to remain almost wholly subordinate in a mythscape where communities must almost always be rescued by physically powerful white men?

Whether one recognizes these as paradoxes or not, and whatever the intent of their creators, the emotional power of the monomythic narratives for a substantial part of the populace is undeniable. The premise of our book is that the vitality of democracy and a full understanding of contemporary religious consciousness depend on an intensive examination of these heroic-redemptive images in popular culture.

Technomythic Development

The modern stories of superheroic redemption arose in conjunction with evolving technologies of presentation that function to preserve their currency and aura of credibility. The format changes of *The Virginian*, an important early-twentieth-century mythic tale, offer an excellent reminder. This archetypal epic of the private gun and the law by Owen Wister began its career as a printed book in 1902. Cecil B. De Mille gave the book its first silent-film treatment in 1914; in that version audiences had to read the Virginian's response to Trampas's insult as a screen caption: "When you call me that — SMILE." By 1929, *The Virginian* had become a sound film, and moviegoers heard those same words spoken with Gary Cooper's cool defiance. In 1946, the movie was remade in color. In 1959, the publisher Gilberton issued the text in comic-book format as a Classic Illustrated (No. 150). Then, in 1962, *The Virginian* became a serialized television production that lasted nine seasons. *The Virginian*-as-novel took on an electronic textual form when the Gutenberg Project published it in 1998 as a downloadable file. And in 2000, *The Virginian*-as-film was recast once again for a world premiere on the TNT cable network. Because remarkable technological advances of this sort in computers, film, and television have enhanced the apparent realism of myth, we have chosen to call our method *technomythic* critical theory. We hope to bring the magic props at least temporarily to the foreground for critical reflection.

To understand our current situation, it is essential for us to take account of voluntary behavior changes that derive from complex webs of motivation and fashion so common in pop culture. The religious quality of such actions has seldom been taken seriously, in part because the artifacts of popular culture that inspire them are not explicitly religious. Cultural interpreters such as Herbert Gans have argued that popular culture merely provides "a temporary respite from everyday life," passing "in one eye and out the other." He also contends that people "use the media for diversion and would not think of applying its content to their lives."[5] In contrast, we believe, with William G. Doty, that "rituals, symbols, and myths establish conservative benchmarks, but at the same time, they anticipate *forms of the future* as they determine and shape ideals and goals for both individual and society."[6] Among those "forms of the future" are the developing styles of religious confession in pop culture's spiritual marketplace. Narratives of superheroic redemption have become occasions for confessional statements of personal transformation and new trajectories of life meaning.

The Werther Effect

In searching out relevant historical precedents and categories to explain fans' imitative behavior, we were struck by an important moment in eighteenth-century Europe. In 1774, Johann Wolfgang von Goethe published a novel that became an important landmark of popular culture in the era of mass-produced literature. Entitled *The Sorrows of Young Werther,* it is the story of a sensitive young man who, thwarted in his passion for a young woman, commits suicide. Within a decade of this novel's publication it had become an international sensation: it was published in many versions and translations, and it evoked hundreds of imitations. S. P. Atkins explains:

> Novelists, playwrights, poets, composers, choreographers, and iconographers ranging from reputable painters and illustrators to anonymous wax workers, all unrestrained by laws of copyright and inspired by their own or others' interest in Goethe's popular novel, quickly appropriated its themes to their peculiar talents. In addition, the cult of Werther was exploited by the trade: *eau de Werther* was sold, and Charlotte and Werther figures . . . as familiar and ubiquitous as Mickey Mouse or Donald Duck today, appeared on fans and gloves, on bread boxes and jewelry, on delicate Meissen porcelain. . . .[7]

The imitation of the Werther character also led to more alarming results in that romantic era. Walter Kaufmann points out that "all over Europe large numbers of young people committed suicide with a copy of the book clutched in their hands or buried in a pocket."[8] Suicide notes referred explicitly to Goethe's novel. In one particularly dramatic case, the young Fanni von Ickstatt leaped to her death from the tower of the Munich Frauenkirche. The unfortunate Goethe was accused of being responsible for this death by a host of preachers and lecturers. One lecturer, Johann Georg Prandl, wrote verses bemoaning her death and condemning Goethe. Goethe was alarmed at the incredible uproar over his novel and its unforeseen impact. Indeed, during his first trip to Italy, where he was both feted and condemned as the author of *The Sorrows of Young Werther,* he expressed the wish that he could destroy his creation.[9] It had apparently taken on a life of its own. Two centuries later, William Shatner and Leonard Nimoy as Kirk and Spock of *Star Trek* would experience similar moments of estrangement from their admirers.

When an artifact enters the arena of popular culture and assumes its own existence in the imagination of fans, a powerful though elusive process begins. We can hardly sort out the causal and motivational influences in the Werther-related suicides. However, they illustrate an interesting interplay between fantasy and reality that begins to obliterate any clear distinction between mere entertainment and seriously contemplated life purposes. Goethe's novel was inspired by an actual suicide, that of K. W. Jerusalem, and also by Goethe's own frustrated passion for Charlotte Buff. The novel, in turn, inspired public interest in the life of K. W. Jerusalem, leading to a published biography of him by another author. But once Goethe's novel captured the popular imagination, a fantasy process had begun that resulted in a wide variety of imitations and personal identifications with the heroes. This process of behavior alteration has its closest analogues in religious ethics, but the particular artifact inspiring it is not itself religious.[10]

We propose to call this paradoxical and elusive result a *Werther effect.* In the Werther effect an audience member (a) experiences a work of fantasy within a secular context that (b) helps to shape the reader/viewer's sense of what is real and desirable, in such a way that, (c) the reader/viewer takes actions consistent with the vision inspired by the interaction between his own fantasy and that popular entertainment. A Werther effect appears to be a form of voluntary behavioral change produced by interaction with a powerful artifact of popular culture. It can be a religiously tinged ethical impulse, within a nonreligious context, that occurs regardless of the intent of the artifact's creators. A Werther effect characteristically embodies a redefinition of the boundary between fact and fantasy.

Throughout this book we will identify *Werther*-like imitative behaviors inspired by materials such as the *Star Trek* television series, Buffalo Bill's Wild West, the *Death Wish* and *Rambo* films, some recent video games, and *The*

Turner Diaries. However, we do not intend to take the censorious line of Goethe's critics: one cannot eliminate fantasy processes by banning works that may have inspired them. The complex interaction between individual imaginations and popular artifacts should instead be brought to consciousness and subjected to balanced criticism.

In the past, puritanical types with keen noses for idolatry have sniffed the religious aura of pop culture. Savonarola ranted against popular entertainments with the same arguments as did Puritan divines in revolutionary New England. They fervently hoped to ban the festivals and theatrical troupes that they felt popularized subversive forms of behavior — polluting the imagination of the faithful. "Christian" in *Pilgrim's Progress* received his most severe testing at "Vanity Fair," where worldly diversions and illicit relations were hawked. Religious zealots throughout American history have promoted bans against the insidious influences of popular culture. From the prohibitions against theaters and pictorial art in colonial days to the recent campaigns against X-rated films, the ire of the faithful has burned against what was perceived as a corrupt, competitive religion. The raging reformers correctly perceived the presence of youth-formative influences under the innocent guise of mere entertainment. But their repressive strategy simply rendered them powerless to deal with the fantasies that appealed to the popular mind. The censorious approach eliminated the possibility of public discussion about fantasy and behavior essential to the health of both the individual and society.

As we have worked out our understanding of the interplay between mythic fantasy and democratic political ideals in this book, we have conceived of its structure in a musical fashion. Section II, "Composing the Mythic Score," looks at the interplay between American historical experiences and fictional reinterpretations of them in the form of heroic tales. The most crucial formations occurred in the early twentieth century with classics such as Owen Wister's *The Virginian,* D. W. Griffith's film *The Birth of a Nation,* and the Swiss story *Heidi.* The *Heidi* narrative offers us the female version of heroism in response to democratic crises — the psychological manipulator; it received one of its clearest expressions in the television adaptation of Laura Ingalls Wilder's *Little House on the Prairie* series of children's books. We devote an entire chapter to Buffalo Bill and his energetic efforts at mythic self-aggrandizement, including the Wild West show, which dramatized America's transition from internal conquest to imperial competition with Europe's great powers.

Section III, "Dancing the Myth of Redemption," looks at the persistent "Werther invitations" — seemingly intentional calls to emulate a fantasy model — in popular materials and some notable cases where the call seems answered. Increasing the scope of community and public institutions with each chapter, we begin with the small town and John Wayne's killing persona in *The Shootist*. A real-life sheriff who embodied the Wayne vision and some of Buffalo Bill's publicity skill was Sheriff Buford Pusser, who parlayed his violent battles into several successful *Walking Tall* movies. Turning to the mythic cityscape, we look at Charles Bronson's durable *Death Wish* series, full of Werther invitations, and Bernard Goetz, New York City's subway vigilante, who was dubbed "the *Death Wish* killer" by the local media. Moving toward the national level, we examine some pop culture attempts to give superheroic powers to a real president, Abraham Lincoln, and to an imaginary one, Judson Hammond, a screen creation who thrilled both William Randolph Hearst and FDR. We also look at two fictional screen presidents from *Independence Day* and *Air Force One* — both of whom take on physically heroic roles. At the abstract level of purging institutions, we look at Theodore Kaczynski, the "Unabomber," as well as Timothy McVeigh, principal bomber of the federal building in Oklahoma City, who responded to the zealous mythic call of William Pierce's book *The Turner Diaries*.

Section IV, "Hymns and Creeds of the American Monomyth," reviews the remarkable range of thematic territories where the mythic score could be performed. In the realm of children's entertainments, we examine the Disney animated cartoons from their earliest beginnings through the triumphant drama of monarchy's rightful restoration in *The Lion King*. Following further the theme of moralized technologies for juvenile control and destruction, we recount the history of video games, from their prenarrative screen blips through their ultra-realistic simulations — games that invite youthful hands to hold and shoot heroically destructive guns. Finally, with *Star Trek's* assorted crews venturing forth four centuries from now, we can view the future's frontier of intergalactic space as the scene for ascetic superheroism under military command. Reflecting further on *Star Trek's* devoted followers, we begin to explore some ways in which the American monomyth is giving rise to new forms of confessional faith. Within fan movements we find individuals claiming new orientations for their lives derived from their encounters with mythic materials. Another focus of pop faith is the *Star Wars* series of films. George Lucas, a friend and follower of Joseph Campbell who tells stories of restored hereditary elites, has developed a kind of religious guru status in American culture, indeed, has even attracted the admiring attention of culture critic Bill Moyers. Campbell and Moyers, like most Americans, are cheerfully oblivious to the implications of superheroism and the aristocratic political values in the materials they celebrate. We conclude our section with the notion of "credotainment," confessional movements based upon entertainment products.

In Section V, "Cadenza: Searching for Democratic Melodies," we listen to the music of catastrophe for the moral and political formulas of the disaster film genre from *Jaws* to the recent Revelation-inspired *Left Behind* series. The artificiality of these cinematic spectacles becomes especially apparent when they are juxtaposed to the moral and heroic complexity that surfaced in the September 11 attacks. In our concluding chapter, we focus on the dangers to democracy in attempts at enacting mythic scenarios, using Oliver North, Jr.'s appropriation of *Rambo* themes as a case in point. We also pose some paradoxes associated with creative culture. Can a democracy generate popular entertainments that celebrate its own core values? We answer in the affirmative by suggesting that films such as *Glory* (1989), *Dead Man Walking* (1995), and *The Straight Story* (1999) embody recognizable but regrettably rare democratic ideals of heroism. We also speculate about the possibility that the forms of heroism with September 11 and the anthrax attacks may contribute to cultural evolution beyond the dominant pattern of the last century.

In seeking a precise grasp of monomythic content, we occasionally compare popular materials with items drawn from what is sometimes called "high culture" — usually the pop culture of an earlier era. We do not mean to suggest that classical literature is always superior to current pop material in its insights, or that the two realms should be kept in hermetically sealed compartments. Both high and popular culture can show self-conscious attentiveness to the myths of their time, each revealing them in distinctive ways. For the vigor of each and the health of the larger culture that contains them both, we suggest that it is preferable that they be responsive to one another.

In this connection we think of a delightful example of contemporary mythic awareness in the recent Claymation film *Chicken Run* (2000),[11] from Great Britain: it both tweaks our American heroic myths and humorously reaffirms democratic mythology. The movie tells the story of an English chicken farm administered by the Tweedys, who run it much like Stalag 17, a World War II German POW camp defined for popular culture by the 1953 film bearing its name. The weary, oppressed chickens are responsive to the plucky Ginger: they accept her belief that "there's a better place out there" — a "fowl Eden," so to speak — and constantly plot their escape despite repeated punishment. Their revolution is ever so timely because the vicious Mrs. Tweedy has tired of administering her hungry flock for mere eggs and wants to run every last one of them through her newly acquired, infernal chicken-pot-pie machine.

An early hope on the horizon comes in the form of the flying Rocky, the

American rooster who miraculously lands in their barnyard. He boasts that he can not only fly but can teach the hapless hens his remarkable skill. Rocky's super power of flight turns out to be a fraud, an illusion that he has exploited after being accidentally shot into the Tweedy chicken space by a circus cannon. When the truth becomes evident, he sneaks away alone — but not without a residue of guilt and a love for Ginger that will bring him back on more honest terms. After Rocky returns, the group accepts the fact that freedom will be possible only through their cooperation and assigned responsibilities. Drawing on the knowledge of fussy old Colonel Fowler (of the R.A.F.) and the pilfered technologies from a couple of thieving rats, the team builds a flying machine that transports them to a promised land, where Rocky and Ginger settle down with the happy community. This fantasy wittily undercuts the redemptive premise of superheroism while affirming the values of collective intelligence, shared responsibility, and the integration of leaders with the communities they assist. As a commercially successful story, it demonstrates the inventiveness of popular culture in producing self-critical perspectives that need not be apologetic in the presence of "high culture's" folklore, literature, and theater.

In any event, our concern is with content and mythic relevance rather than the aesthetic merit of the pop culture artifacts we examine. Our method is ethical and historical. We submit our interpretive techniques, developed from our experience with philosophical, classical, and biblical texts, in the hope that they will serve democratic ethical ideals.

We should make one final comment about the relative importance of the American monomyth compared to other issues faced by the nation. Internationally, we confront wars, terrorism, poverty, famines, epidemics, environmental degradation, and other sources of human suffering; domestically, drug abuse, crime and law enforcement, economic inequality, and resource scarcity are just a few among problems we struggle with daily. Compared to these, a particular mythic pattern in our entertainments will seem to have a lesser urgency. Yet the monomyth's emotional affinity for superheroic redemption may make all such policy problems more intractable. Effective policies require consensus and a solid institutional framework that operates according to publicly accepted laws. We cannot afford to wring our hands, waiting for a Superman or a Heidi to fix our problems.

As we write late in 2001, there are increasing signs that in international affairs the nation is tempted to move with mythic footsteps toward "cowboy" stances. Before the attacks of September 11, the U.S. government took steps to paralyze multilateral efforts to face several issues of international concern: on the environmental front, it renounced the nation's earlier commitment to the

Popular culture often frames U.S. policy issues. When George W. Bush announced that he wanted Osama bin Laden "dead or alive," he may have been reprising the television experience of his youthful years.

Credit: Publicity photo with Steve McQueen, the bounty hunter of "Wanted: Dead or Alive," CBS, 1958-1961.

Kyoto Protocol on Global Warming; it stalled on the Biological Weapons Convention designed to restrain chemical and biological warfare; the U.S. Senate curtly rejected any attempt at moving forward with the Comprehensive Test Ban Treaty; the Bush administration threatens to abandon the Anti-Ballistic Missile Treaty of 1972, with its allied arms-control regimen of the Outer Space Treaty, and the Non-Proliferation Treaty. Instead of these diplomatic agreements, the U.S. government proposes a National Missile Defense, which it proposes to "share" with other countries by offering to shield them. A sentimental thread running through these unilateral thrusts is the expectation that others can see our dominating military power as motivated by purely defensive objectives that will protect the innocent. While critics in other countries view such sentiments as self-deluding, they are perfectly consistent with the image of the selfless superhero encouraged by our most popular entertainments.

Some of our mythic certainties about the special and favored place of America in the world came to expression with the surprise attacks of September 11 at the World Trade Center and the Pentagon and the anthrax terrorism that followed. The official interpretation of these tragic losses has carried an American mythic stamp from the very first moments. Divorcing the events from any connection with U.S. policies, President George W. Bush stated that "America was targeted for attack because we're the brightest beacon for free-

British film makers for *Chicken Run*
parodied the American superhero
in this pre-release poster.
Credit: © Dreamworks SKG, 2000.

dom and opportunity in the world."[12] Taunting the adversary Osama bin Laden, the President embraced a stark, dualistic, and triumphal world view in promising that "this will be a monumental struggle of good versus evil. But good will prevail."[13] Senator John McCain, impatient with the slowly developing military response in the weeks after September 11, echoed the jihadic perspective in calling for a relentless war. With a grim eloquence, he exhorted the nation's leaders to "shed a tear, and then get on with the business of killing our enemies as quickly as we can, and as ruthlessly as we must."[14] While the simplicity of myth and the prospect of vengeance offer special comforts in a time of mass murder, the notion of destroying evil on a worldwide basis may draw us toward spiraling conflicts that we can never hope to control.

Counterbalancing elements of democratic hope in this situation have emerged in a new recognition that America's safety requires it to cooperate with a community of nations. Moreover, President George W. Bush has been courageous in his stances warning against ethnic and religious stereotyping of Arabs and Muslims as a betrayal of democratic respect for minorities.

In our current situation, we believe that examining the American monomyth — the endlessly repeated story of innocent communities besieged by evil outsiders — can help us gain a better perspective on the dangers we face. We invite readers to join in our venture of studying the national mythos. It was never more timely to project our fantasies onto a mirror that renders them with less distortion.

II COMPOSING THE MYTHIC SCORE

In musical composition, creators set down a permanent score that invites repeated performance. The great makers of myth in the past century perfected an American story formula that could be told and then retold to audiences numbering in the hundreds of millions. The stuff of this distinctive American mythic creation came from experiences in rebelling against the English, oppressing slaves, conquering Indians, settling the ever-receding frontier, and finally grasping for imperial power at the end of the nineteenth century. Men and women, with their changing affinities, complementarities, and polarities, were the melodic lines running through these historical events. Chapter 2, "The Birth of a National Monomyth," describes the interplay between these events and the fantasies through which they could be viewed from a more stirring, heroic perspective. Chapter 3, "Buffalo Bill: Staging World Redemption," shows how a clever actor in history could parlay his role into a world-popular celebration of heroic conquest with his Wild West show. Chapter 4, "Heidi Visits a *Little House on the Prairie*," introduces the dulcet tune of feminine redemption: women save recalcitrant individuals and troubled communities with their sweet psychological manipulations in a story tradition that remains alive with the *Touched by an Angel* television series. But this role was not limited to women, as the Pa Ingalls character proved in the long-running *Little House on the Prairie* TV program based loosely and sentimentally on the grittier novels of Laura Ingalls Wilder.

" ' For my sake,' she begged him, ' for my sake.' "

As the American superheroic myth was beginning to form, men still held earnest discussions with their romantic partners about the need for extralegal violence. Here Molly pleads with the Virginian not to face a shootout with Trampas.

Credit: Illustration by Arthur I. Keller in Owen Wister's *The Virginian: A Horseman of the Plains* © 1902.

2 The Birth of a National Monomyth

"It is hard for us, bred on science and rationalism, to grasp how fearsome, how magical, the universe appeared to earlier societies, how full of wonders and portents it was. It could only be controlled by men and women larger than life. Heroes were necessary both as gods and as a part of the ritual that kept the external world secure and tolerable. . . . But epic heroes such as these essentially belong to rural worlds, to societies living near the wilderness. And no wonder then that they are dying, particularly in the Western world, where nature has become benign."

J. H. Plumb, "Disappearing Heroes" (1974)[1]

Reputable scholars such as J. H. Plumb have repeatedly announced the death of mythic heroes with magical powers to redeem the world. This reveals a peculiar analytic lag, because it was written in the heyday of superheroic dramas in popular culture. Thousands of images of heroes and heroines larger than life, with powers every bit as magical as those exercised in classical mythology, were floating about in the American entertainment system, yet they appear to have been unrecognizable to sophisticated minds. Since the traditional, classical mythology was no longer popular, its replacement by a new story form could not be grasped. Perhaps the visual appearance of the modern superheroes and -heroines made them so familiar in everyday life that they simply became invisible. More likely, the seedy products of pop culture, produced for profit and entertainment, lacked the sheen that had been gained by traditional myths, hallowed by centuries of serious scholarship. One thing is certain, in our view: mythology's death notices were greatly exaggerated, to use the phrase of Mark Twain. We therefore provide some of the details that an obituary concerning the allegedly deceased should include.

The Myth of Eden in the American Imagination

Tales of the American monomyth typically begin and end in Eden-like settings. We see small communities of diligent agrarians, townspeople, or members of a work group together in harmony. Then a disruption occurs, one that calls into question the effectiveness of the institutions designed to cope with such challenges. Because those institutions and their leaders conspicuously fail, the mythic vision dictates with clarity that a superhero must act before any likeness of Eden can be restored. Although a few women have taken on heroic stature in the nonviolent stories, the hero is typically a male. *Star Wars* begins in a small farming community on Tatooine, where Luke Skywalker dutifully helps his aunt and uncle on their subsistence farm. Disney's *Lion King* presents us with the newborn cub prince Simba, who lives in a violence-free interspecies paradise until a wicked uncle contrives the death of his father. Simba must endure exile before returning for a miraculous restoration of his own kingship. And the *Star Trek* television series and films have now given us decades of opening scenes with cheerfully bantering crew members on the antiseptic bridge of the peaceful *Enterprise* or the *Voyager*. Suddenly an evil face appears on the screen or a mysterious force seizes their ship, shattering this technological idyll. After the crisis is resolved, the starship is shown back on course, the computer-assisted Eden temporarily restored.

In all these artifacts the state of harmony is the source from which the drama springs, as well as the goal of its resolution. The *monomythic Eden* has distinctive features: it is neither the pure state of nature — the rustic world of small farms and plantations — nor the urban metropolis. It is a small, well-organized community whose distinguishing trait is the absence of lethal internal conflict arising from its members; the surrounding pastoral realm echoes its inner harmony. The citizens are law-abiding and cooperative, without those extremes of economic, political, or sexual desires that might provoke confrontations. A cheerful atmosphere pervades the homogeneous populace, and there is no hint of a tendency on the part of the majority toward evil. If there are evil individuals in the community, they are clearly differentiated by behavior, dress, and physical appearance. The majority's only failing is its impotence in the face of the evil of others.

The obvious model for this monomythic Eden is the Midwestern small town as seen through the lens of pastoralism. Yet, if we examine it more closely, small-town life in the American heartland has hardly been Edenic. Frequent crop failures, depressions, fluctuations in population, and conflicts over school, church, and civic administration have been endemic to Main Street, U.S.A. Farmers commit suicide, murder, adultery, and incest — unpleasant realities set forth with grim realism in Jane Smiley's novel *A Thousand Acres* (later made into a movie). One need only read the novels of Sinclair Lewis to get a sense of the undercurrents of small-town life in early twentieth-century America. Pressures for social and moral conformity cause considerable unhappiness. It is thus unlikely that the monomythic image of a small-town paradise could have arisen from practical experience. This raises the question: how did this myth arise?

Charles L. Sanford's study *The Quest for Paradise* suggests that "the Edenic myth . . . has been the most powerful and comprehensive organizing force in American culture."[2] The myth arose with the discovery of the New World, long before the actual settlement of the continent. Sanford traces this quest for paradise in early tales of exploration and cites Christopher Columbus's conviction that "there is the terrestrial paradise" newly discovered in America. He thus attributed the "innocent qualities of Adam and Eve" to the American Indians (pp. 39-40). Shortly before his last voyage, Columbus claimed the discovery of the new heaven and new earth mentioned in the Bible, placing the discovery of America as a decisive step toward the second coming of Christ and the establishment of the millennial kingdom.

This speculation fed the quest for El Dorado and stimulated Renaissance ideas about Arcadia and the recovery of the Golden Age. Erasmus's *In Praise of Folly* and More's *Utopia* take up these paradisiacal themes. The Reformation linked the quest for paradise even more explicitly with millennial hopes. Luther's *Second Commentary on the Book of Revelation* placed contemporaneous struggles with Catholicism in the penultimate phase of apocalyptic history, which would be followed shortly by a climactic battle and then the dawn of the millennial paradise.[3] These expectations were widely shared by American Puritans. Sanford concludes:

> The most popular doctrine in the colonies was that America had been singled out, from all the nations of the earth, as the site of the Second Coming; and that the millennium of the saints, while essentially spiritual in nature, would be accompanied by a paradisaic transformation of the earth as the outward symbol of their inward state. As Mather put it, "When this Kingdom of Christ has filled all the Earth, *this Earth will be restored to its Paradise state*."[4]

Studies of the American Puritans have shown that the expectation of paradise remained in the rather distant future. The wilderness symbolized temptation, threat, and adversity to early settlers. By 1693, Mather was suggesting that "Wilderness" was the stage "thro' which we are passing to the Promised Land."[5] The Puritans' pessimism about their own evil, as well as that long journey through the wilderness, tempered any tendency toward utopianism.[6]

The Edenic myth came to play a more powerful role in the next century among Enlightenment figures who abandoned the sense of omnipresent evil. Franklin and Jefferson, Sanford observes, combined the Puritan legacy of moral perfectionism with a remarkable confidence in America's Edenic potential. "The image of Paradise in the American myth of Eden has had its greatest development in the moral sphere. The superiority of the United States in quantitative achievements and political skills has consistently been blazoned forth in moral terms."[7] Franklin seems to have been serious when he called his proposed colony in Ohio the future "paradise on earth" (p. 125). In 1836, Thomas Cole proclaimed that "we are still in Eden; the wall that shuts us out of the garden is our own ignorance and folly."[8] Such minor impediments could be dealt with by education, social reforms, and moral endeavors, to which Americans in the first half of the nineteenth century turned with enormous optimism.

The belief in America's millennial destiny, optimism about human progress, and an increasing hope in the perfectibility of man contributed to the idea of America as "The Garden of the World." As Henry Nash Smith defines this image of the American West, "The master symbol of the garden embraced a cluster of metaphors expressing fecundity, growth, increase, and blissful labor in the earth, all centering about the heroic figure of the idealized frontier farmer. . . ."[9] Smith cites an 1827 statement by Timothy Flint that describes happy farmers raising their families "in peace, plenty and privacy, under the guardian genius of our laws. . . . Farmers and their children are strong, and innocent and moral almost of necessity" (p. 140). This mythic image of an agrarian Eden is constantly contrasted with cities, which "are the sores of the political body," as James B. Lanman put it in 1841 (p. 142). This image of the Edenic western garden became embodied in the Homestead Act of 1862, whose strongest appeal, according to Smith, "lay in the belief that it would enact by statute . . . the agrarian utopia of hardy and virtuous yeomen which had haunted the imaginations of writers about the West since the time of Crevecoeur" (p. 170).

The power of this mythic image of the West to disguise empirical reality is illustrated by the reinterpretation of the "Great American Desert" image of the high western plains during their settlement. The treeless region from

Kansas to the Dakotas, whose sparse rainfall had seemed forever to defy cultivation, was advertised as arable after the Civil War by the Department of the
Interior with the motto "Rain Follows the Plough." Farm vegetation and
newly planted trees would increase rainfall sufficiently to produce the promised Eden, according to the ad. David M. Emmons' study *Garden in the Grasslands* cites promotional literature that beckoned millions of immigrants to
the anticipated paradise. Union Pacific Railroad ads compared settlers to
Abraham, Columbus, and the Pilgrims, calling them "the advance column of
civilization . . . a peaceable, even tempered race, who hate war, love peace . . .
honor their wives, raise honest children, live within their income, and grow
rich out of Kansas soil." A Rock Island promotion explained: "It is the garden
spot of the world . . . because it will grow anything that any other country will
grow and with less work. Because it rains here more than in any other place,
and just at the right time," it is the ideal region to settle.[10]

It is scarcely credible today that claims about a rich and trouble-free
western paradise lived on even after most original homesteaders lost their
claims through adverse conditions. The myth was preserved in Western novels and films depicting small communities of peaceful and industrious citizens saved from thieves and blackguards by courageous cowboys. In fact, at
the very moment the Edenic myth was undergoing its most traumatic shock,
during the dust bowl days of the Great Depression, Walt Disney was fashion-
ing animated visions of paradise whose power is still apparent. In his classic
1937 cartoon *The Old Mill,* a fierce storm buffets the idyllic windmill and its
innocent animals just as the economic storms and dust bowl winds had been
striking the midwestern Eden. A loyal pair of birds had laid their eggs in a
gear hole of the unused mill, and the unusual winds drove the creaky wheel
with its great gears over and over — seemingly through the innocent nest. But
the magic of animation preserved the myth as the baby birds magically reappear in the imperiled nest when quiet descends at the end. The same vision
has remained popular at Disneyland in Anaheim, which offers "eternal fun,
infinite holiday and deathlessness — in short, an urbanized Eden," to use
John Seelye's words.[11]

The popular entertainments overlooked by Plumb and an entire generation of classical scholars attest to the virtual omnipresence of the Eden theme.
The decisive correlate to this nostalgic syndrome is a sense of loss, a conviction that the Eden Americans deserve to inhabit is now besieged by insoluble
problems. This theme of a threat to paradise is embodied in the second phase
of monomythic drama.

The Intruding, Evil Other

The action of the American monomyth always begins with a threat arising against Eden's calm. In the popular *Death Wish* films that originated in the 1970s, petty criminals threaten the voyagers from Eden. In *Star Trek's* original series, challenges arise from interplanetary baddies such as Romulans, Klingons, or aggressive gods. In *Star Trek's Next Generation* and *Voyager* series, the disturbances of harmony originate with forces such as the Borg or Q. In the blockbuster success *Jaws*, Amity Island's tranquility is shattered by the marauding supershark. Spiderman and Superman contend against criminals and spies just as the Lone Ranger puts down threats by greedy frontier gangs. Thus paradise is depicted as repeatedly under siege, its citizens pressed down by alien forces too powerful for democratic institutions to quell. When evil is ascendant, Eden becomes a wilderness in which only a superhero can redeem the captives.

The theme of a chosen people under attack emerged in one of the earliest forms of American literature, the Indian captivity narratives. Mary Rowlandson's *The Sovereignty & Goodness of God . . . a Narrative of the Captivity and Restauration,* first printed in 1682, remained popular for a century and a half, along with several similar stories that were bestsellers in colonial America.[12] Rowlandson was living "in prosperity, having the comforts of the world," oblivious of her shortcomings, when the Indian attack destroyed her family and carried her away into the night. Having resisted the temptations of Indian life, she was finally rescued and thus allowed to tell the story of "Israel in Babylon," to use Richard Slotkin's expression. The sense of the chosen people in an alien realm, under attack by the oppressive forces of a demonic Babylon, thus became a central theme in popular literature. "The great and continuing popularity of these narratives, the uses to which they were put, and the nature of the symbolism employed in them are evidence that the captivity narratives constitute the first coherent myth-literature developed in America for American audiences."[13]

The siege of paradise, expressed in the secular terminology of Thomas Jefferson, became central to the Declaration of Independence and America's perpetual pose of innocence: "But when a long Train of Abuses and Usurpations, pursuing invariably the same Object, evinces a Design to reduce them under absolute Despotism," it is the duty of a people to revolt. The Declaration enumerates the phases of this perfidious attack by an unjust King on the innocent colonists: "He has plundered our Seas, ravaged our Coasts, burnt our towns, and destroyed the Lives of our People . . . with circumstances of Cruelty and Perfidy, scarcely paralleled in the most barbarous Ages, and totally unworthy the Head of a civilized Nation." Jefferson portrays these attacks as totally unprovoked, evoking the mildest protestations suitable for a peaceful and law-abiding people: "In every stage of these Oppressions we have Petitioned for Redress in the most humble Terms: Our repeated Petitions have been answered only by repeated Injury."

The paradise and wilderness themes also play decisive roles in the *Leatherstocking* tales, where maidens are captured by aggressive Indians and peaceful frontier settlements are threatened by raiders. The Wild West shows dramatized these themes, showing log cabins and stagecoaches attacked by wild Indians. The dime novels of 1860-1893, which Henry Nash Smith analyzes, concentrated on "rescuing beautiful heroines from the Indians. When the Indians began to yield place in the dime novel to road agents or counterfeiters as the standard enemy, the hunters of the Leatherstocking type lend a hand in fighting the newer foes."[14]

At the root of this shift in the locus of evil was the inability of the western Eden to provide immunity from economic and natural disasters toward the end of the nineteenth century. Smith notes that

> the myths of the garden and of the empire had both affirmed a doctrine of progress. . . . Neither American man nor the American continent contained, under this interpretation, any radical defect or principle of evil. But other men and other continents . . . were by implication unfortunate or wicked. This suggestion was strengthened by the tendency to account for any evil which threatened the garden empire by ascribing it to alien intrusion. Since evil could not conceivably originate within the walls of the garden, it must by logical necessity come from without. . . . (p. 187)

A conspiracy theory thus emerged, projecting all evil outward upon others (or, in today's literary and theological terminology, "the Other"). Whereas Mary Rowlandson had believed her suffering to be a just punishment for her own sins and those of fellow colonists, the myth of an innocent public afflicted by evil foes from outside now began to crystallize. And heroic violence was required to confront these foes. A classic statement of this myth appeared in an early film by D. W. Griffith, appropriately entitled *The Birth of a Nation*.[15]

The opening scene of Griffith's 1915 classic is thoroughly Edenic, depicting plantation owner Ben Cameron gently stroking a pair of puppies. As Gerald Mast observes, "Significantly one of the puppies is black and the other white; also significant is the fact that a kitten soon begins to play with the pups. The animals become visual metaphors for the prewar South's happy mixture of different races and different social classes."[16] The film depicts the Civil War, having been fomented by evil abolitionists who favored miscegenation, as breaking this innocent idyll. As Mast says, "All the evil in the film is instigated by three people" — the abolitionist Austin Stoneman, the mulatto demagogue Silas Lynch, and the "renegade Negro" Gus, whose rape of a young white girl is pivotal. These three seduced others into the evil of the war (p. 86).

The siege of innocent citizens is portrayed through a brilliant series of innovative film techniques that mark *The Birth of a Nation* as a milestone in film history. Film theorists Kinder and Houston note that *The Birth of a Nation* "developed innovations specifically suited to express a dualistic conception of the world."[17] Griffith skillfully blended close-ups, crosscutting, iris shots, split-screen juxtapositions, and unusual camera positions to produce both realism and suspense in the conflict between stereotypical forces of good and evil. One might say that he invented mythic cueing, or at least employed its devices with unprecedented impact. He and his associates discovered "the value of a detail not only as a narrative, attention-getting device, but also as a means of suggesting poetic significance."[18] Despite *Birth of a Nation*'s inflammatory social content, the American Film Institute in 1998 gave it a rank of 44th in its list of "the greatest 100 American movies."[19]

Thus the plight of the innocent South at the hands of carpetbaggers and depraved blacks is conveyed by riotous street scenes, close-ups of lecherous looks at white women, and scenes of war devastation. The mulatto Gus chases Flora Cameron to her death while the camera shifts back and forth from her desperate face to his leering eyes and pursuing body. Griffith used remarkable film-cutting techniques to build the suspense of a concluding scene in which Elsie Stoneman is being forced into marriage with the repulsive mulatto Lynch in the carpetbagger's office. Tension between absolute good and absolute evil is built by short scenes that flash between their two faces and then outside to the gathering Klansmen.

The redemptive resolution provided by these galloping Klansmen derives from a tradition extending back to the Indian captivity tales. When the siege brings the innocent unbearably close to capitulation, Ben and his Klansmen arrive to kill the black militia and free all the captives. Thus the vigilantes bring justice to a threatened nation. The influence of the redemptive scheme popularized by William Cody's Wild West shows (examined in the next chapter) is obvious. The novelty lies in the technical sophistication with which Griffith communicated the mythic paradigm: he made film into a techno-mythic medium immeasurably superior to the storytelling of the previous era. As Arthur Knight observes, the audience "found Griffith's pictures more realistic, more convincing, more human than anything shown upon the screen at that time. . . ."[20]

The closing scene of *The Birth of a Nation* depicts Elsie Stoneman and Ben Cameron in wedding garments, symbolic of the reconciled North and South, gazing at a cloudlike image of the City of God replacing the city of man. A Christ figure replaces the warrior king, who has cut the Gordian knot, confirming the resolution of Eden's siege. Mast observes: "There are several remarkable things about this closing vision — its audacity, its irrelevance, and the passionateness and sincerity of Griffith's commitment to it. . . . Exactly how is this City of God to become a reality? Certainly not by the efforts of the Ku Klux Klan alone."[21] When one takes the emerging monomyth into account, the scene is neither irrelevant nor lacking in efficacy. As Charles Sanford reminds us, the connection between paradise and marriage has long been close in Christian symbolism: "Throughout the New Testament and in the many theological commentaries thereupon the union of the faithful with Christ in the heavenly paradise is depicted by the imagery of marriage."[22] It is also consistent with the tradition of zealous nationalism to believe, as Griffith did, that righteous violence could usher in the millennial age.[23]

Although *The Birth of a Nation* did not contain the isolated, sexually passionless superhero, the monomythic scheme of a restoration of paradise by selfless violence had fully crystallized by 1915. The film was an implicit invitation to emulate the KKK in crusades to make the world safe for democracy. No wonder President Woodrow Wilson, a Southerner who believed in segregation, was enthusiastic about the film's "writing history in lightning." But, as Knight records, "race riots and mob action followed in the wake of its presentation in many cities."[24] A different judgment about this film came from the pen of Ralph Ellison: "The propagation of subhuman images of Negroes became financially and dramatically profitable. The Negro as a scapegoat could be sold as entertainment, could even be exported. If the film became the main manipulator of the American dream, for Negroes that dream contained a strong dose of such stuff as nightmares are made of."[25] The redemption of paradise by lone crusaders would have been unnecessary in American mythology if actual experience with democracy had matched the Edenic expectation. Most of the materials we describe in this book share *The Birth of a Nation*'s pessimistic premise that democratic institutions cannot lift the siege. Citizens are merely members of a *spectator democracy* in which they passively witness their redemption by a superhero. This presumption is dramatized on a world scale in the recent blockbuster film *Independence Day* (1996).[26] In its plot, the United States, even the whole world, is under siege by aliens who want to kill us and suck away our resources for their own use. They succeed in paralyzing the world's military forces. In this situation the President of the United States abandons his constitutional role as Commander in Chief, assuming the role of a superheroic pilot who personally flies sorties against the alien mothership. In response to a super threat against Eden, the normal agencies of a democratic government become invisible.

Like so many other features of the monomyth, this theme of the defenseless "city set upon a hill" seems to have been decisively shaped by cowboy Westerns in the last third of the nineteenth century. At that time the expected Eden of the West was suffering repeated setbacks. The economic disorders of 1873, 1883-84, and 1893-95 were psychic shocks of formidable dimensions to those expecting snug little nests somewhere out in the West. Henry Nash Smith describes the resulting sense of helplessness:

> Since the myth affirmed the impossibility of disaster or suffering within the garden, it was unable to deal with any of the dark or tragic outcomes of human experience. Given a break in the upward curve of economic progress for the Western farmer, the myth could become a mockery, offering no consolation and serving only to intensify the sense of outrage on the part of men and women who discovered that labor in the fields did not bring the cheerful comfort promised them by so many prophets of the future of the West. The shattering of the myth by economic distress marked, for the history of ideas in America, the real end of the frontier period.[27]

Other factors, such as the corruption of the political system and the disillusionment of reformers, contributed to the psychic dilemma as well. But Smith seems to overlook the fact that the Westerns offered an immediate mythic solution. Posed against the failures of democratic institutions, the dime novels and Wild West shows offered unofficial redeemer figures on powerful horses, impartial outsiders whose zeal for the right and sympathy for the underdog would triumph over evil.

The frontier vigilante as protector of a defenseless civilization was given substance by actual conditions in the West. Rapidly expanding exploitation of western resources and the lack of an effective national police system provided an ideal seedbed for vigilante justice. The invention of the six-gun and its successful use against the Indians of the western plains combined with the Civil War experience to produce a heavily armed citizenry. A desperado such as Wild Bill Hickok, who killed dozens of men in frontier duels and ambushes, became a redeemer figure. His repeated service as a U.S. marshal and frontier sheriff blurred the distinctions between vigilantes and public officials. Daniel Boorstin points out:

There were few if any notorious "bad men" who had not at some time or other worn the badge of the law, and risked their lives for what some men in their neighborhood called law and order. Beneath the widespread admiration for the "manhood" of the quick-on-the-trigger desperado was a gnawing suspicion that the desperado himself was often . . . on the side of the right. "The 'bad men,' or professional fighters and man-killers," wrote Theodore Roosevelt in 1888 after one of his trips out West, "are of a different stamp (from the common criminal, horse thief or highway robber), quite a number of them being, according to their light, perfectly honest. These are the men who do most of the killing in frontier communities; yet it is a note-worthy fact that the men who are killed generally deserve their fate."[28]

In Owen Wister's western novel *The Virginian,* which he dedicated to Theodore Roosevelt in 1902, this theme achieved its archetypal formulation. Its original preface introduces the romantic horseman who "rides in his historic yesterday," possessing virtues not found in the "shapeless state" of current democratic morals. "Such transition was inevitable," writes Wister. But he adds: "Let us give thanks that it is but a transition, and not a finality."[29] In the "Rededication and Preface" of 1911, Wister relates his novel to the "half-a-century of shirking and evasion" of political responsibilities. And he insists: "Our Democracy has many enemies, both in Wall Street and in the Labor Unions; but as those in Wall Street have by their excesses created those in the Unions, they are the worst; if the pillars of our house fall, it is they who will have been the cause thereof" (p. vii). In this context of a democracy besieged by mortal enemies, the unknown cowboy from Virginia and those who follow the implied invitation to imitate him provide the only viable defense.

The story of *The Virginian* begins as the narrator encounters the hero from Virginia at the Wyoming train station. "Lounging there at ease against the wall was a slim young giant, more beautiful than pictures. His broad, soft hat was pushed back; a loose-knotted, dull-scarlet handkerchief sagged from his throat; and one casual thumb was hooked in the cartridge-belt that slanted across his hips" (p. 4). His redemptive competence is registered when he saves the narrator from a runaway horse and later shoots a rattlesnake that might have killed him. Similarly, in the cowboy's first encounter with Molly Wood, the Yankee schoolteacher he is to court, he gallantly sweeps her out of a stagecoach sinking into a river. There is prefiguration in these incidents that prepares the way for his ultimate triumph over evil, personified by Trampas, who leads a gang of rustlers threatening to ruin honest ranchers such as Judge Henry. After the Virginian is made foreman of the Sunk Creek Ranch, he undertakes the responsibility of tracking down the rustling gang, capturing two of its members, one of them formerly his best friend. But the frontier code demands that he renounce friendship and hang the thieves. Trampas escapes with a guileless sidekick. When the trackers approach, Trampas shoots his companion in the back so that he can escape on the only horse they have between the two of them.

After an account of the lynching reaches the horrified Molly, Judge Henry visits her to explain its morality. This is a difficult task because "he had been a staunch servant of the law" while serving as a federal judge. "I am partly responsible for the lynching," he admits, but he insists that there is a moral difference between "burning Southern negroes in public . . . [and] hanging Wyoming cattle-thieves in private . . ." (pp. 432-37). Compared with the "semi-barbarous" practice in the South, the recent events are "a proof that Wyoming is determined to become civilized." He contends that, in lynching, citizens are only taking back the inherent powers of government that they have given to the courts:

> But in Wyoming the law has been letting our cattle thieves go for two years. We are in a very bad way, and we are trying to make that way a little better until civilization can reach us. At present we lie beyond its pale. The courts, or rather the juries, into whose hands we have put the law, are not dealing the law. They are withered hands. . . . And so when your ordinary citizen sees this, and sees that he has placed justice in a dead hand, he must take justice back into his own hands where it was once at the beginning of all things. Call this primitive, if you will. But so far from being a *defiance* of the law, it is an *assertion* of it — the fundamental assertion of self-governing men, upon whom our whole social fabric is based. (pp. 438-39)

In an earlier scene, Molly had been horrified to find her schoolchildren playing the lynch game, re-enacting the hanging of Trampas's accomplices. But the judge's words now persuade her to accept the monomythic ethic of circumventing the institutions of law for the sake of saving civilization. Later she even suggests the appropriateness of vigilante violence to the Virginian as they ride past the wordless Trampas into Medicine Bow for their wedding. She remarks that it seems "wicked that this murderer" goes free when others were hanged just for stealing horses. "He was never even arrested!" she says. "No, he helped elect the sheriff in that county," replies the Virginian (p. 450).

Wister's presentation of benign western violence reflects the range war between a cattlemen's association and homesteaders in Johnson County, Wyoming. As Daniel Boorstin points out, the cattlemen's "associations were of course intended to protect the cattle which bore their brands. But they were also protecting the large cattlemen's control over pieces of the open range — the public domain — which, without any legal title, they called their own."[30] W. Eugene Hollon's analysis in *Frontier Violence* describes how the cattlemen came into conflict with small ranchers and farmers, with state and federal officials favoring the ranchers, and the local courts and juries controlled by the homesteaders. When the ranchers' lynch campaigns proved unsuccessful, they arbitrarily seized the small operators' livestock. The homesteaders retaliated with systematic thievery.[31] Harry Sinclair Drago concludes: "It was more than range thievery undertaken for gain: it was rebellion, the oppressed striking back at its oppressors."[32] When the ranchers imported a trainload of Texas gunmen equipped with dynamite to put down this resistance in 1892, the showdown occurred near Buffalo, Wyoming, where federal troops finally intervened. *The New York Times* covered the story in detail, glorifying the big cattlemen's side of the struggle and praising Frank Wolcott, a wealthy cattleman born in Kentucky, whose ranch Wister visited during his first trip to the West.[33] Wister inadvertently reveals the historical content of the novel by allowing the heroic cowboy to explain that his lynched friend "knew well enough the only thing that would have let him off would have been a regular jury. For the thieves have got hold of the juries in Johnson County."[34]

Wister's distortion of the historical reality of western lynching becomes credible in the powerful mythic framework he provides, in which the besieged community is finally redeemed by a duel between Trampas and the Virginian. At the dramatic climax of the novel, the rustler issues a formal challenge to a duel on Main Street. The Virginian seeks the counsel of the bishop, the man who is to preside over his marriage to Molly. The bishop shares the narrator's conviction "that Trampas was an evil in the country, and that the Virginian was a good. He knew that the cattle thieves — the rustlers — were gaining in numbers and audacity . . . that they elected their men to office, and controlled juries; that they were a staring menace to Wyoming. His heart was with the Virginian. But there was his Gospel that he preached, and believed, and tried to live." He reminds the Virginian of the plain command not to kill, and the latter responds: "Mighty plain to me, seh. Make it plain to Trampas, and there'll be no killin'." As they parry about the contradictory demands of religion and communal redemption, the Virginian poses the monomythic question: "How about instruments of Providence, seh?" When the Virginian refuses to give up his honor even for his future wife, the bishop says as the cowboy departs to the battle, "God bless him! God bless him!" (pp. 471-74).

The Virginian then confronts Molly with his painful obligation. She is appalled that he will not simply leave town when he has a chance. He explains that he gave Trampas two chances to get out of the duel:

> "I kept thinking hard of you — with all my might, or I reckon I'd have killed him right there. . . . I spoke as quiet as I am speaking to you now. But he stood to it. . . . He will have to go on to the finish now."
>
> "The finish?" she echoed, almost voiceless. "Yes," he answered very gently. . . .
>
> "If you do this, there can be no to-morrow for you and me."
>
> At these words he also turned white.
>
> "Do you mean —" he asked and could go no farther. . . . "This would be the end?" he asked.
>
> Her head faintly moved to signify yes. . . .
>
> "Good-by, then," he said. (pp. 476-79)

With this last in a series of renunciations in the novel, the hero goes out to his fateful duel — the first "walkdown" in American literature.[35] In this archetypal duel the bad guy draws and shoots first, but he is killed by the Virginian's bullets. The hero's friends marvel, "You were that cool! That quick!" The hero returns regretfully to pack his belongings and return to a bachelor's life. But Molly's "New England conscience" relents, and she capitulates to love.

The bridal pair sets off on their honeymoon, camping the first night on a peaceful mountain island, straddled by a lovely stream. "It belonged to no man; for it was deep in the unsurveyed and virgin wilderness. . . ." Their isolation is celebrated by the Virginian: "The whole world is far from here." After their first blissful night, "she stretched her hands out to the island and the stream exclaiming, 'Nothing can surpass this.' He took her in his arms . . ." (pp. 476-79). In this garden encircled by the stream, symbolic of the biblical Eden surrounded by its rivers, the Virginian confesses his ancient longing: "What I did not know at all," he said, "was the way a man can be pining for — for this — and never guess what is the matter with him" (p. 506). Just as in *The Birth of a Nation*, the resolution of marriage and the entrance into paradise become possible only after evil has been destroyed. Once the vigilante task is completed, whether in the South or the West, the Gordian knot is cut, and the blissful marriage can ensue. The novel ends with the hero and his family ensconced in prosperity and long life. The Virginian becomes a wealthy rancher and mine owner, escaping the "cattle war" of 1892, and passing the redemptive task on to the next generation.

As one of the most influential novels of its time, *The Virginian* became required reading in high schools for decades. More than two million copies were sold, and the novel became the pattern for hundreds of imitations.[36] The success of the paradigm was due in part to the moralizing of vigilante violence by dramatic juxtaposition, impassioned arguments, and the selfless restraint of the hero. For five years the Virginian withstood the villain's provocations, reluctantly killing him at the price of renouncing sexual fulfillment. Gary Cooper played this role perfectly when *The Virginian* was made into an archetypal Western movie in 1929.[37] Robert V. Hine has commented on the "namelessness" of the Virginian, an essential feature in the paradigm: "The vagueness of his past requires the reader to judge the man solely in the present."[38] But more than that, one suspects, it enhances the archetypal power of the story to cast an Everyman in the role of community savior. Facing the siege of paradise, against which mere human force seems unable to prevail, only "the transcendent figure, originating beyond the town," to use Peter Homans' words, is able to redeem.[39]

The Virginian as one of Hollywood's first sound films in 1929 starred Gary Cooper and Mary Brian. The film continued the emphasis on Molly and the Virginian's mutual yearning for life partnership.

Credit: Film poster for *The Virginaian.* Paramount, 1929.

The Axial Decade of Monomythic Development

With 1929 we enter what we choose to call the *axial decade* for the formation of the American monomyth. Here the unknown redeemer on a horse becomes the "Masked Rider of the Plains"; his sexual renunciation is complete; he assumes the uniform and the powers of angelic avengers; and thus he grows from mere heroism to superheroism.

The development of the sexually renunciatory superhero, the most distinctive feature of the monomyth, accelerates to its climax soon after the 1929 release of the sound-film version of Gary Cooper's *The Virginian*. With the technomythic advance of sound film, the embodiment of the monomythic heroism became even more compelling. The shock of the Depression and the rise of unprecedented foreign threats to democratic societies provided the background for the creative advance. In this same year the comic-book version of *Tarzan* appeared. Burne Hogarth, who collaborated with Hal Foster in making Tarzan a household word in the 1930s, sets the scene: "The success of 'Tarzan' owed much to the time when it was first drawn. This was a little after the start of the great depression: big corporations were crashing and misery was widespread. . . . Tarzan finds himself again — like the American people — without weapons to fight off all the perils."[40] But Tarzan, like the many heroes who were to follow him, was more than merely human. The first of the major pulp-novel crime fighters, The Shadow, also appeared in 1929.[41] With the alter ego of Kent Allard the aviator, this mysterious figure performed super feats against the enemies of civilization in some 325 complete novels written over the next two decades. Buck Rogers was also created in 1929, and the ascetic supercop Dick Tracy appeared in 1931. The widely popular pulp imitators of The Shadow, such as Doc Savage, The Phantom, and The Spider, appeared in 1933. Probably the most systematic presentation of a superman appeared in Philip Wylie's novel *Gladiator*, written in 1930, which depicts the prodigy son of scientist parents who proves invulnerable to machine-gun bullets. It was this figure who provided the model for Siegel and Shuster's Superman.[42] The two teenagers developed their comic superhero as a way to counter "the hopelessness and fear in the country" in 1933, but they did not market Superman successfully until 1938.[43]

A decisive factor in the axial decade was the emergence of serialization in the new and more powerful technomythic media. Comic books and radio programs required a heroic format with traditional appeals of adventure and redemption but without marital resolution at the end. Sexual renunciation had to become permanent because, if the hero rode off with his bride into the golden sunset as did the Virginian, it would entail creating a new redeemer figure for the next episode. Once involved in family and business complexities, a hero would have to pass the redemptive torch to the next candidate. The new media offset this problem by allowing a presentation of heroic action more spectacular than any made credible before. Heroes could fly across the frames of comic strips with impunity, or thunder on their mounts at incredible speeds across the sound-effects stages of radio programs. The augmented capabilities ensured the resolution of otherwise insoluble crises. Miraculous redemption thus came to replace the blissful union of married partners as a fitting expression of Eden's restoration.

In *The Lone Ranger* the new, permanently isolated superhero sprang to life in serial form. The program was developed by a Detroit radio station in 1933 to meet the requirements of a regular time slot on a new network. The station owner, George Trendle, wanted a cowboy who would play the role of a "guardian angel," a hero who would be the "embodiment of a granted prayer."[44] The radio version of *The Lone Ranger* ran to 2,956 episodes, ending only in 1954. It has since been replayed in reruns many times, as well as appearing in comic books, a television series running from 1949 to 1961, and films.[45] The genesis episode reveals both the continuity with and the development beyond the Virginian archetype. A voice announces: "This is the legend of a man who buried his identity to dedicate his life to the service of humanity and country. . . . Early settlers in the West had to be brave men and women. . . . There was danger on every side, wild beasts, savage Indians, and the Cavendish gang."[46] Having established the theme of a hero with secret identity who defends humanity from danger, the narrator turns to Butch Cavendish, who orders his gang to open fire on a helpless wagon train: "Wipe them out to the last man!"[47] Later a group of Texas Rangers follows the Cavendish gang into a desolate canyon, where the Rangers are betrayed by their own guide. Just before the ambush begins, the birds are heard twittering in the trees as Captain Daniel Reid asks his younger brother to care of his family if tragedy overtakes them. The Edenic scene is broken by the outlaws' gunfire, which falls upon the trapped Rangers until night. Young Reid wakes up four mornings later in a cave, where he had been carried by an Indian, who introduces himself:

"Me . . . Tonto."

Reid asks, "What of the other Rangers? They were all my friends. One was my brother."

Tonto replies, "Other Texas Rangers — all dead. You only Ranger left. *You lone Ranger now.*" The two men discover that they had been boyhood friends. The youthful Reid had saved Tonto's life, thus providing a prefiguration of his redemptive capabilities, in the style of *The Virginian.* Reid and

The legend of the Lone Ranger, conveyed through publicity as well as his serialized stories, emphasizes the clean, benign exercise of his quest for justice.

Credit: Publicity shot. The Lone Ranger, Inc. © 1943.

Tonto resolve to track down the Cavendish gang and bring them to justice. Jim Harmon describes the scene: "Marked for death by a huge outlaw organization, he decided to disguise himself with a mask, a mask made from the black cloth of a vest in his brother's saddlebags — cloth that has borne the silver star of justice." The narrator intones the litany: "In the Ranger's eye there was a light that must have burned in the eyes of knights in armor, a light that through the ages must have lifted the souls of strong men who fought for justice, for God!"[48] The young man gives voice to his zealous decision:

"I'll be . . . the Lone Ranger!"

As in Owen Wister's story, it is a Southerner who comes west to play the role of national redeemer. In this instance the unification of the symbol system is portrayed by the deep midwestern voice of the Lone Ranger rather than by a marriage to a Vermont schoolteacher. The requisite selflessness in his campaign is portrayed by the dedication of the proceeds from his secret silver mine to pay the expenses for his crusade. The Lone Ranger renounces both wealth and heterosexual love. In his friendship with Tonto there is a remarkable degree of racial reconciliation, in drastic contrast to the reality of an implacable hatred between Indians and the Texas Rangers.[49] Tonto not only becomes the constant companion and follower of the Lone Ranger; he also takes up the crusading ideology, which had played such havoc with the American Indians. A more striking symbol of co-optation could scarcely be imagined, but it provides a powerful confirmation of the white man's vigilante code.

Of equal importance symbolically is the Lone Ranger's taming of the great white stallion Silver after he had saved Silver from death in a battle with a "giant buffalo." The powerful horse responds instinctively to the sound of his name and accepts the gentle mastery of his savior. The narrator describes the wondrous scene:

"As the halter touched Silver, he trembled as if from a chill. Every instinct told him that he must flee at once to preserve his freedom. Yet he stood his ground. It wasn't gratitude that kept him there. It was something stronger. Some mysterious bond of friendship and understanding. He heard the man's voice and he liked it."

"Silver, Silver, we're going to be partners!" says the Lone Ranger.

Tonto is amazed: "Him let you use halter!"

"Give me the saddle."

Tonto replies, "Oh, no horse like that take saddle."[50]

The Lone Ranger then states the mythic point as he places the saddle on the magnificent horse: "There never was a horse like this. Now Silver, we're going to work together."

The narrator reiterates the theme: "No hooves had ever beat the plains like the thundering hooves of that great horse Silver!" The opening lines of the radio program henceforth feature Silver as a full member of the redemptive team. He not only responds to his master's voice without being trained, but seems to "understand" the vigilante work in which he is engaged. The peculiar capabilities of radio sound effects make it possible to render Silver virtually human, whinnying his assent to utterances of Ranger truth. He is the first in a remarkable line of redeemer animals in American popular culture.

The speed of the incomparable horse provides the Lone Ranger with his crucial element of the superhuman: rapid mobility, the most characteristic and coveted form of freedom in America, the ability to transcend space and time. In an early episode the need for such speed was displayed in the Lone Ranger's inability to overtake Butch Cavendish with his former steed. "My next horse must be faster," he says, in order to take the culprit alive and bring him to justice. This theme is touched on, but not fully exploited, in Owen Wister's references to Monte, the Virginian's horse. But in the Lone Ranger series, Silver develops into a symbol of tireless endurance and strength, allowing the vigilante to accomplish miraculous feats that raise him above the merely heroic level of the Virginian.

Extralegal violence and personal vengeance are essential to the vigilante ideology, but in the Lone Ranger's instance there is an elaborate effort to downplay objectionable features of lynch justice. The masked rider is not acting as a law-enforcement officer, despite the black mask of cloth that had borne the star of justice. But he invariably turns his captured crooks over to the authorities for punishment. The program always begins with loud pistol shots interspersed with the *William Tell Overture,* yet the Lone Ranger never kills anyone. With superhuman accuracy his silver bullets strike the hands of threatening bad guys — evoking a mere "yow!" or "my hand!" Yet their evil powers are neutralized. In an elaborate extension of the ideology of cool zeal, which relieves the vigilante of guilt in the exercise of what appears to be "hot" vengeance,[51] the Lone Ranger's powers ensure that he inflicts minimal injury. This is similar to the later theory of nuclear deterrence, where unlimited power is celebrated as the ultimate defense because it presumably will never have to be used destructively. Magical silver missiles will keep the foe from aggression, thus bringing no blame on selfless redeemers. All one needs in order to escape the ambiguity of violent power is more power. Thus *The Lone Ranger* program answers the objections posed by Molly and the bishop in *The Virginian.* The vigilante has become the saint, not merely through superior virtue but also because of superhuman power.

The invitation to imitate that is implicit in the program was articulated when the Lone Ranger found his brother's long-lost son and explained the "great heritage" he was to carry forward:

If the Lone Ranger must fire his silver bullet,
he always makes a clean and mildly disabling shot.
Typical captions in the comics were "yow," "it's my hand."
Credit: *The Lone Ranger* (1951) © The Lone Ranger, Inc., 1943, 1944, 1951.

[Your forefathers] have handed down to you the right to worship as you choose, and the right to work and profit from your enterprise. They have given you a land where there is true freedom, true equality of opportunity, a nation that is governed by the people, by laws that are best for the greatest number. Your duty, Dan, is to preserve that heritage and strengthen it. [Strains of "America the Beautiful" grow louder.] That is the heritage and duty of every American.[52]

In a program broadcast in 1950, that invitation is even more sharply formulated, as a dying government agent tells the Lone Ranger: "Listen to me — carry on. And train someone to carry on in the twentieth century when — when you join your Ranger pals — and me. . . ." The Lone Ranger replies: "Dan Reid is going to meet the twentieth century as a man."[53] The appeal to the audience is to take up the vigilante task with similar manliness.

The final extension of powers into the superheroic scale occurred toward the end of the axial decade. *Superman* began to appear as a feature in the June 1938 *Action Comics*. By the fourth issue, the sales curve indicated that something significant had occurred, and within a few years millions of copies were selling each month, revolutionizing the comic-book industry and making a permanent alteration in the American hero pattern. It was, as Les Daniels puts it, "an instant triumph, a concept so intense and so instantly identifiable that he became perhaps the most widely known figure ever created in American fiction."[54] Ted White refers to the "magnificent sense of wonder" with which these pages were received by readers. Episodes that climaxed with "Look! The bullets bounce right offa him!" virtually replaced ordinary plot development.[55] The August 1939 issue of *Action Comics* emphasizes this theme:

> Leaping over skyscrapers, running faster than an express train, springing great distances and heights, lifting and smashing tremendous weights, possessing an impenetrable skin — these are the amazing attributes which Superman, savior of the helpless and oppressed, avails himself of as he battles the forces of evil and injustice.[56]

As with the Lone Ranger, these extraordinary powers made it possible to carry out vigilante violence without incurring blame. Speeding getaway cars could be stopped dead by Superman's arms — without splattering anyone on the windshield. Superman never kills anyone, thus denying the actual effects of boundless power. If crooks are hurt or killed, it is their own fault. The steel-sinewed fists of Superman can be as gentle as Walt Disney's mill wheel, knocking bad guys unconscious without raising welts on their jaws. Siegel and Shuster's fantasy was even better than silver bullets because their superhero never even had to fire at the enemy. His bulletproof body could grapple with adversaries and bring them to a flawless form of vigilante justice.

In the first years of its comic-book life, Superman's power of flight was limited to prodigious leaps. When the first motion-picture cartoons appeared, however, "he gained the power of pure flight," which was subsequently incorporated in the comics. As we have noted before, the mythic advance goes hand in hand with real-world technomythic breakthroughs, in this instance related to animation techniques. The transcending of human capabilities had reached its apex. When combined with the appealing structure of Superman's plebeian alter ego, Clark Kent, a beguiling fantasy world took form. The redemptive god with superhuman strength was disguised as Everyman, thus breaking out of the bounds of democratic ordinariness. For the first time in modern, secularized America, superhuman powers became widely distributed in fantasy.

In contrast to *The Birth of a Nation* and *The Virginian,* the Superman paradigm exhibits two remarkable features: in addition to vastly exceeding human muscular powers there emerges a full development of what we would like to call "sexual segmentation." Following the pattern of his serialized counterpart, the Lone Ranger, Superman is permanently blocked in his relations to the opposite sex. But the transformation of the redeemer paradigm that surfaces in *The Birth of a Nation* and *The Virginian* exhibits two remarkable features: a transcending of human muscular powers and a completion of the sexual segmentation pattern. Like that of his serialized counterpart, the Lone Ranger, Superman's sexual segmentation is permanent. Although as Clark Kent he is attracted to Lois Lane, he knows that as long as he is Superman, she must always be denied to him. This point becomes emphatic in the *Superman II* movie (1981), in which Superman abandons his celibate vow and takes Lois to the Castle of Solitude for sex. When he returns, he discovers that a loutish truck driver can inflict pain because he now has a vulnerable, soft body. Lesson learned!

The other superheroes of the period were presented with similar strategies of segmenting the element of sexual need out of their personalities. The classic Batman has a permanent relationship with his male counterpart, Robin, but he never forms an abiding relationship with a woman. Billy Batson is called to be Captain Marvel with the injunction, "You are pure in heart. You have been chosen." This purity prevents anything beyond a boyish crush on the well-endowed Beautia Sivana, who has betrayed her own evil father for Captain Marvel. Her feelings for the superhero and his coolness toward her are similar to the perpetually frustrating Clark-Lois-Superman triangle. Torch, Sub-Mariner, Green Lantern, and Spiderman rescue girls but never marry them. The list of single saviors goes on at length: Wonder Woman, Lady Blackhawk, Mary Worth, Rex Morgan, and Marcus Welby. And judging from the fatalities that befall the fiancees of Ben, Joe, and Hoss Cartwright in TV's popular *Bonanza* series, merely planning to marry a fictional redeemer may be the riskiest job in America.

Crowds of Superheroes

Following the phenomenal success of Superman comics in 1938, the axial decade closed with a proliferation of superheroes. The masks, uniforms, miraculous powers, and secret alter egos combine with sexual renunciation and segmentation to complete the formation of the monomythic hero. Batman, Sandman, Hawkman, and The Spirit all sprang to life in 1939; Flash, The Green Lantern, The Shield, Captain Marvel, and White Streak followed in 1940; and Sub-Mariner, Wonder Woman, Plastic Man, and Captain America were born the following year. The opening captions of these comic superhero tales reveal the degree to which the monomythic definition of mission, character, and powers was permanently crystallized by the axial decade. The first episode of *Batman* in May 1939 introduces the disguised isolate as "a mysterious and adventurous figure fighting for righteousness and apprehending the wrongdoers, in his lone battle against the evil forces of society . . . his identity remains unknown."[57] The initial issue of *Captain Marvel* comics announces itself in these monomythic terms: "Whiz Comics proudly presents THE WORLD'S MIGHTIEST MAN — POWERFUL CHAMPION OF JUSTICE — RELENTLESS ENEMY OF EVIL." In the story, Billy Batson is confronted by a divine personage looking suspiciously like the "Ancient of Days" in old Sunday school material. "All my life," the figure says, "I have fought injustice and cruelty. But I am old now — my time is almost up. You shall be my successor merely by speaking my name. You can become the mightiest man in the world — Captain Marvel. Shazam! Blam! Captain Marvel, I salute you. Henceforth it shall be your sacred duty to defend the poor and helpless. Right wrongs and crush evil everywhere."[58] Thus a new superhero takes up the redemptive task from a senile religious symbol, offering for the fantasy life of every schoolboy an opportunity to be transformed by a magic word into the all-powerful redeemer.

The connection of these superhero materials with the American religious heritage illustrates the displacement of the story of redemption. Only in a culture preoccupied for centuries with the question of salvation is the appearance of redemption through superheroes comprehensible. The secularization process in this instance did not eliminate the need for redemption, as the Enlightenment had attempted to do, but rather displaces it with superhuman agencies. Powers that the culture had earlier reserved for God and his angelic beings are transferred to an Everyman, conveniently shielded by an alter ego. Even the most explicit references to the mythology of the ancient world are conditioned by this new superhero paradigm. This can be documented in materials created long after the axial decade. The television version of the goddess Isis began in 1975 with these mysterious-sounding lines:

"O mighty queen," said the royal sorceress, "with this amulet you and your descendants are endowed by the goddess Isis with the powers of the animals and the elements. You will soar as the falcon soars, run with the speed of gazelles, and command the elements of sky and earth."

But as the narrator extends the context, it is clearly the familiar redemption scheme with a segmented superheroine in disguise.

> Three thousand years later a young science teacher dug up this lost treasure and found she was heir to the secrets of Isis. And so, unknown to even her closest friends . . . became a dual person — Andrea Thomas — teacher — and Isis — dedicated foe of evil, defender of the weak, champion of truth and justice.[59]

The references to ancient gods and amulets may sound archaic to some, but the format was shaped during the axial decade of the twentieth century.

As the superhero genre was elaborated in the years following the axial decade, the displacement of traditional religious symbols was frequently articulated. A *Flash* episode of August 1971 seems archetypal: a gang of urban thugs has taken over a church to store and divide their loot; when the faithful nuns pray for relief, one of their oppressors pours scorn on the thought of divine intervention.

> Haw! Whatcha doin'? Askin' your own top man to help you? No way! Nothin's gonna stop us from keepin' this loot!

The gang then accuses the nun's brother of being an informer. Flash arrives just in time to save him from death as they throw him off the roof of a tall building. The boy decides to go straight, but the chief has hidden the loot. The boy confides his problem to Sister Anne, who says that she will pray for help. Flash overhears the conversation and comments: "There's only one way of quickly finding that hidden loot . . . and that's *scientifically!*" The superhero becomes a rapidly moving radar unit, systematically projecting grids over the city and searching until he finds the cave where the loot is hidden. He saves the young informer and his girlfriend from retaliation by secretly warding off hostile bullets and making clubs disintegrate while increasing the strength of the good guy's fists. After triumphing over the crooks, the young man tells his girlfriend, "Might makes right!" The nuns get control of their church again, the juvenile delinquents are reformed, and, as Vic recounts the events, "It all seems like a miracle!" Barry Allen, alias Flash, mutters to himself, "Made possible by the miracle of superspeed!"

In the final scene, Sister Anne expresses her thanks to God for deliverance. As Barry acknowledges that it has been "a *kind* of miracle," the caption reads: "Perhaps, Barry — but to those who believe, 'the moment of a miracle is like unending lightning.'" The miraculous intervention of the modern superhero has confirmed the faith of the naive sister. She thinks God still works in mysterious ways, and if this story is right, he does — through the jet-age counterpart of the Lone Ranger's speedy horse.[60]

The superheroes thus provide a secular fulfillment of the religious promise articulated in the endings of *The Birth of a Nation* and *The Virginian*. They cut Gordian knots, lift the siege of evil, and restore the Edenic state of perfect faith and perfect peace. It is a millennial, religious expectation — at least in origin — yet it is fulfilled by secular agents. The premise of democratic equality is visible in that superhuman powers have to be projected onto ordinary citizens, yet their transformation into superheroes renders them incapable of democratic citizenship. Moreover, total power must be pictured as totally benign, transmuting lawless vigilantism into a perfect embodiment of law enforcement. That such fantasies suddenly became credible in the popular culture is the abiding legacy of the axial decade. Although they had not yet appeared in the minds of their creators, the parameters for Kirk and Spock, Dirty Harry, Rambo, and the Steven Seagal characters were already defined. They were ready to play out their roles of redeeming the American Dream, along with their nonviolent cohorts from Heidi and Mary Poppins to Lassie and Flipper. All that remained was for the subplots to vary and the scenes to change. Henceforth, materials for mass audiences would have to undergo a kind of mythic alchemy to fit the new monomythic consciousness. A story paradigm as potent as Hercules or Odysseus had been born, spawning its offspring in a popular culture that would soon encircle the world. It would not be long before the American monomyth became a subculture of Planet Earth, massaging especially the consciousness of youth and adults, evoking a wide array of imitative behaviors.

By the end of the axial decade, a new mystical consciousness shaped by the American monomyth was already emerging. E. E. Smith's vivid description of the mindset at the end of the axial decade is equally applicable today. Asked to define the meaning of the First International Science Fiction Convention for its participants in 1940, he did so in terms that are disarmingly religious:

> What brings us together and underlies this convention is a fundamental unity of mind. We are imaginative, with a tempered, analytical imagination which fairy tales will not satisfy. . . . Science fiction fans form a group unparalleled in history, in our close-knit . . . organization, in our strong likes and dislikes, in our partisanship and loyalties . . . there is a depth of satisfaction, a height of fellowship which no one who has never experienced it can even partially understand.[61]

Although Smith felt that science fiction fans would never comprise more than a fraction of the population, and that outsiders would have trouble grasping the basis of their fervor, the attitude of credulity and the yearning for fantasy redemption were already visible within the widespread audience for mono-mythic entertainments. A revolution in spiritual consciousness was under way, allowing for the emergence of formal and informal pop religions in which the various superheroic rites could be conducted. Fandom began to emerge as a new form of religious community, and in the alter ego feature of the superhero fantasies every worshiper could become a god.

The Shape of the New Heroic Paradigm

The monomythic superhero is distinguished by disguised origins, pure moti-vations, a redemptive task, and extraordinary powers. He originates outside the community he is called to save, and in those exceptional instances when he resides therein, the superhero plays the role of the idealistic loner. His identity is secret, either by virtue of his unknown origins or his alter ego; his motivation is a selfless zeal for justice. By elaborate conventions of restraint, his desire for revenge is purified. Patient in the face of provocations, he seeks nothing for himself and withstands all temptations. He renounces sexual ful-fillment for the duration of the mission, and the purity of his motivations en-sures his moral infallibility in judging persons and situations. When he is threatened by violent adversaries, he finds an answer in vigilantism, restoring justice and thus lifting the siege of paradise. In order to accomplish this mis-sion without incurring blame or causing undue injury to others, he requires superhuman powers. The superhero's aim is unerring, his fists irresistible, and his body incapable of suffering fatal injury. In the most dangerous trials he remains utterly cool and thus divinely competent. When confronted by in-soluble personality conflicts within the community, he — or more often she — uses nonviolent manipulation. With wisdom and coolness equal to the vigilante counterpart, the female "Heidi-redeemers" (which we describe in later chapters) bring happiness to a desperate Eden.

In these conventions the monomyth betrays an aim to deny the tragic complexities of human life. It forgets that every gain entails a loss, that ex-traordinary benefits exact requisite costs, and that injury is usually propor-tionate to the amount of violence employed. The bold figures of Superman and Flash and the dramatic hoofbeats of the great horse Silver may seem to lack ambiguity; but the paradoxes of the monomyth abound. The American monomyth offers vigilantism without lawlessness, sexual repression without resultant perversion, and moral infallibility without the use of intellect. It features a restoration of Eden for others, but refuses to allow the dutiful hero to participate in its pleasures. The Lone Ranger's laughter was one sound effect never heard after the first program.

The monomythic hero claims surpassing concern for the health of the community, but he never practices citizenship. He unites a consuming love of impartial justice with a mission of personal vengeance that eliminates due process of law. He offers a form of leadership without paying the price of political relationships or responding to the preferences of the majority. In denying the ambivalence and complexity of real life, where the moral landscape offers choices in various shades of gray rather than in black and white, where ordinary people muddle through life and learn to live with the many poor choices they have made, and where the heroes that do exist have feet of clay, the monomyth pictures a world in which no humans really live. It gives Americans a fantasy land without ambiguities to cloud the moral vision, where the evil empire of enemies is readily discernible, and where they can vicariously (through identification with the superhero) smite evil before it overtakes them.

The tapestry of the American monomyth is woven in bold and stirring colors. Its radiant, electronic aura dazzles the beholder's eye and conceals the discordant clash of its components. The intricately crafted message of paradise redeemed by heroes larger than life has appeals far deeper than reason, particularly to a culture believing itself besieged by ruthless foes. To borrow words from J. H. Plumb, the world of the American monomyth is truly "fearsome . . . magical . . . full of wonders and portents. . . ."[62] All things considered, scholarly obituaries for "disappearing heroes" were indeed premature.[63] It seems likely that the portraits in radio, film, television, and the comics are so artful in their technomythic wizardry that even highly sophisticated minds fail to detect the new heroic presences. These dramas of redemption resonate so powerfully with our most earnest hopes that they acquire the semblance of reality. In view of its growth from the axial decade to a position of present ascendancy in global entertainment, the American monomyth is truly alive and well; it reveals a side of modern, scientific man seldom imagined in the dreams of reason that stirred the century in which the American nation was founded. It is surely appropriate now, as we enter the twenty-first century, to investigate this pervasive mythic legacy. In the chapters that follow we will offer a guide to the mythic flora and fauna that have come to populate this increasingly dominant universe of American superheroes.

3 Buffalo Bill: Staging World Redemption

Buffalo Bill was "one of America's strange heroes who has loved the trackless wilds . . . and who has stood as a barrier between civilization and savagery, risking his own life to save the lives of others."

Prentiss Ingraham in a dime novel[1]

The imposing statues of popular heroes are not all the products of imagination alone. In the decisive periods when myths are born, certain historical figures come to assume heroic grandeur, capable of capturing the imagination of the public while the heroes are yet alive. The process of the mythical reshaping of contemporary figures has frequently been described in popular culture — in arenas such as sports, film, music, politics, and military affairs. The shape of the mythical paradigm in American popular heroism deserves closer definition. And the extent to which it arises from denying the reality of "the six-gun mystique" needs clarification. In the story of Buffalo Bill there are some clues to the emergence of a monomythic hero-type, standing with a firearm between threatening savages and innocent damsels, the pattern of the western hero who struggles for law and order against the forces threatening civilization. But if we look toward a less mythically inspired version of history, Michael Straight's *Carrington* provides an imaginative sample of western history-making that does not fall prey to the monomythic paradigm. The task is to discover an approach to the American past that offers hope for moving beyond the illusory ease of six-gun justice.

In this poster for the Wild West show, Buffalo Bill celebrates his contribution
to imperialism as "The Man on the Horse/From the Yellowstone to the Danube/
from Vesuvius to Ben Nevis." Rosa Bonheur, a notable French artist, turns her
gaze from the pudgier, lethargic Napoleon to the trimmer, more erect Cody.
Her banner reads —"Art Perpetuating Fame/Rosa Bonheur/Painting Buffalo Bill/Paris 1889."

Credit: Buffalo Bill's Wild West and Congress of Rough Riders of the World. Courier Litho. Co., 1896.
Library of Congress Prints and Photographs Division. Washington, D.C.

An Instinct for Myth-Making Publicity

The decisive formation of western heroic imagery took place when the daring
and attractive William F. Cody began to style himself as "Buffalo Bill." Show-
man Cody convincingly played the redeemer role for the Wild West show audiences, thundering away victoriously on his horse to avenge civilization's
claim against the outnumbering savages. In the self-portraits of the shows
and the seventeen hundred novels and stories written about his exploits —
many written with his collaboration — Cody developed this heroic image
with brazen exaggerations that even he privately acknowledged were unrealis-
tic. In brief stints as a scout in the Indian wars he participated in historical
events that he then re-enacted in mythic form for the audiences of Europe
and America. John Burke, one of Cody's many biographers, senses the oddity
of this instant transfiguration:

One of the most striking sidelights of the creation of our Western mythology is that it was being fabricated, recast, and enlarged upon almost immediately after the events upon which it was based were taking place. . . . The heroes . . . joined in the process by portraying themselves and re-enacting their supposed deeds. Would Achilles, for instance, have abandoned the forces laying siege to Troy and hurried back to Athens to play himself before a crowded amphitheater? No matter, this was modern America, where a man had the right to cash in on his fame.[2]

This heroic image was developed out of materials and events whose true character required constant suppression of discordant elements.

Will Cody was born on an Iowa farm in 1846 and moved with his family to troubled Kansas seven years later. His abolitionist father died of wounds inflicted by adversaries after only three years in bloody Kansas. At eleven, the strapping boy began working to support his family. Cody recounts, perhaps with considerable exaggeration, the slaying of his first two Indians on a wagon expedition in his first year with a freighting firm. He returned home on foot the following year, after being captured by a Mormon militia company, and was promptly placed back in school. The "swaggering twelve-year-old . . . resisted the educational process to the best of his abilities,"[3] slipping away for several more treks west before returning home long enough to learn to write. By the time he was a teenager, Will could speak Indian dialects and survive alone in the western mountains. After a stint as a Pony Express rider, as a participant in occasional Indian battles and frequent drinking bouts, he served for a while as scout for a Kansas cavalry unit. His exploits in a thieving Kansas bushwhacking unit during the opening days of the Civil War earned him the reputation as "the most desperate outlaw, bandit and house-burner on the frontier."[4]

The fictional celebration of Cody's early life required that the negative implications of these escapades be suppressed in favor of a redemptive idealism. In his waning years Buffalo Bill adopted the line from Prentiss Ingraham's dime novel, "I stood between savagery and civilization most all my early days." Ingraham had described Cody as "one of America's strange heroes who has loved the trackless wilds, rolling plains and mountain solitudes of our land, far more than the bustle and turmoil, the busy life and joys of our cities, and who has stood as a barrier between civilization and savagery, risking his own life to save the lives of others."[5]

The myth of the redemptive mission began after an uproarious celebration with a group of Kansas Volunteers, when Cody woke up the next morning to find himself enlisted in the U.S. Army. Despite heroic tales to the contrary, his major action in eight months of Civil War service was with Louisa Frederici, a spirited young woman who lived with her family in St. Louis. The story of how they met is romanticized in several accounts of Cody's life.[6] He rescues her from a runaway horse in one tale. In another, Bill rescues Louisa from a drunken artilleryman and his cronies. The winged rescue scene prefigures the sexless, caped redeemers of twentieth-century comics.

> But before he [the drunk] could . . . bend his hot, sensual face toward her pure lips, a horse and rider came rushing down the street with the speed of a winged bird. . . . "Oh, sir, you are so brave and good. . . . I would have died before they should kiss me," said the lovely girl.

In reality, Private Cody saved Louisa from nothing more than the completion of an afternoon nap. He jerked the chair out from under her while she dozed in the parlor.[7] After Will's due apologies, the attractive pair fell in love, and a year later they married. Will Cody was twenty years old at the time of his marriage, a circumstance the dime novels all gladly suppress. In the mythical tales Cody remains as pure and unattached as a Christian angel. But the actual Cody alternatively endured, ran away from, and betrayed his impetuous wife for the next half century. A wildly jealous woman unsuited to a harum-scarum life in frontier shacks and hotels, she made Cody's life miserable in his brief stays at home. She fiercely criticized his heavy drinking, crude carousing, and sporadic support of the family. He came home long enough in 1876 to witness the sickness of his daughters and the death of his only son. By 1881, after Louisa surprised him at the end of a Wild West tour as he was ardently kissing his actresses good-bye, a permanent estrangement developed.

Louisa Cody gained final revenge after her husband's death in 1917 by arranging with Harry Tammen of the *Denver Post* for his burial on Lookout Mountain. She reportedly received a fee of ten thousand dollars to disregard Bill's desire to be buried outside Cody, Wyoming; instead, she had him buried in a spot designated by his hated former associate, Tammen. Her revenge for a lifetime of indignities was soured when six of Cody's former sweethearts showed up in places of honor at his funeral, "now obese and sagging with memories . . . beside the grave of hewed-out granite," as Gene Fowler described the scene. "One of the old Camilles rose from her camp chair . . . walked to the casket and held her antique but dainty black parasol over the glass. She stood there throughout the service. . . . It was the gesture of a queen."[8] This was the awkward reality denied in the dramatization of Buffalo Bill as the bachelor who saved girls but was never romantically attached to them.

The transformation of Will Cody from a good-looking frontier rough-neck and successful Army scout to a nationally known redeemer figure began in 1869. Ned Buntline, the prolific author of dime novels, came west to locate the 5th Cavalry, which had just subdued Chief Tall Bull's band. Buntline met Cody and used his name in the title of a dime novel series that attributed many of the legendary exploits of Wild Bill Hickok to him. Buntline's *Buffalo Bill: The King of the Border Men* was a daring piece of legend-making. It must have been surprising to Will Cody that his heroization included abstinence. In one of Cody's little sermons that Buntline wrote, the bibulous Bill declares, "There is more fight, more headache — aye, more heartache in one rumbottle than there is in all the water that ever sparkled in God's bright sunlight. And I, for the sake of my dear brothers and sisters, and for the sweet, trusting heart that throbs alone for me, intend to let the rum go where it belongs, and that is not down my throat, at any rate."[9] To Cody's credit, it is conceded by his contemporaries that he never spoke or acted in this abstemious and sexually ascetic way outside of the novels. But the denial pattern nevertheless stamped the cowboy tradition with the image of a milk-drinking superhero who saves his kisses for his horse.

Buntline's use of the nickname Buffalo Bill was apt. The year before meeting the author, Cody had worked as a buffalo hunter for the Kansas Pacific Railroad. In a single eighteen-month period he claimed to have killed some 4,280 of the beasts on which Indian survival depended.[10] Cody's autobiography describes a shooting contest in which he killed 69 buffalo in a single day, a vivid account of how the West was "redeemed":

> I was using . . . a breech-loading Springfield rifle — caliber .50 — it was my favorite old "Lucretia." . . . My great *forte* in killing buffaloes from horse-back was to get them circling by riding my horse at the head of the herd, shooting the leaders, thus crowding their followers to the left, till they would finally circle round and round. On this morning the buffaloes were very accommodating, and I soon had them running in a beautiful circle, when I dropped them thick and fast. . . . I had "nursed" my buffaloes, as a billiard-player does the balls when he makes a big run.[11]

This "sport" was suitable for eastern socialites, and Cody began escorting millionaires and European royalty. His gifts as a raconteur, scout, and hunter, together with his ability to dress splendidly for the stylish expeditions, made him a popular figure. He was beginning to act the heroic role of the dime novels. Invited by his millionaire acquaintances, Cody made a grand tour of Chicago and New York in 1872, witnessing performances of Buntline's play about the life of Buffalo Bill. Cody returned to lead a cavalry unit into a successful attack on a Sioux village near the South Fork of the Loup River. He earned the Congressional Medal of Honor for his dauntless charge into the camp and killing at least one Indian with his hunting rifle.[12] He suffered a slight graze wound — the only one ever received in battle, according to Mrs. Cody, an account that differs from later newspaper accounts of 137 bullet, arrow, and tomahawk scars incurred in the defense of civilization.[13]

Blending History and Myth

Cody's dramatic duel with Chief Yellow Hand permanently formed the emerging heroic paradigm. Buffalo Bill was working with the 5th Cavalry to head off a band of Cheyennes who sought to join Sitting Bull in the wake of Custer's demise in 1876. Cody claimed that, in a skirmish between scouting forces, young Chief Yellow Hand rode forward with a challenge to personal combat: "I know you, Pa-he-haska (Long Yellow Hair): if you want to fight, come ahead and fight me."[14] This remark, if historical, implies an expectation of hand-to-hand combat, but when Buffalo Bill's horse stepped into a hole and fell, a fellow officer, Lt. King, reported that "Cody coolly knelt and, taking deliberate aim, sent his bullet through the chief's leg and into his [Yellow Hand's] horse's head. Down went the two, and before his friends could reach him, a second shot from Bill's rifle laid the redskin low." Despite a few flourishes in later accounts by Cody himself, his conquest of Yellow Hand — as he came to be known through mistranslation — was about as chivalrous as the way he shot buffalo. His ruthless use of the .50-caliber buffalo gun allowed little doubt about the outcome of the "duel." This episode's mythical power derived from the dramatic setting, the cool efficiency of the hero (whose Bowie knife "scientifically" scalped Yellow Hand), and the colorful outfit Bill selected from his theatrical trunk.[15] In Henry Nash Smith's words, "It consisted of a Mexican suit of black velvet, slashed with scarlet, and trimmed with silver buttons and lace. . . . These costumes, fictional and actual, illustrate the blending of Cody with his theatrical role to the point where no one — least of all the man himself — could say where the actual left off and where dime novel fiction began."[16]

This incident became the model of countless duels in which cool and "peace-loving" superheroes always won. Elements of chivalry were inserted to fit the premise of "civilization" triumphing over "savagery" and to deny the actual aggression of Cody and his allies against the Indians. In some accounts the running skirmish became a formal duel reminiscent of archaic European rituals. As Cody re-enacted the incident in Wild West shows and told it repeatedly to audiences, he fired the first shot at Yellow Hand's horse while still on his own; then his horse stepped into a hole, and he fired from a standing position at the same moment that Yellow Hand sent his bullet whizzing past his head. Eyewitnesses reported that Yellow Hand had no firearm, but this could not be allowed in the mythical re-enactment. It had to be made into a duel with a bad guy who fired first.[17] Further embellishing details, such as the fictions that Yellow Hand was wearing an American flag as a breechcloth and flourishing the scalp of a blond woman, helped make it Buffalo Bill's fight against a perfect symbol of Indian aggression. In another fictional account that Cody helped create for a dime novel, the Yellow Hand paradigm of a chivalrous duel against an evil adversary is visible:

> Face to face, knee to knee, and hand to hand, Raven Feather and Buffalo Bill met. Twice the borderman parried the deadly thrusts of the wily chief — twice again the steel of the savage drank his blood, but weak from twenty wounds, the Indian's eyes were not sure, and soon the knife of the brave borderman reached his body with a fearful thrust. . . . Buffalo Bill, anxious as he was to hurry back to his loved ones, had to delay to have the blood staunched which poured from many a sad gash in his noble frame. . . .[18]

This passage emphasizes both the aggressive thrusts of the Indian and the pacific character of the redeemer figure; the hero has no thought for himself, but he gladly risks his life for his mother and family.

The theme of a hero whose gun saves civilization assumed central importance in the plays and Wild West shows Cody developed. Immediately upon returning from the Black Hills campaign, he toured with a melodrama entitled *The Red Right Hand; or, Buffalo Bill's First Scalp for Custer.* He re-enacted the chivalrous duel with Yellow Hand, and his victory helped take away the sting of the Custer "massacre." When the spectacular outdoor shows were developed in the 1880s, this violent ritual "achieved an immeasurable impact on the national consciousness."[19] Buffalo Bill toured England and the Continent, was feted by royalty and blessed by the Pope.[20] His tours helped place the stamp of monomythic redemption on the consciousness of the entire Western world. The show featured Cody and his scouts rescuing careening stagecoaches from howling Indian attacks, re-enactments of Custer's Last Stand, and the marksmanship of Annie Oakley.[21] Cody always carried with him the scalp of Yellow Hand and delighted in re-enacting the duel for his fans. The highlights of the Wild West shows "were the spectacles. An immigrant train,

complete with oxen and mules, was attacked by whooping Indians. . . . A settler's cabin was attacked by savagely painted Indians."[22] These were dramatic
rituals of denial in which the reality of the invasion of Indian lands was trans-
figured into redemption.

A few critical voices were raised in Cody's time. Newspapers carried stories, editorials, and reviews that occasionally compared Cody's claims with
historical facts or raised moral objections. His public display of Yellow
Hand's scalp elicited protests against "the blood-stained trophies of his murderous and cowardly deeds."[23] But this was distinctly a minority opinion.
Even the sophisticated Mark Twain, who knew the West from personal experience and loved to debunk inflated myths, wrote Cody that "down to its
smallest details the Show is genuine. . . . It is wholly free from sham and insin-
cerity. . . ."[24] General Sheridan, the commander of the Western Theater during the Indian wars, obviously placed more credence in the redemptive exaggerations than in his military reports when he "proclaimed that Buffalo Bill
had killed more Indians than any white man who ever lived." Theodore Roosevelt was well versed in Western history and surely recognized the enlarge-
ments of the Wild West shows, yet he applauded Buffalo Bill as

> . . . one of those men, steel-thewed and iron-nerved, whose daring progress
> opened the great West to settlement and civilization. His name, like that of
> Kit Carson, will always be associated with old adventure and pioneer days
> of hazard and hardship when the great plains and the Rocky Mountains
> were won for our race. . . . He embodied those traits of courage, strength
> and self-reliant hardihood which are vital to the well-being of our nation.[25]

The basis of popular credulity is visible in these statements about white
civilization's triumph through the exploits of its western scouts. Intelligent
people believed in Buffalo Bill, despite the evidence to the contrary, because
he dramatically embodied the Redeemer Nation concept.[26] The Manifest
Destiny of the nation to bear the burden of civilization against the irrational
resistance of savages was so widely believed that accepting Buffalo Bill was
virtually automatic. Joy S. Kasson has accurately called the Wild West an enterprise in "performing national identity."[27] To question the deeds of the winner of a Congressional Medal of Honor was to cast the nation's zealous ideals
into doubt. It was downright un-American. Even for highly critical minds,
Buffalo Bill's successful visualization of the western redeemer myth had a
massaging effect. What they could no longer accept in the form of stated ideology, full of Manifest Destiny jargon, they readily believed when reduced to
its visual basics. When Cody brought back real Indians from recent military

engagements to stereotypically re-enact their defeat by him and the U.S. military, the critical impulse found it easy to surrender. Accepting the mythic stature of Buffalo Bill had an additional advantage of implicitly denying the sordid facts about Western genocide. Thus those who might otherwise have argued about the means of western expansion were relieved to see that it was always the Indians who attacked the whites first and that Buffalo Bill was merely redeeming the innocent by killing the aggressive.[28]

The fact that the Wild West shows so perfectly embodied the emerging monomythic ideals lent credence to their advertising claim of educational value. The shows were not presented as mere entertainment, but as ritual evocations of the national ethos. When Buffalo Bill continued touring in his shows instead of volunteering for the Spanish-American War, his publicist, Major Burke, replied to charges of cowardice:

> Damn it all, what we are doing is educating you people! I am not afraid to say, sir, that the Wild West symposium of equestrian ability has done more for this country than the Declaration of Independence, the Constitution of the United States, or the life of General George Washington. Its mission is to teach manhood and common sense. We are not traveling to make money, sir, but only to do good. (p. 15)

This denial of personal self-interest and the profit motive, ridiculous as it may sound, is congruent with the other denials we have noted. They are the incipient stages of an elaborate doctrine of selflessness that marks the fully developed monomyth.

Historian Kent Ladd Steckmesser has summarized the traits that surfaced in this development of the Western hero: "genteel qualities" of Puritanical virtue; "clever traits" such as skill with weapons; "prowess" in the sense of always prevailing against numerous foes; and "epic significance," or the glorification of individual exploits.[29] These motifs are linked together in the definitive case of Buffalo Bill with a redemption scheme that Steckmesser overlooks, in which the hero relieves the community of its mortal threat from aggressive savages. The chivalric code makes it necessary to ritually deny the superior firepower of the white invaders. The symbol of a redeemer seeking nothing for himself ritually represses the invaders' desire for profitable western lands. A more flattering version of current events could hardly be imagined.

Don Russell, a leading authority on Buffalo Bill, observes that the legendary West of his theatrical shows became the norm against which popular portrayals of the period measured themselves:

It spawned many competitors and imitators, but the Cody show remained the biggest and best of the lot in its heyday — initiating an on-going process of illusion-making that has made its image of the West a part of our heritage. The Wild West show in its beginning was a representation of a historical era that was still contemporary. As time went on dramatization continued the illusion, as did the accompanying popular literature and its eventual translation to movies and television. The resultant legendary West derived in large part from the Wild West show.[30]

We should add here that the "illusion" involved a denial of aggression that was highly appealing to an expansionistic culture, and that from this denial was emerging the American monomyth.

Teddy Roosevelt and Manifest Destiny

An important mythic crossover toward enactment in American politics and diplomacy came quickly. Teddy Roosevelt, a friend of Buffalo Bill, was enamored of the myth. He shared Cody's passions and rhetoric of the subjugation of inferior peoples everywhere. In *The Winning of the West* he expressed his demeaning view of native culture: "The most righteous of all wars is a war with savages, though it is apt to be also the most terrible and inhuman. The rude, fierce settler who drives the savage from the land lays all civilized mankind under debt to him."[31] And surveying the victims of conquest around the world, he threw in his lot with the paler-skinned bloody hands: "American and Indian, Boer and Zulu, Cossack and Tartar, New Zealander and Maori — in each case the victor, horrible though many of his deeds are, has laid deep foundations for the future greatness of mighty people."[32]

As Assistant Secretary of the Navy in the McKinley administration, Roosevelt was in a position to transform the myth of a Redeemer Nation into an international reality. Caught up in the concept and rhetoric of Manifest Destiny and the imperialism he shared with leading figures such as Alfred T. Mahan and Henry Cabot Lodge, he developed visions of controlling territories in Latin America and the Pacific. It seemed downright unmanly to stand idly by while Europe colonized Latin America, Africa, and Asia. In 1898, his impulses in sympathy with the bellicose publisher William Randolph Hearst and many Americans, TR was contemptuous of McKinley's failure to declare war against Spain immediately after the sinking of the *Maine:* "The President has no more backbone than a chocolate éclair."[33] In fact, after the *Maine* blew up, TR almost single-handedly started hostilities with Spain by ordering Admiral Dewey, commander of the U.S. Navy in Hong Kong, into position against the Spanish in the Philippines — an order he gave while the real Secretary of the Navy was out of the office at a doctor's appointment!

When the war he had prayed for came, Roosevelt, like Buffalo Bill, was ready to translate his bellicose talk into action. He assembled a volunteer unit of cavalrymen, the Rough Riders, and installed himself as its leader. And he led the Rough Riders and other U.S. cavalry regulars in the charge up Kettle Hill near Santiago in the early fighting in Cuba. Roosevelt, as good a performer and p.r. man as there was at the time, had his own publicist and historian along with him on the Cuban campaign, one Richard Harding Davis, who regularly sent dispatches back to Hearst's papers. He also brought along a camera crew to ensure that the latest image-making technology would capture the glory of his exploits.

After having borrowed the "Rough Riders" label for his own military unit from Cody's Wild West show (partly to pay homage to the Congress of Rough Riders that Buffalo Bill had featured in his show since 1893), Roosevelt passed back the imperial torch to Buffalo Bill in 1899 after the victories of the Spanish-American War. The show replaced "Custer's Last Fight" with the "Battle of San Juan Hill," a commemoration of TR's courage. The show thus formally acknowledged the surpassing of mere internal conquest as a goal and celebrated America's acceptance of its global assertions of power. As more battles and attempted conquests came, the Wild West show replaced its Indians, and then its Spaniards, with other groups of "savages" who would have to yield to America's civilizing impulse for the world. Richard Slotkin tells of a series of rapid changes of the show's personnel designed to express animosity toward Filipinos (for their resistance in the Philippines) and then toward Chinese. "The Battle of Tien-Tsin," a 1901 innovation, was "a re-enactment of the capture of that city by the Allied army that suppressed China's 'Boxer' Rebellion and rescued the 'captives' in the Peking Legation Quarter."[34] In this performance the Indians assumed the role of the Boxers, and the Wild West's soldiers and cowboys represented all of White civilization" (pp. 85-86).

Carrington

The life of Buffalo Bill reveals a denial of self-interest in providing a monomythic shape to the task of hero-making. In glorifying of weapons as the barrier between savagery and civilization, in pretending restraint in their use, and in renouncing affections, Buffalo Bill and his Wild West actors attain redemptive powers matching those of legendary gods. Readers may object, however, that we assume a simplistic distinction between myth and history that betrays our own illusion that we can confront history with a post-mythical perspective. And perhaps our selective discovery of facts at variance with monomythic images reveals nothing more than a different set of mythic sensibilities. In searching for a plausible alternative to the monomyth, we find it instructive to examine Michael Straight's attempt to cope with Buffalo Bill's legacy in his historical novel *Carrington* (1960).[35]

Straight's subject is the Fetterman Massacre of 1866, which occurred near Fort Phil Kearny in Wyoming. Eighty-three soldiers led by Lieutenant Fetterman were slain near the Lodge Trail Ridge by a large group of Sioux warriors. The central figure of the novel, Colonel Carrington, was commanding officer at the fort. From Straight's perspective, Carrington was a judicious and admirable man, but his occasional vacillation prevented his ever earning the respect of the men he commanded. As a former abolitionist, he lacked the sense of racial superiority that most of his men felt. He also realized what no one else cared to admit: that the 700 badly trained and ill-equipped soldiers at Fort Phil Kearny were no match for 30,000 braves. His refusal to fight and his attempts at conciliation with the aggrieved Indians helped to provoke the fatal mutiny.

Lieutenant Fetterman, an audacious officer sent to strengthen Carrington's deteriorating unit, became an attractive competitor for the loyalties of the men in the regiment. He shared their impatience with the indecisive, conciliatory, and militarily maddening actions of the colonel. Not grasping the military dilemma, despite his proven bravery in Civil War battles, Fetterman decided to play the heroic role that Buffalo Bill would have staged theatrically with greater success. Defeated Indians in the later Wild West shows were a good deal less menacing and motivated than those Fetterman envisioned slaughtering. Colonel Carrington had received intelligence from the Cheyenne that the Sioux planned to attack Fort Phil Kearny with minor but provocative guerrilla raids, by which they hoped to lure the soldiers beyond Lodge Trail Ridge, where an overpowering force could quickly annihilate them. Yet Fetterman, boasting that "with eighty men I will ride through the entire Sioux nation," mutinously defied Carrington's orders not to move beyond the ridge. He led the entire company to death. His emasculated body was found at the bottom of the heap of his comrades.

Straight's picture of the men who went to their deaths is disturbing and complex. Some were drunkards, tortured by their war memories and aching wounds; some were sympathetic with the Indians and disgusted by the genocidal hatred that flared so frequently among the other men of the regiment. Straight was conscious that he was defying the mythic conventions so decisively stamped upon popular tastes by cowboy Westerns. In his tragic vision, there was no war between savagery and civilization, as in the tradition of Buffalo Bill and Teddy Roosevelt. It was rather the clash of two proud cultures, each possessing its own savagery. Straight moved beyond the popular stereotypes of good and evil, responding this way in an interview with John R. Milton: "No one in this novel . . . is villainous, in the sense that he wills evil. Everyone in the book . . . tries to carry out his duty. . . . They brought about evil . . . because they could not understand the nature of their actions, or else, because they had no sense of good and evil."[36]

This conclusion about the massacre was shaped by an unusual degree of historical discipline. Straight spent long days walking and photographing the landscape in the region of the battle, untangling the hidden military logic that had acted itself out in 1866. He camped at the site during the relevant seasons, and he studied letters, military dispatches, diaries, and medical reports at the Old War Records Branch of the National Archives. He spent long hours with Indians, discussing their understanding of the events and observing their sign language as they re-enacted for him the dialogues he had reconstructed between the chieftains and the U.S. military. He spent time with muleskinners and did research on Irish speech. But in presenting his fictional story of the massacre, Straight recognized the role of his own imagination and selectivity. While making no claim to have discovered the final truth, he refrained from the mythic denials required by the Buffalo Bill tradition.

Straight's portrait struck mythic nerves, as he discovered during the early 1960s, when the novel was considered as the subject for a Hollywood film. Since the royalties from the sale of his novel had earned Straight a meager fifty cents per hour, the suggestion to make the novel into a film was appealing. But he found that the very historical accuracy he had attained made the novel unacceptable as Hollywood film material. Living comfortably in Buffalo Bill's historical shadow, with its morally stereotyped conflicts between white civilization and red savagery, filmmakers found *Carrington* too unyielding. Straight describes their reactions:

> The novel, they said, would make a very good movie; it was set in the right country; it had the requisite number of battles with Indians; and so on. Only, they had three very serious reservations. . . . The first was that the leading character in the novel was an intellectual; that was very bad, they said. I agreed, but I added that there wasn't much that I could do about it. . . . The second matter that bothered them was that the central character had a number of weaknesses. I said, that's right: he did. . . . So then they

came out with the third reservation; and that was the gravest of all. The fact was, they said, that my novel had an unhappy ending. I said, that's right; but there's nothing very cheery, after all, in the deaths of eighty-three men. At that, they were very glum.[37]

The mythical expectations of the audience were such that they might not pay the price of admission. The novelist's fifty cents per hour seemed generous compared to the market value for historical realism in Hollywood. In subsequent years "new" Westerns, such as *Little Big Man* (1970), *Soldier Blue* (1970), *Dances with Wolves* (1989), and *At Play in the Fields of the Lord* (1991), have been produced, reversing the stereotypes so that Indians assume virtuous roles. Robert Altman's film *Buffalo Bill and the Indians; or, Sitting Bull's History Lesson* (1976)[38] fits this tradition of revision, exploring in a fantasy way the relationship between Cody and Sitting Bull in the years of the Wild West productions.[39] But one wonders whether historical realism of Straight's caliber is marketable even now.[40]

The difficulties in separating the monomyth from the history of the American West are symbolized in the epilogue to Straight's novel (with its ironic presaging of Hollywood's rejection of it). Retired General Carrington, who had been relieved of his command after Fetterman's foolhardy attack on the Sioux, returned to the scene decades later for official ceremonies sponsored by the city of Sheridan, Wyoming: a monument was to be dedicated on Massacre Hill. The old and unfairly treated Carrington seized the opportunity to relate what he knew about the mutiny and its subsequent cover-up. "In a quavering voice he cried, 'Here is the place and this is the hour for justice to historical truth.'" It was a long and sordid tale and, like the events themselves, did not lack its complexities.

> The General's voice dwindled, and when at last he stood rocking on his cane, no one was certain whether he had finished or given out. By then many of the spectators had moved away, for, interesting as the General's arguments were, he had spoken too long.

After a picnic lunch, ceremonial speeches by others reverted to the heroic imagery of the West. A congressman gazed at the monument to the dead soldiers and remarked that "truth and justice prevail with the running of the years." Sergeant Sam Gibson, retired, told how "he had come West as the youngest soldier in the Second Battalion — and stayed on to avenge the dead." As in the Buffalo Bill stories, the side of right is ever triumphant despite occasional reverses. Then ceremonies were cut short because the audience was hot and un-

Buffalo Bill ("the Hero of the Wild West") has had long tenure in the world of
pulp novels and comic books. In this German episode from the 1970s,
Buffalo Bill interrupts torture and "bloody revenge" against a white
gun trader who has swindled the Apaches.

Credit: *Buffalo Bill — Der Held des Wilden Westens* © Bastei-Verlag, 1970.

comfortable. Sgt. Gibson found his way back into town and attempted to tell some of the patrons in a crowded bar about how it was at the time of the mutiny. No one listened. He tried to order a drink that had been a favorite at the old fort. "'Give me an Old Tom, just like we had up at Phil Kearny!' The bartender shook his head. 'Never heard of either one.'"[41]

Here is perhaps the most characteristic form of denial in monomythic culture. Certain that history conforms to mythic expectations and that civilization has subdued savagery, most Americans have little interest in the details. The myth of Buffalo Bill's West is kept intact by denying even the memories that would convey the manner of its enactment. In the year of the American Bicentennial, a group of high school students in California proposed that the nation's capital be moved to the site of Buffalo Bill's ranch. Their teacher explained in an interview: "We feel the nation's capital should be in North Platte, but I think a name like Buffalo Bill or something like that would be more appropriate." Nebraska Secretary of State Allen Beerman applauded this campaign with a monomythic declaration about restoring paradise: If federal officials were moved to Buffalo Bill's town, he said, with its "clean air, water and open spaces, perhaps they would end up with clean and open minds."[42]

Clinging to such hopes blinds one to the sobering message of western history. As Michael Straight suggests, the true heroes were the Carringtons, who sought to avert the fatal clash between the races, not the killers who were certain that civilization would be redeemed by buffalo guns. Straight maintains that "if Carrington had succeeded, in that winter of 1866, the whole course of the Indian Wars would have been altered."[43] Belief in the possibilities of conciliation and peace admittedly also contains some mythical elements, but it may prevent us from following the next generation of Bill Codys right over the Lodge Trail Ridge.

4 Heidi Visits a
Little House on the Prairie

"Heidi is going to stay here and make you happy. We shall want to see the child again, but we will come to her. We shall come up to the Alm every year, for we have reason to offer thanks to the dear Lord in this place where such miracles have been wrought for our child."

grandmother of the girl healed in *Heidi*[1]

" 'Who's your boss?' the tough galoot asks Michael Landon. 'God,' he replies. For Michael [Little House on the Prairie] *Landon is nothing if not perpetually sincere."*

People Weekly on Landon's angel role
in the *Highway to Heaven* TV series[2]

Violence is not the only means of redemption through which monomythic material expresses its bias against the democratic ethos. One finds problem solvers and miracle workers using less forceful means; but the transformations they accomplish are no less dramatic. In the most complex human dilemmas, against the barriers of sloth, jealousy, and hardness of heart, the domestic superheroes work their magic of happy endings. Like Heidi, they contrive to heal the sick and bring happiness to the lonely. A grateful world

"Put your foot down firmly once," suggested Heidi.
(*Page* 344)

In *Heidi*, the miraculous young healer and her friend Peter
lead Klara to make her first steps.

Credit: Heidi © McKay Co., 1922. Illustration by Jessie Willcox Smith.

heaps upon them blessings and honor because their purity and cheerful helpfulness are the catalytic agency for modern miracles.

Popular females such as Dorothy in *The Wizard of Oz*, Maria in *The Sound of Music*, Little Orphan Annie, and Laura of the *Little House on the Prairie* television series have female literary predecessors in the European literary tradition of Dickens' Little Nell, Florence Dombey, Little Dorrit, in P. L. Travers' Mary Poppins, and in Johanna Spyri's Swiss character Heidi. American counterparts include Pollyanna and Little Eva in *Uncle Tom's Cabin*. In American television, male counterparts emerged in the 1960s and 1970s, with characters such as Dr. Marcus Welby and Charles Ingalls of the long running *Little House* series (NBC 1974-1983 followed by syndication on TBS). In the 1980s NBC offered the durable *Highway to Heaven* series (1984-1989). These tales featured Landon as Jonathan Smith, Angel, accompanied by his sidekick angel, Mark Gordon. *Highway to Heaven* shows heavenly heroes who miraculously change people with behavior problems — fixing them every time. Perhaps the oddest male appropriations of the Heidi role came in the film *To Wong Foo, Thanks for Everything! Julie Newmar* (1995), featuring three drag queens stranded in tiny Centersville, Nebraska: they immediately cure problems of alcoholism, muteness, stuttering, spousal abuse, and sexual dysfunction through a mixture of psychological manipulation — and physical intimidation. At the film's end, all the townspeople gather on Main Street to affirm that they are all "drag queens." Carol Ann, one of the beneficiaries, heartfully says to the departing Vida, "I don't think of you as a man and I don't think of you as a woman. I think of you as an angel."[3]

In recent years this tradition of redemption through controlling love has been seen most often in the *Touched by an Angel* series (CBS, 1994-present). The social function of these nonviolent domestic redeemer figures, both male and female, is to intervene in dreadful situations where the merely human powers of reconciliation and healing have failed. In contrast to the violent males, the means of redemption change — but the pattern of sexual renunciation, selfless virtue, and miraculous powers remains intact.

Heroines in the Protestant Tradition

The origin of current domestic redeemers can be traced to the Protestant piety of the nineteenth century. In contrast to earlier Puritan piety, it concentrated on the domestic realm and the transformation of individuals. Issues of public justice and problems of managing a "commonwealth" receded from sight at the same time that the traditional doctrine of the depravity of man was being replaced by utopian dreams of the perfectibility of man. Early Puritans had accounted for human flaws in the commonwealth by meditating upon universal depravity, the presence of those chosen for damnation, and the unfortunate sloth of the saints. The recession of these answers in the nineteenth century, visible both in Protestant liberalism and in the circles of secular Enlightenment, left an uncomfortable anomaly for those who believed in the perfectibility of man and society. If everyone is perfectible, why are there so many irascible and disruptive persons in one's family and community? If salvation is to be universal, why do so many seem to reject it? If the pursuit of happiness is blessed by Providence, why are so many people so unhappy?

An increasingly optimistic Protestantism answered these questions by emphasizing the need for both evangelism and loving works. Both would convert the unhappy and achieve the promised perfection of society. Wave after wave of revivals and reform movements in the nineteenth century spread the conviction that a selfless, loving act would melt the hardest heart and solve the thorniest problem. The exhortation "If everyone practiced love, these problems would disappear" replaced the jeremiads of an earlier generation. A self-reliant and optimistic public was thus granted the responsibility for societal redemption at the same time that the notion of miraculous divine intervention in human affairs was becoming old-fashioned. "God has no hands but our hands" was the newly popular refrain. But the knotty question still remained: What about those dilemmas that resist the application of well-intentioned love and admonition?

The classical Catholic tradition had possessed an idea that might have been usable here — that of the "saint" who through special divine gifts is a channel of miraculous redemption. But earlier Protestantism had fiercely rejected the concept of special saintliness declared efficacious by churchly authority; they replaced it with the "priesthood of all believers." Early Puritans applied the term "saint" to every believer who took up the pilgrimage of faith, while they rejected the notion that any son or daughter of Adam could be redemptive for others. "Christian" in *The Pilgrim's Progress* could be exemplary for others in his successful struggle but never redemptive. The best of the Puritan "saints" had forever to retain the introspective quest for secret sins. Thus only the "word of God" communicated by the Spirit could redeem, said the Protestant divines of early America. But as the nineteenth century repeatedly demonstrated, the Word alone did not suffice, either for incorrigible individuals or complex conflicts in society arising out of the structure of the family or the economic system. There was a need for embodiments of redemptive love that would have a superhuman capacity to redeem, yet still remain democratically ordinary. A culture that had given up the belief in the Virgin Mary and guardian angels stood ready for their democratic replacements.

The popular literature of Protestant culture spawned a new redeemer figure, a superheroine — often a mere child — who solves problems by selfless love and virtuous cheerfulness. She is a model of moral purity, seeking nothing for herself, while loving others in a generous but sexually chaste manner. Female redemptive power requires a soul and body uncontaminated by sexual passion. We can witness the emergence of this sexless heroine pattern in the novels of Charles Dickens, which were widely popular both in England and America during the nineteenth century. Scores of other heroines were born in the minds of authors inspired by Dickens. He would surely have been astounded by such fertile propagations from his angelic virgins.

Little Nell in *The Old Curiosity Shop* was the first of Dickens' characters

Little Nell of Dickens' *Curiosity Shop* is shown as an angel after her early death.
Her great uncle, The Single Gentleman, muses: "If you have seen the picture gallery
of any one old family, you trace the same sweet girl through a long line of portraits . . . the
good Angel of the race — abiding by them in all reverses, redeeming all their sins."
Credit: Illustration from Charles Dickens' *The Old Curiosity Shop*, 1841. Text from Chapter LXIX.

to embody the new scheme. With utter selflessness, this pretty fourteen-year-old spends her frail life trying to save her degenerate grandfather. Harassed and finally foreclosed by the villainous dwarf Quilp, the lonely pair — Nell and her grandfather — escape London by night and begin a desperate pilgrimage. Like a pathetic Moses, Nell leads her confused grandfather out of danger. She had hoped to regain a peaceful solitude where happiness would be possible, but in the end Nell gains only her own death. As Dickens scholar Steven Marcus points out, "That 'fresh solitude' for which Nell prays is also her original state, her destination, that earliest home. The idyllic recollection of Eden, of life restored to its pristine harmony, has here developed clearly on the side of its tendency toward death."[4] For the sake of this redemptive mission to recover Eden, Little Nell repeatedly forces her dissolute grandfather to flee temptation and vice. When, for example, she discovers that his companions have involved him in a planned robbery, she awakens him to insist on immediate flight:

> The old man rose from his bed, his forehead bedewed with the cold sweat of fear, and, bending before the child as if she had been an angel messenger sent to lead him where she would, made ready to follow her.[5]

Dickens uses angelic imagery throughout the book to refer to the purity of Little Nell. When her friend Kit finally locates Nell in her dying moment, he explains, "I have been used, you see . . . to talk and think of her almost as if she was an angel."[6] Sexual purity combines with a selfless renunciation of happiness to make the angel imagery appropriate.

While Nell remains the innocent suffering servant whose angelic virtues provide only temporary respite for her grandfather, later Dickens heroines are more effective. Florence Dombey's selfless love for her cruel, hardhearted father effects a miraculous moral transformation; this occurs after Paul Dombey, having driven his wife and unwanted daughter, Florence, from his mansion, has lost his fortune. He is embittered at the world for the death of his only male heir, on whom the dynastic hopes of Dombey & Son rested, and unfairly blames his daughter for rivaling his dead son in health and vitality.

In an amazing gesture of Christian charity, Florence seeks out her fallen father, asking his forgiveness for having left home (though he had cruelly driven her out in rage over her sympathy for his second wife, Edith). The gesture breaks his hardened heart, and he responds, "Oh, my God, forgive me . . ." (p. 421).

The redeemed Paul Dombey returns with Florence to live out his life in her home, expressing to his grandchildren the affection he had withheld from his own daughter. Florence also redeems the alienated Edith, who replies thus to her selfless overtures: "Florence! . . . My better angel . . . purest and best of natures, whom I love . . . [you] who might have changed me long ago . . ." (p. 445). As a result of her encounter with Florence, Edith sends a message of reconciliation to her husband. So in the most irreconcilable domestic conflicts, the intervening love of selfless redeemers like Florence Dombey is effective in the end.

In *Bleak House* the wisdom and virtue of Esther Summerson triumph over a decadent world, redeeming all whom she touches. A. E. Dyson observes that "her intelligence is chiefly moral and intuitive. . . . She can 'smell out' people's moral natures by instinct. . . . She is also given a high degree of self-knowledge and unusual gifts of self-sacrifice . . . a convincing depiction of moral goodness. . . ."[7] The same pattern holds for Little Dorrit, who, as J. Hillis Miller suggests, is pictured by Dickens as "a person who is altogether good. And this miraculous goodness is imagined as the persistence into adult life of the purity of childhood. . . . Little Dorrit derives all her power to help her father and others around her from her preservation of the simplicity, lovingkindness, and faithful perseverance of childhood."[8] It is miraculous because Dorrit is an adult who "understands the wickedness of the world, and is able to accept and love even that" (p. 241).

Dickens' angelic redemption scheme is particularly prominent in *Hard Times,* where Rachel's selfless love for Stephen Blackpool and his alcoholic wife saves him from a desperate act of murder to free himself from an intolerable marriage. He falls on his knees before the lovely Rachel and says, "Thou art an Angel. . . . Thou changest me from bad to good. Thou mak'st me humbly wishfo' to be more like thee, and fearfo' to lose thee when this life is ower, a' the muddle cleared awa'. Thou'rt an Angel; it may be thou hast saved my soul alive!"[9]

This image of the ideal woman as an angelic redeemer figure communicating divine love to a fallen world became a crucial tenet for Victorian literature in the wake of Dickens. These angelic girls give us an image of selfless love devoid of sexuality, combined with a perfect conformity to the post-Puritan virtues of cooperativeness, cheerfulness, and submissiveness. Redemption here takes the form of adjustment to circumstances rather than the annihilation of incorrigibles.[10] The suffering servant replaces the horseman with the avenging weapon. Except for the seemingly instinctive need of these Victorian heroines to submit to male authority, they betray no sense of female sexual identity. As H. R. Hays wittily puts it, this literature makes women into "the bell-shaped angel" who, given the "conspiracy of silence" concerning sexual relations, presumably "produced young by parthenogenesis."[11]

Heidi Comes to America

A series of female writers took up the presentation of the superheroine in the wake of Dickens. Harriet Beecher Stowe modeled her depiction of Little Eva in *Uncle Tom's Cabin* after Little Nell. Beginning in 1868, Martha Farquarson developed the female redeemer figure in the *Elsie Dinsmore* series: Elsie was the pious heroine who redeemed others by bursting into tears at hardness of heart. She brought her irreligious father to repentance by fainting at the piano when he tried to force her to play secular music on Sunday.[12]

For many Americans of the twentieth century, perhaps the best known of such literary heroines is Heidi in Johanna Spyri's book of that title, first translated into English in 1884. This perpetual favorite has often been translated, published, and filmed in America, once featuring Shirley Temple in the title role (1937).[13] More recently it appeared as *Heidi's Song* in a Hanna Barbera animated version (1982), and it finally received the Disney blessing in 1993.[14] Its appeal to audiences in the United States seems to reveal an American appetite for tales of redemption effected by stereotypically feminine powers of love and psychological manipulation.

In the Spyri classic, the orphan Heidi is brought to the Alps to live with her old grandfather, a recluse who is at odds with religion and society. Her cheerfulness and transforming machinations turn the forbidding mountains above Dorfli into a veritable Eden. After rescuing the neighbor boy Peter and his goat from a precipice, Heidi offers him her lunch in exchange for his promise not to punish the errant animal. "You may have it all. . . . But then you must never, never beat Distelfinck, or Schneehopli, or any of the goats."[15] This manipulative strategy succeeds in permanently altering Peter's treatment of the goats: bribing was never more redemptive. Heidi also keeps Peter's blind grandmother company, giving her something to live for once again. After Heidi's very first visit, the old woman goes to bed, saying, "If she will only come again! Now there is something still left in the world to give me pleasure!" (p. 44). Heidi talks her previously antisocial grandfather into repairing the shutters on the primitive house where the old woman lives — to the amazement of all. As Heidi humbly controls the older males, one by one, the process of beneficent domestication is well on its way.

The Alm-Uncle's resistance to sending his eight-year-old granddaughter to school or church brings about a fall from Paradise. Heidi is taken to Frankfurt, where she becomes the companion of the crippled Klara. Desperately homesick in the lowlands, Heidi feels "as if she were in a cage behind the long curtains. . . . Like a little bird placed for the first time in a handsome cage, she flew from one window to another. . . . She felt that she must see the green grass and the last melting snows on the cliffs" (p. 61). Heidi selflessly becomes Klara's friend and brings joy to her life but constantly runs afoul of the rigid disciplines of the governess. The governess becomes convinced Heidi is mad because she lashes out against the crowded city, which seems so antithetical to life in the Alps: "If the robber-bird should fly over Frankfurt he would scream still louder, because so many people live together and make each other wicked, and do not go up on the cliffs where it would be good for them" (p. 76). As a corrupted urbanite, the governess lacks the mythic bias toward the more Edenic alpine life. Poor Heidi! Convinced that she would never see her beloved mountains again, and fearing she would appear ungrateful if she complained, the child who has begun to bring such remarkable changes in her companion falls into despondency. "Heidi dared tell no one that she was homesick. But in her heart the burden grew heavier and heavier. She could no longer eat, and every day she grew a little paler. At night she often lay awake for a long time thinking of the Alm" (p. 89).

In terms conventional for both European and American pietism, Heidi is told by Klara's grandmother that religious submission would provide a happy solution to her desperate loneliness. "You see, Heidi, the reason you are so sad is because you know no one who can help you. . . . If you pray every day and trust Him, everything will be made right for you, and you will soon have a happy heart again" (p. 90). The child replies, "I will go now, right away, and ask God to forgive me . . . and I will never forget Him again" (p. 94). Shortly thereafter Heidi begins sleepwalking and betrays to the summoned doctor that she dreams of being in the mountains again with her beloved grandfather; whereupon the good doctor prescribes the Alpine meadows for her health.

After her return to the mountains, Heidi's role as a selfless redeemer develops rapidly. She uses the money she's received from Herr Sesemann to buy white rolls for the blind grandmother, who has trouble eating the hard black bread. After Heidi tells her grandfather how the "dear Lord" must have planned for her to return with money for the rolls and the ability to read to the blind woman, a miraculous change comes over him. He climbs up to Heidi's loft that night and finds her lying there with folded hands, having thanked God as she had promised. "Then he, too, folded his hands and bowed his head. 'Father,' he prayed, 'I have sinned against Heaven and before Thee and am no more worthy to be called Thy son!' And great tears rolled down his cheeks" (p. 123). The next morning he puts on his coat with the silver buttons for the first time in years and takes Heidi to church — to everyone's amazement. The community welcomes him back as if the years of hostility and alienation had somehow disappeared. The old man confesses, "The dear Lord was indeed good to me when He sent you up on the Alm" (p. 127). The simple faith that God uses her to achieve the happiness of others keeps Heidi from reflecting on her own role in this miraculous melting of a hardened heart. She remains as pure and selfless as the first day she skipped up the Alm to her grandfather's hut.

The climactic miracle is the healing of Klara. She is brought to the Alm the spring after the doctor's visit, along with her wheelchair and other paraphernalia. The bright sunshine and goats' milk begin a process of natural healing, which Heidi and her grandfather encourage. One day the old man carries Klara up to the meadow and leaves her with Heidi and Peter, not knowing that Peter has spitefully pushed Klara's wheelchair over the cliff. When Klara wants to see the flowers higher up, Heidi's moment has arrived. Ordering Peter to help, she commands Klara to take her first steps. "Klara did so . . . and suddenly she cried out excitedly, 'I can do it, Heidi! Oh, I can! See! I can take steps, one after another'" (p. 191). Later, when Klara's grandmother comes to witness the unexpected miracle, she explains to Peter how his sin in destroying the wheelchair had been turned into good. This scene resonates with the healing miracles ascribed to Jesus in the Gospels. The requirement for this miraculous transformation of evil into good is a child-like female saint. The natural healing processes and providential coincidence are galvanized by the selfless good works of Heidi and her associates.

The redemptive score of our innocent superheroine is thus perfect. She conveys the wondrous powers of the Alpine Eden to everyone she encounters: her bitter old grandfather, the lonely doctor, the illiterate Peter, his lonely grandmother, and now the crippled Klara. This redemptive paradigm matches the monomythic outline at every point. The unselfish redeemer, lacking in any sexual consciousness, achieves marvelous solutions through which she restores Edenic happiness, and everyone lives happily ever after. This mythical plot varies from the masculine heroic patterns only in the means of redemption, which are psychologically and religiously manipulative rather than violent. Whereas the men achieve sexual segmentation through renunciation, superheroines like Heidi simply remain in a prepubescent state forever.

A surprisingly large number of figures in American children's literature and popular culture fit the Heidi model. Pollyanna is a sort of Yankee Heidi: she redeems an entire town and brings frustrated lovers together by teaching and living the "Glad Game." Little Orphan Annie fits the same pattern of permanent prepuberty arrest, playing the role of a thoroughly secularized Heidi whose miracles are sometimes wrought by her superhuman associates like Daddy Warbucks. Maria in *The Sound of Music* is the asexual, childlike woman who softens the heart of the militaristic Baron von Trapp. Dorothy in

The Wizard of Oz transforms the Scarecrow, the Tin Man, and the Cowardly Lion before returning to Kansas without having grown perceptibly toward feminine maturity. Mary Worth, whose popular comic strip has endured since 1938, is a postmenopausal variant of the selfless redeemer guided by fate from crisis to domestic crisis — reliably bringing the miracle of happy endings. Jessica Fletcher, the widowed detective of *Murder She Wrote* (1984-1996), extended the Mary Worth tradition of kindly meddling to the criminal scene.

Television's Pa Ingalls as the Heidi Man

One of the most striking developments in American pop culture is the emergence of male Heidi figures who redeem by nonviolent manipulations. It is possible that Santa Claus, shaped by the Victorian yearning for domestic happiness, is a predecessor in this regard. The most important figure in popular culture to carry on the Heidi tradition was Michael Landon, who played the Charles Ingalls father character during the long-playing *Little House on the Prairie* series, which remains in syndication with TBS nearly two decades after its final program in 1983. When that series expired, Landon figuratively went to heaven as his own executive producer for the *Highway to Heaven* television series (NBC, 1984-1989). Portraying an angel continued the domestic redeemer role he had played so convincingly.

In the *Little House on the Prairie* novels by Laura Ingalls Wilder, Charles Ingalls is barely able to support his family as a farmer and jack-of-all-trades. In the television series, Pa spends the bulk of his time and creative energy solving the problems of the community. The long, monotonous days and years behind the plow and building shelters with primitive tools have disappeared from view, while a series of domestic crises each finds neat resolution within the 48-minute-program time space. In one episode Ingalls almost single-handedly relieves Walnut Grove of a typhoid fever epidemic after the doctor and minister prove incapable of coping with the deadly threat. He finds that the source of the infection is the cut-rate grain being sold in the community. Ingalls' taste for a different type of flour had protected him and his family from the epidemic. Once he has established why they are exempt from the plight of other mortals in Walnut Grove, Ingalls leads the campaign to heal the community, using the church as a hospital. His issuing of orders symbolizes the status of the domestic redeemer above the traditional redemptive agencies of society: "Reverend, bring shovels. We will have to bury the dead right away." The episode concludes with a touch of Heidi pietism after the plague subsides. "God lets it happen to strengthen us," remarks the minister.[16]

In another television episode, Ingalls' coolness and moral sense keep the community from an unjust lynching. The man entrusted to buy seed corn from a distant town is accidentally pinned under his wagon; but the ever-stupid citizens of Walnut Grove immediately conclude that he has made off with their money. They scorn Ingalls and discuss violent retribution; meanwhile, Ingalls himself retraces the route and finds the injured man in the forest, saving both him and the community. Like Dickens' Esther Summerson, Ingalls has an unerring ability to tell "good guys" from "bad guys" and thus assures perfect solutions to moral dilemmas.[17]

The monomythic structure of these domestic redeemer tales is stamped into a *Little House on the Prairie* episode such as "Ebenezer Sprague," which opens with the typical Edenic scene of the Ingalls children romping over the unspoiled prairie.[18] Arriving from the wicked city like a hardhearted capitalist, the Scrooge-like Ebenezer Sprague begins spoiling paradise by demanding a penalty payment because the completion of the new bank building is forty-eight minutes late. In a coldly hostile manner, he turns down Ingalls' friendly invitation to dinner.

The next day, the women of Walnut Grove gather to consider how to remedy the lack of school texts for the poorer children of the community. They resolve, after the intervention of the selfless Mrs. Ingalls, to take up a community collection; she also volunteers to approach the difficult banker. When she does, however, Sprague immediately accuses her of attempting to use "the wiles of a woman" to get a loan her husband had applied for and had been rudely refused. "My only duty is to run an honest bank and make a fair profit for myself. . . . Children will grow up without books." And thus a domestic impasse arises in the innocent town: the banker hinders the progress of farmers like Ingalls, and his refusal to contribute dooms the effort to provide books for needy children. What could possibly alter this Scroogish impediment to paradise?

The monomythic plot at this point calls for the emergence of a super-hero. Sure enough, Laura unwittingly strikes up a friendship with the newcomer to Walnut Grove and innocently sets about the task of miraculous transformation. She has taken up fishing, which is Sprague's only hobby. Her first encounter with the unknown man at the pond is inauspicious, but eventually she persuades him to use some of her doughballs for bait, so that he can catch as many fish as she has. They end up riding back together in the buggy, and she reports to her family at supper that this unknown fisherman is now her best friend.

The next day, Laura discovers the identity of her fisherman friend, with whom she had innocently discussed the problem of the mean banker who would not contribute to the book fund. She returns to the fishing hole to confront Mr. Sprague with his deception. But rather than admitting it, Sprague accuses her of feigning friendship to get Pa's loan. She replies with perfect integrity, "All I wanted to have was a good friend."

Pa Ingalls strides into the bank the next morning as the cool avenger who must administer a proper verbal lashing.

> "You broke that little girl's heart. She went down to that pond every day to see her best friend. . . . My little girl gave something to you. Friendship. You took it and threw it right back in her face."
>
> "I don't need friends," Sprague replied.
>
> "Well, that's good for you, Mr. Sprague, because you don't have any. You know, I feel sorry for you. You can't take anything, and you can't give anything except money. And as far as I am concerned, that means you don't have anything at all."

This denunciation recalls Heidi's harsh verbal punishment of Peter. The banker spends a sleepless night in his barren room, much as Scrooge dreams of his empty life without friends or family. In a miraculous conversion indebted far more to Dickens and Spyri than to Laura Ingalls Wilder, the television program depicts Sprague secretly sending a crateload of books to a surprised school. Laura is reconciled with the banker, and the program ends with Ebenezer Sprague in the bosom of his newly adopted family, much like Dickens' Scrooge in the house of Bob Cratchit. The formerly hardhearted bachelor is hugging little Carey, who replaces Tiny Tim in the festive scene. The camera fades back through the window, showing the Christmas-like celebration in the Ingalls home, with a lovely cake at the center of the scene. Laura's reprise confirms the restoration of paradise through psychological manipulation: "I kept Mr. Sprague's secret about the books. And Pa got his loan and bought the forty acres. Mr. Sprague said I sure didn't lie about Ma's cooking. It was the best in the whole world." Johanna Spyri would have blushed to find so many Heidis around a single cake.

The Retreat from Realism and the Ascent of Angels

Perhaps the most remarkable facet of the domestic redemption scheme in the television version of *Little House on the Prairie* is its departure from the starkly realistic novels of Laura Ingalls Wilder. Her chronicles of the pioneer experience in the Midwest encompassed a great variety of topics that children have found fascinating: Ma's wonderful cooking, Pa's fiddling for family singing in the evening, the many journeys to different homestead locations, the experiences of struggling with adverse weather, the encounters with insects and animals, and the struggles of survival as a farm family in the perpetual throes of bankruptcy. The opening lines of *On the Way Home* convey the somber and realistic material characteristic of these Wilder chronicles.

> For seven years there had been too little rain. The prairies were dust. Day after day, summer after summer, the scorching winds blew the dust and the sun was brassy in a yellow sky. Crop after crop failed. Again and again the barren land must be mortgaged, for taxes and food and next year's seed. The agony of hope ended when there was no harvest and no more credit, no money to pay interest and taxes; the banker took the land. Then the bank failed.
>
> In the seventh year a mysterious catastrophe was world wide. All banks failed. From coast to coast the factories shut down, and business ceased. This was a Panic.[19]

These lines from Laura's diary convey the blunt, courageous, unsentimental spirit that is characteristic of this entire series of children's books. The social order does not escape criticism, though the tone is never ideological. There are moments of comfort, security, and joy in the stories, but the predominant tone is of hardships, some self-imposed by the failure of family schemes to live well on the adverse prairie, and there are no miraculous redemptions of evil bankers.

When one compares these stories with the television episodes, one can clearly see that a process of *mythic alchemy* has occurred. By *alchemy* we refer to the purging of elements that do not fit monomythic premises. The novels are cleansed of their realistic components and transformed from tragic sagas to happy, sentimentalized melodramas. When desperate circumstances arise, they are always neatly eliminated at the end of an hour program by miraculous redemption. Elements that might prevent an audience from being intoxicated by the mythic brew are filtered out.

In the novel *By the Shores of Silver Lake*, for example, Laura's older sister barely survives scarlet fever and suffers permanent blindness. The family tenderly cares for her with its limited means, saving pennies for years before Mary can be sent to a school for the blind. She learns to do housework without her sight, while Laura takes over chores and becomes "her eyes" by describing events, weather, and scenery. It is a courageous, ennobling story of coping with harsh reality. In September 1975, Lewis K. Parker described his interview with producer-actor Michael Landon and his cast on the *Little House* set in California. He asked whether the TV Mary would go through the ordeal of blindness. "No, but Mary will get glasses. . . . That'll happen in a show about her grades mysteriously dropping — all because she can't see the blackboard and doesn't want to tell anyone."[20] Sure enough, the next television episode, "Four Eyes" (Sept. 17, 1975), showed Pa finding Mary studying late at night in the wake of a bad report card. He writes the answer to a problem on her slate and says, "See that?" She looks puzzled and must step closer to the slate to read what it says. Pa then devises an experiment to test her sight, and he subsequently takes Mary to Mankato to be fitted with glasses. Mary's schoolmates tease her as "four eyes," so she hides her glasses in a hollow log. Her chief tormenter, naughty Nellie Olsen, begins to boast about winning the forthcoming history contest. But Mary retrieves her glasses at the last minute and wins the highest grade. To make the neat resolution complete, Mary has to wear the glasses for only a month or so until her strained eye muscles are eased. The television producers/writers have distilled the permanent affliction of blindness into a temporary and minor problem solved by the ingenuity of superdad. It was not until the fourth season that this sugary treatment was surpassed: Mary is allowed to go blind in a state of anger that requires the family to send her away. But she quickly meets Adam at the school, finding him so attractive that her rage disappears.[21]

For children who have read the realistic Wilder novels for the past three generations, the years of the *Little House* television series ranked as a flagrant violation of historical consciousness. The large viewing audience, however, was assured that they were witnessing historical reality. Michael Landon explains:

> So we take incidents from the books and build stories around them. We've pretty much shown how the real Ingalls family lived. . . . I got together with the art director and we researched more than fifty books on frontier life in Minnesota in the 1870's. . . . As a result, our show is probably the most visually authentic of any ever made about the Old West. (Parker, pp. 12-13)

Thus pseudo-empiricism is part of the program's believability strategy. But even here the alchemy process is apparent. In place of mud and drought there are clean streets and barnyards and green fields. Instead of frequent tornadoes, grasshoppers, and blizzards, there are occasional bouts with adverse weather that always end happily. But the cumulative result of the transmutation is that the raw, threatening prairie and the ugly, raucous towns become Edenic. Natural evils that strike everyone without discrimination in the novels are distilled so that the Ingalls family is either spared or quickly retrieved by its virtue, hard work, and redemptive skills. The Pa Ingalls of the novels — the foolish, loving, bearded man plagued with mortgages, disasters, and crop failures — is alchemized in the television series into a handsome, smooth-skinned savior who devotes most of his time to rescuing the community. Historical details such as Pa's stealing food for his family in *The Long Winter* and his fist fight at the land claim office in *By the Shores of Silver Lake* have been eliminated. The historical Ingalls family leaves behind a succession of abject failures; they miscalculate, lose their land, and have to move on. But the process of TV's mythic alchemy makes them always triumphant in adversity, abiding in a stable paradise where children grow up romping over green meadows. The orchestra always comes in on cue to sweep the audience into a nostalgia for paradise.

Touched by an Angel

The Heidi scheme surfaces in more recent television programs that feature angelic teams as the superheroic restorers of paradise. Ruth Shalit's essay on the history of angels throws light on this development. She describes with discernment the great variety of angels in the ancient and medieval worlds. Some were agents of apocalypse and lesser judgments, others offered messages of hope or acts of assistance. She points out that in the recently surging angels market, the bestsellers feature helpful creatures inclined to satisfy human desires for everything from prosperity to sexual fulfillment. "Even as Americans have increasingly absented themselves from the disciplines and encumbrances of traditional religion, angels have returned with a vengeance, but less as a manifestation of faith than an objectification of need."[22] Shalit sees in this a confirmation of Richard Hofstadter's prediction from *Anti-Intellectualism in American Life* that psychological redemption in this life would replace salvation in the next one.

The *Touched by an Angel* series has fulfilled this prophecy with plots that repeatedly offer the domestic version of the monomyth. The superheroic characters are the boss angel Tess (Della Reese), who is the postmenopausal matriarch of a holy threesome; her aides are the youngish Monica (Roma Downey) and Andrew, Angel of Death (John Dye). Though Monica and Andrew must occasionally spend intimate time together, their sexual chemistry is muted — because they are both actually dead. The stressful situations in which they perform their miracles are a result of individuals who respond belligerently toward others and also self-destructively. The family members or other agents within that person's community show themselves deficient in responding to such a vicious or despairing person. They are too judgmental, too unloving, or too baffled to give that person the love he or she needs — or the self-esteem that comes only through awareness of God's redeeming love.

When the angels come to intervene in these deficiently therapeutic communities, they must initially disguise themselves while they study the situation and develop a strategy. Reminding us of the superhero's uniform or mask, they typically take on institutional roles as social workers, judges, lawyers, and so forth, so that they can inconspicuously launch their miracles. The manipulative aspect generally comes with a tinkling shower of angelic light on Monica's reddish hair along with the message that "I am an angel who has come to tell you of God's love." The magic of confronting an actual angel who accepts each individual and expresses the love of God always prevails, resulting in the individual's rehabilitation. The redeemer team joins in a group hug as a dove — the program's icon — flutters off into the sky. The angels are free to go back to heaven to pick up another assignment and a new disguise that will go with it. This formulaic element echoes the formula of the cowboy riding away from the saved community.

This redemptive recipe can be seen with shining clarity in a *Touched by an Angel* episode entitled "The Penalty Box."[23] Jeff McHenry, a clever student and talented hockey player headed for Harvard, attends expensive St. Crispin's Academy. He drives a new BMW coupe to school, parks in a red zone, and responds arrogantly to the security person who politely complains about it. Through quickly sketched scenes at home and at school, we see that he does nothing for himself and expects others to provide personal service without any gratitude from him. He abrasively dominates other students in social situations and acts possessively about the girl for whom he competes with "Mr. Jennings," another hockey player and the son of a banker. Tess, Monica, and Andrew have been tipped off by God that Jeff will soon experience a great anger and sense of betrayal, so they come around to steer him toward greater maturity and humility. Jeff's dad, a widowed venture capitalist, has "leveraged a lot against a deal" and will quickly lose the family wealth; Jeff's car will be repossessed. He can no longer play hockey in the arena for which his father provided the naming gift. He will have to leave St. Crispin's and attend the plebeian East High. The full angelic team is needed for such a bitter, humiliated young man.

To meet this crisis that no human agency can resolve, Tess becomes the lunch-room lady, Andrew becomes the history teacher, and Monica becomes the hockey coach at competing East High. Each is there to observe and to plant the needed spiritual seeds that will redeem Jeff. As the news of financial distress unfolds, Jeff is immediately shunned by the rich St. Crispinites. When he learns that the money for Harvard has evaporated, Jeff is furious with his father: "So you're nothing but a gambler. You have just gambled my future away." In hopes that he can make it to Harvard anyway, he joins East High's hockey team, where he feels contempt for the other players and obnoxiously hogs the puck in a game against his old St. Crispin team (where a Harvard hockey scout is said to be present). During the game Jeff and Jennings, his former teammate, begin a brawl and Jeff must go to the penalty box for two minutes. Tess snaps at Monica, "Go, now!"

Time freezes in the arena as Coach Monica confronts a disoriented Jeff with her radiant gold-lit hair and these words: "God has called a timeout. I'm an angel, an angel sent by God." When she asks why he is failing to play as a team member, Jeff replies, "I've got to go to Harvard." Monica says, "It's character that decides what you are and what you become." Jeff reveals that he is obsessive about going to Harvard because it "will set [him] up for life." But a deeper reason is that getting to Harvard was a promise he made to his dying mother, giving her momentary comfort. Monica tells him that, despite his pledge, this game is not about winning but about respecting his teammates. "Become a future leader, not just a Harvard man," she exhorts. Jeff returns to the team huddle and hands the captain's helmet back to the former captain, a much less talented player. "I've been an idiot. I don't deny it. I've been selfish." Then he gives a rousing Henry V–St. Crispin's Day speech that lifts his team to play with real spirit. They do not win.

However, Tess and Andrew have placed themselves near the Harvard hockey scout and have badgered him to pay attention to the amazing Jeff. At game's end, the scout approaches Jeff with the news that Harvard is out of money for the fall semester but that he thinks he can get some hockey scholarship money for him in the spring. Finally, against all probability, Jeff and his dad are reconciled at the end of the episode.

While it's sentimentally satisfying to see these instant character adjustments, we find ourselves in agreement with Ruth Shalit's judgment that *Touched by an Angel* consistently embodies "a cynical optimism." "Evil, misfortune, even death: in this upbeat cosmos, all may be avoided or reversed. Tragedy is nothing but a plot device. Pain is real only so that it may be repealed. Rescue is inevitable. Inconclusiveness and uncertainty are banished."[24] All it takes is a smiling team of angels, a momentary flash of glowing hair, and some well-chosen words about acceptance, love, and accepting responsibility. The God of these stories is a narcissistic projection completely lacking in the transcendence confronted by virtuous Job. In place of human maturation gained through self-understanding, exertion, and suffering, instead of robust freedom and responsibility, these stories promise that super agencies will solve our problems and make us happy. This is truly a religious opiate, more potent and more illusory than the targets aimed at by Marx and Freud.

Life without Heidi

The most serious question to be raised about these schemes of domestic redemption concerns their efficacy in helping mere mortals cope with reality. What is their likely impact on persons facing the irremediable conditions of disability, accident, natural catastrophe, financial loss, human evil, and death? What message do these stories offer to the poor, the defeated, the frustrated, and the disappointed?

Materials such as *Heidi,* the *Little House on the Prairie* series, and the *Touched by an Angel* series imply that if superheroes were present, they would solve a vast array of problems quickly and painlessly. But since there are no such figures outside of popdom, there really seems to be little that can be done. Passivity in the face of adverse circumstances becomes linked with a tranquilizing nostalgia for Eden. The message is that all good people — and even a few vicious ones — deserve happy endings, no matter what their limitations; however, since such happiness is not available in real life for most people, the natural conclusion is that something must have gone dreadfully wrong. A selective, nostalgia-drenched presentation of the past thus erodes the ability to live in the present and awakens the yearning for total solutions offered by the modern propagandists of redemption.

The impact of the domestic redemption scheme on communal and familial leaders may be equally problematic. Those who identify with the redeemer figures and seek to emulate their feats in real life will find that targets of redemption are not as easy to change as one might expect. Nor is adversity easy to alter. Without overlooking the need for and potential of benevolence, we can nevertheless perceive that cheerful Heidis do not generally succeed in reconciling alienated oldsters to church and community. Innocent Lauras usually fare no better using homemade fish bait to soften the lonely and embittered hearts of bankers. The manipulative techniques of pious abnegation and well-devised tongue lashings rarely evoke the miraculous transformations promised by the myth. They are more frequently the source of additional alienation. But since an illusion of perfect selflessness is essential to the redemptive scheme, the mythic alchemy denies one's personal motivations in order to mask manipulative campaigns. The myth teaches those seeking to emulate superheroes not to place their cards on the table, not to admit their own emotional needs, and hence always to assume the attitude of the injured servant when thwarted. When the stance of the innocent savior proves futile, explosions of indignation are imminent. Frustrating reality can turn domestic manipulators into male and female bitches. Massaged by the myth to believe that they require no growth or adjustment to adversity, would-be superheroes and -heroines have a disconcerting tendency to withdraw from sustained encounters with reality.

The Laura Ingalls Wilder novels are a more reliable resource than their television distillations for coping with real-world adversity. As popular and charming children's novels, they remain deeply grounded in human reality because they assume a realistic and tragic rather than a melodramatic and sentimental stance. Tragedies treat limitations both in the worst and best of humans, bringing them face to face with their flaws. Sartre's line from *No Exit* is suggestive as we consider the limitations of the domestic redemption scheme: "Hell is other people." There is a limit to our ability to change others to suit our standards, and those who strive hardest at this task make the most perfect hells for themselves and their victims. While pop redeemer tales disguise this by the illusion of selflessness, tragic materials open us to reality and give us strength to endure without happy endings. Tragic heroes such as Socrates and St. Paul suffer death as a consequence of actions they have freely chosen. In an orbit far beyond happy endings and miraculous escapes, their heroism consists in the disciplined acceptance of their own limitations, a remorseless exposure of the illusions of superiority, and a firm but modest defense of the truth as they saw it. The simple perfections of the pop redeemers are unattainable in this classic tradition. Heroes of the Greek tragedies, such as Oedipus, for example, fall because of their pride (hubris) or because of a fate intimately linked to the virtues they possess. Their glory is the capacity to rise to moments of truth, to acknowledge their flaws and sins, and to live with the consequences — often paying the price of death.

These resources of tragic realism are required to cope with contemporary adversity. That they can be embodied even in popular materials suited for children is shown by the Wilder novels. There can be no facile assignment of tragedy to high culture and melodrama to popular culture. The Ingalls family of the novels deserves to stand in the company of Sisyphus and the Loman family in *Death of a Salesman*. Such materials may provide the vision needed to live with domestic struggles as well as circumstances inflamed in part by our own flawed efforts to redeem. They reveal that life can be deeply satisfying without monomythic Glad Games, happy endings, and bountiful rewards bestowed by virtuous Heidis. Rejecting this strand of mythology should reduce the patriarchal expectation that women need to be the angelic servants of men, accepting the abuse that such roles entail. These myths are a self-destructive hindrance to maturation for both men and women. While loving angelic miracles carry less collateral damage than do violent heroics, they advance the ethos of democracy no more than does the brute force of the Virginian or Buffalo Bill. By abandoning the hope for problem solvers with super powers, we may develop the courage to accept our communal responsibility for those structures of family, economy, politics, or religion that are essential for the maintenance of a humane world.

III DANCING THE MYTH OF REDEMPTION

A dance uses overt body movements that respond to musical rhythms and phrases. When a man dances our mythic score, he attacks an evil threatening the community — most often with fists and deadly weapons, not with the manipulative love of the sweet feminine redeemers. Along with the growing stature of the nation, the stage for this violent drama's choreography became increasingly large. We see a small, rustic tableau in Chapter 5, "John Wayne and Friends Redeem the Village," where the legendary actor John Wayne and the legend-making real-life sheriff Buford Pusser destroy the wicked agents who terrorize cowering small communities. Chapter 6, "Cleansing Perilous Cities with Golden Violence," looks at Paul Kersey, Hollywood's *Death Wish I-V* vigilante, who stalks and kills the street punks of New York and other cities; the chapter also views the real world's Bernard Goetz, dubbed "the *Death Wish* vigilante" by the popular press for his shooting of youths he feared on a New York subway; finally, it investigates the real-life Joe Clark, who, like Buford Pusser, posed with symbols of physical intimidation for his fight against evildoers in the big-city schools — his baseball bat paralleling Pusser's big hickory stick. Also, like Pusser's, Clark's exploits became grist for the Hollywood mill. Chapter 7, "Superheroic Presidents Redeem the Nation," moves to the national plane, giving us a view of American presidents with powers that overcome the threats from internal, foreign, and even alien adversaries. The most physical of these presidential ballets comes when President Marshall of the film *Air Force One* kills several terrorists with his bare hands and finally kicks his principal opponent off the aircraft and into the sky. The most planetary of the presidential superheroes is Thomas Whitmore of *Indepen-*

dence Day: he flies nuclear combat missions against alien spaceships. In Chapter 8, "Lethal Patriots Break the Rhythm," we review the progress of the masculine myth as it responds to feminism, gun control, and other perceived threats to the ideal of redemptive violence; the response is an attack on government itself. Mel Gibson's screen persona, from *Lethal Weapon* to *The Patriot,* shows us the man liberated from feminine socialization — capable of the higher slaughter that protects the community. Finally, we explore a couple of real-life enactors of this mythic imperative, Timothy McVeigh and Theodore Kaczynski (the "Unabomber"), lone individuals who exhibit the traits of men freed from female influence — a profile chillingly similar to the agents of the Taliban.

5 John Wayne and Friends Redeem the Village

"The archetypal American is a displaced person — arrived from a rejected past, breaking into a glorious future, on the move, fearless himself, feared by others, killing but cleansing the world of things that 'need killing,' loving but not bound down by love, rootless but carrying the Center in himself, a gyroscopic direction-setter, a traveling norm."

> Garry Wills on why John Wayne remained the
> number-one movie star for many years after his death[1]

"There's nothing wrong with a gun in the hands of the right person."

> Buford Pusser on letting his
> nine-year-old son play with a rifle[2]

In the evolution of the American myth system, the cowboy western provided an archetypal template for cleansing little villages beset by vicious evildoers. In an earlier chapter, we analyzed the most important of these stories — *The Virginian*. This persuasive story of an armed savior stirred the American appetite for ritual recastings of its wisdom. Within a decade of the publication of *The Virginian*, the exceedingly popular Zane Grey published *Riders of the Purple Sage* (1912), which featured a cowboy hero named Lassiter, who confesses his gun-based faith to Jane Withersteen, whom the wicked Mormons

The John Wayne International Airport pays sculptural tribute to the moment when the righteous but swift hand is poised to kill one more bad guy.
Credit: Sculptor Robert Summer; picture © Seeing-Stars.com, Gary J. Wayne.

want to pull into their polygamous fold. Jane, still ambivalent about the Mormon patriarchy to which her own father belongs, is horrified about the prospects of bloodshed. Lassiter asks rhetorically: "Where would any man be on this border without guns? Where, especially, would Lassiter be? Well, I'd be under the sage with thousands of other men now livin' an' sure better men than me. Gun-packin' in the West since the Civil War has growed into a kind of moral law. An' out here on this border it's the difference between a man an' somethin' not a man."[3]

Echoing the sentiments of novels such as those by Zane Grey, directors of and actors in the cowboy movies that were common in the early days of film reworked the sagebrush saviors with embellishments that repeatedly made their narratives feel new — but reassuringly sensible. In addition to entertaining, the myth sometimes suggested the possibility of moving its premises into the practice of life. Two adept mythic translators who aimed their dramatic fictions toward action were John Wayne and the lesser-known Buford Pusser. Wayne was a renowned performer of myth who consistently wove the values he enunciated through film character into real-world political stances he took in national life. As a symbolic educator, he developed a preference for stories in which his character mentored the next generation of heroes. And, like the Virginian, he repeatedly demonstrated that transcending the deficiencies of mere law required a manliness liberated from female influence. In his concluding film, *The Shootist* (1975),[4] Wayne coherently pulled together the monomythic themes of failed institutions, righteous vigilante killing, and the rejection of women's values. Here as in several other films where his character interacts with young people, he acts out the process of bringing the next generation to the task of purging the village.

By contrast, Buford Pusser was a real-life Tennessee sheriff who found in the contours of myth an opportunity to become a national legend of fearless integrity and opposition to evil. Living in Adamsville, Tennessee, whose population was under 2,000, Pusser was to play out a life of unsurpassed violence in law enforcement that inspired the *Walking Tall* film trilogy and a *Walking Tall* television series. Because of his untimely death at age 36, Pusser just missed the opportunity to become a movie star who would play himself in the sequel to the first film. Pusser is commemorated in written biographies,[5] popular songs, and other memorials in Tennessee that survive long after his death.

The common beat shared by Wayne and Pusser was the intimidated village that hungered for a more decent life. In their mythos, safety could never be provided by ordinary democratic means of law enforcement; it always required extralegal actions. Together they give us a monomythic model of how to make small towns safe when timid citizens lack the courage to confront evil in their midst.

Training for Manhood

John Wayne was a craftsman who first learned to dance the monomyth at the request of others. His graceful enactments slowly became far larger than life under the direction of those poets of the dusty Western mythscape, John

Ford, Raoul Walsh, and Howard Hawks. Encouraged to make military morale-building movies during and after World War II, Wayne eventually exercised his growing professional autonomy to embrace film roles for himself that expressed personal ideals linked to the redemptively violent heroes he played. His films regularly presented plots that distanced the hero from any female influence, while imploring young men and women to accept the roles defined for them by the myth: sacrificial death for the male and quiet domesticity for the female.

A blunt articulation of Wayne's favored mythic persona as mentor came in his 1949 film *The Sands of Iwo Jima*.[6] While far removed physically from a western village, this movie worked out several themes that would reappear in later films with frontier settings. In *Sands*, Wayne plays Marine Sgt. John M. Stryker, a lonely man whose wife has abandoned him and cut off his relationship with his son. The circumstances trigger nostalgia, self-pity, and a career-impairing pattern of alcoholism in the sergeant. After leading his rifle company in fierce fighting at Guadalcanal, Stryker's job is to take a group of new recruits in New Zealand and blend them with a handful of survivors who have had battle experience. His most difficult charge is Pfc. Peter Conway, the son of a colonel who has died in combat while Stryker served under his command. He wants to befriend the young man because of his admiration for the father, but finds himself severely rebuffed. Conway rejects all military values, telling Stryker that he believes in education and literature — "Shakespeare instead of a Marine manual," as he puts it. Then, during a leave from the base, the young man falls in love with a New Zealander. Accepting the comfort of a woman's company is simply one more way of expressing his alienation from the military values vital to his rifle company's survival. Stryker gently warns him that it's "no time to be getting serious with a girl"; but Conway insists on marriage before the company leaves port for combat. Stryker is absent from the wedding.

In an episode that begins drunkenly, Stryker further clarifies the irrelevance of women to the life mission that eventually leads him to death on Mount Suribachi. After accepting an invitation to drink at the prostitute Mary's apartment, he gives her money to go out and purchase more liquor. ("By the long arm of coincidence," as Stryker puts it, her name is the same as his wife's.) In her temporary absence he discovers a baby rattling its crib behind a closed door. When Mary returns, a suddenly sober Stryker feeds pablum to the baby, throws money in the crib, and after hearing Mary complain that "there are a lot tougher ways to make a living than going to war," Stryker seems to get over any longing for the comforts of women and domesticity. He tells the sidekick who protectively shadows his boozy diversions that he has no more regrets about his disloyal wife. At his death, we learn that he still cares deeply about his son, but he is far beyond thinking that women deserve an important place in his world.

Another episode in the film reinforces skepticism about the call of domesticity. During a training exercise, a live grenade rolls toward Conway, who is dreamily reading a letter from his wife. Stryker alertly leaps on him to save his life, taking a fragmentation wound himself. The significance of this lethal distraction seems to make no impression on Conway at the time. When Stryker's death comes on Suribachi, it converts Conway's reluctant tolerance of him to filial love. At the end of the film, Stryker has gained the admiration of all the men who formerly found his treatment of them abusively cruel.

In one of his last films, *The Cowboys* (1972),[7] John Wayne returned to this teacher's task of bringing hard discipline into the lives of young men — this time in the Western setting. Wayne's character, the single rancher Wil Andersen, must manage a cattle drive with the assistance of teenage boys on vacation from school. He becomes a tough but caring mentor to these youngsters, who are really surrogates for his own dead sons. When his raw crew comes under siege by a gang of rustlers, Andersen dies at the hands of their cruel leader. But the boys are not helpless in this situation because they have learned their lessons well. At his burial, one of them reflects his code: "It ain't how you're buried, it's how you're remembered." The young boys proceed to track down Andersen's killers and gain revenge. It is a fitting tribute to the man who wished to be a father to them.

Villages under Siege

In *The Man Who Shot Liberty Valance* (1962),[8] John Wayne and John Ford collaborated in presenting one of the starkest pictures of the village crying out for a righteous gun. The story is told almost entirely in flashback at the time of the death of the pauper Tom Doniphon (John Wayne). We learn that a few decades earlier the village of Shinbone was a tiny burg in the midst of small farms; its visible assets were stagecoach service, a newspaper, a saloon, a boardinghouse with a pretty young cook, and a handful of citizens. Among them is the charismatic Tom Doniphon with a Tonto-like black servant named Pompey. Statehood had not yet come to Shinbone's territory, and it lacked both churches and schools. These farming people feared the ranchers' desire to preserve open range for their cattle, and they frequently found themselves terrorized by the vicious Liberty Valance, who worked as the ranchers' hired gun. The town's marshal, Link Appleyard, is portrayed as a whiny, gluttonous coward who titters with fear when anyone suggests that he use his office to protect Shinbone's people from the crimes Liberty Valance is committing out in the open. He complains that "the jail's got one cell, and the lock is broke." Only Doniphon is tough enough to make Valance stand down in a confrontation.

Toward this fearful community comes a stagecoach carrying Ranse Stoddard, a law graduate from the East who intends to practice in Shinbone. As the stage nears the town, a masked Liberty Valance and his cohorts rob the passengers. When Stoddard objects and tries to protect a woman, he gets a beating from Valance's silver-handled whip. As Valance rummages through the passengers' belongings, he discovers Stoddard's law books. "Law, huh?" he snarls contemptuously, tearing out the book's pages and throwing them on the prone Stoddard. "I'll teach you the law — Western law." Whereupon he savagely beats Stoddard again, and is only prevented from killing him by his companions.

This scene, showing the impotence of the law as a force in the town, raises the question that hangs over the film: How can the town be saved when those who speak for the law are so weak? Doniphon, who favors peaceful civility, is also skeptical about the relevance of law, constantly calling Stoddard "Tenderfoot" and "Pilgrim." He patronizingly says: "I know that those law books mean a lot to you. But out here a man solves his own problems." He warns Stoddard that to put up his sign for the practice of law is to invite Valance to shoot it down. Doniphon also intervenes angrily when Stoddard, with his naïve beliefs, starts teaching a class with an emphasis on learning to read and on the sacred documents of America's founding. He is most angry that his "boy" Pompey and Hallie, Pompey's intended wife, attend; he orders Pompey to get back to work on the farm and tells Hallie to get back in the kitchen of the boardinghouse — "where you belong."

Yet the quirky Stoddard persists in his crusade to create a literate and lawful place, finally provoking a crisis with Valance whose resolution will only come from a shootout on the streets of Shinbone. Valance has demanded election as delegate to the territorial convention as the ranchers' spokesman, but he loses to Stoddard in a public election and wants to settle the score in the streets. Stoddard can hardly aim a pistol, despite help from Doniphon, and he seems doomed. However, when the confrontation comes, Doniphon stands unseen in an alley and fires a rifle shot that kills Valance.

Stoddard acquires fame as "the man who shot Liberty Valance"; however, he becomes queasy at a regional convention when nominated to represent the claims of statehood before the U.S. Congress. As a lawyer and spokesman for peaceful ways, he is unwilling to cash in on his reputation as a killer. At that point, Doniphon takes him aside and explains that it was *he* who killed Valance. He explains that "it was cold-blooded murder, but I did it for Hallie." It's clear that Doniphon had longed for Hallie, because he goes home to his farm and tries to commit suicide — beginning by setting aflame the room that he had built to please her.

The Man Who Shot Liberty Valance has the flavor of tragedy rather than melodrama. Within its own mythic frame, the symbolic message is that civilizing the Western village means adopting feminine values. At a moment when Valance enters the café where Ranse wears an apron as kitchen helper, he comments, "Look at the new waitress." Hallie, who craves to read, is won over by the literacy of a man who can wear an apron. Doniphon, whose vigilante shot has made law, statehood, and the marriage of his love to another possible, becomes the anachronism. The man who can "solve his own problems" can no longer be part of the feminized village. Yet the film suggests the heartrending injustice of that. The dejected, self-destructive Doniphon is a better man than those who have profited from his sacrifice.

The Shootist's Disciple with a Gun

In his final film, *The Shootist*, John Wayne again successfully wove together the themes of manliness, righteous violence, and the call to young discipleship. The story borrows many of its details from the life of the notorious nineteenth-century Texas gunman John Wesley Hardin, who killed with good conscience between twenty and forty men before he was shot from behind at the Acme Saloon in El Paso, Texas. The film imagines a turn-of-the-century Carson City, Nevada, in 1901 — brimming with new technologies such as the telephone, the trolley car, and the horseless carriage, but still lacking credible law enforcement. Wayne's last will and testament to his disciples, so to speak, is to challenge them. And for one final time, John Wayne's film persona challenges them to save the village through violent means. The tendency of John Wesley Hardin to kill people everywhere he went is transmuted by this film into a socially redeeming virtue.

As a cultural artifact, *The Shootist* presents an exceptionally clear illustration of the artistic desire to break out of the fictional frame. Since Wayne had become an international icon of American popular culture, his film may be seen as a significant expression of the informal civic faith in the purifying powers of violence. Further, one can see in the film's subject and style a deliberate effort to cloud the distinction between John Wayne as actor and Wayne as cultural symbol.

In his last years, John Wayne suffered several times from cancer, losing a lung in 1964 and experiencing other cancer-related discomforts in his final films. Filmed three years before his death, *The Shootist* is regarded as his "death film," since the plot is about a cancer-stricken gunfighter who travels alone to Carson City to die at the end of his career. The blurring of actor and mythic persona begins from the first moments of the film, where we see clips from earlier Wayne films *(Red River, Hondo, El Dorado,* and *Rio Bravo)* in a progression that "ages" him from the early black-and-white films to the color medium of his later career. In each cut he guns down a bad guy. The name of Wayne's gunfighter character, J. B. Books, obviously refers to the Book of Job — though it becomes clear that the Book of Wayne carries a different message from the biblical book. His "Code of Law," as he refers to it, says: "I won't be wronged, I won't be laid a hand on, I won't be insulted. I don't do these things to others and I require the same of them." When we meet this legendary gunman as he approaches Carson City, we learn that he has already killed thirty men. When a bandit stands in the road and demands his wallet, he coolly shoots him in the stomach; the hapless crook stumbles into a stream,

The Shootist is the story of a legendary gunfighter's death. Like the film, the poster focuses on the urgency of killing a few more men — rather than the gunfighter's own experience of death. "He's got to face a gunfight once more to live up to his legend once more TO WIN JUST ONE MORE TIME." Killing even in a time of death is winning.

Credit: *The Shootist*
© Paramount Pictures, 1976.

where he will probably die. Once in town, Books encounters the insulting Cobb, who blocks his path in the road with a delivery wagon and refers to him contemptuously as a "tuckered out old man." In a quick cut to a tavern scene we learn that Marshal Thibodeux is gleefully ineffectual in his law-enforcement role. When the tavern owner Pulford shoots one of his customers, the marshal celebrates the distance (eighty-four feet!) and accuracy of the single bullet "straight through the heart."

Once Books has gone to see Doc Hostetler (Jimmy Stewart) about his pain, he learns of his impending, painful death from colon cancer. Doc says these suggestive words: "I wouldn't die a death like I just described, not if I had your courage." The bad guys he meets around town give him the determination to kill a few more persons worthy of death before he accepts his own. The marshal eggs him on with the fatuous remark that "once we get rid of people like you, we shall have a garden of Eden."

By using a false name ("William Hickock"), Books contrives to take residence in the rooming house of the attractive widow Bond Rogers (Lauren Bacall). True to his character as a monomythic hero, Books must resist temptations that would thwart his destructive but morally purifying mission in this little village. At first Mrs. Rogers places several obstacles in his path, not the least being the comfort of her companionship. But once she learns that he is the famous killer, she is repulsed by his presence and orders him to leave. He refuses. Bond pleads with him to become pacific; she also wants him to attend her church, and when he refuses, she asks that he at least accept counsel from Pastor Saunders. Books refuses because "my church has been the mountains, solitude," but also because to accept solace or spiritual redirection from an advocate of the Sermon on the Mount would be a timid surrender of his honor as a lone gunfighter. He remarks that "death is the most private thing in my life" and that "my soul is what I've made of it." The cowardly Marshal Thibodeux warns Books: "Carson City is full of hard cases who'd sell their souls to put your name on the wall. You dally here and you'll draw trouble the way an outhouse draws flies." But fleeing from these "hard cases" would be shameful for a man who already has thirty notches on his gunbelt. As Books remarks to the horrified widow Rogers, a Sunday School teacher, "I don't believe I ever killed a man who didn't deserve it."

Besides his quest to purify the village, Books' principal human interest is directed toward Mrs. Rogers' awkward, unpromising son Gillom (Ron Howard). Gillom rides with the degenerate Cobb on his delivery route, frequently nipping from a whiskey bottle. However, he is thrilled with Books' reputation, swagger, and weapons, and he is eager to learn the secrets of handling a six-shooter. Books apparently senses that his still-imposing presence will draw Gillom toward his own life mission of righteous killing. In response to Gillom's question about how he killed so many men, Books encapsulates the secret as follows: "It's not always being fast or even accurate that counts, it's being willing. . . . [M]ost men . . . aren't willing. They blink an eye or draw a breath before they pull the trigger — and I won't." As a token of his affection, Books buys back his treasured horse Dollar from the stable and gives it to the lad.

The moment of truth comes when Books feels himself at the edge of a steep physical decline that will erode his shooting powers. He has to nip more frequently on the laudanum from Doc Hostetler. He sends Gillom with an invitation to the town bad guys: they are to meet him at the town's tavern on Monday morning. Symbolically, Gillom is so eager to be Books' messenger of death that he breaks away from his mother, who is taking him to church. Books also requests Bond to have his suit brushed and not to "use her woman's intuition" and "make surmises" about what he's going to do. She silently defers. For his part, the marshal collaborates by letting the arrogant Cobb out of jail for the occasion and avoids the scene by going to an interview for a *New York Times* story about how Carson City is reacting to the presence of the dying Books.

At the tavern shootout, Books kills all three bad guys, while he himself is seriously wounded. The moral premise of the shootist's innocence is masterfully played out: although Books has obviously contrived the situation that will lead to the death of all three men, he never fires until the other has made his move. So he carries no moral burden of being either a precipitous aggressor or a laggard retaliator. Having fairly vindicated his honor one last time, he is shot in the back by a sneaky bartender. As Books lies helpless, the curious Gillom bursts into the saloon, pries Books' dying fingers off his pistol, and uses it to kill the bartender. He has shown his "willingness" in the spirit of Books. And then to affirm a peace-making message of his own, Gillom tosses the gun down and gets a final wink of approval from Books. The audience can see that the crusader's mantle has been passed on to a worthy disciple. *The Shootist* thus has the structure of an extended invitation to join in righteous killing, with the successful acceptance depicted in the film's concluding fantasy. Gillom walks away from the Metropole, ignoring his peace-loving mother as he wordlessly walks past her toward the mountains of solitude from whence superheroes of the American west rise. He has found in Books a spiritual godfather to give focus to his life. As in *The Cowboys,* the ideal of mythic enactment has taken root in the next generation of young disciples.

In the real world beyond Hollywood, Wayne also managed to bequeath a legacy to his culture. In addition to receiving the Presidential Medal of Freedom posthumously, Wayne received countless accolades at his death, including this eulogy from President Jimmy Carter:

> He was bigger than life. In an age of few heroes, he was the genuine article. But he was more than a hero. He was a symbol of many of the qualities that made America great. The ruggedness, the tough independence, the sense of personal courage — on and off the screen — reflected the best of our national character.[9]

And for Carter he had also become more than a mere symbol: "He embodies the enduring American values of individualism, relentless bravery and perseverance in pursuit of what is right." The Medal of Freedom, we should point out, had been granted only eighty-three times in U.S. history, reserved for individuals of rare stature, such as George Washington and Andrew Jackson.[10] Jimmy Carter, so often a man of sincere Christian conviction who championed peaceful solutions, seems utterly out of character in this sort of adulation. The same leader who led successful negotiations over the Panama Canal, at Camp David in reconciling Palestinians and Jews, in advancing the Strategic Arms Limitation Treaty (Salt II) with the Soviets, here praises the embodiment of someone waiting to explode in righteous rage and take the law into his own hands, just itching to shoot to kill. One could hardly ask for more convincing evidence that the American monomyth persuasively disarms both the intellect and the emotional stance of peacefulness.

In its contribution to the Wayne hagiography, *The New York Times* concentrated on the public response to Wayne's film roles: "They loved the man with the powerful walk, red bandana, old-fashioned good manners and the half-deep voice. It all suggested not great wit or stirring sensuality but decency, common sense, good humor, and America."[11] In this farewell editorial, the *Times* overlooked the element of the crusading, suicidal violence that *The Shootist* so deftly condensed. The U.S. Mint, which issued the official John Wayne Commemorative Medal, was closer to the popular understanding of Wayne in placing his image from the film *The Alamo* on the coin. The Wayne artifact industry that grew in the wake of his death was also sensitive to his deep cultural identification with guns and violence. Consequently, we now have the "John Wayne Commemorative Carbine," "The Colt John Wayne Presentation Edition" (in "The Rampant Colt" design), "The Duke" (a .22-caliber single-action "Frontier Revolver"), and "The John Wayne Commemorative Holster and Gun Set." These weapons come with replicated engraved signatures, Wayne likenesses, and film images that remind us of the hero who settled issues with weapons.[12] The John Wayne International Airport in Orange County, California, features a bronze statue of Wayne standing in a gunfighter pose, with one hand reaching for his revolver. Wayne's popular acceptance as the village cleanser, the gunfighter-redeemer, outlived all the criticisms of his stolid acting and his politics.

Tennessee Moonshine, Gambling, and Whores

It may be tempting to smile condescendingly at the muddled vision that can celebrate Wayne's killer persona as one of our greatest Americans. One might hope that Americans of recent decades would surely not be as blind to the mythical recasting of current events. However, it is myth's nature not to reveal its presence to those it enthralls. Myth need not carefully argue its case, but requires little more than the embodiment of what we want. A glance at the *Walking Tall* films of the 1970s and the continuing life of their legend may help to dispel any illusion of immunity. The *Walking Tall* movies depict the legendary exploits of Sheriff Buford Pusser, a man styled as a selfless ascetic who risks his life to redeem his small-town community from villainous spoilers. When the original *Walking Tall* (1973) appeared, Pauline Kael noted its similarity to the tradition established by Buffalo Bill: "The Western cowboy hero hasn't disappeared: he's moved from the mythological purity of the wide-open spaces into the corrupt modern cities and towns."[13] The success of these films among some Americans and their continuing life in video formats indicate that the psychic resonance of the man standing between civilization and savagery is still sonorous.

Although Pusser, a huge bear of a man at 6'6" and 250 pounds, has been dead for more than a quarter of a century, his legend lives on. The original *Walking Tall* movie was followed by *Part II: Walking Tall* in 1975. *The Final Chapter: Walking Tall* appeared in 1977; but it was quickly superseded in 1978 by the made-for-TV *A Real American Hero*. A television series named *Walking Tall* ran for a period in 1981.[14] In addition to his video immortality, there remains a Buford Pusser Home and Museum in Adamsville, Tennessee; the latter contains a fence post he allegedly used to pound on bad guys in one of his bone-crunching enforcement actions — and the basis for Hollywood's "hickory stick," which it adopted as his icon.[15] Carbo's Smoky Mountain Police Museum in Pigeon Forge, Tennessee, displays the "death car" in which Pusser made his last drive in 1974. His daughter Dwana operates Pusser's Restaurant and Gift Shop, which deals in memorabilia from his career in law enforcement.[16] A stretch of U.S. Highway 64 in McNairy County, Tennessee, was designated the "Buford Pusser Highway" by the Tennessee legislature, and the city of Adamsville has an annual "Buford Pusser Festival."[17] He is also commemorated on several Web sites. What kind of man in late twentieth-century America could stretch his fifteen minutes of fame into decades of immortality?

According to W. R. Morris's "authorized biography," *The Twelfth of August*, Pusser was injured in a fracas at a dice game in Tennessee in 1957. He moved to Chicago and took up wrestling as preparation for the revenge he planned to inflict on the casino where the incident occurred. Three years later, Pusser and two friends returned and administered a beating to casino employees, using a hickory stick as a weapon. The three were indicted for assault, battery, and robbery, but they got off with alibis based on doctored timecards from their jobs. Pusser later admitted to newsman Charles Thompson: "I beat hell out of the two bastards who cut me. I hospitalized them something awful. Then I got in my car and drove back to Chicago, leaving them like they left me." Not long afterward, in 1962, Pusser got a break that allowed him to come back to Tennessee: his father, who had been Adamsville Police Chief, now wanted his son to take over. He said: "Son, my leg has been bothering me a lot lately. I think you'd be the ideal man for the job."[18]

Later Buford won elections for constable and then county sheriff in 1964. As part of his campaign for sheriff, he staged an illegal raid outside his jurisdiction. His father, whom he had hired as a jailer, describes the action: "We didn't have any money and we needed to attract attention. We loaded up with guns and kerosene and hit the place. We busted hell out of their operations. It was the first time anyone around here had ever touched those people, and voters knew we meant business."[19]

After Pusser took office as sheriff, the picture becomes a bit cloudier. There's no disagreement that Pusser and his father clamped down on bootleggers (despite their stated sympathy with moonshining) in order "to get the money they needed for equipment and men" by selling confiscated vehicles and liquor.[20] And there is no doubt that Pusser was physically courageous in his battles with armed criminals who aimed to kill him. He was badly wounded several times, and during one arrest he killed two men who were trying to kill him. A particularly tragic episode in his life occurred in 1967, when his wife, Pauline, was assassinated by gunmen as she rode in the car with him during an investigation. Pusser became ineligible for office in 1970 because of a term limitation; when he ran again in 1972, he was unable to win re-election. Charges of excessive brutality certainly played some role, since he boasted that he "wore out more pistol barrels banging mean drunks over the head than the county would pay for."[21] He died in a high-speed, loss-of-control auto accident in 1974, just at a time when he was planning to play the role of himself in the movie sequel to the original *Walking Tall*.[22]

While the facts of Pusser's life are more than dramatic, the mythic trans-mutation of them tells us a great deal about the American taste in heroes. The film trilogy shapes Buford's life according to the mythic template; and it was this stylization that gave him temporary fame. Although he was a well-known character in Tennessee law enforcement, the film backs away from the facts when its prologue warns us that the story is "suggested by the life of Pusser" and that "the fictitious characters and incidents are not intended to refer to actual persons or events, and any similarity is unintentional and purely coin-cidental."

Taken as a trilogy, the story arc constructed for *Walking Tall* is an epic re-venge tale. In the first film we are introduced to Buford Pusser as a family man driving down the highway with a camper trailer, a happy wife snuggled by his side, and children in the back seat with a dog. They are headed toward the Edenic farm home of Buford's parents. Sick of the "organized dishonesty" of the professional wrestling business, he wants to settle down. Like so many other heroes, he prepares for the later battles we will witness by announcing, "I'm not going to fight with anyone anymore." With his parents' financial as-sistance, he quickly settles down on a peaceful farm with a couple of fishing ponds. We learn almost immediately that Pauline disapproves of guns when Buford invites his young son, Mike — in the den of his parents' home — to pick up his rifle, aim it, and feel the trigger. To his nervous wife Buford says, "There's nothing wrong with a gun in the right hands." Pauline is just one dis-tracting female force along the road of righteous mayhem that lies ahead. (The real-life Pauline had actually encouraged Buford to take on the sheriff's role.)

When Buford's old pal Lutie McVeigh invites him to go gambling with him, the trilogy's plot gets a vector that drives it to the last scene. The Lucky Spot casino cheats Lutie, who has blown some of Buford's borrowed money at the gaming table. In the ensuing fight to get the money back, Buford is beaten, slashed many times with a knife, and left to die on the side of the road. Sheriff Thurman proves to be corrupt by refusing to take any action. Buford comments: "There it is again, the System. Live my way or don't live." Deciding to seek personal justice on his own, Buford returns with a giant hickory stick, savagely beats his tormentors, and collects the value of his stolen car and gambling losses from the cashier.

For this he later stands trial; but he is acquitted when he rips off his shirt to show the jury his permanent scars. After his acquittal, Pauline pleads with him, "No more fighting!" She wants to stop "the senseless life-and-death grudge fight." But Buford now has the courage to run for the office of sheriff himself, and he wins after Sheriff Thurman kills himself trying to run him off the road.

This simplification of the real Buford Pusser's career bypasses his period in the police department, his work as a constable, and his father's role as former sheriff.

The rest of the trilogy pits Buford in battles against "the State Line gang," and against the corrupt or gutless judges and state officials who constantly employ a version of the law that favors criminals. He faces sexual temptations from hookers, one of whom wants to set him up for assassination and another who pleads to marry him after the death of his wife. By *The Final Chapter*, Buford experiences poverty as a result of so generously subsidizing his enforcement activities. But his quest to completely avenge Pauline's murder, getting every last participant, drives him onward. Even the kingpin who has ordered Pusser's assassination is shown dying at the hands of associates because of his increasingly demented quest to kill the near immortal Pusser.

Departing from the predictability of the mythic formula, *The Final Chapter* gives us something new. It reprises scenes from the making of the first film and shows the Pusser family attending the premier performance. It also shows us how Hollywood fame lifted the Pusser family out of their poverty. The narrative even suggests that the rage of the enemy kingpin, John Witter, over Buford's fame and newly gained Hollywood wealth — even though he no longer held office in Tennessee — resulted in a vengeful "fix" on his Corvette that caused his fatal accident.

A notable feature of *Walking Tall* was its brazen denial when components of the myth were questioned — how it verbally or visually countered any objections to the myth-making. The denials seemed meant to immunize the audience against criticisms leveled at the historical Pusser. The writers deny any motivation for vengeance when they depict Buford returning to work after Pauline is killed, having won re-election while recovering from his own wounds. His deputies ask what they should do "to get those bastards who shot you and your wife." Pusser replies: "The only thing any of us gonna do is keep the law for the folks who pay our salaries. I ain't about to use this office to get vengeance on the people I owe it to." The denial of Pusser's violent tendencies is also communicated by repeated scenes of tenderness and touching among acquaintances and family members. The notion that Pusser would use his great physical strength brutally or for mere retaliation, that he would succumb to his own rage, is hidden.

An interesting sidelight of the denial-of-violence theme is the account of the advertising campaign for the first *Walking Tall*. It emphasized the "raw violence" in the film, with the result that audiences were very sparse in the opening weeks after its release. Charles Pratt, the president of the film company, consulted with Cinerama officials to develop a new ad campaign "that played down the violence and depicted an embrace between the hero and his wife. . . . The result was a complete turnaround."[23] Audiences began to pack

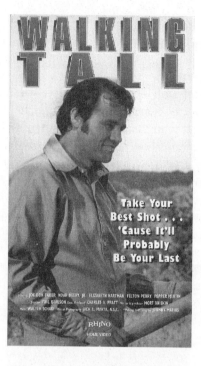

The images for the boxed *Walking Tall* videos, like the films themselves, emphasize the deadly anger of Pusser. The idea of his official role in law enforcement is missing.

Credit: Video box packaging © Rhino Home Entertainment; film © 1975 Bing Crosby Productions.

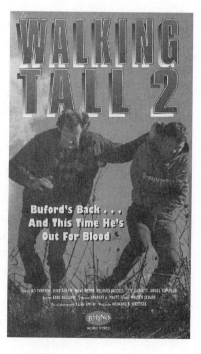

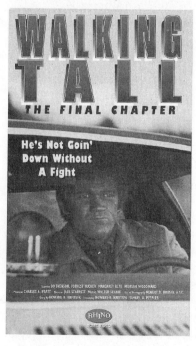

the theaters. It appears that the violence became more acceptable when it was symbolically denied. Later audiences were able to respond favorably to the violent ads for successor films because Pusser's nonaggressive character had been firmly established by the original *Walking Tall*. There is nothing wrong with a little violence as long as it stands between civilization and savagery.

The public adulation of Buford Pusser fits the pattern we discovered with Buffalo Bill. The comparison with cowboy heroism was made by the *Nashville Banner*: "Wyatt Earp, Bat Masterson and Wild Bill Hickok tamed a lot of mean desperados. The name of Buford Pusser now joins the list of those fearless lawmen."[24] He was named "outstanding young man of the year" by the Tennessee Jaycees, "Honorary Sergeant of Arms" by the Tennessee House of Representatives, and was chosen "National Police Officer of the Month" by a detective magazine. Pusser received "reams of law-enforcement credentials" from governmental units around the country, including more than a hundred deputy sheriff commissions. He had acquired a kind of mythic license to attack offenders everywhere. Local religious leaders also applauded his battles in terms reminiscent of the ever-triumphant Buffalo Bill. The real-life Reverend E. E. Thomas, who frequently held services in the county jail, told Pauline:

> The Lord is not going to let some criminal snuff out his life. . . . Remember, David, too, had a tough battle with Goliath, but he won because God was on his side. Sheriff Pusser is a lot like David. The only difference is that the sheriff has many Goliaths to fight while David had only one. The sheriff will win because God is with him![25]

This comparison of the 6-foot, 6-inch, 250-pound Pusser carrying a .357 Magnum pistol and AR-15 automatic rifle with the diminutive David and his five smooth stones is proof of the power of monomythic denial.

At Pusser's funeral, the Reverend Russell Gallimore compared the deceased to another man "who walked tall," Jesus Christ. The two men were equally nonviolent, he stated, taking up big sticks for the sake of peace. Like Pusser, Jesus "took for his weapon a stick — a stick that was used against him — and in the final analysis, it took the form of a cross." Gallimore called on "the Christ who walks tall on this earth to help us pass through this valley of grief."[26] So powerful had been the technomythic presentation of Buford Pusser that his stick, transformed by the movie from a weapon of personal vengeance to an emblem of restraint in the enforcement of law, becomes symbolic not just of his life but also of the Christian religion itself. The crucified Christ himself is validated by comparison with the monomythic Pusser. It is a status to which neither John Wayne nor Bill Cody would have aspired.

6 Cleansing Perilous Cities with Golden Violence

"VIOLENCE IS GOLDEN WHEN IT'S USED TO PUT DOWN EVIL."

> *Dick Tracy Comics* on the day following
> Robert Kennedy's assassination[1]

"I was a monster. I don't deny it. I wasn't a monster until a few years ago. But you have to be a monster to survive in New York City. New York City doesn't give a damn about violence."

> Bernard Goetz, dubbed the *"Death Wish* Vigilante"
> by New York's popular press[2]

"In this building, everything emanates and ultimates from me. Nothing happens without me."[3]

> Joe Clark, the bullhorn- and baseball bat–toting
> principal in Paterson, New Jersey, and subject
> of the movie *Lean on Me* (1989)[4]

The superheroic path as response to human evil has beckoned to travelers in every generation, offering clues about proper responses to threatening circumstances. The present violent age is no exception. Heroic forms from the past give shape to popular materials and invite emulation by current audiences. The approach of Rollo May, an interpreter of contemporary consciousness, offers a suggestive point of departure. He believes that rising violence in our society is directly related to the abandonment of a mythic road system. Convinced that there are no modern equivalents of the classical myths, May points to the resulting apathy and impotence as the sources of aimlessly destructive actions. Violence, according to May, arises when myths and symbols, which provide maps of order and meaning, fall into disrepair. The self, deprived of the myths that confer meaning on its existence, feels an impotence and frustration that easily boil over into rage. Violence results from a lack of mythic coherence.[5]

Our overview of the monomyth's career in the past two centuries has indicated that popular entertainments contain mythical elements comparable to the classical myths whose demise May laments. In some of the materials violence is presented in carefully wrought golden imagery. The presence of these seductive images, not the absence of older myths, accounts for some of the destructive turmoil in our midst. Violence, we submit, increases when a mythic system, intact though perhaps unacknowledged, channels frustration and aggressive impulses into destructive avenues. Mythical violence suggests to its audience the possibility of achieving a negative form of integration through zealous retribution. It can even issue invitations to enact the behavior displayed in the mythic narrative.

In this chapter we will focus on revenge films and the city-cleansing genre in which violence occupies an honored place. We will also look at some people living in the real world who have been responsive to the imperatives of this form of the cleansing myth. One of these is Bernard Goetz of New York City, who was immediately called the "Death Wish Killer" when he fired the gun he owned illegally at four panhandling youths on the New York subway, wounding all of them. Although the court system penalized his rashly retributive behavior, Goetz remains a hero to many advocates of a belligerently armed citizenry. We also examine the lionized New Jersey high-school principal Joe Clark, the subject of the movie *Lean on Me,* who adapted the cleansing myth to the urban school situation.

Death Wish Times Five

The *Death Wish* movie (1974) is archetypal in that it adapts the dominant American myth of the Western village cleansers to the modern urban situation. It is archetypal in a second sense as well, because it laid the foundations for a mythic franchise — a series of formula films about urban vigilantes who save the community through righteous killings that the police are too cowardly to commit themselves. Coming as it did at a time of national concern about urban crime, *Death Wish* (1974) thrilled audiences with its precise, swift, and fatal punishments. The Paul Kersey character (played by Charles Bronson) continued in the sequels *Death Wish II* (1982), *Death Wish 3* (1985), *Death Wish 4: The Crackdown* (1987), and, finally, *Death Wish V: The Face of Death* (1994).[6] Critics of the sequels frequently commented that the aging actor Bronson seemed bored — or even dead; perhaps their attentiveness to quality in acting led them to overlook ritualized drama's power to capture an audience that shares its mythic premises.

The vigilante killings in the *Death Wish* series complemented the themes of other urban cleanser-avenger franchises: Clint Eastwood's *Dirty Harry* (1971) was followed by other "Dirty Harry" films, which feature an out-of-control cop who violates protocols to deliver the deadly street justice that people really want. *Magnum Force* (1973), *The Enforcer* (1976), *Sudden Impact* (1983), and *The Dead Pool* (1988) all contributed to a remarkable body count. Another cool, avenging killer to ride the formula toward stardom has been Steven Seagal, with his movies *Above the Law* (1988), *Marked for Death* (1990), *Out for Justice* (1990), *Under Siege* (1992), *On Deadly Ground* (1994), *The Glimmer Man* (1996), and *Fire Down Below* (1997). An African-American superhero detective, John Shaft (played by Richard Rountree), was permitted to join the deadly team: *Shaft* (1971) led to *Shaft's Big Score* (1972), *Shaft in Africa* (1973), *Shaft, the Executioner* (1973), and finally, *Shaft* (2000), in which the actor Samuel L. Jackson replaced Rountree as John Shaft, an avenger nephew of the original Shaft.[7] There was even one heroine who was allowed to join the vengeful male mayhem: in the movie *Eye for an Eye* (1995), a mother (Sally Field) listens to the rape-murder of her daughter over the phone; she then murders the killer herself after he is legally freed from prison on a technicality. In this zealous genre, where the law must always be circumvented to kill the right person, we can see the mantle of mythic leadership pass from one set of cool trigger-fingers to another.

A stream feeding these retributive rivers of urban blood first trickled out of Brian Garfield's novel *Death Wish*.[8] Garfield wrote the novel as a cautionary tale about the psychotic potential of privately administered justice. When one examines the transformation of Garfield's novel into the movie *Death Wish*,[9] one can perceive how easily a text with a pacific message can become a mythic prism throwing a golden aura onto the path of violence. Garfield protested the movie made from his novel and its commercial success; he even

This film poster for *Death Wish* celebrates Bronson's role as the avenger who stalks through darkness on a mission of righteous killing.

Credit: Film @ Paramount, 1979.

wrote a successor novel entitled *Death Sentence*,[10] which proposed less violent options for dealing with crime. *Death Sentence* never even found filmmakers who wanted to pervert its message — as they obviously had with the *Death Wish* novel.

The original *Death Wish* story opens with Paul Kersey and his wife vacationing in Hawaii, enjoying themselves in a paradisiacal setting. When he resumes work at his architectural firm the next day, Kersey's family is stricken by tragedy: his beautiful wife and his daughter-in-law are attacked by three hoodlums in their East Side apartment; the wife is brutally murdered, and the daughter-in-law is raped. Kersey buries his wife and returns to work with stoic coolness. He inquires at the police station about the killers, only to be told that they may never be apprehended. While fretting about his powerlessness to cope with this anonymous malevolence, Kersey gets several rolls of quarters from the bank and puts them in a sock. Before long he has to use this primitive weapon to beat off a mugger. Returning home shaken, he tests his sockful of quarters once again. It shatters on a living-room chair, indicating his need for a more reliable weapon.

Kersey's boss sends him on an assignment to Tucson, hoping that different scenery will relieve his traumatic memories. There Kersey encounters a successful real-estate developer with frontier attitudes. The developer takes Kersey, who has been a conscientious objector, to a gun club for an experience with the West's tradition of pistol firing for self-defense. In a pivotal episode, the two men visit Old Tucson and witness a staged shootout between good guys and bad guys. Impressed more than his liberal biases can admit, Kersey returns to New York after brilliantly completing his architectural assignment. On a visit to the hospital where his daughter-in-law is supposed to be recuperating, he discovers that she has moved from shock into an incurable psychosis. Returning home to his now lonely East Side apartment, he finds a gift from the Tucson developer in his suitcase: a pearl-handled revolver in a velvet-lined case.

In a significant conversation with his son, while they are returning from a hopeless visit to his daughter-in-law in the sanatorium, Kersey secretly resolves to take up the "uncivilized means" of vigilante defense.

"What do you call people who just sit by and do nothing when attacked?" Kersey asks.

"Civilized?" responds his son.

From that point on, Kersey systematically offers himself as a target for muggers. When they attack, he responds with his new revolver. Reluctantly and with sickened revulsion at first, he soon becomes a cool executioner who gains a sense of personal fulfillment and manhood. He redecorates his apartment in bold colors as a sign of his personal rejuvenation. Meanwhile, his campaign to redeem the city from muggers produces a citywide, then a nationwide, sensation. An enormous outpouring of sympathy from the public and even from the police department wells up; people are even inspired to act in their own self-defense when encountering thugs, and this produces reduced crime statistics. As Paul, the reborn vigilante marksman, attempts his eleventh killing, he is wounded and taken to the hospital. There the police captain promises not to reveal his identity if he will simply leave town. The movie closes with Paul Kersey arriving at O'Hare International Airport to witness four Chicago toughs harassing a comely girl. Helping her pick up her parcels, Kersey responds to the obscene gestures of the retreating thugs by aiming down his trigger finger at them with a gleam in his eye. The traveling vigilante in the businessman's suit has arrived in yet another desperate, lawless community.

The successor stories in the *Death Wish* franchise follow the pattern of the original. Each begins with the Paul Kersey character who has reverted to a quiet, productive life. But soon he has acquaintances or fiancées who are menaced or viciously murdered by street thugs or organized gang members whom the police hesitate to confront. Any woman who loves Kersey/Bronson has trouble surviving more than a few film minutes after she has expressed it. The killers are always dressed to type and commit acts of sadistic brutality. In the last of the *Death Wish* quintilogy, filmed when Bronson was 72 years of age, a mob criminal dressed as a woman follows a lovely lady into a restroom, then gags her and crunches her face against a shattering mirror. In the nauseating retaliation that follows, the head mobster, Tommy O'Shay, is immersed in a volatile, flesh-eating acid. The audience gets to see him bob up, with less of his flesh in each showing.

Death Wish as "Regeneration Through Violence"

If stories in the righteous vigilante genre appeared in a primitive culture, they would undoubtedly be classified as mythical. We use the term "mythical" here to refer to dramatic stories told to convey a people's sense of reality and proper response to threat. In classical and primitive cultures, such narratives dealt with the interaction of men and higher powers, disclosed ultimate realities and norms, and offered adherents models for behavior and answers to agonizing questions. These myths need not be explicitly religious. Henry Tudor notes that "there are many myths in which the sacred plays no role whatsoever. . . ."[11] An essential mark of mythic thinking is the ordering of present experience as "an episode in a story, an incident in a dramatic development" (pp. 7-8). A story from the past is presented as a model of how life should be understood and lived, and is generally accepted uncritically as a kind of revelation. Richard Slotkin has offered a valuable summary of how the narratives of a particular culture produce a mythology capable of channeling subsequent behavior:

> A mythology is a complex of narratives that dramatizes the world vision and historical sense of a people or culture, reducing centuries of experience into a constellation of compelling metaphors. The narrative action of the myth-tale recapitulates that people's experience in their land, rehearses their visions of that experience in its relation to their gods and the cosmos,

and reduces both experience and vision to a paradigm. . . . The believer's response to his myth is essentially nonrational and religious . . . he feels that the myth has put him in intimate contact with the ultimate powers which shape all of life. . . . Myth . . . provides a scenario or prescription for action, defining and limiting the possibilities for human response to the universe.[12]

In these terms, *Death Wish* is unquestionably mythic, even though it does not feature duels with dragons or struggles among the gods. It explicitly offers an "Old West" prescription for understanding and dealing with modern crime. The plot of this myth is distinctly American, belonging to the genre described by Slotkin as the "myth of regeneration through violence" that developed out of the Puritan colonists' tales of Indian wars and captivities. Showing the alien Indian culture as a demonic threat, these stories depicted violence as the means of both cleansing the wilderness and regenerating true faith in the believing community. They reveal an ambivalence about the Western paradise that is similar to the Eden-civilization theme in *Death Wish*. The wilderness was both the source of licentious temptation and the stage for the millennial drama of world redemption. It is in post-Puritan materials such as *The Leatherstocking Tales* and the later cowboy stories that the West came increasingly to be viewed as the unspoiled source of vitality and regeneration. Cooper's Deerslayer, for example, derives his identity and power from the wilderness, becoming the self-reliant killer that nature presumably has taught him to be. Like Charles Bronson in the character of Kersey, the Deerslayer remains true to his own private standards despite pressures: he remains the isolated, celibate figure that his heroic tasks demand.

Victor Turner suggests that mythical material provides the community with "symbolic enrichment" in adapting to threatening new circumstances. The mythic instruction is thus "essentially a period of returning to first principles and taking stock of the cultural inventory," and "often the cultural knowledge is transmitted by the recital of mythical narratives."[13] Hence in *Death Wish* the urban hell is cleansed by the adaptation of the Old West ritual (which Kersey brings back from Old Tucson), but not through a conscious process on the part of the audience. Most viewers simply feel captured by a film like *Death Wish* or *The Shootist*. They are not aware of being ritually instructed, because myths derive from and appeal to the unconscious rather than the conscious mind. Although the process within an individual may be largely unconscious, the mythical paradigms of his culture have already been implanted, so that an American responds to one kind of mythical plot and a Chinese person to another. Ernest Becker's definition of "the unconscious" seems most appropriate in this context: "The Unconscious is not a reservoir of animal drives; rather, it is the unexamined residue of our early training and feeling about ourselves and the world."[14] In the case of the American viewers of *Death Wish,* we would suggest that the impact of the modern myth is largely determined by the "unexamined residue" of the Old West and superhero paradigms.

According to Becker, the unconscious mind provides the unreflective, uncritical motivation for subsequent behavior:

> Since the Unconscious represents our basic organismic conditioning about the kind of world we are comfortable in, the kind that is "right and true" for us, we must understand that it comprises the gross and deep going motives of our behavior — motives which are not amenable to reflective, symbolic scrutiny. Since our Unconscious is our basic emotional identification with the kinds of feelings and acts which make us comfortable, we can say that it contains the motives that *determine* our behavior, whether we consciously will it or not. (pp. 183-184)

Now if traditional myths play a role in shaping the unconscious mind, and if revenge-killing films such as *Death Wish* serve as a transitional bridge for adapting an archaic myth to current needs, the entire process has immense cultural significance. The ever-recurring fantasy of redemptive violence may provide a key to the high incidence of violence on the part of virile males — or weak male outcasts — and the passivity on the part of the general public, both of which seem to be characteristic of current American society.

How might young men come to see their behavior in the mythic light of golden violence? Surface realism in *Death Wish* — the "look" of reality as vigilantes gun down bad guys — cannot by itself compel assent to absurd images of action in a familiar terrain. Something else must account for the power of the violent mythic images in a movie such as *Death Wish.* We detect here a mythic paradigm that includes the subtle use of three components: *mythic selectivity, mythic massage,* and the *invitation to emulate.* It is these processes that allow the audience's encounter with urban hell to be mythically productive, offering appealing patterns for thought and action.

Making the *Death Wish* Scenario Credible

Mythic selectivity is a process whereby an artifact defines the factual realities in a given situation. *Death Wish* has struck audiences as highly realistic in its depiction of urban violence and pastoral tranquility. But an examination of the selectivity with which the film presents "the facts" reveals substantial elements of distortion. For instance, paradise is supposed to be located in Hawaii and Tucson, whereas New York and Chicago are simply urban hells. Selective elimination of contrary features is required to sustain such a conclusion. New York is pictured only during the most miserable part of the year; its neighborhood beaches and parks, its beautiful buildings and cultural facilities are overlooked. Muggers lurk in every alley. Couples drop exhausted into bed, too overburdened by urban chaos for sexual enjoyment. Arizona and Hawaii are pictured as idylls of safety, whereas their actual crime rates per 100,000 population were roughly comparable to New York's in 1974 (when the first *Death Wish* was filmed). By the mid-1990s, when the elderly Bronson moved about in his urban jungle, the murder rate in New York (at 13.4 per 100,000) was a good deal lower than Phoenix's (16.3) and only slightly higher than Tucson's (9.7). The rape scene in *Death Wish* was made to look routine in New York, whereas the actual incidence per 100,000 population is 42.8 for New York City, 27.4 for Honolulu, and 49.3 for Tucson. And the 1990s produced even higher crime rates in the Old West paradise. By 1996, Tucson's forcible rape rate (59.9) was almost double that of New York (31.8).

In *Death Wish* the Hawaiian beach is so isolated during the high tourist season that Kersey and his wife are tempted to make love in the open. The beach presumably has only one hotel, no other visitors, and no "natives." Tucson likewise has neither smog nor nonwhite Americans. Its housing developments are idyllic. Its developers presumably care nothing about profit, unlike those in the New York office, because they are motivated by love of the "natural" way of life.

The muggers in the *Death Wish* film have been pictured with equal selectivity. The first three villains appear stereotypically like thugs in older cowboy movies: they knock over groceries in the supermarket and bump innocent damsels, just as cowboy thugs pushed maidens off the boardwalks. The thugs leer at Kersey's lovely wife and daughter-in-law, their appetites as close to the surface as those of the bad cowboys in the saloon scenes of old Westerns. The bad guys of all the *Death Wish* movies fit their evil mold in a way that makes it easy to cheer when they lose their lives: they are bullies when they pull a knife on a presumably unarmed victim, but they're cowardly when they find that he is ready for self-defense. They always draw first but never mortally wound our hero. John Cawelti has described this conventional "last-minute precision" of the cowboy films: "The hero never engages in violence until the last moment and never kills until the savage's gun has already cleared his holster. Suddenly it is there and the villain crumples."[15] In one instance a *Death Wish* mugger with a drawn weapon cannot even manage to get a shot off before our vigilante draws and kills him with the neat predictability of the sheriff's shotgun dropping the bad guys in Old Tucson. This pattern of bluntly sketched stereotypes persists throughout the entire *Death Wish* series.

The police are portrayed as mediocre at best, but the beat policemen are, of course, better than their overseers. The chief is an overweight, clumsy degenerate, his burned-out cigar and chronic wheezing corresponding to the bumbling of the force as a whole. They cannot even effectively stake out Kersey's house after warning him to stop his killings: he slips out the back door with ridiculous ease while the chief himself is parked out front. The district attorney and police commissioner chew candy with the chief and indulge themselves in walnut-paneled offices rather than biting the bullet on crime. They want only to disguise their incompetence and avoid making Kersey a martyr; but they do not really wish to enforce the law.

In a world of cunning predators and incompetent law-enforcement officials, *Death Wish* offers a hero selectively pictured as larger than life. Despite his urban attire, he is really a superhero in the cowboy tradition. Naturally, the first time he fires an archaic weapon in the Tucson gun club, a muzzle-loading .45-caliber pistol, he hits the bull's-eye. This is clearly a mythical feat, wildly improbable with an untested, primitive weapon, particularly for a man who had not touched a gun since his youth. Kersey is portrayed as having sworn never to touch a gun after his father's death many years before. The pacifist who hates guns is elected by fate, by his incredible sharpshooter's eye. The unwilling vigilante, stoically accepting his duty but taking no pleasure in the killing, reflects the traditional pattern. His duels with the bullying muggers also fit the paradigm of the Main Street shootout. Even though he faces virile adversaries three at a time, he guns them down with ridiculous ease. His bullets strike the mark, and only in the final duel is he wounded. Even then, the hero can be only superficially harmed.

Most people would agree that these features are biased when they are pointed out to them; but while the images flicker on the screen, they arouse not a ruffle of doubt. Pseudo-empiricism accounts in part for this remarkable credulity. The viewer has the illusion of actually seeing muggers in every alley; he witnesses the brutal rape scene as a real occurrence; his eyes convince him of the cowardice and incompetence of the muggers. When one considers how difficult it would be to sustain a similar credibility while reversing the patterns, making the bad guys shoot straight and the hero miss, one can recognize mythic forms at work. The audience accepts selective details because those details fit a mythic paradigm.

The Reassurances of the *Death Wish* Myth

Mythic massage is a process of assuring viewers that the gap between myth and reality can be bridged. In *Death Wish* the vigilante actions of the modern superhero solve the knotty problem of urban crime. Mythical redemption works out in everyday life according to mythical expectation. Complex social problems are neatly solved with a single gesture; tangled human relations are sorted out and resolved; evil is eliminated with a single heroic stroke. In *Death Wish* the elements of mythic massage touch the fate of villains and vigilantes, the achievement of justice for the community, and the redemptive impact on the world.

That justice can be achieved by the vigilante method is the assurance produced by the mythic massage of *Death Wish*. As the press accounts in the movie make clear, each of the victims of Kersey's executions has a prior criminal record. Each criminal attacks the seemingly passive Kersey without provocation, thus fully earning the fate he receives. Moreover, a dramatic drop in violent crimes is reported and discussed repeatedly in the film: law and order are achieved for the community through vigilantism. If a more realistic picture of vigilante miscarriages of justice were presented, the sense of closure would dissipate. What would the impact on the audience be if one of the "muggers" turned out to be Kersey's peaceful neighbor on a midnight stroll? Or what would be the effect of revealing the reason why sensible police departments discourage vigilante practices, namely, that it invariably increases rather than decreases violence? The film pictures the New York City Police Department as having merely political reasons for dissuading the vigilante: they are embarrassed that Kersey alone could do more in the fight against crime than their entire organization could. So the movie, through technomythic artifice, skirts the objections that common sense would make against the mythic redemption scheme.

The most blatant proposition in *Death Wish's* mythic massage concerns world redemption. Reporters from all over the world are pictured as clamoring to get the message about the vigilante and his dramatic campaign against urban villains. Crime is a worldwide problem, and here is the means of redemption — not just for New York but for all the world. The traditional American sense of being a "city set upon a hill" as the moral example for the world is combined here with the naive narcissism typical of the superhero cult. Public acclaim of the superhero's exploits, though usually shown to have no appeal to the hero himself, provides a powerful confirmation of the myth. Paul Kersey is shown several times devouring media reports about his vigilante exploits. He is too cool to need the assurance of such acclaim, but he takes a grim pleasure in receiving confirmation that the redemption he has wrought is efficacious for the entire world. America's restoration to moral leadership among the nations is explicit in the scenes with foreign reporters and newscasts. They speak many languages, but all praise the same redemptive achievement.

The power of mythic massage is enhanced by its unavailability in the real world. Most people experience life as an endless series of difficulties in which gratification is seldom more than temporary. In the arena of communal problems, where the requirements of order and justice are constantly in tension with individual needs and desires, final solutions are even more elusive. But when redemption from these limitations is offered in a powerful modern embodiment of a familiar and appealing myth, nostalgia combines with a yearning for easy solutions to bring off the massage.

The Call to Discipleship in *Death Wish*

Occasionally, popular materials issue a call that seems aimed at courageous viewers. This is what we call the *invitation to emulate,* or Werther invitation. Some of those who participate vicariously in the mythic drama internalize the behavior patterns and subsequently follow them when they face analogous situations in their lives. In the case of *Death Wish,* the archetypal model of the Old West vigilante provides the invitation for responding to the modern urban situation. Kersey's modeling his behavior after a mythical paradigm suggests to the audience that they do likewise in becoming a superhero vigilante. The other option presented by the film is to remain an expectant but passive public waiting for salvation-by-vigilante. In the latter case, the public in the movie reinforces the spectator stance of the audience.

The origin of mythical redemption in *Death Wish* is Edenic. The vigilante solution is first advocated by the Tucson developer, who considers self-reliance and six-gun self-defense as a law of nature, the powerful secret of Western vitality and tranquillity. The Tucson advocate of these rural virtues is himself an embodiment of the paradoxical elements that comprise the traditional American sense of paradise: he unites love of nature and a fascination with the machines that domesticate nature; love of guns and a yearning for law and order; disdain for the profit motive and an obvious delight in the expensive pleasures of life; and a love of unspoiled nature and pride in tract real-estate development. Apparently single, though seemingly well-integrated, he becomes for Kersey the source of redemptive wisdom. And it is he who provides the pearl-handled pistol that starts Kersey on his redemptive mission in the urban no-man's-land.

The visit to Old Tucson is the moment of recognition in which the invitation of the mythical Western paradigm strikes home to the grieving, liberal Kersey. The tourist crowd stands around while the sheriff shoots it out with the bad guys between the saloon and the jail. As six-gun and shotgun cut down the invaders with divine efficiency, the camera pans to Kersey's face to show that something has clicked to overcome his civilized reticence. The look of total conviction on his face communicates the power of the mythical model, and from this moment on the audience is certain that he will take up the invitation to become a vigilante-redeemer in his own beleaguered city. The behavioral emulation is both immediate and compelling.

Once Kersey embarks on the mythical path, his behavior becomes an invitation for others in the movie. As details about each victim are reported, previously cowardly and demoralized citizens begin to take action for themselves, and their more passive neighbors applaud them. A stalwart old black woman is reported to have turned on a purse snatcher and driven him off with her hatpin. A crew of construction workers catch a criminal and give him a suitable beating before the authorities arrive. Everywhere heroes would now arise from the common people to pattern themselves after this example. The traditional idea of America as the redeemer nation echoes in this story, both for the hero and for a helpless world that is yearning for the redemptive age to dawn.

Bernard Goetz as Old West Disciple

Bernard Goetz was a 37-year-old man who recycled the *Death Wish* pattern back into its urban birthplace of New York City in 1984. Confronted by a group of four subway panhandlers who demanded five dollars in a way that seemed menacing to him, Goetz pulled out a gun he was carrying and opened fire. The four young men — Barry Allen, Troy Canty, James Ramseur, and Darrell Cabey — were armed with only a sharpened screwdriver, but Goetz shot all four of them. When two of them fled after his first volley, he shot them in the back. In a taped confession that he gave to police in New Hampshire, he recounted approaching Cabey and saying, "You seem to be doing all right; here's another." Then Goetz left the startled passengers on the subway with these words: "They tried to rip me off."[16]

With an appropriate nod to Bronson's movies, the *New York Post* called Goetz "the *Death Wish* killer" and "*Death Wish* Vigilante."[17] Describing his frame of mind at the moment of his explosive attack, Goetz said:

I became a vicious animal, and if you think that is so terrible, I just wish anyone could have been there in my place. Anyone who is going to judge me, fine, I was vicious. My intent was to kill 'em, and you just decide what's right and wrong.[18]

Goetz was self-righteous about his "vicious" behavior because of his earlier experiences with law enforcement as a crime victim. He worked as an electronics repairman in the city, and during 1981 he had experienced a mugging in which he was seriously injured. He was extremely dissatisfied with the behavior of the police, who detained him as a victim longer than they held the perpetrators, who had been arrested at the scene. After that, Goetz sought a license to carry a handgun but was denied; later, he purchased a pistol in Florida and brought it back to New York, carrying it on his person whenever he moved about in the city.

From the moment of his surrender and detention in New Hampshire nine days after the shooting, Goetz was lionized by many Americans as the living incarnation of the *Death Wish* scheme. For many, his behavior — regardless of the facts — was immediately assimilated into the mythic story of the righteous gunman purging the city of its evildoers. One citizen said: "I don't give a damn where he shot 'em or how he did it. Those lousy punks deserve to die. God bless that man. When he pulled that gun, he was shooting for all of us." Someone scrawled on the East River Drive wall, "POWER TO THE VIGILANTE. N.Y. LOVES YA!" Ugly racial dimensions appeared in signs such as "Goetz Rules Niggers"; but many blacks, including the well-known Roy Innis, an executive for the Congress of Racial Equality, themselves accepted the notion of Goetz's healthy effect on the climate of citizen fear in the city.[19]

As the cult of righteous assault grew, a Bernard Goetz Legal Fund was established, to which people from across the nation contributed. A merchandising industry quickly flourished to satisfy desires for adulation: one could buy Bernard Goetz T-shirts, baseball caps, backpacks, and bumper stickers — all with messages like "Go Get 'Em, Goetz" and "Goetz 4, Crooks 0." A number of songs were played on the radio: one song, "Thug Busters," was released with a related T-shirt; a group called Ronny and the Urban Watchdogs created a song called "Subway Vigilante." Goetz also became a celebrity whose views were sought out for newspaper columns and interviews on radio and television. He appeared with Geraldo Rivera on the *20/20* program and with Barbara Walters of CBS. He gave lectures to groups on how to confront thugs. In one he said: "You've got to teach them how to get the gun out quickly. You can't have a guy fumbling with the weapon, trying to get it out of his pocket and dropping it. Crimes just happen too quickly for that."[20]

At the height of this fervor, Charles Krauthammer wrote a prophetic essay, "Toasting Mr. Goetz," about a likely decline in his fame once the legal system reviewed his behavior. As Krauthammer put it: "No one remains, no story remains abstract forever. . . . As soon as reality sets in, the glamor will fade, and the people will come to their senses."[21] Like other legal observers, he pointed out that even if Goetz had been under attack, his deadly response to the panhandlers wanting five dollars was hardly proportional. Furthermore, his confessions suggested that he wanted to punish the muggers who had harmed him in the earlier episode. A New York grand jury eventually indicted Goetz for attempted murder and illegal weapons possession. Standing trial in 1987, Goetz was acquitted of all charges except the relatively trivial one of carrying an unregistered weapon, an offense for which he served an eight-month prison term. Darrell Cabey, who had been paralyzed with brain damage, brought a civil suit against Goetz for $50 million twelve years later. In the civil trial, the jury found that he had "acted recklessly and without justification"; Goetz lost the imaginary sum of 43 million dollars and immediately declared bankruptcy.

During this trial Goetz clarified his state of mind for the jury by declaring that he "felt he had performed a public service in the shootings, that the mothers of his victims should have had abortions, and that society would be better off if certain people were killed or locked up or used in forced labor."[22] Had Goetz not progressively revealed such an aberrant state of mind, *Death Wish*'s mythic legacy of city cleansing with summary executions might have surged toward the vitality he hoped for.

Cleansing the Urban School with Joe Clark

As 1980s New Yorkers saw themselves besieged by harassment and disorderly conduct in the subways and on the streets, students and parents at many inner-city schools during the same period felt hopelessness about drugs, weapons, teen pregnancies, shabby facilities, and low academic expectations. Despite the obstacles, some inner-city educational leaders had improbable successes in lifting morale, discipline, and academic achievement. For example, Jaime Escalante, a Bolivian immigrant to the United States, made his mark as an innovative educator who convinced his students from the Los Angeles ghetto that they could master mathematics. He even led them to competitive performances on national Advanced Placement Tests of calculus. His teaching style insisted on classroom order, imagination in translating abstract concepts, and relentless encouragement. A docudramatic film, *Stand and De-*

liver (1988), offered a tribute to his dedication and achievement — without painting him as a classroom saint.

Another impressive public school figure to emerge in the 1980s was Joe Clark of Eastside High in Paterson, New Jersey. Like Escalante, he became the subject of a semidocumentary film, *Lean on Me* (1989). Although Clark, like Escalante, was presented as a hero, the film offers a complex moral character-ization that Clark himself praised. Clark's personal life and approach to school administration presented facts that a popular filmmaker could render as monomythic heroism — to public acclaim. The initial scenes of the film establish Clark as a loner whose wife has deserted him but who cares deeply about his students' learning and future. Unlike his fellow teachers, who wear suits and ties, he wears a dashiki in his middle-school classroom and focuses on the historical injustice of racism. However, his abrasiveness in dealing with higher authority has alienated him from his school's administration and also from his union. In order to be cooperative with their administration and get a raise, his fellow teachers secretly make a deal to have him demoted and sent away to an elementary school. There he works effectively, but in obscurity.

Then a community crisis comes. Eastside High has done so poorly in high-stakes testing that the state of New Jersey is about to take it over. The school district will lose substantial funding if this happens. After protesting, the mayor of Paterson reluctantly allows Dr. Napier, a school official, to per-suade the equally reluctant Clark to take the job. When he arrives at Eastside High, Clark finds chaos: the building is covered with graffiti, inside and out; a teacher intervenes to stop a fight and is savagely beaten, leaving the building on an ambulance stretcher; open drug deals take place at the school door; a girl is stripped of her blouse and bra by a gang and shoved screaming out into the hallway.

Then Joe Clark takes over. He asks his assistant to gather the names of ev-ery student who has been in the office for misbehavior over five years — or has brought guns or dealt drugs. He gathers the entire student body in assem-bly and puts the 300 "miscreants" onstage. He announces that they have "done nothing" in their five years, and declares: "You are all expurgated, you are out of here. I wish you well." To the remaining students he says, "You are going to defy the expectation that you are all failures."

The brashness of Clark's move in cleansing the school leads to meetings with angry parents, who question the legality of what he has done. Clark flatly says that the students are all "rotten to the core." Then he switches to a preacher's voice and tells them that, in learning of his assignment, he had complained, "God, why hast thou forsaken me?" God has answered him by telling him that he must "do whatever he can to transform and transmogrify this school into a special place where hearts and minds can blossom. . . . And that's why I threw the bastards out." In the world of *Lean on Me*, as defined by Clark's vision, there are good kids, bad kids, and one weepy borderline kid, Thomas Sams, who begs to come back to school. After urging him to jump from the school roof to kill himself — as a way of giving him a vision of his future with drugs and bad associates — Clark readmits him to Eastside.

Clark is equally brash in establishing his absolute authority with his staff. At his first meeting with them, he takes on a demeanor that stems from his Marine drill instructor's background. When a teachers' representative says that the teachers want to tell him what they have "done in anticipation of your arrival," Clark snarls: "Sit down, Mr. O'Mally. Think you can run this school? If you could, I wouldn't be here, now would I?" He shouts: "No one talks at my meetings. No one! You take out your pencils and write!" From this moment on, Clark is at war with his teachers. He announces: "This is not a democracy, this is a state of emergency. . . . My word is law. There's only one boss in this place and it's me." Clark establishes his physical dominance of the entire school by carrying a bullhorn and a baseball bat as symbols of his toughness. In one scene, he easily slams to the floor one of the drug-dealing, expelled students who has attacked him with a knife.

At one point Clark decides that the school must begin building pride by learning to sing the school song. In the hallway he hears the strains of beautifully sung classical choral music. He bursts into the room and discovers that the teacher, Mrs. Elliot, is rehearsing Mozart for a concert the following week at Lincoln Center. (The choir turns out to be one of the few successful programs in the school.) When the teacher resists interrupting the rehearsal to work on the school song at that very moment, Clark explodes. He cancels the concert and suspends the teacher on the spot. Later, when the assistant principal, Ms. Levias, says, "Nobody knows what you're doing," Clark replies, "That's exactly the way I like it." After taking a substantial amount of personal abuse from Clark, Levias tells him that he has exaggerated his influence at the school and that she wants a transfer: "You do not do it all alone; you are constantly abusive, thoughtless and cruel." Clark later acknowledges her criticism in a very indirect way and wins her back to his staff.

Clark also wins the political battle with his community critics, led by the evil Mrs. Barrett, whose son he has tossed out. Mrs. Barrett presses the mayor on how Clark has violated fire codes by chaining the school doors to keep drug dealers out. (The city of Paterson will apparently not provide the kinds of emergency doors with alarms that white schools have.) As a result, when the fire chief appears on a surprise inspection, Clark is arrested, cuffed, and put in jail. Mrs. Barrett begs the school board to fire him. However, *Lean On*

Me ends on a happy note when thousands of students march in the streets of Paterson, demanding Clark's release. As the prospect of a riot threatens, the mayor begs Clark to leave the cell and urge the students to go home. When he does, Eastside receives simultaneous word that it has received a passing score on the state competency exam. So the cleansing of the evil people from this urban school has preserved the autonomy and permitted the happiness of the surviving community.

In describing this docudrama's plot, it is important to note that much in it has been invented or compressed for dramatic purposes. This is a clear instance of mythic selectivity. For example, Joe Clark was never arrested or sent to jail. His school's passing rate on academic achievement exams remained below the norm for urban schools in New Jersey.[23] Furthermore, the student dropout rate increased during his tenure.[24] But like Clark's own publicity, the movie conformed to a myth of redemptive school cleansing that much of the public finds gratifying. The audience expected that the selfless superhero would have to work outside the system, resisting the pressures of democratic institutions, and taking the rules into his own hands in order to redeem. His achievements had to be magnified by the myth makers in order to make such a feat credible.

Before the release of *Lean on Me* in 1989, Clark had already become a national celebrity. Ronald Reagan commended him as the kind of leader needed in the schools. Reagan's secretary of education, William Bennett, sided with Clark in his battles with the school board over the legality of his student "expurgations" and his arbitrary firing of teachers. According to a *Time* magazine cover story, Bennett telephoned Clark to tell him to "hang in there." Commenting to the press about his agreement with Clark's methods, Bennett said, "Sometimes you need Mr. Chips, sometimes you need Dirty Harry." Gary Bauer, the White House policy development director, offered Clark a White House policy adviser position.

Another career did in fact become necessary for Clark in 1989, when the school board of Paterson felt it could no longer tolerate his methods or prolonged absences for personal speaking and film promotion. The very man who had brought Clark to Eastside High, Dr. Robert Napier (a fellow African-American who was prominently featured in the film), was the one who insisted on his dismissal. Ironically, the last straw was a school assembly celebrating the movie *Lean on Me*, which occurred while Clark was away in Los Angeles taping an appearance on the *Arsenio Hall Show*.[25] The offensive element was a strip act at the high school, in which a female stripper removed the clothing of two male strippers. While Clark had not planned the program, he was held to be derelict and fully accountable.[26] Subsequently, he became the director of the Essex County Youth House, a juvenile detention facility.

This graphic for *Lean on Me's* video box emphasizes the mixture of care and intimidation that Joe Clark brings to the task of school leadership. The picture of Clark with the bullhorn, backed up by the bat, asserts the need for physical forcein rescuing schools.

Credit: *Lean on Me* film © 1989 Warner Bros.; packaging © 1989 Warner Home Videos.

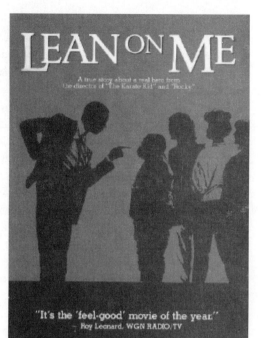

Despite the fact that Clark succeeded in creating a safer, cleaner school for those he permitted to stay, his Manichean identification and classification of students meant that he probably discarded many students who could have been saved by other methods. Viewed from a community perspective, expelling those students simply relocated the problem of how to bring them into the circle of law-abiding, productive citizens. As was the case when Bernard Goetz undertook to cleanse the city, a detailed awareness of what the savior actually thinks and does can be repellent. In the end, Paterson city officials complained that Clark had become a "loose cannon" and that having him on board had "cost the city of Paterson more than it has achieved." That is the price to be paid whenever a monomythically styled hero offers to purge the community of its evildoers. Despite its mythic glitter, golden violence always proves itself a far baser metal than democracies can tolerate.

7 Superheroic Presidents Redeem the Nation

"The United States in Congress assembled, shall have the sole and exclusive right and power of determining on war and peace."

> Ninth Article of Confederation adopted
> by the Continental Congress (1777)

"I think that the President (Harrison Ford) kills four or five guys, one of them with his bare hands."

> Roland Emmerich, Director of *Air Force One* (1997)[1]

The U.S. president, standing so often at center stage during historic crises, has been woven into the fabric of national mythology. Legend-making about presidents emerged as soon as the nation had presidents to ponder. However, the development of fantasies about the president as a violent superhero — a man who can bare-handedly strangle the nation's enemies — occurred only at the end of the twentieth century. If the mythic imagination of the 1930s could transform reporters, cowboys, cops, and ordinary citizens into community saviors with superpowers, why did the office of the presidency have to wait so long? Perhaps it was the widely held awareness that the job ordinarily consists of activities such as speaking, consulting, party building, electioneering, and correspondence. Or maybe there was a deference, a feeling that the

126

President James Marshall (Harrison Ford) bucks protocol, ignores his advisers, and tells all terrorists of the world, "Now it's your turn to be afraid." A Vietnam vet, he is ready to fight them in hand-to-hand combat.

Credit: *Air Force One*, © Columbia Pictures, 1997.

President Hammond in *Gabriel Over the White House* — suddenly transformed by the impulse to help America's poor — confronts Congress, requesting "four billion dollars to restore buying power, stimulate purchases, restore prosperity." When murmurs of resistance are voiced, he demands "to assume full responsibility for the government."

Credit: *Gabriel Over the White House* © Turner Entertainment, 1993.

office should be honored for what it is and not the fantastic imagining of what it might be. And surely the United States' late-twentieth-century supremacy arising out of the Cold War victory may have provided inspiration.

Whatever the reason, the transformation into a super-presidency occurred when the American monomyth provided templates for the action-adventure film presidencies of Thomas J. Whitmore (Bill Pullman) in *Independence Day* (1996)[2] and James Marshall (Harrison Ford) in *Air Force One* (1997). In both movies, the presidents play the role of world cleansers. In *Independence Day*, President Whitmore himself flies combat air missions against alien spacecraft to rescue a universally grateful planet earth. In *Air Force One*, President Marshall becomes his own armed force when he kills terrorists, rewires the fuel system, commands U.S. missile attacks on his own plane, and then flies it during a tricky rescue operation. His victory over terrorists is accompanied by the message that terrorists everywhere should fear the super power of the U.S. president himself.

These movies, released during the tenure of President Bill Clinton, offered an alternative image of the presidency as the union of physical heroism with moral perfection. The box-office payoff was astonishing: the profit for these films exceeded any other films about the U.S. presidency. Behind the startling success of these films lie questions about the historic paths that led to such mythifications of our highest office, and the more speculative issue of how such films might affect the expectations for a U.S. president.

It should not surprise us that the comic-book-style scenarios of these two films found important predecessors in the American monomyth's axial decade. The president as an outsized fantasy hero first emerged in the movies *Gabriel Over the White House* (1933)[3] and *The Young Mr. Lincoln* (1939).[4] But it would be many decades before a president on screen would show the super powers that comic books routinely assigned to other men in tights and capes.

The American Presidency and the Monomyth

The American presidency is not a very promising terrain for nurturing the dramatic conventions of the monomyth. The election of a limited-term president with constitutionally limited powers sets up an immediate tension between the requirements of legality and the frequently urgent need for innovation. Why restrain a president with limits except in fear of what he might otherwise do? But why elect new presidents at frequent intervals unless there is fear of a leader who might become dictatorial with the passage of time? In

Stephen Skowronek's view, this tension between innovation and restricted powers is even built into the president's oath of office:

> Each incumbent swears both to "execute the office of the President of the United States" and to "preserve, protect, and defend the Constitution of the United States." In the first instance, he is charged to exercise expansive powers for independent action; in the second, he is charged to affirm the fundamental order of things. Somehow the order-shattering implications of the exercise of power have to be reconciled with the order-affirming expectations of its use.[5]

These countervailing pressures reflect both the origins and the subsequent history of presidential experience.

The office was born in debate about the extent of presidential power — or whether there should even be such an office. The Continental Congress displayed a bias, engendered by the experience of an abusive monarchy, toward collective rather than focused executive leadership. The Articles of Confederation (1777) repeatedly identify the agency in their new government as "The United States in Congress assembled" or "The Committee of the States." These Articles made no provision for a presidential executive. When the U.S. Constitution was being written, ten years later, a consensus had emerged that the Republic needed an executive officer for greater vigor in achieving its purposes. Alexander Hamilton had a fulsome, monarchical conception of executive power, while others were more interested in devising restraints. As Michael A. Genovese summarizes it, "Making the presidency too strong would jeopardize liberty; making the office too weak would jeopardize good government."[6] The Constitution's Article II only vaguely defined the responsibilities and powers of the president: the president possesses "executive power"; he is commander-in-chief of the armed forces for occasions defined by Congress alone; he informs Congress about the state of the union and makes recommendations; he makes treaties (with advice and consent of the Senate); he has the duty "to see that laws are faithfully executed." The president would have limited powers and a limited term of office. How such a complex constitutional theory could function was determined in large part by the first incumbent in the presidential office.

George Washington as Selfless Savior

The dilemmas of articulating the presidency as an effective office were temporarily resolved by George Washington, who provided a decisive precedent for the later development of the American monomyth's notion of the selfless redeemer of the democratic community. Many of Washington's contemporaries understood him mythically as a reincarnation of the Roman Cincinnatus. According to that legend, the small farmer Cincinnatus had been called upon in an emergency to assume the dictatorship. His task was to rescue a consular army surrounded by enemy forces. Dispatching his job in a single day, he immediately returned to his little farm — despite Rome's astonished acclaim for his leadership. Representative of many visual and literary artists of the Revolutionary period, Jean-Antoine Houdon accepted a commission to render Washington as a marble figure entitled "Cincinnatus," a statue that he completed in 1788 and that can still be seen at the Virginia state capitol. He was just one among many who felt comfortable in portraying Washington as a selfless agrarian unmoved by the prospects of fame or power.[7]

Washington gave convincing substance to his status as the American Cincinnatus of the Revolutionary War, trumping his predecessor's single day with nine years on the battlefield. And bespeaking his modesty, when the Continental Congress offered him the commander-in-chief position in 1775, he seemed sincerely embarrassed by his qualifications, asking them to remember his self-confessed inadequacy if he failed. Finally, he demonstrated his sacrificial approach to public responsibility by refusing to accept a monthly salary. As compensation, he asked only to be reimbursed in accord with an exact accounting of his personal expenses.[8] Surrendering his command after the war, he returned home without loot or office. Even England's King George III commended Washington for his renunciation of office, declaring that he was "the most distinguished man living" and "the greatest character of his age."[9] When Washington's moment to serve as president came, he seemed, in the words of Clinton Rossiter, "perfectly suited for the delicate task of finding the right balance of authority and restraint in the executive branch."[10] At a time when his charismatic popularity would have permitted him to exceed the Constitution's rather vaguely defined grant of authority, he managed to be assertively firm without violating the spirit of checks and balances that had defined the office. After Washington's death, Jefferson wrote in tribute to his "singular destiny and merit" in managing the affairs of the United States "through the birth of a government, new in its forms and principles, until it had settled down into a quiet and orderly train." Washington had achieved this through "scrupulously obeying the laws throughout the whole of his career, civil and military."[11]

Abraham Lincoln as Legitimate Law Breaker

Abraham Lincoln inherited circumstances calling for a different attitude toward the powers of the office. Washington's task of lending stability to a hopeful beginning had been displaced by an unraveling union of the states. Lincoln's predecessor in office, James Buchanan, while opposed to slavery and to Southern secession, felt no constitutional authority to confront their rebellion. Buchanan expressed his passive view of the presidential role in a parting statement to Congress: "After all, he is no more than the chief executive officer of the Government. His province is not to make but to execute the laws."[12] Lincoln was acutely aware of the paradoxes associated with such passivity and stated it this way in his Special Session Message on July 4, 1861: "Must a government, of necessity, be too *strong* for the liberties of its own people, or too *weak* to maintain its own existence?" In another formulation, Lincoln queried: "Are all the laws but one to go unexecuted, and the Government itself to go to pieces lest that one be violated?" He knowingly took actions of doubtful legality when he blockaded ports, suspended habeas corpus, arrested newspaper editors, and issued the Emancipation Proclamation on his sole authority as a commander-in-chief in a time of war. This is the way he expressed himself in a letter to Samuel Chase: "These rebels are violating the Constitution to destroy the Union; I will violate the Constitution, if necessary, to save the Union; and I suspect, Chase, that our Constitution is going to have a rough time of it before we get done with this row."[13]

Despite the pattern of what Clinton Rossiter has called "constitutional dictatorship," Lincoln did succeed in holding the Union together and extending the meaning of equal citizenship under the law. While acting so tenaciously, he acted as teacher for the nation, repeatedly justifying the extraordinary actions he had taken as well as clarifying how best to preserve the republic. He also behaved without the abolitionist zeal that identified its side as wholly righteous. His moral sense was subtle enough to recognize that both sides prayed to the same God in behalf of their cause — and sinned grievously in pursuing it, as his eloquent Second Inaugural Address made clear. Lincoln submitted to the electoral process in 1864, renewing his authority by once again satisfying the will of the people. Lincoln, of all people, would have denied that the nation can be purged of evil.

Taken together, the presidential experiences of Lincoln and Washington remind us that the American monomyth as it developed in the twentieth century addresses genuine political issues of the tensions between legality and community redemption as well as the importance of personal character. Furthermore, Washington and Lincoln helped to popularize two important elements in the monomyth: Washington's character as selfless savior of the country and Lincoln's behavior as the man who deliberately circumvented laws to serve a higher purpose. We see variations of these traits in every monomythic hero.

The Emergence of the Superheroic Presidency in the Axial Decade

As much as any election in U.S. history, the choice of president in 1932 felt momentous to voters. The stock market crash of 1929 had resulted in 80 percent shareholder losses; among banks, 11,000 of 25,000 had become insolvent; manufacturing had declined to nearly half its 1929 level, resulting in unemployment for 25 to 30 percent of U.S. workers. In international finance, a halt in the outflow of war reconstruction credits for Europe resulted in its declining vitality and the inability to pay war reparations.[14] Franklin Delano Roosevelt won a smashing electoral victory over Herbert Hoover in 1932, taking 472 electoral votes against the incumbent's puny 59. Hoover lost both his home state, California, and his home county of Santa Clara.[15]

Unease about the American political system had stimulated widespread interest in the fascist programs of Italy and Germany. Father Charles Coughlin of Detroit took to the national airwaves with anti-Semitic interpretations of the nation's distress, praising Hitler and Mussolini. The newspapers of William Randolph Hearst employed both Mussolini and Hitler as paid foreign correspondents in the Sunday section "March of Events." Hearst's wife, Millicent, visited with Mussolini in Rome and secured his commitment for a series of articles, each one scheduled to earn him $1500. She wrote a favorable article about Il Duce, with whom she had spent many hours: "Mussolini is a great executive, a true leader of men, and the great works he has accomplished are his genuine fortification to a high place in history and in the hearts of his people."[16] By 1932, Hearst had extended Mussolini's contract with a commitment to publish 26 articles and in 1935 raised the offering to $1750 after Italy's invasion of Ethiopia.[17] Hitler was also a favored Hearst correspondent, beginning in 1930 with "Adolf Hitler's Own Story; He Tells What Is the Matter with Germany and How He Proposes to Remedy It." Although Hitler eventually proved unsatisfactory to the Hearst organization because he failed to meet his submission deadlines,[18] Hearst felt comfortable with the emphases of both Hitler and Mussolini on rebuilding their national countries and with their attacks on the Versailles Treaty concluded at the end of World War I.

Accenting the era's flirtation with fascism, Columbia Pictures released the propaganda film *Mussolini Speaks* during the first week of FDR's term in 1933. The film's narrative voice was that of Lowell Thomas, notable radio commentator for CBS and the author of numerous books based on exciting reporter assignments, including adventures with Lawrence of Arabia. John Kreuckeberg describes the argument of this film for "successful fascism" as a three-part exposition: "The bringing of order to Italian society; the securing of economic prosperity and modernity for Italy; and finally, ensuring the future of 'the race' through militarized expansion."[19] After running through fascism's achievements in restoring order and regenerating industrial and agricultural production, the film concludes with an emphasis on "the philosophy of action" and the "future of the race." The Black Shirts from the film's beginning are matched at the end by images of boys with swords and knives at training camps — preparing themselves for future war. Kreuckeberg sums it up: "Thus the future for Italy was secure. 'We have nothing to fear,' Thomas translates for the audience as Mussolini bombastically pronounces the success of fascism to Italians and threatens, 'If there are any influences that attempt to break the understanding between our regime and the people, we will crush them.'" Columbia Pictures disclaimed any objectivity about Mussolini with its screen dedication: "To a man of the people whose deeds for his people will ever be an inspiration to mankind — Benito Mussolini."

Mussolini Speaks was an unusual box-office success. Favorable film reviews and cheering audiences were matched by its phenomenal $1,000,000 gross on a mere $100,000 investment.[20] In an era when a film could be seen for as little as 15 cents, *Mussolini Speaks* was remarkably popular and helped to shape a political environment for extraordinary presidential powers in the United States.

A Hearst-Roosevelt Collaboration

Nearly simultaneous with this American hymn to Mussolini, William Randolph Hearst's Cosmopolitan Studios, in concert with MGM, released *Gabriel Over the White House*. Like *Mussolini Speaks*, it was publicly screened within days of Franklin Roosevelt's 1933 inauguration. Despite its fascist themes — unsurprising in a Hearst endeavor — this film received script review and approval from the White House. It came about through an improbable but known convergence of interests between Hearst, Roosevelt, and the film's content.[21] This was a period when Hearst and Roosevelt had an amiable relationship, which was based in large measure on a common understanding of the need for federal economic intervention. Hearst was one of Roosevelt's largest financial supporters in the 1932 election: he gave Joseph Kennedy $25,000 along with instructions to buy radio time for FDR.[22]

The script for *Gabriel* derived from an English novel written by Thomas F. Tweed, a former assistant to British Prime Minister David Lloyd-George. Titled *Rinehard: A Political Melodrama of the Nineteen-Thirties* in England, it became *Gabriel Over the White House: A Novel of the Presidency* in the United States. The 1933 book depicted unmistakable social and political features of its publication year and seemed to predict that America would crumble during the Depression. To emphasize the accuracy of its contemporary setting, the film version of *Gabriel* used newsreels and carefully constructed White House interiors.

The protagonist of *Gabriel* is a recently elected machine politician named Judson Hammond (played by Walter Huston). Willingly manipulated by his secretary of state, Jasper Brooks, the man responsible for his election, Hammond is indifferent to the quality of his appointees and callous toward the plight of America's luckless citizens. Several times he indicates his deference to "the party" — rather than the interests of the people — in setting a course for government. In an early scene, he plays hide-and-seek at the White House with his nephew while blotting out the radio pleas of a spokesman for jobless veterans. In his personal life, he is a bachelor who obviously feels a sexual attraction toward Pendola Malloy, the woman he brings in as his personal secretary.

Early in the film a scene presents an anxious reporter who paints a dismal economic context for his query to the president:

> Starvation and want is everywhere, from coast to coast and from Canada to Mexico. Men and women are begging for bread. Men are freezing without coats while cotton rots in the fields. Thousands of homeless. Millions of vacant homes. What does the new administration say to this? What different plan has the government to this indictment; this state of misery and horror — of lost hope, of broken faith, of the collapse of the American democracy?[23]

Hammond answers with platitudes that evoke Herbert Hoover's responses to the challenges of the Great Depression. And he tops it off with a denial of the reporter's right to quote what he has just said:

> Young man, I shall answer you directly, and through you I shall speak to all my countrymen. America will weather this depression as she has weathered other depressions. Through the spirit of Valley Forge, the spirit of

Gettysburg, and the spirit of the Argonne. The American people have risen before and they will rise again.[24]

The film's determination to hammer away at Hoover while favoring a more activist government reflects not only Hearst's temporary leaning but also that of the film's producer, Walter Wanger, who hoped the film would advance the cause of FDR and his programs.[25]

The cynical President Hammond, like so many comic-book figures who became caped superheroes in the 1930s, undergoes an accident that suddenly transforms his life. While recklessly driving the presidential limousine in a prankish attempt to outrun his own protective motorcade, Hammond pushes the speed up to 100 miles per hour and crashes the car. As he lies in bed, certified by his doctors as dying, the curtains of his room blow as the spirit of "Gabriel, the Revealer" passes through the window and revitalizes him. Not only does he recover from his seemingly fatal injuries, but he begins to exhibit the marks of a monomythic hero. His first demonstration of new character comes when he cringes at the warmth of Pendola Malloy's caring touch. He rejects his former partner with cold formality, addressing her as "Miss Malloy." After two weeks of being sequestered, he finally emerges from his bedroom devoid of any Hooveresque platitudes about promised prosperity. With ghostly, "burning eyes" (the doctor's words), Hammond is now ready to save America — even though this will require "cutting through the red tape of legal procedure." He stands in the well of the Congress and demands a suspension of legislative activities while he restores the country to order; he also demands that he be made "Dictator." Congress responds with an impeachment threat, but they capitulate to his burning fierceness when he delivers this statement:

> We need action. Immediate and effective action. I ask you gentlemen to declare a state of national emergency and to adjourn this congress until normal conditions are restored. During that period of adjournment, I shall assume responsibility for the government. I think, gentlemen, that you forgot that I am still the President of the United States and as Commander-in-Chief of the Army and the Navy, it is within the rights of the President to declare the country under martial law.

Suddenly the camera fades to a newspaper proclaiming Hammond's status as "Dictator of the United States." He abolishes the Eighteenth Amendment and thus ends Prohibition, creating a "mobile federal police" in battle wagons to fight organized crime. He creates a new banking system and makes a stirring, sympathetic speech to the Bonus Army in Baltimore, declaring that he will create an "Army of Constructions" for the jobless. He goes directly to the people via radio with explanations of his actions.

Hammond deputizes his secretary, Harley Beekman, to command a roving military unit that will attack gangsters. They track down the racketeer Nick Diamonds (actually an immigrant named Anton Brilawski, who had organized an assassination attempt at the White House); when captured, the gangsters are given a summary court martial by Beekman, and then an execution by firing squad against the background of the Statue of Liberty.

A final sequence of the film reflects the views of William Randolph Hearst on foreign relations. In a speech reflecting Hearst's own scriptwriting for the production, Hammond demands that foreign governments disarm and immediately repay their war debts to the United States. He gathers foreign emissaries on a yacht, from which they can see the dramatic destruction by aerial bombardment of two U.S. warships. The threat is clear: disarm and use the savings to repay your war debt; otherwise, America's air power will destroy your navies.[26] Hammond's final act is signing an agreement with cheerfully submissive foreign governments who have capitulated to his bullying. They agree to disarm and to pay war debts to America. Once he has accomplished this, Hammond retires to his study and dies — whereupon the angel Gabriel whooshes the curtains again, apparently to claim the expired soul of a now great president.

Roosevelt himself was so enthusiastic about this movie that he showed it to a group of senators from the U.S. Congress. FDR, who struggled through later life in a wheelchair, must have warmed to *Gabriel*'s vision of a president who emerged from his disability with larger-than-life political powers. Roosevelt also seemed to perceive it as congruent with his own political purposes early in his administration: he had a great sense of urgency about "action and action now." In his First Inaugural Address on March 4, 1933, he warned that the constitutional division of powers might thwart responses to the developing emergency:

> It is to be hoped that the normal balance of executive and legislative authority may be wholly adequate to meet the unprecedented task before us. But it may be that an unprecedented demand and need for undelayed action may call for temporary departure from that normal balance of public procedure. I am prepared under my constitutional duty to recommend the measures that a stricken nation in the midst of a stricken world may require. These measures, or such other measures as the Congress may build out of its experience and wisdom, I shall seek, within my constitutional authority, to bring to speedy adoption.

But in the event that the Congress shall fail to take one of these two courses, and in the event that the national emergency is still critical, I shall not evade the clear course of duty that will then confront me. I shall ask the Congress for the one remaining instrument to meet the crisis, broad Executive power to wage a war against the emergency, as great as the power that would be given to me if we were in fact invaded by a foreign foe.

Roosevelt is not predicting here that he will become a dictator; but he does promise that if Congress fails to act as he hopes it will, he will ask for broader executive powers to cope with circumstances that he likens to war.

In addition to showing the New Deal–friendly film to senators at the White House, FDR personally expressed enthusiasm for the film. In a letter to William Randolph Hearst, the President wrote: "I want to tell you how pleased I am with the changes which you made in *Gabriel Over the White House.* I think it is an intensely interesting picture and should do much to help. Several people have seen it with us at the White House. Some of these people said they never went to the movies or cared for them but they think this is a most unusual picture."[27]

In addition to pleasing the president, *Gabriel* did well at the box office and received favorable comment in numerous publications. *Film Daily's Yearbook* asked 384 critics to rate 1933's offerings, and *Gabriel* ranked sixteenth among 507 feature releases.[28] Mordaunt Hall, reviewer for the *New York Times,* described it as "a curious, somewhat fantastic and often melodramatic story, but nevertheless one which at this time is very interesting."[29] Like so many other reviewers, he does not mention the issue of fascism as an alternative to constitutional leadership so prominently raised by the film. There were at least two voices, however, that sounded warnings about the narcissistic and anti-democratic features of this film that was proving to be so congruent with the emergence of the monomythic presidency. Walter Lippmann was one critic who felt the mythic pulse of "the infantile world of irresistible wishes." He was also offended at the movie's "dramatization of Mr. Hearst's editorials."[30] *The New Republic* noted the "half-hearted plea for fascism."[31] These voices provided a kind of early warning system about the dangerous interaction between superheroic fantasy and the American presidency.

Monomythic Expansion in *The Young Mr. Lincoln*

Judson Hammond was not the only monomythic president of the axial decade. The director John Ford's well-known film *The Young Mr. Lincoln* (1939) offered an unusual and well-received version of Lincoln as a physical hero possessed of extraordinary powers of psychological manipulation. Lincoln as superhero capped a long development of Lincoln fictionalization in American arts.

Ever since his election to the presidency in 1860, Abraham Lincoln has steadily provoked creative response within popular culture. Frank Thompson's encompassing study *Abraham Lincoln: Twentieth-Century Popular Portrayals* lists the dramatic poem *Ahab Lincoln* (1861), the play *The Irrepressible Conflict* (1862), and *King Linkum the First: A Musical Burletta* (1863) as immediate attempts at fictional rendition.[32] At the distance of almost a century and a half from his term of service, we now find hundreds of books, plays, poems, feature films, and television dramas that place Abe Lincoln's life in the foreground. It is puzzling that Lincoln as fictional subject so far outdistanced impressive rivals such as Washington or Jefferson. Thompson speculates that Lincoln remains intriguing because of "his ability to be all things to all people, even as he remained resolutely true to himself. He is a truly unique historical figure, yet he lived his life and dealt with others in a way that told them he was just a common man, like themselves." Seen in this way, Washington and Jefferson are too individualized to be "one of us." Thompson adds, however, that "history and myth have become so inextricably entwined that we can never truly separate the two."[33]

What does lie in the realm of historical fact are Lincoln's public statements and acts as candidate and as president. They reveal a logically powerful mind, a passion to hold the country together, a compassion for the victims of war on both sides, and a bent toward self-deprecating humor. His correspondence, like his public demeanor, reveals a sense of moral complexity and self-criticism. In these respects, Lincoln surpasses the "common" qualities of his character to achieve a humanly flawed moral and political genius.

John Ford's *The Young Mr. Lincoln,* however, propels Lincoln from the uncommon to the superhuman in the range of his powers, almost placing his hero alongside the axial decade's men in tights and capes. This is certainly not what one might have expected from this particular filmmaker. During his long career, John Ford drew on and contributed clichés to the Western film genre, but his stories usually transcended the melodramatic moral simplisms at the heart of the monomyth. His 1939 film *Stagecoach* offered a western pilgrimage experience for nine travelers, a long and perilous journey through the big landscape that featured Indian attacks, a philosophical doctor, a crooked gambler, a greedy banker, a virtuous whore, an unfairly jailed outlaw, and a showdown gunfight. But the plot resolution in *Stagecoach* lacks the ethical closure of ritualistic drama. In the end, the outlaw Ringo Kid (played by John Wayne) and the prostitute Dallas (Claire Trevor) slip away to Mexico for life on a ranch. No community has been restored by their virtue; and the passengers on the stagecoach have failed to form even a temporary solidarity. The ending of *Stagecoach* has the moral ambiguity of most lives. An even subtler resistance to moral formula is evident in Ford's revisionist Western *The Searchers* (1956), where the audience is initially encouraged to identify with Ethan Edwards (John Wayne again), who sets off to find a niece whom Comanche Indians have taken captive. It initially appears to be another vengeful confrontation between civilization and savagery; but Ford shows us things about Ethan's money, his loyalty to the Confederacy, his racist hatred of Indians, and his obsessive violence that encourage us to withhold our admiration. And then the film surprises us again when Ethan, who wants to kill his niece for having become a Comanche wife, finally confronts her and feels compelled to rethink the justice of his plan. He does not kill her.

In the light of John Ford's cinematic achievements, one might have expected an auteur as wise and skilled as this to press for a script that would rise to the moral complexity of Abraham Lincoln. But *The Young Mr. Lincoln*, released in the same year as *Stagecoach* — and drawing on the superb acting talent of Henry Fonda in the title role — is a bizarre monomythic rendition. The film does remain faithful to several standard elements in the Lincoln legend: Abe the rail-splitter, the store keeper, the devoted reader, the laconic humorist, the lover devoted to Ann Rutledge and stricken by her death, and the doleful partner of a shrewish Mary Todd. But it is in the movie's treatment of Lincoln's practice of law that it so clearly embodies conventions of monomythic heroism.

Ford's aptly named film focuses on Lincoln's coming of age as a young attorney. This narrative strand begins when Lincoln discovers his life's interest and takes up the study of law, and it ends with his victory in a dramatic criminal trial where he serves defendants in a murder case. Abe's legal awakening occurs as a store clerk when the penniless Clay family arrives in New Salem, Illinois. Abe generously provides for their needs in exchange for the chance to pull some books out of a barrel in their wagon. When he finds *Blackstone's Commentaries*, he reveals his excitement. And as Abe later sits by the river reading *Blackstone*, he comments on its grand revelation: "By jing! That's all there is to it: right and wrong. Maybe I should take up this legal thing." That the sharply critical mind of even a young Abe Lincoln, contemplating the complexity of mid-eighteenth-century common law, would come to such a naïve conclusion, is hardly plausible. But the linkage of the law with moral simplicity serves the movie plot that unfolds.

The film's first clients in Lincoln's law practice are a pair of quarrelling farmers. Instead of leading them to court or considering the legal merits of their claims against each other, he threatens to knock their heads together. Norman Rosenberg suggests that Lincoln is "threatening violence in order to avoid legal trouble,"[34] but the monomythic preference for superheroic interventions as opposed to the slow, imperfect process of the law is already in view at this point in the film. Moreover, Abe is actually impatient to arrive at the fair, where he will further demonstrate his physical supremacy in several contests. At midnight on the same day, he finds his second clients in the same Clay family from whom he had earlier obtained his *Blackstone*. The tipsy Clay boys have been involved in an altercation with the bullying, lecherous deputy sheriff Scrub White, who, after having pulled a gun, turns up mysteriously dead of a knife wound. Mrs. Clay was at the scene of White's death, and Lincoln quickly arranges with her to defend her sons. But the town's mob is an-

In *The Young Mr. Lincoln*, Abe expresses his indifference to the formal proceedings at the murder trial of his clients. He lolls in the gallery and browses in the law books.

Credit: *The Young Mr. Lincoln* © 20th Century Fox, 1939.

gry about the death and threatens the ineffectual sheriff with lynching the boys. Recognizing the impotence of law, Lincoln stands at the steps of the jail and interrupts the mob's use of a battering ram. He interposes his own violent threats against mob members, while moderating them with self-deprecating humor: "You wouldn't want me to lose my first clients, would you?" Since Lincoln has so decisively reminded the town that same day about his physical strength, his threat of violence is effective and credible.

The movie's highlight is the trial of the Clay brothers. Strangely, they are unable to describe exactly what they did, and Lincoln does not seem to consult with them at all. Mrs. Clay, who was an eyewitness, refuses to speak because she is afraid of saying something that will spare one son at the expense of the other. At trial, Lincoln's performance is hardly lawyerly. He mocks the judge and the opposing attorneys with country humor. As other participants perform their legal roles according to the rules of the court, Lincoln lolls around the periphery of the courtroom in a way that suggests his amusement at the foibles of law and his superheroic certainty of a happy outcome. As Rosenberg points out, he uses no legal arguments that would vindicate or extenuate his clients' deeds.[35] Nor can he shake the testimony of Palmer Cass, one of the eyewitnesses for the prosecution. Since White was a visible bully in the community, a self-defense argument could be compelling. Or Lincoln could explore collusion between Cass and White. It's difficult to avoid the conclusion that Lincoln's reluctance to employ the normal processes of law constitutes a reckless gamble with their lives. The judge who presides in his case seeks him out to give this very warning, but Lincoln disrespectfully ignores him.

Ford's Lincoln resolves the seeming impossible dilemma by means of a courtroom trick that presages the later Perry Mason television dramas. Using a *Farmer's Almanac* — also obtained from the illiterate Mrs. Clay — Lincoln suddenly impeaches the testimony of Palmer Cass, the presumed pal of Scrub White. Even though Cass is only a witness and not a defendant, Lincoln badgers him until he breaks down and confesses to stabbing Scrub White. Cass is not even on the witness stand when he does so; nor has Lincoln had to address the jury to make the case for his clients. The superheroic Lincoln wins his victory by a manipulative psychological ploy. His shouting "plain talk" that evokes the surprising confession beats the lawyer talk of those who play by the normal court rules. In the words of Rosenberg, "*Young Mr. Lincoln* marks its hero as someone who works *within* but is not really of the legal machinery."[36] In our view, this feature is typical of the American monomyth in preferring extralegal means of redemption rather than the normal processes of the law. John Ford's Lincoln is actually more of a loner than Perry Mason, who although always working against a corrupt or incompetent system, at least relies on staff work from the secretary Della Street and the investigator Paul Drake to discover the evidence or the loophole that wins the case.

The movie ends with a powerful symbol of Lincoln's distance from the institutions of law and other people. He wanders off on a lonely road, heading for a stormy sky. It is a monomythic hero moving beyond the community he has just spared from committing an injustice against innocents. This Lincoln is a man above the law. It is not the Lincoln who sued and defended railroads, who represented creditors and debtors, or the Lincoln who argued several hundred cases at the appellate level before the Illinois supreme court. This is a superman whose physical threats and actual psychological violence restore moral balance. The Lincoln of Ford's film would have no interest in writing eloquently of the demands of maintaining an equality of laws and the original union of the United States; such a president could never somberly remark, "I claim not to have controlled events, but confess plainly that events have controlled me."[37] The historical Abraham Lincoln defended the principle that all men are created equal and sought to preserve the constitutional system, but not as superhero. He brought decades of patient experience in reading, listening to claims, and framing complex legal arguments to the tasks of his presidency; he was a supreme politician who carefully weighed the views of his constituents as he improvised new policies in the midst of the greatest crisis of American history. But the miraculous powers displayed in *The Young Mr. Lincoln* are nowhere evident in his life.

The President as Action-Adventure Hero

In the years during World War II and immediately thereafter, filmmakers were reluctant to touch the presidential office or character with John Ford's boldness, a reluctance particularly understandable during the McCarthyist inquiries into political loyalties in Hollywood. Biographical films located safely in the more distant past became dominant. Typical were *Tennessee Johnson* (1943), *Wilson* (1944), and *The President's Lady* (1953), which dealt with a socially ostracized romance of Andrew Jackson. *Sunrise at Campobello* (1960) gave a stirring picture of FDR's struggle with polio in the 1920s — before he became president. Only in the 1960s did the irrationality of Cold War nuclear plans and the Cuban missile fright succeed in stimulating movies about presidential behavior in an unthinkable now. Nuclear presidents-in-crisis, for example, appeared in three widely seen films of 1964: *Seven Days in May*, *Dr. Strangelove*, and *Fail Safe*.

While creators of fiction temporarily became more guarded in their presidential depictions, the twentieth-century momentum to symbolically equate
the national government with the presidency continued. A long-term study
of periodicals reveals that feature articles on the president grew from 109.5
per year during Roosevelt's terms to 200 for Kennedy and 407 for Jimmy
Carter; Ronald Reagan's presidency moved to the 500 level.[38] In a true quan-
tum leap, measured at the end of the year 2000, *Magazine Index* indicated
more than 14,000 articles on the subject of Bill Clinton, a large proportion of
them stemming from the Monica Lewinsky affair and the impeachment effort. While presidential focus intensified, studies of the U.S. Congress went
into recession. An analysis of Congress in television network coverage
showed a decline of approximately 50 percent in the decade between 1975 and
1985.[39]

Beginning in the 1970s, several events coalesced to bring presidents back
to the Hollywood screens in an increasingly monomythic guise. Richard
Nixon's unpopularity and fall made his presidency unusually juicy as a starting point for tales of villainous ambition and dishonesty. Thomas Monsell's
book *Nixon on Stage and Screen* (1998) lists hundreds of productions, including fiction films, puppet shows, operas, and docudramas — not one of them
depicting him in a wholly favorable light. After Nixon, Americans became less
obliged to maintain a reverential attitude toward occupants of the Oval Office; and the stature of the presidency slipped another salacious notch with
Bill Clinton's philandering sexual proclivities. Creators felt additional license
for imagining an American president immersed in tabloid-style scandals.
Clinton's lack of military service and significant military achievement in his
terms offered additional grounds for sneering at his subheroic stature. Hollywood sensed in these weakened defenses for the office an opportunity to give
us more films featuring an American president than in any previous decade.
Among the hundred or more "president films" of the 1990s, *Pelican Brief*
(1993), *In the Line of Fire* (1993), *Clear and Present Danger* (1994), *Independence Day* (1996), *Air Force One* (1997), *Deep Impact* (1998), and *Armageddon*
(1998) all earned box-office grosses in excess of $100,000,000 dollars. *Wag the
Dog* (1997) and *Primary Colors* (1998) both drew significant public attention
because their plots coincided with the titillating themes of Bill Clinton's legal
entanglements.

The most commercially successful of these films — *Air Force One* and
Independence Day — present their presidents as action-adventure heroes.
Their narratives repeatedly evoke the formulas of the American
monomyth. In accounting for their box-office triumphs, one finds it difficult to isolate the crucial ingredient. Is it musical score, star power, special

effects, cleverly suspenseful story, or nationalistic flattery? Without pretending to assign proportional credit, we can see that these fictional presidents conformed more tightly than ever to the monomythic model of the nation's highest office.

Independence Day

Independence Day[40] presents the United States president in a science-fiction genre film that uses twin American crises as theme: the challenges to American masculinity and the destruction of the entire planet. All of the film's principal men have been abandoned, impeded in career, or unfairly demeaned by women, and this includes President Thomas J. Whitmore. Whitmore's wife maintains an independent professional career, traveling and leaving the President at home with their daughter. A female pundit of television's McLaughlin Group quips that the nation "elected a warrior but got a wimp." The sad news of his sagging status in the polls is delivered to Whitmore by one of his female advisors, Connie Levinson, a woman in a power suit who has deserted her own husband.

The external crisis occurs on July 2, when a giant, alien-controlled spaceship appears over Washington, D.C., and other major American cities. Whitmore tries to communicate in a friendly way by sending a helicopter as an emissary, but it is immediately destroyed. The president himself manages to escape before the White House explodes and burns. He is taken to a remote base, Area 51, where he learns that this is the very same species of alien that had descended at Roswell, New Mexico, in 1948. What he learns from a brief and frightening encounter is that the aliens have come to extract earth's resources and have decreed that all humans must die. Whitmore then knows that the earth faces an apocalyptic battle. His wife dies after the alien attack on Los Angeles, a consequence of disregarding her husband's request that she leave immediately once the threat became apparent. She whimpers in death like a little girl: "I'm so sorry I didn't come home when you told me to."

Undeterred by environmental arguments against using nuclear weapons in the near atmosphere, Whitmore gambles as he launches an attack on the spaceship hovering over Houston. The attack destroys Houston, but the aliens remain. All humanity now hangs in the balance. One of the computer programmers, David Levinson (Connie's abandoned husband), conceives the idea of transmitting a computer virus to the aliens' command center. Perhaps this will temporarily disable their defenses, permitting effective attacks. The president himself, a Gulf War pilot, steps aside from his strategic role as commander-in-chief and volunteers to fly a tactical missile raid against one of the space ships. His rationale, expressed to a puzzled general, is: "I'm a combat pilot; I belong in the air." This makes absolutely no sense, except that in conformity with the American monomyth, the president must now function as a superhero to redeem the world.

Fortune favors the plan to transmit the computer virus to the womb of the mothership. The window of vulnerability permits another abandoned male, the drunkard Russell Case, to send the decisive missile thrust that destroys the aliens' command and control. As he flies to his own kamikaze-like death, he shouts, "In the words of my generation, 'Up yours!'" The happy resolution comes when the alien ships, cratered by nuclear hits, fall smoking to the earth, permitting the human avengers to admire their destructive work. Thus a suicide raid comparable in mythic motivation to that of September 11, 2001, helps to save the world.

Looking at these events in the movie as an exercise in presidential power, we can see an assortment of constitutional circumventions that are rendered acceptable in this monomythic drama. In addition to the president's desertion of his own decision-making post, most other institutions of democratic government go missing in action. For example, the president does not consult with Congress about declaring war on the aliens, nor does he consult with state or local governments about their emergency capabilities, nor with party leaders. His military is peculiarly truncated, consisting principally of a "Marine Air Force"; the Army, the Navy, and the regular Air Force play no prominent role.[41] The president dismisses Nimzicki, his secretary of defense, as a "sniveling little weasel" and does not bother to replace him. He also takes on the role of world leadership without working through any visible international institutions. We simply see that other military forces on the globe are coordinating in response to the president's leadership.

President Whitmore offers a florid Shakespearean-Churchillian affirmation of American centrality to the world's hopes, which comes before the final battle: "We will not go quietly into the night. We will not vanish without a fight. We're going to live on! We're going to survive! Today we celebrate our Independence Day." He proposes that "our 4th of July" become humanity's Independence Day from the tyranny of aliens — once those aliens have been successfully destroyed. The film scans several times through villages, mosques, and synagogues that show frightened people in prayer, obviously hoping that the U.S. will succeed. In the end, the world has been restored to safety, and the women we see in this movie are either dead or redirected to better serve the needs of the men in their lives. Their day in all this might be called "re-dependence."

Independence Day was one of those rare films that became entangled in a political campaign. In 1996, when incumbent Bill Clinton ran against Bob Dole, both candidates seemed eager to be associated with the world-redeeming presidency. During this campaign, Clinton hosted *Independence Day*'s Dean Devlin (producer), Roland Emmerich (director), and Bill Pullman (who played the fictional President Whitmore) at the White House. Even though it was a mere two years after the destructive blast at the Murrah Federal Building in Oklahoma City, President Clinton praised a film in which we witness the White House being incinerated. "I recommend it," he declared. And Bob Dole, who had come off as a stuffy old moralist for his earlier attacks on Hollywood, issued statements of praise for *Independence Day*'s patriotism and its battle between good and evil. Dole's spokesman explained that the violence was "socially redeeming" because "it promoted the greater good."[42] However, in view of the very real challenge to global stability and security posed by the September 11 attack, this film and the ideology it represents seem thoroughly corrosive.

Air Force One

Although *Air Force One* presents no alien invasion, it too presents the American president as a world-redemptive figure who has a monomythic contempt for the pragmatism of diplomacy and consulting with his own advisers. President James Marshall (Harrison Ford) has been summoned to Moscow for a celebration of a joint U.S.-Russian raid to capture a Kazakh, General Radek, who threatens to bring back nationalistic Communism. Disgusted by his own government's delay in intervening, Marshall announces: "Never again will I allow our political self-interest to deter us from what we know to be morally right." And then he issues a boastful challenge to all enemies in the world:

> Atrocity and terror are not political weapons. And to those who would use them, your day is over. We will never negotiate. We will no longer tolerate you and we will no longer be afraid. It's your turn to be afraid.

Marshall's speech has a sensational effect in Moscow. Russians line the streets to wave American flags as the presidential motorcade passes.

The president's national security adviser fumes about not being in on the decision to take such a bold stance; but his chief of staff gloats about the new mood of implacability and the publicity: "They're already calling it the 'Be Afraid Speech,'" he says to the president. And then he tells someone on the phone that "the president is ready to take Congress on. He's not going to kiss their ass for each vote." Consulted about a new crisis in Iraq, the president simply says: "Let's not waste any more time. Let's send the *Nimitz* back in."

The triumphal mood does not last for long, because the champions of General Radek have made a deal with Gibbs, an agent of the Secret Service, which quickly permits them to control Air Force One. They execute passengers and threaten the president's wife and daughter as tactics in gaining the release of General Radek. In the first confusion of the hijacking, the president — just at the moment when he was expected to take his exit using the ejection pod — has hidden on the plane. He was, as we learn, a Vietnam helicopter pilot who won the Medal of Honor. He has stayed on Air Force One to fight unarmed, in hand-to-hand combat with men who are thirty years younger than he. He eventually kills five of them as he stalks the lower deck, luring the armed men to their death below. One he strangles to death.

These extraordinary feats alone are not enough to save the plane. The president must then use the telephone with a weak battery to get wiring instructions on dumping the fuel; he must use the fax machine to order a missile attack by U.S. forces on his own plane. He arranges for many passengers to parachute to safety. And then, because all the pilots are dead, he flies the plane himself in a tricky mid-air rescue operation.

Back in Washington, a different struggle is taking place: it revolves around Vice President Kathryn Bennett (Glenn Close). Will she take the full power of the presidency, as she might? She is urged to do so by the secretary of defense, who first wants to sacrifice all passengers because he hates General Radek so much; and then he wants to have the president certified as incompetent. Everyone eventually signs on except the vice president, and she has the pen in hand to do so. After all, she is angry at the president for failing to get in the escape pod as he was supposed to: "He's taking a risk with his life." Thus one of the suspense elements is whether the United States will get its first woman president. But she shows faith in this president: when it becomes clear that he has survived every threat posed by the terrorists and the disloyal Secret Service agent, she tears up the paper. Because she stands tough in defense of her president as commander-in-chief, he gains the necessary time for all the crafty maneuvers required to destroy every terrorist on board his plane.

Air Force One symbolically vindicates the notion of the president as the one man who can take huge risks — physical, moral, and political — and is capable of winning triumphant victories in each arena. But does such a person, let alone a president, exist? Does such a president symbolize democratic leadership? Are we justified in being concerned about the political influence of the images offered by *Air Force One* and *Independence Day*?

Youthful Voters and the Mythic Presidency

The vitality of political institutions depends on the acculturation of the younger generations. A great crisis emerged in the Soviet Union's sphere of influence when it became clear that the young people of East Germany, Hungary, Czechoslovakia, and Poland lacked any sense of identification with the Stalinist regimes that ruled them. Opportunists would always step forward to exercise authority, but how many citizens would accept it?

In a less dramatic way, the United States shows signs of a declining political participation in American presidential elections. Recent history would include a belated legitimation of the Vietnam draft (and a potential stimulant for youth voting) when Congress sent the Constitution's Amendment XXVI to the states on March 23, 1971; by July 1 of that year, the amendment reducing the voting age to eighteen had been ratified by the states. War protestors could not complain that men too young to vote were being sent to their death in Vietnam.

In the presidential election of 1972, the first in which an eighteen-year-old could vote, the participation of those between eighteen and twenty-four (49.6 percent) almost matched the 21-24 cohort's rate in 1968 (50.4 percent). Thereafter began a steady decline: the 1976 participation dropped to 42.2 percent and fell again in 1980 to 39.9 percent. Despite a bump back up to 42.8 percent in 1992, the youth cohort looked pretty unengaged again by 1996, with a mere 32.4 percent participation rate.[43] By the 2000 presidential election, a mere 48 percent were registered.[44]

Could superheroic images of the presidency play some role in this decline? In the uncertain enterprise of cultural interpretation, it is difficult to say with confidence that mythic artifact X causes behavior Y. A further complicating factor here is that so many recent images of the American president have conformed to the pattern of the monomythic supervillain. As a case in point, the film *Absolute Power* (1997) dramatizes an adulterous president Richmond (Gene Hackman) who sexually brutalizes the wife of the very friend who made him president, permitting her murder by Secret Service agents when she uses a knife to fight back. Then he allows his vicious chief of staff to orchestrate a cover-up that results in several attempted murders of those who know the truth about the president. Richmond is thwarted by the superhero Luther Whitney (Clint Eastwood), who outsmarts the cadre of corrupt assistants protecting the president. *Absolute Power* is merely one of several films in the 1990s — including *Dave* (1993), *In the Line of Fire* (1993), *Clear and Present Danger* (1994), and *Wag the Dog* (1997) — that portray degenerate U.S. presidents. Depicting the president as a villain with outsized

powers of manipulation may appeal to audiences disgusted with recent in-
cumbents, but the monomythic structure of such films strengthens despair
over democracy itself. Why should one take the trouble to vote if the system
itself is hopelessly corrupt?

The most obvious critical observation to be made about Presidents
Whitmore and Marshall is that we don't need such presidents because we
have chosen to have laws and democratic institutions instead. And even if we
needed them, we couldn't elect such paragons of physical and moral perfection. The circumstances of action for these fantasy presidents have been simplified so as to make a physically heroic action seem necessary to save the
world or the presidency. But the world of presidents can never be that simple.
To the extent that youthful voters are encouraged by popular entertainments
to expect an uncomplicated world that demands a leader with visceral instincts, they shall be disappointed. The Hollywood film industry seems to
stagger in recent years between the unbearable criminal and the unattainable
superhero.

If our popular culture were thoroughly imbued with the mythic premises
of democracy, we would see women and men in the imaginary Oval Office
who exemplify a fuller array of abilities required by the Constitution and the
demands of public leadership. In this regard, the widely watched television
series *West Wing* presents a textured, policy- and politics-oriented presidency
that exemplifies many of democracy's working values. President Josiah Bart-
lett, while cast in the heroic role, is merely wise rather than superhuman in
his struggles with the endless series of large and small problems that rush toward his desk. He occasionally wins a battle over his conservative detractors,
but, as audience members, we don't witness a redeeming of the world or even

President Marshall kills
several attackers during
Air Force One's flight of
terror; this burly terrorist
dies in his bare-handed
strangle.

Credit: *Air Force One* © 1997
Columbia Pictures.

the nation. This president has trouble saving himself from his allies and from some of his own instincts. His presidency is thus scaled down toward a credible representation of democratic leadership.

As President George W. Bush confronts the issues posed by the terrorist attacks begun on September 11, 2001, he has oscillated between the poles of superheroism and realism. In his remarks at the Washington National Cathedral service on September 14, he announced a world-scale purgation of evil, announcing that "our responsibility to history is already clear: to answer these attacks and rid the world of evil." He has repeatedly referred to members of the Al Qaeda network simply as "the evil ones." Bush also suggested initially that the mixture of national virtue and anger would give us extraordinary control in the conflict with terrorists: "This nation is peaceful, but fierce when stirred to anger. This conflict was begun on the timing and terms of others; it will end in a way and at an hour of our choosing."[45] This rhetoric echoed an earlier taunt of President Reagan to terrorists — "You can run but you can't hide." It also had the flavor of Harrison Ford's confidently delivered words for terrorists in *Air Force One*. "We will never negotiate. We will no longer tolerate you and we will no longer be afraid. It's your turn to be afraid." This sort of mythic bluster cannot be the basis for public expectations about the outcome of conflict, particularly when the adversary welcomes death in the service of his cause. President Bush and his officials seem to realize this, as they have repeatedly urged the public to be patient and to anticipate years of struggle in attempting to create a more secure international environment. We hope that the latter message prevails as the basis for presidential acts and policy making.

8 Lethal Patriots
Break the Rhythm

"I know in my heart that I am right in my struggle, Steve. I have come to peace with myself, my God and my cause. Blood will flow in the streets, Steve. Good vs. Evil. Free men vs. Socialist Wannabe Slaves. Pray it is not your blood, my friend."

Timothy McVeigh, in a farewell letter to a boyhood friend[1]

GABRIEL MARTIN: *"Father, what changed you?"*
BENJAMIN MARTIN: *"It was your mother. I had trouble breathing around your mother."*
GABRIEL: *"A woman has the strangest effect on men."*

dialogue between father and son in
Mel Gibson's *The Patriot* (2000)[2]

"Women should neither be present at my burial nor at any later date should visit my grave."

from the will discovered in the luggage of Mohamed Atta,
suspected of piloting American Airlines Flight 11
into the World Trade Center, September 11, 2001[3]

151

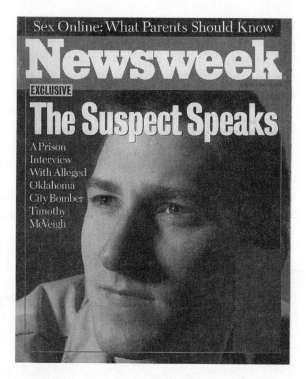

Timothy McVeigh took on a kind of stoic charm for the media. Newsweek's cover article, which offered no important disclosures about the crime of Oklahoma City, presented him as a kind of celebrity.

Credit: Newsweek, Inc. © 1995.

Throughout the American monomyth's development, its creators have found new realms from which to purge evil. Beginning with villages and then adding cities, the cleansing process eventually moved to encompass the nation and then the world. The fictional heroes of these earlier battles recognize the failures of community, but they spare its institutions from the explosive violence or manipulative sweetness they direct toward the evil Others. Thus their license to operate outside the law does not prevent them from cooperating with its elected or appointed authorities. At most, the heroes walk away at story's end from the badges or leaders that they despise. In the innocence of the axial decade, for example, the Lone Ranger and Superman always turn over the bad guys they capture to the sheriff or the police — and remain mute about the incompetence that demanded their assistance.

Since the 1980s, however, a more pessimistic strand of the monomyth has emerged: in this strand, government itself is the oppressive, irredeemably corrupt Other. Rather than being an Edenic paradise corrupted by outsiders, the community is shown in a fallen condition linked to evils within its own leadership. The mythic solution thus lies in confronting it with the deadly violence previously dealt to intruders, a violence that will break the rhythm of ordinary government. This discovery of the evil at the heart of institutions lies close to the surface in Sylvester Stallone's *Rambo* series and in Clint Eastwood's much-lauded *Unforgiven* (1992). We also see it in Mel Gibson's medieval epic film *Braveheart* (1995) and his movie about the American revolution, *The Patriot* (2000). For the *Left Behind* series (1995-) and the novel *The Turner Diaries* (1978), the war to destroy governments and leaders corrupted by unlimited evil becomes the overt, consuming mission of the heroes.

A leitmotif in most of these fictions is the imperative to escape from women's restraints in responding to evil. The premise is that women are too conciliatory, too likely to acquiesce in an evil rather than destroying it. As texts about manhood, these fictions echo and amplify themes from the men's movement of the 1990s, suggesting that men must distance themselves from their mothers and other women so that they can re-establish contact with their "inner warriors" and with older men.[4] These stories are thus a double denial of the democratic hope that our governed life consists of a community of all adults with equal rights. This articulation of the myth demands that the corrupted community, rather than setting itself right through a pragmatic politics of relative equals, be purged by spasms of violence controlled by lone males. As Mark Juergensmeyer has shown in his study of religious violence, this holy terror by "cowboy monks" — men alienated from women — has become a global pattern involving Christians, Jews, Hindus, Muslims, and Sikhs. Mohamed Atta's will (cited above) bespeaks the motive of escaping from females in the service of apocalyptic schemes of purging the world's evil. The Taliban of Afghanistan is only the most visibly extreme of these men preoccupied with destroying secular government so that women can be more fully subordinated.[5]

During the period when popular fictions offered these plots of lashing out at government, the United States lived through the deeds of two homegrown terrorists, Timothy McVeigh and Theodore Kaczynski (also known as the Unabomber). Both lived out unique scenarios of confronting "the System." McVeigh, who seemed to be inspired by monomythic tales, chose to live and to accept death quickly as an acknowledged disciple of *The Turner Diaries'* fiery ideals. The Unabomber, in contrast, devised a script of mysteriously selected bombing targets over a seventeen-year period. It seemed to be his envy of the attention McVeigh received that led him toward self-promotional publicity, which eventually resulted in his identification and capture. Both men felt that they were bringing redemption to a world indifferent to its own well-being.

These two terrorists audaciously enacted significant elements from our widely applauded mythic scenarios. The lamentable death of so many unsuspecting people is a comment on how such violence works out in practice.

Pairing these cool, effective terrorists with their mythic counterparts from contemporary popular culture reveals a deep schizophrenia in our land: on our mythic holidays from the formal ideals of democracy, we celebrate visions that horrify us when translated into action by those who enact purgative deeds of the monomyth. In this chapter we examine this tension between what we mythically honor and what we find intolerable when it becomes social fact.

Men without Women

With the exception of the asexual Heidi and some female redeemers discussed in Chapter 4, females always looked troublesome to the American monomyth. During its formative years, tales of relationships between men and women showed a dialogical complexity: women were to be reasoned with. In *The Virginian,* for example, Judge Henry and the Virginian must persuade Molly to reject legality in favor of vigilante justice. In the film *High Noon* (1952), Will Kane must choose between the certainty of family life with Amy Fowler, the Quaker teacher, and the prospect of a deadly shootout with Frank Miller's gang. Initially deserting Will because of his readiness to face a violent confrontation, Amy ends up as the only person in Hadleyville who gives assistance. She saves his life by shooting one of Miller's bad guys in the back. Despite the rejection of women's sentiments about violence, we can detect optimism that sufficient evidence of evil will eventually persuade women to accept the use of violence. And the underlying premise of such stories remains romantic. Women are desirable partners for the life-after-violence — once the community is safe again.

As we saw in Chapter 5, John Wayne helped define the way toward a symbolic world where women's influence is diminished by rejecting the romantic ideal. A suggestive early film (with John Wayne in a nonspeaking role) was entitled *Men Without Women* (1930),[6] a story about a heroic man whose career was destroyed through his misplaced trust in a woman who betrayed his military secrets to the enemy. Earlier we reviewed John Wayne's Sergeant Stryker of *The Sands of Iwo Jima,* a man who drowns in self-destructive pity over being rejected by an unloving wife — before a prostitute finally makes it clear to him that no woman could really matter to him. At that moment he becomes fully liberated to die sacrificially for his country.

A cluster of social changes in the 1970s and 1980s nudged the purveyors of mythic violence into more extreme postures about the place of women. Central to the culturally constructed "crisis of masculinity" were these factors: failure to win the Vietnam War; the nation's diminished economic power following the Arab oil embargo of 1973; assertive gay and lesbian movements; and unemployment stresses when minorities and women appeared to advance while white men saw themselves languishing. Perhaps the most provocative factor for male heroic ideals was feminism, with its critiques of bloody masculinities in both war and in domestic violence. Philosophically, one kind of answer came from writers such as Warren Farrell, a feminist-turned-masculinist who wrote *The Myth of Male Power,*[7] where he suggests that the apparent power of men is actually a form of victimization that literally kills them. The proof lay partly in the differing mortality statistics for men and women. He audaciously claimed that the slavery of men should be compared to the slavery of African-Americans.[8] Consciousness-raising and assertiveness about men's victim status was Farrell's answer.

A more hands-on approach for impaired men came in a series of activities and products designated as "The New War" in James William Gibson's book *Warrior Dreams.* In addition to gun shows, *Soldier of Fortune* conventions, and paintball combat, Gibson describes the pulp fiction and films offering fantasy warfares of restored manhood. An important symbol in these New War creations is the "Black Widow," the fatal seductress who must be resisted or destroyed. He puts it this way: "All women are black-widow women. To be sure, there are different subspecies, but all are dangerous creatures, enemies of one kind or another who are either to be avoided, mastered, or killed."[9]

In this spirit of resisting or mastering women, numerous action films since the 1980s have either eliminated women from their script or, if they were present at all, quickly disposed of them. John Rambo, the Sylvester Stallone character who appears in *First Blood* (1982), *First Blood: Part II* (1985), and *Rambo III* (1988),[10] functions almost entirely outside any relationship that includes women. The Vietnamese character Co Bao, in *Part II,* is killed almost as quickly as she has had her first snuggle with Rambo. Martin Riggs, Mel Gibson's character in *Lethal Weapon* (1987), begins his journey in a recurrently suicidal state resulting from his wife's death. This void in his life permits a reckless fury for his lethal and often illegal law-enforcement practices. He gets surrogate family satisfactions from those of his obsessively cautious partner, Roger Murtaugh (Danny Glover). Gibson embroidered further on the formula of dead wife/relentless attack on government in his movies *Braveheart* (1995)[11] and *The Patriot* (2000). A similar plot is worked out in *The Unforgiven* (1992),[12] in which Clint Eastwood's Will Munny character regenerates himself through a final spasm of violence — after finally achieving emotional distance from his dead wife's demands to stop drinking and stop killing people.

The bluntest expression of this rage toward women occurs in William Pierce's neo-Nazi novel *The Turner Diaries*. There Earl Turner, a low-level revolutionary racist, has a lover, Katherine, who is killed by "the System" that Earl is working to destroy. But his affection for her does not indicate any concession about the changing character of gender roles in America. He laments:

> Liberalism is an essentially feminine, submissive world view. Perhaps a better adjective than feminine is infantile. It is the world view of men who do not have the spiritual strength to stand up and do single combat with life.[13]

This "single combat" depends on access to unlimited quantities and types of weapons that Jews, blacks, and feminized liberals want to take out of the hands of real men, exposing them to the depredations of inferior races. The

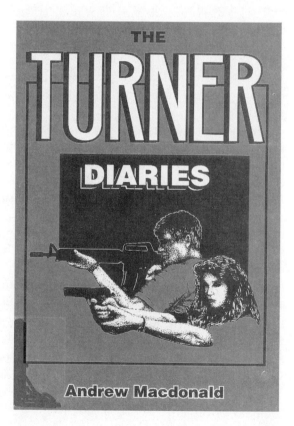

The plots of William Pierce's white supremacist novels (written under the pseudonym "Andrew Macdonald") focus on the power of the gun to purify America through the extermination of non-caucasian groups, feminists, and Jews.

Credit: *Turner Diaries*
© 1978, 1980 William Pierce.

author later adds this "Note to the reader" as a clarification of Turner's resentments about the world he is prepared to destroy:

> "Women's lib" was a form of mass psychosis which broke out during the last three decades of the Old Era. Women affected by it denied their femininity and insisted that they were "people," not "women." This aberration was promoted and encouraged by the System as a means of dividing our race [white] against itself. (p. 45)

In Pierce's Hitler-inspired vision of racial purification, liberal feminism gets its proper punishment on "the Day of the Rope" in 1993. In his grisly vision of a purified Los Angeles, "thousands of female corpses" are hanging throughout the city, all wearing placards indicating their sexual association with "Blacks, Jews, or with other non-White males" (p. 161). Earl Turner's group eventually gets access to nuclear weapons, which permit it to wage an all-out racial assault to cleanse major regions of the U.S. and of the world as well.

It may be comforting to realize that Pierce is the most extreme among the widely known creators in this new tradition of masculine violence. But his cluster of values — the definition of masculinity through the subordination of women, combined with explosive attacksDdddd on authority — became the mythos from which box-office gold and Hollywood Oscars could be manufactured for more than two decades. Examining some of the most successful of these fantasies allows us to trace the bizarre careers of Tim McVeigh and the Unabomber along the contours of a more familiar mythic map.

The Crusade against Government in the *Rambo* Films

The Rambo stories have been one of the great successes in American cinema, temporarily making Sylvester Stallone a focus for patriotic pride and one of the world's leading box-office attractions. As an evil-purging hero, John Rambo possesses infallible moral instincts about whom to disable or destroy. Although critics trashed Stallone's films as having comic-book plots, Rambo popularized the explosive turn against one's own society as the source of corruption. It is not surprising that the young Timothy McVeigh was a fan of Rambo and of Chuck Norris's similar *Missing in Action*. In their interview-based biography entitled *American Terrorist*, Lou Michel and Dan Herbeck report McVeigh's admiration for these fantasy characters: "These were men's men, in McVeigh's eyes, and he wanted to be like them."[14] What were the Rambo plots that he found so attractive?

In *First Blood,* John Rambo is a vet who has returned from the Vietnam war. Although he is a Congressional Medal of Honor winner, he feels thoroughly alienated from American society. Unlike Stallone's *Rocky* character from an earlier decade, who needed a supportive wife to help him rebuild his will to win, Rambo is a pure loner. Like other Vietnam veterans, he is shown to be unwelcome in his ironically named hometown of Hope, Washington. When he returns to this community, the malevolent, slovenly sheriff, Will Teasle, treats Rambo like a criminal. When a deputy sheriff arrests him as a vagrant and treats him brutally, Rambo's imagination flashes him back to when he was among the Vietcong. He breaks out of the Hope jail and becomes a one-man army in the local wilderness, carrying but a single-bladed knife. As he flees, he battles rats in a mine, spears a boar, survives army rockets, and steals an army vehicle. Although he gets incredibly cut up, scarred, and dirty, he single-handedly defeats a whole army of sheriff's deputies, state troopers, and national guardsmen. He even sutures his own wounds on the fly. The symbolism of Rambo's oppression tells us that the same hero who struggled to save the nation from its most vicious enemies must strike at the institution of law enforcement itself merely to preserve himself. At the film's end, Rambo has trashed the local law-enforcement center and burned down part of the town.

The premise that national government itself must be attacked and cleansed with bursts of bullets was the next step for Rambo in Stallone's enormously popular successor film, *First Blood: Part II.* Here Rambo is dropped into a jungle on a strictly reconnaissance mission for the CIA — after being explicitly told that he is "not to engage the enemy." Discovering a camp where an American POW is being tortured on a cross, Rambo defies orders and decides to rescue him. He then finds himself abandoned by his timid superior officers, who desert him in the jungle because he has disobeyed their cowardly and politically motivated orders not to rescue prisoners. The logic is that rescuing them would acknowledge that the government had abandoned them in the first place. Rambo, of course, has too much personal honor to participate in such betrayal. He discovers a whole camp of POWs in North Vietnam, finds a bedraggled American helicopter to escape in, and rescues the whole lot all by himself.

A crucial political moment in *First Blood: Part II* comes when Rambo returns to Thailand with the rescued POWs. He has said to Murdock, the craven CIA boss, "I want to kill you." Instead, he takes an M-60 machine gun into the CIA command center and sprays the computers and radio equipment with a devastating shower of lead. Just as they did at the climax of *Star Wars: A New Hope,* when Luke Skywalker blows up the Empire's Death Star, movie audiences stood to applaud this scene. Rambo's attack fell not on an alien enemy's headquarters but on a democratically established institution of his own country — presented here as the symbolic enemy of democracy.

The *Unforgiven* Redeemer

Another of Timothy McVeigh's film favorites was Clint Eastwood's *Unforgiven* (1992).[15] In the letters he wrote from prison to the journalist Phil Bachrach, he twice commented that he thought it the best film ever made. As in the Rambo tales, the theme of *Unforgiven* is congruent with McVeigh's sense of mission to kill authorities who try to disarm citizens. We also see a superheroic killer in *Unforgiven* who escapes from the orbit of the women who emasculate his redemptive capacity. Unlike the Stallone creations, this film carries the prestige of having garnered nine Academy Award nominations; in the end it won the Oscar in four categories, including Best Director and Best Producer for Clint Eastwood, who was also a candidate for Best Actor. In addition, the movie was showered with awards from the Golden Globes, the Los Angeles Film Critics, and the National Society of Film Critics.[16]

This poster for *The Unforgiven* film distills its message into a stark icon: community justice requires placing a gun in the right private hands.

Credit: Warner Brothers © 1992.

The point of departure for *Unforgiven*'s story is that one of the prostitutes, Delilah, in Big Whisky, Wyoming, has had her face slashed by resentful cowboys. Little Bill Daggett (Gene Hackman), the sheriff who regards the women as the property of their pimping saloonkeeper, will not punish this crime beyond requiring the cowboys to give some horses to the women's "owner." Angered at this disregard for their standing under law, the prostitutes, whose income will now be diminished by Delilah's "cut-up face," offer a thousand-dollar bounty for anyone who will provide vigilante justice.

A young man who fantasizes about being a Western gunslinger and calls himself the "Schofield Kid" recruits Bill Munny (Clint Eastwood) and his partner Ned Logan (Morgan Freeman) to kill the two cowboys who have abused the "lady." The Schofield Kid has come looking for Munny because of Munny's Civil War reputation for being the "meanest goddam son of a bitch alive." Munny is reluctant to get back into the killing game that he played so well, claiming that he was formerly effective only when drunk and that he is truly ashamed of what he did in acquiring his earlier fame. He confesses that he killed "women, children, animals — everything that walks and crawls." He renounced that life after his marriage to the reform-minded Claudia Feather, who has since left him a widower. However, economic despair pulls him toward the reward for the prostitutes' vengeance scheme. "Just need the money, to get a new start for them youngsters," as he sees it. As they set out on their venture, Munny is haunted by the idea of betraying Claudia with this renewal of his old self. And Logan rubs it in: "You know, Bill, if Claudia was alive, you wouldn't be doing this."

Unforgiven is a somewhat altered version of the archetypal plot of the American monomyth: at the story's beginning, paradise has already been sullied by the abuse of prostitutes; and the gunfighter Munny — rather than being a selfless servant — is motivated by his desire for reward money. Nor is there any veneer of religious justification. But the story of William Munny is typical of superheroic tales in the circumstance of his double identity. When his wife died of smallpox, Munny was left to raise their two children on an impoverished Kansas farm. The film's beginning scenes show this hapless widower farming ineptly, falling down in the barnyard mud when he tries to pursue his hogs. His renunciation of the temptations of sex, whiskey, and cursing also holds true to the monomythic paradigm of the pure, self-controlled character — which Munny is until the moment he discovers that the brutal sheriff and his deputies have killed his partner, Ned Logan, who proved too peace-loving to harm anyone. Munny takes a big swig of whiskey and returns to town, dropping the empty bottle in the rain. He passes Ned's body, which is displayed in a casket in front of the saloon with the sign: "This is what happens to assassins around here." With this provocation, the scene is now set for the violent retribution.

A corrupt government that tolerates the mutilation of women and the torturing of prisoners cannot be allowed to stand. When Will Munny comes into the saloon with his shotgun, the sheriff is briefing the posse for the next day's hunt. The humiliated prostitutes are looking on as their redemption unfolds. In an incredible scene of cool marksmanship Munny shoots at close range the sheriff, his deputies, and the saloon owner. Without suffering a scratch, Munny escapes a town full of armed men. One deputy has a final chance to shoot the killer but shies away. Munny rides off shouting, "Any son of a bitch who takes a shot at me, I'm not only going to kill him, I'm going to kill his wife, all his friends, and burn his damn house down." This threat of terroristic violence shields him. Delilah and Alice come out of the saloon, with the other prostitutes behind them, to watch their redeemer ride off into the rain. The camera pans to the face of the abused prostitute, Delilah, gazing at the superhero, her scarred face radiant with satisfaction and admiration as Munny disappears into obscurity, completing the mythic cycle.

The printed epitaph-like statement at the end of *Unforgiven* confirms the disappearance of the disguised superhero, lifting up the irony of redemption through disreputable violence:

> "William Munny had long since disappeared with the children . . . some said to San Francisco where it was rumored he prospered in dry goods."

Part of this film's appeal — cited by critics as the key to revitalizing the Western film genre — is its ambivalence about idealizing the Western hero. It manages to reinstate vigilante violence sympathetically without placing the white hat on the savior's head. It also reprises the ritual humiliation of the superhero that was a trademark of the Clint Eastwood "Spaghetti Westerns" of the 1960s. This is but a prelude that dramatizes the inevitable, violent resolution in which the restored superhero slowly recovers from his beating and kills the villainous torturers. The protection of the weakest and most shameful members of society is the moral imperative that ultimately justifies the violence against hard-hearted representatives of the government.[17] Undergirded by the American superheroic paradigm, which requires a hero with a secret identity to redeem an otherwise helpless society, this is the classic American story of regeneration through violence — both for the hero and for the community that profits from his violence. It also reprises the Western's traditional message about the necessity of private guns for social justice. Big Whisky lives under "Ordinance 14," which declares that all guns must be surrendered to Sheriff Daggett. The posturing assassin English Bob comes to town to kill the cowboys, bringing along a journalist to build his legend. However, he allows the sheriff to take his weapons away and then is nearly kicked to death in the sheriff's sadistic display of power. Munny suffers a similar humiliation, but comes back for revenge with a clumsy shotgun, actually better suited to his wavering aim after years of inactivity.

At the time of the Academy Awards ceremony, Clint Eastwood professed to thinking that his movie had eliminated the last remnants of glamour in gun-fighting. He told a reporter: "This story preaches that it isn't glamorous to take up the gun. It is not glamorous to kill people, it's not beautiful, and I think that's very, very current on people's minds today."[18] This apologia deals with the surface texture of *Unforgiven*, while it overlooks the movie's conformity to the plot of the American monomyth. It is true that the film has taken beauty away from the gunman and his massacres. But Tim McVeigh, who saw his bombing in Oklahoma City as retaliation for the death of women and children at Waco, probably had a more accurate appreciation of the film's message: that violence can restore community, and that English Bob was completely ineffective once he'd lost his gun to the sheriff who was eager to trample on him.

Lethal Broadsword, Lethal Hatchet

In his *Lethal...* series, Mel Gibson has created one of the most successful franchises of the action-adventure genre, taking the monomythic plot from the contemporary police detective realm of those movies and later extending it backward in time to medieval Scotland *(Braveheart)* and the American Revolution *(The Patriot)*. His Martin Riggs character appeared in four *Lethal Weapon* films between 1987 and 1998. Riggs's fluctuations between comic goofiness and manic ferocity has repeatedly attracted large audiences. Riggs, as we mentioned earlier, was archetypally monomythic in his original appearance. He lacked a domestic anchor because of his wife's untimely death, steadily contemplating a gun he was tempted to turn against himself. Like Bill Munny of *Unforgiven*, this redeemer needed to find his own redemption. Aided by the more stable Roger Murtaugh, who aspires to live a comfortable middle-class family life, Riggs regenerates himself as he violently tramples on suspects and villains who cross his path. The emotional trigger for his rejuvenation is a moment of extreme personal victimization when his partner's daughter, Riane, is kidnapped by the corrupt CIA dropouts who are running a major drug operation.

An imaginative leap was required to take the "lethal" character formula from its urban crime setting and apply it in the construction of historical epics; but Gibson did just that in his films *Braveheart* (1995) and *The Patriot* (2000). More surprising, *Braveheart* outdid *Unforgiven* in critical and popular acclaim. At the 1995 Academy Awards, *Braveheart* collected ten Oscar nominations, winning five, including Best Director and Best Picture for Mel Gibson. It earned numerous other nominations and awards from other organizations for its story content and directing. Although the Pict-inspired blue face paint was a first for an Oscar make-up award, the success probably had something to do with the way it gave the monomyth a new set of medieval clothes.

Braveheart is a romanticized account of the famous Scots patriot and resistance fighter William Wallace, who lived between 1270 and August 23, 1305, the date of his execution by the English King Edward I. Because Wallace is one of Scotland's most important national heroes and because he lived in the very distant past, much that is believed about him is probably the stuff of legend. But there is a factual strand that historians agree to. Important points of reference for thinking about the mythic elements of *Braveheart* include these facts summarized by the Scots scholar Matt Ewart:

- Wallace was born into the gentry of Scotland;
- his father lived until he was 18, his mother until his 24th year;
- he killed the sheriff of Lanark when he was 27, apparently after the murder of his wife;
- he led a group of commoners against the English in a very successful battle at Stirling in 1297, temporarily receiving appointment as guardian;
- Wallace's reputation as a military leader was ruined in the same year of 1297, leading to his resignation as a guardian;
- he spent several years of exile in France before being captured by the English at Glasgow, this resulting in his trial for treason and his cruel execution.[19]

Given the drama of Wallace's life, it is surprising that there had been no earlier film about him. Since *Braveheart*'s filmmakers did not see a sufficiently compelling story in the history at hand, they added an overlay of American monomythic ingredients. Several of these have been precisely mapped by Elizabeth Walker Mechling and Jay Mechling in an essay dealing with *Braveheart*'s film fantasy and its relationship to the Oklahoma City bombing. They identify these elements of invented history:

- Since Wallace's parents lived well into his adulthood, he could not have been a motherless boy who loses his father when he is seven or eight years old, as portrayed in the film; the effect of this stylization is to make Wallace a "wild child" over against the tame, effete English he opposes in the film. *Braveheart* also presents the other principal males as "mother-less" men.

- As a middle son in his family (the film depicts him with a single older sibling), he would likely receive a classical training aimed toward the priesthood — not the warrior training we see.
- Since Wallace had a mother, his separated-from-women masculinity is an artificial construction, heightened in the film by the nearly instant murder of his wife by the English after their union.
- The invented romance with Princess Isabelle, the wife of "the sodomite" English Prince Edward II of the film, is really not possible, thus guaranteeing that he cannot ever settle down from his patriotic warfare.
- Since Wallace belongs to the gentry, he cannot be the outsider figure — as he is in the movie — to the "bickering Scottish nobles," who knight him into a leadership role as a result of his success at Stirling.
- Wallace's sacrificial death in 1305 "becomes the redemptive act for Scotland," immediately spurring the Scots to reassert their autonomy. The liberating battles in fact did not come until 1314.[20]

The Mechlings, who viewed the *Braveheart* epic only a few weeks after the Oklahoma City bombing, were struck by the similarity between the rhetoric of the American militia movements and the Scots "freedom fighters." The movie's message, so congruent with the Patriot movement with which McVeigh associated himself, legitimates violence against the state. And it does so against a background in which the Scottish do their military training with mere rocks because England has rounded up all their weapons (p. 162).

While the analogue of American militia ideology may be accidental for *Braveheart*, Gibson's film *The Patriot* explicitly celebrates the notion of militia-based guerillas destroying government. This recounting of the American Revolution in 1776 offers as its central character Benjamin Martin, a recently widowed farmer with seven children in South Carolina. As the film immediately introduces us to his Edenic farm, wrapped in a golden haze and worked by African-Americans who are exclusively freedmen, we find Martin tinkering with one of many rocking chairs that collapse when he sits on them. Imminent trouble for this little paradise is posed by his eighteen-year-old son Gabriel, who wants to join the Continental Army. Benjamin disapproves because he experienced combat in the French-Indian War, in which he became known as "The Hero of Fort Wilderness." He remains troubled by his morally painful reflections on what he did in that war and thus resists his son's pleas to approve his enlistment. Benjamin has become a pacifist.

When the South Carolina legislature convenes to discuss a war of rebellion against the British, he attends, objects, and clarifies himself at length. In urging patient discussions with the English, he says, "There are alternatives to war." And he explains that his own personal situation rules out his participation: "I have seven children; my wife is dead. Who is to take care of them?" Then he flatly declares: "I will not fight and I will not vote to send others to fight in my stead." When pushed about his underlying beliefs, he says sharply: "I am a parent. I haven't got the luxury of principles." He also makes it clear that he is averse to making war for the sake of a new independent national government. He quips, "Why should I trade one tyrant, three thousand miles away, for three thousand tyrants, one mile away?" He believes that "an elected legislature can trample on a man's rights as easily as a king can." His fellow citizens are shocked, and his hot-blooded teenage boys, thrilled by the prospect of patriotic warfare, feel humiliated. As the Martin family leaves the legislative session, Gabriel sees his father's stance as a show of cowardice and remarks caustically, "When I have a family, I won't hide behind them."

As is typical for monomythic plot development, this pacifism endures only a few minutes of the film until evil arises to threaten Eden. When a battle between the Redcoats and the Continental Army erupts in one of Martin's fields, soldiers from both sides are dragged to the porch of his home for medical care. Gabriel Martin, now a courier for the Continentals, also shows up with a serious injury. Then the evil British Colonel Tavington appears. He takes Martin's employees, identifies Gabriel for hanging, and then kills Gabriel's 15-year-old brother on the spot for a mild, unarmed gesture of opposition. Benjamin's legalistic attempt to explain the rules of war protecting a courier falls on disdainful ears. Because the Martin farmstead has sheltered wounded Continentals, the Colonel orders it to be torched. Benjamin rushes into his burning house, rescuing some guns and his engraved metal hatchet — obviously a weapon he used at Fort Wilderness. From this point forward, the movie unfolds as a monomythic tale of revenge and redemption.

The lethal hatchet is a token of the awakening inner warrior that has been locked away by prolonged domesticity. It is Benjamin's connection with wildness of the sort conveyed by William Wallace's shaggy hair and ragged clothes in *Braveheart*. Benjamin immediately gathers two of his weeping boys, gives them rifles, and tells them that they are going to calmly shoot at Redcoats. With them in tow, he sets out to ambush the convoy that is taking his son Gabriel for a hanging. Before the battle is over, he and his simpering boys have killed twenty of the stunned enemy, rescuing Gabriel in the slaughter. Fur-

Packaging for *Braveheart* video game issues a fantasy Werther invitation: take up the sword and become a medieval strategist and freedom fighter.

Credit: *Braveheart* © 1995, 1996 Paramount Pictures and 20th Century Fox Film Corporation. © Eidos Interactive Limited 1999.

thermore, the former pacifist Benjamin has astonished his sons with his frenzied use of the hatchet, severing the spine of one Redcoat, cleaving the skull of another, and finally chopping the last living soldier into a bloody pulp that is smeared on his own clothing and skin. The maniacal slaying in this episode later prompts Gabriel to pressure his father to tell exactly what happened at Fort Wilderness — and how Benjamin had changed into the man who resisted war at the legislature's meeting. The answer, of course, lies with the dead wife. "I had trouble breathing around your mother," he says, and his son immediately understands because he has already noticed that women have "the strangest effect on men." Just as Bill Munny was dtamed by Claudia Feather, Benjamin had been temporarily feminized into peaceful ways of dealing with conflict.

The Redcoat crimes at his farm have instantly dissolved the pacifism of Benjamin Martin. The question remains about how he will serve. The regional commander, Colonel Burwell, knows him well from the French-Indian War and wants him in the regular forces. But just as he distrusts any democratically elected legislators, he distrusts the Continental Army. It accepts the tactics of ritual sacrifice, dictating that troops march toward one another's lines on an open field. Martin wants to be a militiaman, giving himself and his men the freedom to come and go freely, to wear what they please when they fight, and to use the tactics of the guerilla raid.

Martin has repeated successes in harassing British shipping and carrying off outrageous tricks of war. So Colonel Tavington decides to punish the town where he is known to have supporters. He gathers all the town's citizens, forces them into a church, locks the doors, and torches it. Benjamin Martin's new daughter-in-law is incinerated with the rest of the townspeople in that church, and his son Gabriel is killed in a revenge quest. Martin declares that he is quitting the war entirely, yet he quickly musters the courage to fight one more time, rousing the troops by carrying the flag of the colonies into a battle that appears to end the war. It is the kind of neat closure that is characteristic of the monomyth: the oppressive government is defeated and expelled, while the surviving community is free to continue its previously happy way of life. Once again the almost lone hero, freed from the restraints of pacifying women, has redeemed the community through furious acts of vengeance against governing authority.

Saving Democracy with Bombs

Does the form of the American monomyth that targets government authority have an impact on American culture? Without claiming a full grasp of individual human motivations, we can see the fantasy of redeeming violence — floating untethered from philosophical or domestic restraints — reflected in the deeds of Timothy McVeigh and Theodore Kaczynski.[21] Like the heroes of myth, they claimed to act in behalf of social freedom. But their deeds caused enormous suffering and fear, and in many ways added intrusive restrictions on mailing practices, on travel, and on the design of our public buildings. As we detail those consequences, we can see the deep reality gap between mythically scripted violence and the chaos of real-world applications.

Timothy McVeigh was a person with a deep love of weapons that began in his teens. His mastery of battle guns enabled an outstanding military performance in the Gulf War. He returned as a medal-bearing, tired hero who quickly washed out of the Green Beret training camp to which he came directly from the battle zone. Dissatisfied with the regular stateside army after such a dramatic period of conflict in the desert, he left the army and drifted into security work and eventually gun-dealing. His biography, *American Terrorist,* reports an early fascination with *The Turner Diaries* as part of his post–high school reading. In addition to owning guns and doing target practice, McVeigh seemed to have a restless mind immersed in texts from American popular culture — the music of Nine Inch Nails,[22] the *Red Dawn* (1984) and *Blown Away* (1994) movies, *Star Trek* and *Star Wars*. He reported getting his first impressions of military life from *Rambo: First Blood* and the similar Chuck Norris POW-rescue fantasy *Missing in Action* (1984). In his prolonged interviews from prison after receiving the death sentence, he used plot details of movies several times as points of clarification or justification for his own actions and state of mind.[23] It is no stretch of the imagination to perceive McVeigh responding to a Werther invitation from *Star Wars* (1977). Michel and Herbeck explain:

> McVeigh saw himself as a counterpart to Luke Skywalker, the heroic Jedi knight whose successful attack on the Death Star closes the film. As a kid, McVeigh had noticed that the *Star Wars* movies showed people sitting at the consoles — Space-age clerical workers — inside the Death Star. Those people weren't storm troopers. They weren't killing anyone. But they were vital to the operations of the Evil Empire, McVeigh deduced, and when Luke blew up the Death Star those people became inevitable casualties. When the Death Star exploded, the movie audiences cheered. The bad guys were beaten: that was all that really mattered. As an adult, McVeigh found himself able to dismiss the killing of secretaries, receptionists, and other personnel in the Murrah Building with equally cold-blooded calculation. They were all part of the evil empire. (pp. 224-225)

McVeigh also used this *Star Wars* comparison in attempting to recruit Michael Fortier to come along on the mission to Oklahoma City. When Fortier questioned McVeigh about the range of victims, McVeigh "explained to me that he considered all those people to be as if they were storm troopers in the movie *Star Wars*. They may be individually innocent, but because they are part of the — the Evil Empire, they were guilty by association" (pp. 332-333).

McVeigh was especially enthusiastic in his praise of *Unforgiven*, commenting on it in his prison letters to the journalist Phil Bacharach: "*Unforgiven* still gets my vote for best overall movie."[24] The zeal for destroying a corrupt government that disarms its citizens resonated with him. But during the years before the Oklahoma City bombing, *The Turner Diaries* was his steadiest mythic companion at workplaces, in the military, and at gun shows, where he sold copies below cost to spread its vision of rebellion against governmental controls. One collector reported seeing McVeigh asleep in his car at a gun show with *The Turner Diaries* under his pillow.[25] He occasionally expressed a desire for a different kind of bed mate, but he settled into a restless pattern of travel for the gun shows he worked. Any kind of long-term relationship with a woman seemed incompatible with his primary commitment to the world of guns and revenge against those who sought to restrict their availability.

Because the incidents at Ruby Ridge, Idaho (1992)[26] and the Branch Davidian compound in Waco, Texas (1993)[27] were law-enforcement actions against illegal weapons, they especially infuriated him. For McVeigh, the ban on silencers, flash suppressors, grenade launchers, and the like were outrageous violations of the Second Amendment. And like millions of other Americans, he was appalled at the government's killing of children at both sites. The Waco conflagration stirred a sense of urgency, prodding him to turn his reckless courage toward "declaring war on the federal government."[28] The apocalyptic *Turner Diaries* gave McVeigh a kind of blueprint for strategy and a design for the exploding truck: passages in the novel offer detailed ideas about how to give the fertilizer ammonium nitrate the blasting power of TNT for the destruction of an FBI building in Washington, D.C.[29]

The *Turner Diaries* also gave McVeigh the spiritual model of Earl Turner, a man whose "name is inscribed in the Record of Martyrs"[30] because he had the suicidal courage required to destroy the Pentagon with a nuclear weapon. The novel constantly intones the spiritual dimensions of this task of destroying government, interspersed with incidents such as staging a mortar attack on the U.S. Congress. Earl Turner's diary affirms that "only by making our beliefs into a living faith which guides us from day to day can we maintain the moral strength to overcome the obstacles and hardships which lie ahead" (p. 9). And the men who accept the discipline of The Order wear monk-like garments in a ceremony that identifies them as "bearers of the Faith" who are "born again" (pp. 73, 74). A grand sense of divine mission is attached to the ceremony. In Turner's words, "Everything that has been and everything that is yet to be depends on us. We are truly the instruments of God in the fulfillment of His Grand Design" (p. 71). This crusading rhetoric explains in part the attraction of the Christian Identity movement to *The Turner Diaries*.[31] Although McVeigh reported that he was attracted less by *The Turner Diaries'* racism than its affirmation of the rights of gun owners, he did fully assimilate from his fictional hero the apocalyptic sense of importance and the stoic discipline.[32] So shaped by this book was McVeigh that he sent copied pages of *The Turner Diaries* to his sister as his parting explanation for his expected death. He also carried this chilling terroristic passage in his escape car so that investigators would find it:

The real value of our attacks today lies in the psychological impact, not in the immediate casualties. More important is what we taught the politicians and the bureaucrats. They learned this afternoon that not one of them is beyond our reach. They can huddle behind barbed wire and tanks in the city, and they can hide behind the concrete walls of their country estates, but we can still find them and kill them.[33]

McVeigh survived the sudden death that he had predicted for himself that day. His pride and the advice of counsel led him to say nothing in his own defense at his trial. He remained defiant about the righteousness of his mission until the moment of his execution in 2001.

The delayed and well-publicized execution of McVeigh doubtless added something to the mythic stature of the apocalyptic *Turner Diaries*. It had earlier been the inspiration for Robert Matthews in the early 1980s to found The Order, which carried out a counterfeiting scheme, armed robberies, and the anti-Semitic murder of Alan Berg, a Denver radio personality.[34] Matthews created an initiation ritual for his *Brüder Schweigen* (Silent Brotherhood) — a name borrowed from the Nazi SS[35] — that resembled the ceremony depicted in *The Turner Diaries*. During a two-year spree of crime, they planned a truck bombing against the Murrah Building in Oklahoma City that McVeigh eventually chose. Matthews died in an armed confrontation with the FBI in 1984. *The Turner Diaries* also offered a template for the Aryan Republican Army, which committed robberies and bombings between 1992 and 1996.[36] And in the murder of James Byrd, Jr., who was tortured and then dragged to his death by a pickup truck in Jasper, Texas, testimony was given that John William King, the pickup's driver, explained to his companions that "we're going to start *The Turner Diaries* early."[37]

In his study of millenarian religious movements in the U.S., Jeffrey Kaplan contends that "the [radical] right wing talks a better revolution than it is prepared to fight."[38] It may be that "theologies of violence" are acted on infrequently. But the few who, like McVeigh, Matthews, and King, believe in a participatory apocalypse are quite enough to seriously damage the social framework. They are the American counterparts of Osama bin Laden's terrorists, enacting a similarly apocalyptic form of revenge against democratic societies. Referring to the airline hijackers of September 11, bin Laden proclaimed: "God has blessed a group of vanguard Muslims, the forefront of Islam, to destroy America. May God bless them and allot them a supreme place in heaven."[39] Zealots of this mindset make it clear that no crusade against external enemies can suffice to provide a secure protection.

The Unabomber's Crusade for the "Freedom Club"

The Unabomber's character is more difficult to decipher. The garrulous, evangelical McVeigh left a stream of evidence about his ideology and his actions. But the young and shy Kaczynski disappeared rather quickly from everyone's social grid. As an assistant professor of mathematics at University of California-Berkeley from 1967 to 1969, he made a decision to leave teaching and live as a hermit in the woods — somewhat on the pattern of Henry David Thoreau.[40] Eventually situating himself in rural Lincoln, Montana, he led a lonely subsistence existence while reading a handful of books about technology and behavior control. They helped him solidify his belief that contemporary technology, managed by elites in metropolitan mazes, was the enemy of freedom. Apparently deriving some inspiration from Joseph Conrad's novel *The Secret Agent,* which is about an anarchist bomb-maker, he fabricated sixteen exploding packages that detonated in various locations between May 25, 1978, and April 25, 1995. Three people were killed, several were permanently maimed, and others temporarily injured. The only "message" of these bombs came as an "FC" stamped into a portion of the metal positioned to survive as a fragment. (The FBI did not decode the "FC" to mean "Freedom Club" until 1995.) What the victims shared were loose connections with technology, behavioral science, or environmental damage — such as students, secretaries, mail-room attendants, researchers, publicists, or lobbyists — all perceived by Kaczynski as freedom's foes.

After years of sending these mail bombs and placing explosive devices in labs or parking lots, Kaczynski promised a truce in his war if *The New York Times* and the *Washington Post* would publish his personal manifesto, a 65-page typescript of some 34,000 words. After much national debate about offering such a platform to a terrorist, "The Unabomber Manifesto" appeared in both papers on September 19, 1995.[41] Many pages into his text, the Unabomber gave the following rationale for killing and maiming his victims — before unveiling his plan to save the world:

> To make an impression on society with words is . . . almost impossible. . . . Take us (FC) for example. If we had never done anything violent and had submitted the present writings to a publisher, they probably would not have been accepted. If they had been accepted and published, they probably would not have attracted many readers. . . . Even if these writings had had many readers, most of these readers would soon have forgotten what they had read as their minds were flooded by the mass of material to which

the media expose them. In order to get our message before the public with some chance of making a lasting impression, we've had to kill people. (§96)

In other words, the mere publication of his ideas in such a corrupted society would not allow them to make any impression, unless they were accompanied by years of terror induced by his bombs. As instructed by a monomythic system assumed by Kaczynski along with so many other Americans, violence was required to cleanse the world.

The ideas of the *Manifesto* were themselves mostly commonplaces of cultural criticism. What he had taken from his brief Berkeley stay was a loathing for the activists he saw there. He devotes many pages to "the psychology of leftism," suggesting that the leftist has "feelings of inferiority" and that "he hates America and the West because they are strong and successful" (§16). He rejects the art preferred by leftist intellectuals because of "its sordidness, defeat and despair." He dismisses feminism because he thinks women "are nagged by the fear that women may NOT be as strong as men" (§14). Echoing Nietzsche's analysis of "objective reason" a hundred years later, he despises scientists wholesale because their motives generally reflect a desire to participate in the self-serving "power process" — not curiosity or the desire to benefit humanity (§89). But lest one think the Unabomber is just another unhappy conservative, he says that "conservatives are fools. They whine about the decay of traditional values, yet they enthusiastically support technological progress and economic growth" (§50). The FC man sits selflessly above politics, because his target is technology itself rather than obnoxious, deluded social groups (§193).

A scheme of reverting to a natural Eden is the point of fighting against technology. Here the rationale is that a technology-based society requires regulation (§114-116), that "the 'bad' parts of technology cannot be separated from the 'good' parts" (§121ff), and that "technology is a more powerful social force than the aspiration for freedom" (§125ff). FC's own positive ideal is that of "wild nature" — the earth "independent of human management" (§183). To return to this ideal, it is "necessary to get rid of industrial society." Thereafter, people who "feed themselves must be peasants or herdsmen or fishermen or hunters" (§184). In getting back to this more primitive state, the "industrial system should be attacked in all nations simultaneously" (§195). The revolutionaries who carry out the worldwide task cannot use technology for any goal other than destroying technology itself (§200-202). This anti-technological revolution will bring freedom by destroying all social power that depends on technology. Thus people who live without refrigeration, heating, medical technology, and so forth, will live small-group lives in a reversion to the subsistence mode of existence that Kaczynski himself had practiced for many years. This is the shivering Edenic state[42] that will return after elites and their technologies have been purged.

When Kacznyski wrote the first draft of his essay in the early 1970s, he had modestly stated on its first page: "I make no claim to originality."[43] While his thinking progressed in the intervening years before he released the Manifesto, this diminutive characterization remained largely true. The uniqueness of the Unabomber redemption scheme lies in a more thorough destruction of technology than even the Luddites had considered. His social isolation had hidden from him the subtlety and vigor with which many of his ideas about technology's ill effects were being expressed by others who chose not to terrorize anyone.

The Unabomber's tactics of revolution presuppose that "the unthinking majority" prefers its ideas formulated "in simple, black-and-white terms: THIS is all good and THAT is all bad" (§186). While a few rational people will prefer FC's dry, rational discourse, "propaganda of the rabble-rousing type may be necessary when the system is nearing the point of collapse and there is a final struggle between rival ideologies to determine which will become dominant when the old world-view goes under" (§188). FC is thus pessimistic that most people waiting for their liberation will ever understand the need for it: "History is made by active, determined minorities, not by the majority, which seldom has a clear and consistent idea of what it really wants" (§189). Here we see the impulse of the mythic warrior who is determined to save the innocent community whether it wants to be saved or not. The goal is an abstractly defined, historically reversionary state that few of the rescued would recognize as freedom.

Kaczynski never got the chance to argue for his scheme of social salvation in a court of law. His court-appointed attorneys, supported by his family, insisted on using an insanity defense to preserve his life. To avoid the humiliation of that defense, he pled guilty to a single killing in exchange for a life sentence in a federal prison.[44] As a prisoner with the most stringent security status in the federal prison system, Kazcynski eventually met and had several conversations with Tim McVeigh at the Supermax facility in Colorado. In fact, he wrote a letter to the authors Michel and Herbeck in which he offered this assessment of McVeigh's action:

> If violence were to be used to express protest, it could have been used far more humanely, and at the same time, more effectively, by being directed at the relatively small number of people who were personally responsible for the policies or actions. . . . Such protest would have attracted just as much national attention as the Oklahoma City bombing and would have involved relatively little risk to innocent people.

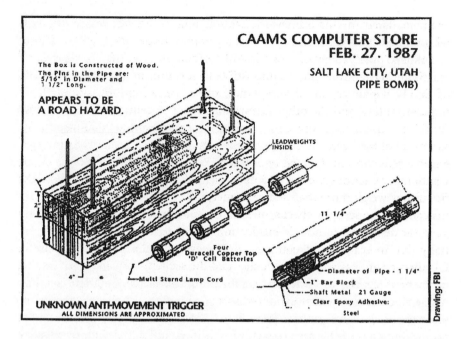

CAAMS COMPUTER STORE
FEB. 27. 1987

SALT LAKE CITY, UTAH
(PIPE BOMB)

The Box is Constructed of Wood.
The Pins in the Pipe are:
5/16" in Diameter and
1 1/2" Long.

APPEARS TO BE
A ROAD HAZARD.

LEADWEIGHTS
INSIDE

11 1/4"

Four
Duracell Copper Top
'D' Cell Batteries

Multi Starnd Lamp Cord

Diameter of Pipe - 1 1/4"
1" Bar Block
Shaft Metal 21 Gauge
Clear Epoxy Adhesive:
Steel

UNKNOWN ANTI-MOVEMENT TRIGGER
ALL DIMENSIONS ARE APPROXIMATED

Drawing: FBI

Although Theodore Kaczynski's "Freedom Club" had a single member, his surprise attacks caused injuries, death, and great terror. This FBI drawing reconstructs one of the "road hazard" bombs — apparently a board with projecting nails. Placed in a parking lot near a Salt Lake City, Utah, computer store, it was meant for any civic-minded person who touched it.

Credit: FBI.

Kazcynski added that "many anti-government people . . . [who] might have accepted violence that was more limited and carefully directed were repelled by the large loss of innocent life at Oklahoma City."[45] It is ironic, of course, that a man who so thoroughly botched his own separation of "innocent" and "guilty" targets should deliver this appraisal. Despite the evidence about the actual victims of his devices, the Unabomber could still delude himself by reaffirming his commitment to the myth of a clean violence that efficiently punishes evildoers while sparing the innocent — thus redeeming the world for freedom.

Fueling the Myth with Ammonium Nitrate

Tim McVeigh and Ted Kaczynski show us how determined men can craft the premises of the American monomyth into a program of action against government. Their mythic framework has startling similarities to the terrorists who piloted the planes on September 11, hoping to destroy a satanic power and thus to purify the world. As with the Columbine High School killers, Eric Harris and Dylan Klebold, it's impossible to sort out the relative importance of family dynamics, social acceptance, career opportunities, stimuli from popular fantasy, and the other factors that affect a young person's ability to function constructively in a community. But we can say with confidence that as a result of their zealous, self-righteously motivated actions, we have experienced a reduction in the quality of freedom in American life. Because of the Unabomber's actions, we can no longer drop off packages at the U.S. Post Office if they weigh more than sixteen ounces. We must present them to a clerk instead. Airline security checks, questions about the control of personal baggage, the demand for photo identification, and so forth — all are legacies partially due to fears about compact, lightweight bombs. McVeigh's blast in Oklahoma City has also further cultivated the security state of mind, leaving permanent legacies in stone barriers and additional security personnel. The high school terrorists have produced some high schools in America that imitate prisons, with every entering student subjected not only to searches but to the confiscation of the most trivial of personal effects. Building designs are evolving, making compromises with convenience to ensure that entryways and parking zones are less vulnerable to truck bombs. More surveillance cameras and guards are being used, reducing our privacy and demanding of us more taxes — and exposing us to more weapons that can be misused. These trends were accelerated after the destruction of the World Trade Center, not only for the United States but also for the entire industrialized world. Mythicized zealotry in its various guises now threatens to undermine the possibility of democratic institutions everywhere.

The ironies in the lives of our own domestic zealots McVeigh and Kaczynski, told separately or together, would make a movie that does not conform to monomythic expectations. Its plot would play out the consequences of stolidly motivated men who have severed their emotional and social ties not only with family but also with the "feminine" cooperative and conciliatory values that can be so constructive in times of crisis. Such a film might help us to understand what those men lose when they leave the social orbit in which men and women are bound together, contributing to one another's lives. It would expose the illusion that humans can become "super" and that they are ever justified in taking the law into their hands; it would reveal the profound misconception of believing that violent destruction will advance the cause of freedom.

In a sense, the outrageously violent movie *Fight Club* (1999)[46] has already told this story with considerable skill. The film staggers through puddles of blood spilled with strange joy in its movement toward an unusual reconciliation of a man and a woman. The narrator of *Fight Club*, Jack, loses his apartment to an explosion; feeling disoriented, he ends up spending his time in a bare-knuckled "fight club" introduced to him by new friend Tyler, much bolder than he, who has taken him in. He and Tyler have a philosophical discussion about women and decide that they are dispensable. As Tyler says, "We are a generation of men raised by women. I wonder if another woman is really the answer we need." At the "club" young men beat each other into bloody forgetfulness to forget the pain of consumer-themed lives that feel meaningless. Their self-destructive behavior seems to be a taunting response to the culture of self-improvement that several of them explore. Then, inspired by a zealous vision of corporate evil, they begin "Project Mayhem," an anarchic program of blowing up credit-card companies and coffee franchises. But Jack's epiphany about the dead-end toward which all this violence is leading begins to come when he tries to blackmail his corporate boss for assault by inflicting injuries on himself; he correctly understands that he has been mutilating himself. He turns to Marla, the strange woman he has allowed into his hyper-masculine world, and decides that she, with him, is the future. He also realizes that his domineering, violent friend Tyler Durden, the person who seduced him into the spiral of devastation, was an imaginary companion expressing his own fantasies. In her review, Susan Faludi commented that "*Fight Club* could be seen as a savagely violent reprise of *American Beauty* (1999), in which another corporate male conformist rebels, quitting his job and thumbing his nose at his image-obsessed wife." Faludi encapsulates the ending: "For men facing an increasingly hollow, consumerized world, the path lies not in conquering women but in uniting with them against the hollowness. . . . In *Fight Club*, the man and woman clasp hands in what could be mutual redemption."[47]

Romance is hardly a cure for personal crises of meaning or for meaningless work; but compared to lethal crusading, clasping hands seems like a step in the direction of social integration. Movies made in the spirit of *Fight Club* can help us imagine the impact of entertainments that seek to move beyond the ruling mythic paradigm. Unfortunately, *Fight Club*, like *Natural Born Killers* (1994), may so closely resemble what it critiques that it simply adds more fuel to the inviting fire of stylized violence. Some critics saw it as the embodiment of "fascism,"[48] failing to note Jack's insights about his violent deeds and their unredemptive consequences. These are insights whose enactment in the social realm we would truly enjoy.

IV HYMNS AND CREEDS OF THE AMERICAN MONOMYTH

Folk songs tell stories, often dealing with fateful episodes. Given a stable core of stereotypical characters, roles, and plots, creative adapters can sing a song's wisdom in realms distant from its origins. In Chapter 9, "Cheerful Saints and Melodious Lions," we see how Walt Disney and his corporate successors have steadily given animated and animal expressions to the myth from the time of the shrill Mickey Mouse to the triumphant Lion King. The Disney enterprise repeatedly uses the Heidi model of feminine sweetness and innocence as the means of triumphing over evil. Chapter 10, "The Sound of One Hand Killing: Monomythic Video Games," traces the history of computer-based games from primitive bouncing balls to the most recent developments, in which the youthful player holds and fires the weapons that save imaginary communities. Chapter 11, "*Star Trek*'s Humanistic Militarism," describes the vision of its creator, Gene Roddenberry, who sought to make secular humanism attractive in his utopian vision — a vision firmly grounded in the myths propagated by popular entertainments that preceded his franchise. As a musical form, the hymn appeared among the ancient Greeks as a song celebrating gods and goddesses or heroic men. Variants survive in America's "spiritual marketplace," where fans seek enlightenment from inspiring entertainment products and communion with other fans. Chapter 12, "*Star Trek* Faith as a Fan-Made Religion," describes the evolution of *Star Trek* fans from the goofy costume and convention period to the sober adults who quietly confess, "*Star Trek* has given meaning to my life." Chapter 13, "Fascist Faith in the *Star Wars* Universe," tracks the rise of *Star Wars* belief systems, its kinship with European fascism, and the emergence of George Lucas as cultural and spiritual

177

guru. Chapter 14, "Monomythic Credotainment," looks at the new recreational temples that are forming in cyberspace around *The Matrix*, the films of Steven Seagal, and the popular television series *Touched by an Angel*. Although encouraged by the civilized give-and-take that focuses on mythic values, we lament the absence of a commitment to brick-and-mortar churches, with their greater potential for building the skills of democracy.

9 Cheerful Saints and Melodious Lions

"[Disney's art] reaches greatness, a degree of perfection in its field which surpasses our best critical capacity to analyze and . . . succeeds . . . in pleasing children and simple folk."

Mortimer Adler, *Art and Prudence*[1]

"I'll stack 'Mary Poppins' against any cheap and depraved movie ever made."

Walt Disney[2]

After years of studying exotic foreign cultures, the distinguished anthropologist Hortense Powdermaker returned to Hollywood to live among the people of the film colony. During the period from 1947 to 1948 she examined their mores and artifacts and found strange taboos against "all biological aspects of the human species."[3] Her informants helped trace this to "the Code," a voluntary scheme of self-censorship adopted by the Motion Picture Association of America. "The showing of toilets is rigidly prohibited. They are always missing in any bathroom scene. Even the sound of an out-of-scene toilet being flushed is deleted" (p. 61). This ban alone could hardly have retarded the development of screen art, but there were more serious prohibitions, including the nearly total suppression of sexual love. This remarkable colony, though it

179

The Simba toy lion is soft and cuddly. His grin conveys the innocent sweetness through which the lion — like so many other Disney heroines and heroes — earns the right to rule.
Credit: Mattel, Inc., Arcotoys, Inc. © The Walt Disney Company.

was called "Sodom by the Sea" in its periods of greatest sexual scandal, forbade the depiction of the activities that presumably afforded the greatest pleasures for the actor-natives. "All suggestions of intimacy in and out of marriage are taboo. . . . In one film, the MPAA asked for the deletion of dialogue that indicated that a husband wanted to sleep with his wife. Even gestures of affection between a man and wife are taboo. The MPAA asked for omission of a scene in which a man was buttoning his wife's dress and kissed the back of her neck . . ." (p. 59).

According to Powdermaker, the taboos were hypocritical because they did not "represent the actual beliefs, values or behavior of the people practicing them" (p. 55). It was an unusual situation for an anthropologist, since among the so-called "primitive" peoples "taboos are an integral part of behavior and values . . ." (p. 67).

With hindsight, we can now see that Hollywood has overcome these sexually hypocritical discrepancies by heaving the old Code overboard. But at the moment of her reported observations more than fifty years ago, there was already a serious flaw in Powdermaker's ethnography. The filmmaker she overlooked in her assessment was Walt Disney: he was exceptional in that he accepted the taboos with the sincerity Powdermaker observed in primitive cultures. Walt Disney needed no censor because he had internalized the values of the American public that had given the Code its distinctive shape. He operated happily within the limits of "the Code" because it expressed his own sense of decency and artistic merit. Disney thereby became America's greatest popular creator, an international pop institution in himself whose work is considered uniquely suitable for children. One can hardly understand the American taste for a new form of the monomyth without a comprehension of the founder's vision of his artificial but highly profitable world.

The Code of Sanitation in Disney's Land

Like the Ten Commandments of the Old Testament, the Motion Picture Production Code (1930-1968) was largely negative. The "nots" and "forbids" generously season every section. "No picture shall be produced which will lower the moral standards of those who see it." "Lustful and open-mouth kissing, lustful embraces, suggestive posture and gestures are not to be shown. . . . Blasphemy is forbidden. Reference to the Deity, God, Lord, Jesus, Christ, shall not be irreverent."[4] But mere conformity to negative prohibitions can no more inspire art than it can inspire life. A key to Disney's creativity is that he did not feel restricted by these negative limits. He understood how the revulsive feelings that lay behind the Code could be used to create characters with mythic appeal. But, above all, Disney displayed unsurpassed gifts of storytelling and developed complex innovations for presenting visual images. His genius was recognized by some of the most serious artists of his day. Leopold Stokowski and Deems Taylor respected his work enough to collaborate with him in the creation of *Fantasia,* a remarkable experiment in using abstract forms to illustrate musical ideas. Composer Jerome Kern said: "Cartoonist Walt Disney has made the twentieth century's only important contribution to music. In the synchronization of humorous episodes with humorous music, he has unquestionably given us the outstanding contribution of our time."[5]

Mickey Mouse was Disney's first great creative achievement, demonstrating the potential of the animated cartoon genre. Sergei Eisenstein, the great Russian film director, declared that Mickey Mouse was America's most original contribution to culture.[6] In 1935, L. H. Robbins described the mouse as "the best-known and most popular international figure of his day."[7] It was a figure remarkable in part for its lack of sexual differentiation. Mickey's pants and lack of shirt are the only clues to his masculinity. His speech, provided by

Walt Disney himself, was similarly sexless. Fritz Moellenhoff noted that "the larynx contains a most peculiar voice. It is crowing, thin, without modulation and we are unable to tell whether the character is a man, woman or child. . . ."[8] Mickey lacked both whiskers and beastly paws. Instead, he was given four-fingered hands, always neatly clothed in a pair of white gloves. Mickey's romantic partner, Minnie, was equally sexless in appearance. Though consciously modeled upon the human being in her upright stance and skirt, her upper torso was as devoid of mammary development as Mickey's lower torso was in genital protuberances. None of Disney's funny animals has embarrassing and potentially dirty orifices or appendages.

Richard Schickel connects this peculiar sanitizing approach to animal life with a revealing episode in James Agee's novel *A Death in the Family,* in which a mother expresses her disgust for Charlie Chaplin: "That horrid little man . . . he's so *nasty . . . so vulgar!* With his nasty little cane; hooking up skirts and things, and that nasty little walk!"[9] Here is the revulsive feeling behind the censor's code that Disney avoided in his mythical animal creations. The transmutation of the human body, with its unavoidable sexual features, made Disney's animal comedy less intimate, not as objectionable as Chaplin's films. By eliminating biological realities, Disney was able to present a version of sexuality that was highly entertaining for squeamish audiences.

It is therefore puzzling that one can repeatedly observe anal sexual play in Disney cartoons. In *Moving Day,* Donald Duck gets his rear end repeatedly stuck in a goldfish bowl and struggles mightily to release himself. He gets a toilet plunger stuck on his rear, which he then thumps, tugs at, and twists in a long episode. This anal preoccupation of Disney was so strong that Richard Schickel was prompted to observe evidences of a fetish in which sexuality is transferred to infantile buttocks. He mentions the concluding imagery in *Fantasia:* "The sequence ends with the most explicit statement of anality ever made by the studio, which found in the human backside not only the height of humor but the height of sexuality as well. Two of the little cupids who scamper incessantly through the sequence finally — and blessedly — draw a curtain over the scene. When they come together, their shiny little behinds form, for an instant, a heart."[10] This form of sexuality was presented as more innocent and wholesome than anything that humans could ever expect to experience. Sex had become sufficiently innocent, trivial, and enjoyable that every family knew it could trust itself to go to the movies.

Disney's discovery of sex without sex inspired some of his outstanding technical achievements in the field of animation. In 1932 Disney released his first color cartoon, *Flowers and Trees.* It received an Academy Award as Best Cartoon for its ingenious presentation of a romance in the woods between two trees. Beautiful flowers and animals celebrate the trees' courtship, while a wicked, gnarled old tree becomes jealous and starts a fire that threatens to destroy the forest. The ugly, wicked tree is burned by the fire it has started; but a timely rainstorm, triggered by birds flying through a cloud, rescues everyone else. The two trees are united in loving joy, hugging and kissing each other. The entwinement of the woody, anatomically undifferentiated bodies at the conclusion is a satisfying embodiment of antiseptic sexuality. The pulsing glowworm who has volunteered to serve as nuptial ring is the only sign of warmth.

It was in 1937 that Disney's sanitizing effort achieved its first definitive expression: *Snow White and the Seven Dwarfs*[11] appeared that year and received a "special" Academy Award for "screen innovation."[12] The mythic transmutation of the Grimm Brothers' fairy tale clearly indicates the interest in both cleanliness and sexual purity. The Grimms describe the dwarfs' house as immaculate, "small but indescribably neat and clean." Snow White, in fact, angers the fastidious little men by messing up their house, drinking up their wine, and dropping off to sleep in one of their beds. It is they who suggest that she can earn her room and board if she promises to keep "everything orderly and clean in our household. . . ."[13] In Disney's film, Snow White finds the little house a pigsty: "The sink was piled high with cups and saucers and plates which looked as though they had never been washed. Dirty little shirts and wrinkled little trousers hung over chairs, and everything was blanketed with dust." She resolves to clean up the mess because they "need someone to take care of them. . . ." She and her "forest friends" become a veritable Heidi team, quickly solving the household crisis of the hapless dwarfs. When the latter return from the mine, Snow White is asleep, worn out from her household miracles. Disney's princess then awakens, miraculously names the little men, and then insists that they wash and change their clothes before supper. After the miracle of sanitation and the baptism into cleanliness, the dwarfs dance around their princess with utter delight. Like the males in *Heidi*, they achieve fulfillment by mere proximity to their sweet reformer. The final detail in the sanitizing campaign is to erase any possible doubt about the sexual implications of a young lady living with seven dirty old men. Whereas the Grimms allowed the lucky dwarfs to sleep in their beds adjacent to the princess, Disney sends them all downstairs to sleep on the floor. It is as if Walt had stood before the fabulous dwelling of the Brothers Grimm with Snow White's words on his lips, "Let's clean their house and surprise them."[14]

Another of Disney's triumphs, the perpetually successful *Bambi* (1942),[15] was billed as "A Great Love Story."[16] Here Disney moved beyond anal humor, tree romance, and White Magic cleanser to the subject of mating, but without the distracting and presumably unwholesome motif of masculine desire. In the de-eroticized love story, Bambi's first love is stirred by Felice's sexually aggressive approach. Felice nuzzles the passive buck as the colorful symbols of cartoon love radiate around them. Then the selfless and impassive Bambi is thrust into competition with another stag. In one of the most dramatic scenes of the film, the competing stag steps between Bambi and Felice, and the hero is "forced to battle against his will with the other deer."[17] In the duel, which plays itself out like a scene in *High Noon,* the reluctant but powerful Bambi pushes the aggressor over a cliff. The fate of death is here assigned to the stag possessing normal animal instincts for mating and dominance. The pacific Bambi, lacking either sexual passion or the instinct to rule, thus becomes a father and the Prince of the Forest at the film's happy ending.

The sexual paradigm in *Bambi* is virtually identical to that in the *Playboy* magazine fantasy, where cool males in elegant dress observe far less clothed women in states of sexual desperation. The male is neither the aggressor nor the initiator of sexual relations. He waits to respond obligingly to female sexual needs. But in neither male nor female does there seem to be an expression of ego needs. Sexual union is the result of Felice's sexual void being joined with Bambi's sense of duty to help those in need. Conflict is thus inconceivable except when a bad stag slips into the scene. Sexual fears are eliminated, jealousy is rendered obsolete, and passion is permanently out of style.

The comfortable myth of Bambi-sex points to a recurring paradox in such material. Disney strove mightily after realism in the development of the technical aspects of his films. He made careful photographic studies of forest areas in Maine, working with live fawns as models for the cartoon illustrators. So exacting was the animation that the film was delayed several years in its release. But on the point central to the love story, Disney could not resist mythic alchemy. Sanitized of nasty animal characteristics, Bambi becomes a heroic figure who brings decency to the forest wilds.

Disney's nature films present the same paradox of painstaking photographic realism and mythic story line. He would shoot thousands and thousands of feet of film in order to construct a story in which animals act out human dramas. In the *Legend of Lobo* (1962), Disney presents a young wolf whose mother has been killed and father trapped. Lobo joins a different pack and, after proving himself, becomes its leader. Lobo's mate is captured by a hunter, who then uses her to lure Lobo into a trap. Lobo leads his entire pack of wolves in a raid on the rustler's hideout, but rescues his mate instead of falling into the trap. Similarly, in *The Moon Spinners* (1964), the youthful Nikki and Mark seek refuge in an ancient Greek temple as they flee from the wicked Uncle Strato. There are vicious cats living there but they leave Nikki and Mark unharmed; when the wicked Strato comes, they fall on him, scratch him, and drive him away. These are schemes that transform animal species into something they can never be: it is anything but realistic to sentimentally depict animals with redemptive instincts; indeed, it is kitsch rather than art.

But the final irony in Disney's work is that he sanitizes fantasy life itself, as evidenced by such features as the mermaid without nipples in the "Small World" section of Disneyland. Such a world is truly small, but its popularity is undeniable.

Disney's Creation of a Super Mouse

L. H. Robbins raised the rhetorical question of Disney's remarkable popularity as early as the thirties:

> Why is it that university presidents praise him, the League of Nations recommends him, *Who's Who* and the *Encyclopaedia Britannica* give him paragraphs, learned academies hang medals on him, art galleries turn from Picasso and Epstein to hold exhibitions over his monkey shines, and the King of England won't go to the movies unless Mickey is on the bill?[18]

Part of the answer is that Disney created a charming and novel means of film presentation whose animated motion and color had great appeal. Disney also displayed editorial genius in relating humorous episodes without wasting a single frame of imagery. But beyond these visual considerations, Mickey seems to embody what Robbins calls the "release from the tyranny of things. . . . He declares a nine-minute moratorium on the debt that we owe to the iron facts of life. He suspends the rules of common sense and correct deportment and the other carping, conventional laws, including the law of gravity, that hold us down and cramp our style."[19] During this same period, Burne Hogarth was creating a comic-book Tarzan with a similar function: "He is the incarnation of our secret desire to be free from every form of insignificance, frustration, degradation. . . ."[20] Hogarth gave Tarzan hyperbolic powers of movement and struggle that could be plausibly attributed to his education in the jungle among higher apes.

Mickey Mouse, hardly a match for an ape, surpasses Tarzan and King Kong in his ability to do anything. His normal screen life is one of leaping, climbing, and manipulating as no human being ever could. Like a diminutive David, he always overcomes his adversaries, regardless of their stature. Robert D. Feild wrote a moving account of Mickey's genesis and miraculous powers in 1942, after the first decade of the mouse's cartoon life. He describes how Disney concocted the mouse as he worked in Kansas City:

> The original mouse, the spiritual ancestor of Mickey, is reported to have made friends with Walt years before in the garage that served him as workshop. He came to offer consolation during periods of despondency. Some say, even, that he trespassed on the master's drawing board, cleaning his whiskers with unconcern or hitching up his imaginary pants. The impression he left upon Walt's mind was such that it needed only a crisis for him to reappear in the form of a savior. Be this as it may, Walt had accepted a challenge, and he needed help. It was at this moment, on the train for Hollywood, that Mickey appeared. . . . Straightway he stretched out his gauntleted hand and said, "Put it there, pal," and a friendship was cemented for good and all.[21]

This momentous apparition of a mouse sounds more laden with significance than the encounters between St. Francis and his animal friends. Disney's faith in the mouse allowed him to move mountains of capital and to thrill a worldwide audience with screen miracles. Feild pays extravagant tribute to the cultural effect of Mickey, referring to his genesis years as "a period of history in which civilization is going through pangs of rebirth while mankind struggles in a strange darkness, uncertain of its destiny." Disney's mouse played a virtually redemptive role in leading the world out of this "strange darkness." Here is Feild's description of Disney's contribution to the mythic development during the period that we have called the axial decade for the American monomyth:

> During those few short years between 1928 and the present [1942] it will be found that Mickey played no mean part. Not only did he give us courage when we most needed it, forcing us to laugh to hide our tears, but also he opened up new worlds of experience and contributed to the refashioning of our ideals. Without precedent, this imaginative little symbol frisked his way into the hearts of all. There is no corner of the earth into which he has not penetrated; there is no type of man, from crowned head to primitive savage, that has not been won over. (p. 38)

The age-old dream of a single, universal religious image seems, according to this account, to have been achieved by the frisky mouse. Icons bearing Mickey's sacred image multiplied by the millions: dolls, toothbrushes, pencils, sweatshirts, beanie caps, toys, and tableware all came to bear the licensed imprimatur.

Mary Poppins' Heidi Touch

Mickey Mouse was not, however, the greatest financial success for Walt Disney. Live-action films proved even more profitable. Disney achieved a perfect synthesis of film miracle and sanitized sexuality in *Mary Poppins* (1964).[22] It was his most successful creation, critically and financially, embodying many of the values of his earlier, animated films. Emboldened by his reductive experiments with sexuality, Disney took the charwomanish Mary Poppins from the Travers novels and assigned the role to Julie Andrews. Travers's Mary, often bad-tempered and unpredictable, underwent a mythic alchemy to acquire Heidi's angelic sweetness. Rather than being blown to the door of the Bankses' home by a gusty wind, Disney's Mary Poppins descends from the heavens on her umbrella, coming on the clouds in biblical style to set things right. Disney thus created a redemptive story line absent in the Travers novels. Whereas the original Mary Poppins creates chaotic situations with her erratic comings and goings, Disney's heroine causes a confrontation with the wicked, calculating bankers and precipitates the dismissal of Mr. Banks, who then renounces his mean-spirited, pecuniary outlook and becomes a father to his children. Disney's Mary, despite her physical charms and the availability of Bert, played by the handsome Dick Van Dyke, shows absolutely no romantic inclination. She remains, in her own words, "practically perfect." It is the perfection of a Heidi redeemer manifest in a figure no one would mistake for a child. At the film's conclusion, this superheroic paragon ascends like an angel, her redemptive task completed, in a scene that replaces her inexplicable departures at the conclusion of the Travers novels.[23]

Audiences and critics have been utterly disarmed by the sense of the miraculous with which Walt Disney so richly invested his story. Critics referred to "the technical wizardry of the film," to Disney's "vast magic-making machinery," and to the "magical moments" in *Mary Poppins*.[24] One critic lavishly suggested that *Mary Poppins* "showed why movies were invented." The film re-created the sense of the miraculous that has disappeared from most modern religion, invading an allegedly secularized nature by cinematic manipulation. When the untidy nursery is to be cleaned up, Mary assures the Banks children: "In every job that must be done . . . we find an element of fun. We find the fun and *snap!* the job's a game!"[25] Straightaway, the toys and clothes move magically to their appointed places, accompanied by the opening and shutting of drawers. It is a miracle more automatic and charming than anything Johanna Spyri could have imagined. It has also been more rewarding: by the year 2000, *Mary Poppins* had earned $102 million from its worldwide distribution, not to mention the secondary income from the sale of records, music, and other items licensed through the film.[26]

Disney's Beautification of Violence

One aspect of Walt Disney's work that perhaps deserves even more intense critical evaluation is his treatment of violence. It is closely related to what Glenn Gray noted in his book *The Warriors*. There is in human nature, according to Gray, a positive aesthetic delight in the experience of destruction:

> While it is undeniable that the disorder and distortion and the violation of nature that conflict brings are ugly beyond compare, there are also color and movement, variety, panoramic sweep, and sometimes even momentary proportion and harmony. If we think of beauty and combat without their usual moral overtones, there is often a weird but genuine beauty in the sight of massed men and weapons in combat.[27]

Disney understood this fascination with destruction, and many of his early animated films, particularly *Bambi, Snow White,* and *Fantasia,* show scenes of apocalyptic terror. Many children shudder at seeing the murder of Bambi's mother and the great forest fire. But Disney also understood those "usual moral overtones" of revulsion that audiences might bring to scenes of destruction, and mitigated them with happy endings.

The technique of animated drawing allowed Disney to retain a satisfying level of violence while removing the elements that might make his audiences squeamish. Given the freedom to make funny animals behave without following the laws of nature, he was able to immunize them against the effects of violence. Heads could be bashed in and bodies rolled flat, only to bounce back alive in the next instant. Destructive actions against the bodies of others became the stock device of cartoon humor. For instance, in *Steamboat Willie* (1928), a goat eats some sheet music, and Minnie cranks the tail to produce a calliope version of "Turkey in the Straw." Other animals are then converted to musical instruments as Mickey squeezes them, bangs on them, and twists them. Music was never produced by more cheerfully sadistic means. In *Moving Day* (1936), Goofy is smashed flat by a piano, and later his head and legs are crushed through a refrigerator door by the same malicious instrument. The cartoon ends when the hideous Sheriff Pete lights a cigar in front of an open gas vent, having maliciously struck the match on Donald Duck's beak. Everything is destroyed, including Pete's hide. He is shown suspended nude in a bathtub above a thoroughly wrecked house from which he had just dispossessed the innocent Goofy, Donald, and Mickey. These extreme varieties of bodily violence, which would obviously be fatal for human foreclosers, are defused by animation to permit the audience to have the good, clean fun they have come reverently to expect from Disney.

Disney discovered an important principle in these reductive experiments with animated violence: Never confront an audience with the uglier aspects of conflict that might cause feelings of unhappiness or ambiguity. Disney resolved to keep happiness as the cardinal value in his universe. Even in the films where stereotyped forces of good and evil confronted one another, he banned unhappiness and required cheerful endings. When he created Disneyland late in his career, he was fond of calling it "The Happiest Place in the World." The liberal use of this claim in advertisements indicates the appeal of a land populated by figures associated with defused violence that can be enjoyed without aftereffect. It is indeed happier than anything in the real world.

The Moralization of Nature and War

The discovery of the limitless plasticity of the animated cartoon gave Disney an unsurpassed ability to depict moral judgments in his artifacts. He could alter and stylize physical characteristics so as to convey simplified moralizations. In fact, Disney seems to have had little interest in moral gradations. For instance, Robert Feild relates Disney's comment about the little town at the foot of menacing Bald Mountain in *Fantasia:* "It sort of symbolizes something. The forces of good on one side and of evil on the other is what I'm trying to see in the thing. What other reason can there be for it?"[28] Disney's cartoons convey stereotypical messages by having trees, plants, and animals sway or sing sympathetically when virtuous characters appear. They shrink in revulsion or fly away on cue when a wicked wolf or witch appears. The appearance of good and evil characters could be so completely stylized as to embody the moral judgment Disney wished to have his audience pass on them. The stereotypical potential is much greater than is possible for melodrama, for example, because the latter is limited by the fact that human beings must play the roles.

Disney's skill in visual moralization is evident in the creation of the witch in *Sleeping Beauty* (1959). Bob Thomas relates the process of the artist working on Maleficent: "Because she was to turn into a dragon later, he gave her a horned headdress with a collar that resembled bat wings. Her cold but beautiful face was encircled by black cloth, giving her a mask-like look. Continuing her evil appearance, her robe was black with folds of purple revealed. The lines of the robe carried out the vertical motif, and the train curved with a snaky feeling."[29] The animation process helped Disney reaffirm his hostility toward adult sexuality. The story outline he wrote for *Snow White* specifies: "THE QUEEN: A mixture of Lady Macbeth and the Big Bad Wolf — Her beauty is sinister, mature, plenty of curves — She becomes ugly and menacing when scheming and mixing her poisons — Magic fluids transform her into a witchlike hag."[30] The "curves" of the wicked Queen are played off visually against the pure, straight lines of Snow White. A similar effort to associate curvaceous femininity with evil is made in *Fantasia's* (1940) "Night on Bald Mountain," where demonic hags are presented with bare breasts and extended nipples — the only occasion in Disney's film-making career that he unveiled these menacing anatomical structures. With every detail controllable, Disney's animation allows a transcendence of the subjectivity and ambiguity that usually afflict moral vision. Stereotypes that would be laughable when presented by live actors and actresses assume a strange, mythic power and believability.

The surpassing of burdensome subjectivity through technical manipulation is particularly evident in Disney's propaganda film *Victory Through Air Power* (1943).[31] Disney was an early proponent of strategic bombing in World War II. He felt that the American government was insufficiently alert to its potential for winning the war. Consequently, he collaborated with Major Alexander Seversky in making a film about strategic bombing, taking the career and ideas of Billy Mitchell as the point of focus. The film opens with a message that casts General Mitchell in the role of the redeemer: "Our country in the past has struggled through many storms of anguish, difficulty and doubt. But we have always been saved by men of vision and courage who opened our minds and showed us the way out of confusion."[32] The narrator goes on to show how Mitchell was "ignored and ridiculed" and concludes with a dedication to the memory of Billy Mitchell and other gallant airmen. The film develops an extended and often animated argument for strategic bombing, using comic presentations of Axis stereotypes. It graphically portrays Seversky's scheme of a single united air command encompassing the entire globe and guaranteeing victory. Film historian Leonard Maltin summarizes the concluding scene:

> The final animated sequence shows Seversky's idealized air force in action, taking off for Japan, bombing the cities and factories and crippling their power. Then a giant eagle soars through the air, aiming for an octopus on the ground below: the eagle jabs at the head of the octopus, again and again, until it retreats and loses its grip on the map under it. The eagle triumphantly perches on top of the globe, and a zoom backward shows it to be the top of a flagpole flying the American flag in victory.

Maltin comments about the character of this "powerful" and "crystal clear" propaganda: "When Seversky refers to a shield of air power, we see an actual shield atop a relief map of Europe and see just how it works. When he talks about Hitler's wheel-like stronghold, the wheel is shown and the metaphor made real. The film is perfect propaganda because it leaves no room for argument; it shows you that what it says is true" (p. 63). Disney further strengthened his propaganda by sanitizing the violence he advocated. By drawing his argument to give it concreteness, he was able to eliminate elements that might arouse objections from his audience. James Agee noticed, for example, "that there were no suffering and dying enemy civilians under all those proud promises of bombs; no civilians at all, in fact."[33] Disney's animated leap from military metaphor to visual "reality" thus was able to serve whatever goals its creator wished to espouse, leaving the horrible human wreckage out of sight.

Victory Through Air Power may have been a significant factor in shaping the attitudes of its audience, whose leaders had early in the war declared themselves morally opposed to the fascist atrocity of strategic bombing. On the first day of American participation in World War II, President Roosevelt had called for each warring nation "publicly to affirm its determination that its armed forces shall in no event, and in no circumstances, undertake the bombardment from the air of civilian populations or of unfortified cities." In the following year he reiterated this: "The bombing of the helpless and unprotected civilians is a tragedy which has aroused the horror of all mankind. I recall with pride that the United States consistently has taken the lead in urging that this inhuman practice be prohibited."[34] H. C. Potter, one of Disney's film directors, reports the following anecdote as told by Disney:

> The British Air Force thought this [film] was the greatest thing that ever came down the pike, and the picture was much better known in England than it was here, in official circles, and early in the game Walt told me this story, and swore this was what happened. When Churchill came over to the Quebec conference, they were trying to get Roosevelt interested in this long-range bombing idea, and Roosevelt didn't know what the hell they were talking about. Churchill said, "Well, of course, you've seen *Victory Through Air Power*. . . ." And Roosevelt said, "No, what's that?" Air Marshal Tedder and Churchill worked on Roosevelt until Roosevelt put through an order to the Air Corps to fly a print of *Victory Through Air Power* up to Quebec. Churchill ran it for him, and that was the beginning of the U.S. Air Corps Long Range Bombing.[35]

This is the kind of claim Leni Riefenstal could have made about her skillful and powerful *Triumph of the Will* on the theme of Nazi rallies, "which channeled the psychic energies of hundreds of thousands of people" in Hitler's Germany. In both instances the filmmakers used the most sophisticated film techniques to serve idealistic causes, resulting in the needless deaths of thousands of innocent people.[36] This also reveals an ominous side to the allegedly harmless violence in Disney's cartoons, a subject that deserves more careful scrutiny than it ordinarily receives.[37] Entertainment in the form of violence-without-consequences works out more happily in the animated films than in history.

When Disney turned to live-action films, he transferred the techniques and mythic patterns he had developed through animation. The technical wizardry that had allowed him to reinstate the credibility of miracles allowed him to completely moralize the world of his films. With special-effects photography, skillful stunts, and ingenious gadgets, Disney could make the entire universe comply with his mythic vision. This effort has been faithfully continued since his death by the Disney Studio. In *The Love Bug* (1969) the studio created a redemptive Volkswagen possessing the human tendency to protect the weak. In *Herbie Rides Again* (1974), the heroic car leads a whole pack of driverless Volkswagens in thwarting the greedy ambitions of a real-estate developer, Alonzo Hawk, who wishes to deprive a poor, sweet widow of her charming firehouse home. Herbie even brings together a young pair for marriage, though they are naturally wholesome and lack sexual passion. These moralized Volkswagens even attend the wedding at the end of the film, rearing on their hind wheels to pay tribute to the pair united by the heroic Herbie. These films moralize technology just as thoroughly as Disney had moralized nature in his earlier films. The mythic treatments of nature, animal life, and technology have a profound kinship to the antihistorical spirit displayed in television's *Little House on the Prairie* material. Every element of human experience must be transformed to suit the requirements of the monomyth.

The Cultural Supremacy of Walt Disney

Disney's efforts to create a sanitary form of happiness were regarded as the finest examples of educational entertainment. The hundreds of accolades he received prompted the question posed by his promotional literature: "What kind of man is this who has won the Medal of Freedom — highest civilian award in the United States; twenty-nine motion picture Academy Awards; four TV Emmys; scores of citations from many nations, and some 700 other awards; who has been decorated by the French Foreign Legion of Honor and again by the Art Workers Guild of London; has received honorary degrees from Harvard, Yale and the University of Southern California . . . ?" The piece provides the answer to its own question: Disney's mission was "to bring happiness to millions. It first became evident in the twenties, when this lean son of the Mid-West came unheralded to Hollywood [and] began to animate his dreams. . . ."[38] That mission has seemingly been accomplished, as witnessed by the millions who have watched Disney's movies, television programs, and cartoons and who visit his amusement parks every year. They comment frequently on the remarkable feats of sanitation that keep Disneyland spotless despite hordes of littering tourists.

Far be it from us to carp at cleanliness, but the sanitizing urge is central to the power of Disney's mythic artifacts, and even the most sophisticated minds have been willing to surrender themselves to its power. Mark Van Doren wrote that Disney's "techniques, about which I know little, must of course be wonderful, but the main thing is that he lives somewhere near the human center and knows innumerable truths that cannot be taught. That is why his ideas look like inspirations and why he can be goodhearted without being sentimental, can be ridiculous without being fatuous. With him, as with any first rate artist, we feel that we are in good hands; we can trust him with our hearts and wits."[39] When minds of Van Doren's critical caliber are eager to accept the massage, we know that we are confronting artifacts of wondrous power.

Because Disney credibly reinstated the sense of the miraculous, it is not surprising that the growing empire of theme parks in Florida, Japan, and France have become, in effect, shrines that celebrate the founder's vision. What is not explicit at these sites is Walt Disney's contribution to the goal of the Motion Picture Production Code: "Entertainment which tends to improve the race, or at least to re-create and rebuild human beings exhausted with the realities of life. . . ."[40] This holiday of the spirit seldom reflects the democratic spirit, as we can see in the most recent triumphs of the Disney Corporation.

The Restoration of Beastly Dynasty

At the time of Walt Disney's death in 1966, this question hung in the air: Could the Disney Corporation profitably survive without the founder's sense that allowed him to connect with such a wide American public? We now know that even greater riches lay ahead. Carefully guarding the vault that contained the classics such as *Snow White, The Three Little Pigs, Cinderella,* and *Mary Poppins*, the Disney Corporation refused to sell the treasures to television, as so many other studios had, but worked at becoming an independent television power in its own right by creating successful series such as Disneyland, Walt Disney Presents, and The Wonderful World of Color. By 1996, the Disney Corporation would acquire Capital Cities/ABC, Inc., owners of the network giant ABC.[41] By the year 2000 it had become the third largest entertainment-broadcast conglomerate in the world, with 120,000 employees and revenues of $25.4 billion.[42] Disney Studios also took on stage productions, refurbishing the New Amsterdam Theater on Broadway in New York City. There it successfully restaged its film *The Lion King* as a musical to great critical acclaim and commercial success. But what about the firmly established mythic traditions that Walt brought to animated films? Does today's Disney Corporation still hew instinctively to the mythic tradition of the American monomyth?

Looking at the critical and commercial triumphs of the past decade, we must conclude that the answer is a somewhat qualified no. Several stories from Disney's assorted studios have escaped from the sexually antiseptic formulas that built the empire. To broaden its market, Disney established Touchstone Pictures, which released *Pretty Woman* (1990), a fairy tale about an impoverished prostitute who provides erotic therapies to a sexually impaired rich man; in gratitude, he showers her with shopping privileges and claims her as his wife. Another subsidiary, Miramax Pictures, released *Priest* (1994), an exploration of the spiritual struggles of a gay Catholic priest. This film provoked boycotts organized by Catholic media watchers. And David Lynch's production *The Straight Story* (1999), we will argue in our final chapter, is a rare and moving story of redemption — without superheroic powers of any kind.

Moreover, the animated heroic tales of the 1990s — *Beauty and the Beast* (1991), *Aladdin* (1992), *The Lion King* (1994), *Pocahontas* (1995), and *Tarzan* (1997) — are all framed by the romance genre, where sexual fulfillment and partnership are linked with some acceptance of permanent responsibility for the welfare of a community. In effect, these stories revert to the pattern of the classical monomyth. But like most traditional stories of departure-testing-return, they have nothing to do with the symbolic affirmation of democratic ideals. And they are told with Old Walt's starkly simplistic understanding of good and evil, which can be overcome only by those who exhibit the sweet innocence of stereotypically feminine love.

The plot of *The Lion King*,[43] a feudal restoration drama transposed to the African savannah, illustrates this enduring set of Disney values. The film begins in a kind of peaceable kingdom. The lion King Mufasa rules a beautiful land, and the animals who are normally the breakfast, lunch, and dinner for lions gather for a ceremonial blessing of the legitimate successor to Pride's Rock, the cub Prince Simba. In this scene the animals are introduced one by one, with their place in the hierarchy of dominance clearly implied. In a nice gesture toward art's traditional role in legitimating the dominance of elites, Simba's presentation is commemorated with a cave painting.

As Simba grows toward adolescence, paradise is destroyed by an evil uncle, Scar, who has a plan to murder both Simba and his father, Mufasa. Scar's "outsider" status is conveyed by his British accent (provided by Jeremy Irons) and the use of stereotypically homosexual traits. In his moment of supreme treachery, Scar triggers a wildebeest stampede and pushes Mufasa into it, thus succeeding in killing the King but missing his opportunity to kill little Prince Simba. But he does psychically disable Simba by encouraging his belief that his trek into the forbidden elephant graveyard was responsible for the tragedy. Simba accepts Scar's suggestion that he go into exile as punishment. Once he is gone, a violent anarchy, led by hyenas, envelopes Pride Land. Nature itself becomes barren because of a drought, and the result is a desperate struggle to survive. Scar allows his goose-stepping hyenas — formerly excluded from Pride Land — to terrorize the savannah kingdom. And indulging his own laziness, Scar forces the lionesses to do all the hunting for the pride.

In jungle exile, Simba first adopts the "hakuna matata" philosophy of the little comrades who take him in — "no worries for the rest of your days." However, after he has attained adulthood, Nala, his lioness pal from earlier days, seeks him out and urges him to accept his responsibility to return and to rule. Prompted by Nala, Simba gradually becomes convinced that he is the rightful ruler, that he is the very image of his father, Mufasa, and that he must become the savior of his father's old fiefdom. He returns, confronts Scar, and then pushes him to his death among his disloyal hyenas. Echoing apocalyptic themes, *The Lion King* features a grand fire that comes to purify the land of Scar's evil, followed by regenerative rains. The hyenas, who represent the outsiders that cannot be tolerated within the kingdom, are once more excluded. Simba marries his Nala, and they become the parents of a new cub — thus renewing "the circle of life." The assembled kingdom chants, "Simba, you must rule with peace, you must rule with love." The good lion, who has established his lack of aggressiveness through an early experience of victimization and his benign disposal of Scar, has morally triumphed over the bad lion, who wanted to triumph through predation.

At all points the film tells this story with beautiful animations that are remarkably faithful to the physical appearance of nature, stirring music, perfectly crafted voices, and the irritating wisecracks salted in for the adult spectrum of the audience. It may sound harsh to say, with Matt Roth, that *The Lion King* is just one more example of "Disney-fascism."[44] But the symbolism of the fable is inescapable: the most powerful, provided they show a little compassion, shall rule the rest; and the ruled shall be happiest when they festively celebrate their oppressors. This film raises and quickly resolves the question of animal aggression and its role in the normal dominance of lions. The curious young Simba had early raised questions about the beastliness of their cruelly predatory way of life, but Mufasa finesses the question with a tidy ecological lesson:

> MUFASA: Everything you see exists together, in a delicate balance. As king, you need to understand that balance, and respect all the creatures — from the crawling ant to the leaping antelope.
> SIMBA: But, Dad, don't we eat the antelope?
> MUFASA: Yes, Simba, but let me explain. When we die, our bodies become the grass. And the antelope eat the grass. And so we are all connected in the great Circle of Life.

The Disney studio could have terrified young audiences with the sounds of screaming antelopes being attacked by roaring lions, but they sanitized reality with the melodious sounds of circling life. The film thereby provides a model for human interaction that sanctifies domination and violence.

Other Disney Kingdoms

The Disney film *Tarzan* (1997) offered a variation on this theme of "natural" domination. Tarzan, the Caucasian human, becomes an "accidental" gorilla with extraordinary jungle smarts that elevate him to the top of his hairy, lazy tribe. Only Tarzan is clever enough to protect his hirsute friends from the predatory European hunters. (Not a single African appears on the screen of this film about Africa.) In good monomythic fashion, Tarzan proves his worthiness to gain acceptance as leader of apes by initially rejecting Jane's companionship, for he must stay to accept custodial responsibility for his threatened apes. But the story does end in a kind of romantic paradise: Jane and Tarzan together, living among the animals who acclaim their natural superiority.

With the exception of *Mulan* (1998), which tells the story of an assertive girl warrior in China who challenges the males around her, the other Disney animations of the 1990s skirt these themes of natural patriarchal power by featuring characters who fit well into the Heidi mold. Belle, in *Beauty and the Beast,* transforms the beast with her selfless, compassionate love. Aladdin eventually moves to the top of his kingdom in Horatio Alger fashion by sweetly befriending a persecuted princess, Jasmine, who wants to marry for love in defiance of her father and her evil Uncle Jafar. Aladdin demonstrates his worthiness for royal companionship by demonstrating his charitable instincts toward hungry children who search the garbage for food. He gives them his bread — which he has just stolen — and remarks wistfully to his monkey companion: "Someday, Abu, things are going to change. We'll be rich, live in a palace, and never have any troubles at all."

Pocahontas,[45] who presents the physical appearance of a Native American Barbie® doll, lives out the legend of saving Captain John Smith so that she can bring about more peaceful relations between the English and her people. The Disney studios consciously sought to create a revisionist story of encounter between Native Americans and their conquerors, employing consultants and prominent figures to that end. Russell Means, for example, whose voice was used in the film, commented that he was "overwhelmed" by the script: "It tells the truth about the motives for Europeans coming to the so-called New World. I find it astounding that Americans and the Disney Studios are willing to tell the truth."[46] As Gary Edgerton and Kathy Merlock Jackson point out, the Disney studio gave the story their familiar grounding in a girl's search to fulfill a dream. Uncertain about whether to accept a tribal companion, Kocoum, "she falls in love with the first white man she sees."[47] The film leaves her at the point of longing for John Smith, who is returning to England after being saved by her love. What it omits from her life story are the complexities of colonial subordination that quickly befell her: her kidnapping by the English; her becoming an English Lord's wife, Lady Rebecca Rolfe; her conversion to Christianity; and, finally, her death in England at the age of 21. To its credit, Disney did break unfamiliar ground in attempting to walk for even a short distance in the moccasins of a famous Powhatan. But the world of animated sentimental romance, ruled by innocent love, is hardly a vehicle in which to inspire much serious thought about colonial conquest or its aftermath.

Disney as Democratic Educator?

The Disney enterprises have consistently presented themselves to the American public as educators. With global reach in storytelling, theme parks, and merchandising, Disney could be a potent force in celebrating democratic ideals. Is there much more to Disney than tales of dominance by powerful "natural" elites such as the Lion King, Tarzan, or Hercules? Or sentimental tales of triumph by sweet princesses such as the Little Mermaid, Pocahantas, or Belle? In an attempt to answer our own question, we visited Disney.com's "Edu-station,"[48] where the corporation vends materials "For Your Classroom." We found a cluster of social science units and clicked on "Great Minds Biographies," suspecting that we might find one of our great democratic leaders from the past. Unfortunately, Pluto greeted us with "SORRY. THE PAGE YOU REQUESTED WAS NOT FOUND. . . ." So we searched for "democracy" within the site and found a reference to the "Audio-Animatronics spectacle" called "Great Moments with Mr. Lincoln," introduced at the 1964-65 World's Fair. Then a Disneyland® Resort™ "Fun Fact" popped up to tell us that "Lincoln's *Disneyland®* address is composed of excerpts from speeches actually made during his presidency." So far as we can tell, that's about the only remnant of democracy that can be found in the land of Disney. As the little troops so cheerfully sing there, "It's a small world."

10 The Sound of One Hand Killing: Monomythic Video Games

"We advise that parents should monitor the use of video games by their children. If you or your children experience any of the following symptoms: dizziness, blurred vision, eye or muscle twitches, loss of consciousness, disorientation, any involuntary movement or convulsion, while playing a video game, IMMEDIATELY discontinue use and consult your physician."

from the EPILEPSY WARNING for the *Braveheart* video game[2]

The Emergence of a Games Technology

As we have seen, the American monomyth's history is intertwined with the technology of twentieth-century entertainment. The latest technomythic platform is the computer. Developing quickly in the past few decades, the personal computer and the arcades now offer high-fidelity sound and an assortment of interactive controls for hands, feet, and voice. Recent heroes of the digital screen can fly, shoot, shout, punch, and kick in response to a user's

199

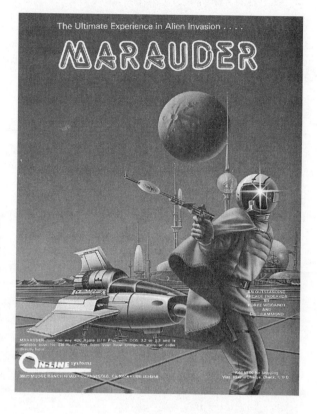

Early computer-based games offered the traditional mythic appeals of mobility, powerful weapons, hidden identity, and defending against aggression. *Marauder*'s advertising in 1982 promised the experience of superheroics.

Credit: *Softalk* magazine advertisement in 1982 for the Apple II game *Marauder,* from On-line systems.

promptings. So compelling are the actions of these superheroes that the U.S. Army in 2001 abandoned its durable "Be All You Can Be" marketing slogan for the oxymoronic "An Army of One." The theme of the campaign, as suggested by the real Sgt. Joseph Patterson of its advertising, is that you can become a high-tech superhero in the army.

These computer games offer a new style of mythic socialization with intense personal involvement in a monomythic scenario. The interactive game experience now allows the participant to *be* a savior and to feel viscerally the pleasures of redeeming a situation from threat. And by opening their codes for constructing scenarios to the game-playing community, some companies are permitting users to further customize myth in the direction of personal taste.

U.S. culture has found much to celebrate in these startling evolutionary achievements. Computer-based games are addictively popular and hence profitable, both at home and in international markets. When the Sony Corporation released its new PlayStation 2 consoles in 2000, eager consumers camped out for more than twenty-seven hours at San Francisco's Metreon Center, overnighting in a rainstorm. The few who could make their purchases did so at 12:01 a.m., a pilgrimage experience of waiting for the latest game technology that was replicated all over the country.[3]

The games have been more than a mere commercial success. They also make claims of educational respectability. Game producers, educators, and players plausibly extol the learning potential: chip-based fun demands the development of keyboard skills in addition to teaching eye-hand coordination and spatial sense. Beyond the mere physical, players learn mastery of rules, sense of strategy, tolerance for intellectual complexity — not to mention the experience of losing. Everyone who plays such a game for more than a few minutes is impressed by its demands for physical skill and tactical judgment.[4]

The Columbine Questions

Despite the above wholesome effects of these computer-based games, clouds of suspicion have always gathered around them. In the 1970s parents were alarmed by the darkness of arcades, the cost of playing, and by the unwholesome-looking adults they often saw there. Some communities passed restrictive ordinances against them.[5] In 1982, C. Everett Koop, the conservative surgeon general of the United States, accused video games of causing "aberrations in childhood behavior" and having a destructive effect on family life.[6] Sherry Turkle's book *The Second Self* (1984) explored the cognitive aspects of these games while noting their addicting tendencies and the "altered states" of many who entered this fantasy world.[7] And because some highly popular games had violent themes and starkly gendered roles, social scientists quickly began to explore their potential for aggressive and sexist behavioral influences.[8]

National anxiety about fantasy violence as entertainment crested in the spring of 1999 during a remarkable period of mythic coalescence. The sudden juxtaposition of popular mythic materials with monstrous criminal events posed anew questions about links between culture and behavior, mind and hand, playing at killing and murder itself. The following events took place over a thirty-day period during the spring of 1999:

- *The Matrix*, a popular movie that was to become a cult film, was released on March 31, 1999. As we mentioned in chapter one, its redemptive climax features a pair of shooters, Neo and Trinity, dressed in long black coats, lugging bombs and guns into a building for a destructive raid on the powers of "the matrix." During the firefight Neo first dies and then experiences a resurrection. In his resurrected state he kills with a magical, flying fury that liberates all of humanity from tyranny.

- On April 12, the parents of three Paducah, Kentucky, students killed by Michael Carneal brought a $130-million suit against Time Warner, Inc. and Polygram over an alleged incitement to murder because of a fantasy scene in *Basketball Diaries,* where the character played by Leonardo DiCaprio enters a classroom wearing a trench coat and blasts away with a shotgun. Their families also sued the producers of the violent video games *Doom, Quake,* and *Mortal Kombat.* Jack Thompson, attorney for the families, offered this broadside taunt to America's pop culture: "We intend to hurt Hollywood . . . the video game industry . . . the sex porn sites."[9]

- The June cover of *Computer Gaming World,* mailed to subscribers on April 19, depicted a flying gunman wearing a long black coat. This imaginary DEA agent, Max Payne, aims two guns at the magazine's readers, one blazing with a radiant burst of light. The cover's caption, "Playing G.O.D.," refers to the inspired acronym adopted by the Gathering of Developers group, which produces first-person-shooter (FPS) video games. These games allow the player to view victims through a gun sight that tracks their movements. In addition to evoking a wrathful Jehovah, the phrase "God mode" describes an option of some games in which the shooter becomes invulnerable to death.

- On April 20, Dylan Klebold and Eric Harris, both known as admirers of Hitler and dedicated players of the FPS games *Doom* and *Quake,* entered Columbine High School in Littleton, Colorado, dressed in long black coats that concealed their weapons. They slaughtered twelve classmates and a teacher before killing themselves.[10] In a posthumously discovered videotape, Harris sits with his shotgun "Arlene" (a *Doom*-derived name) and says: "It's going to be like f---ing *Doom.* Tick, tick, tick . . . Haa! That f---ing shotgun is straight out of *Doom.*"[11] The murdering pair made approving references to the film *Natural Born Killers* (1994) as they contemplated their revenge against the offenses, real or imagined, committed against them. They also foresaw a special kind of glory for themselves, imagining that their lives would become a major movie, with directors Steven Spielberg and Quentin Tarantino fighting for the film rights.

These cultural fragments associated with the Columbine massacre evoke numerous questions. Does the synchronicity of these events tell us something about the behavioral contagion of mythic imagery? Were Harris and Klebold deliberately re-enacting the ecstasy-in-purifying-destruction so conspicuous in shooter games such as *Doom?* Had they taken spirit from the blazing guns and bone-crunching kicks of *The Matrix's* Neo and Trinity? And did Harris and Klebold, so thoroughly immersed in the slaughters of their game world, become desensitized to the elements of parody and critique in *Natural Born Killers,* seeing it as a model instead of as satire?

Even the normally slaughter-jaded readers of *Computer Gaming World* were disturbed by the grim juxtaposition of "God" with its visual echo of Columbine. The magazine received enough complaints about its cover that it responded to some of its disappointed readers. *CGW's* "G.O.D. cover" was merely "a bizarre coincidence," according to its editorial director, Johnny Wilson. And surely we can accept that. But Wilson wanted to defend the magazine's artwork and trade territory when he suggested that games actually have "a positive, cathartic effect in simulated violence. Violence in computer games is not intended to encourage the slaughter of unarmed innocents." Instead, according to Wilson, violence is merely "used as graphic hyperbole to raise the stakes and make us pay attention." Wilson went on to highlight a range of factors affecting real-world violence, but finally conceded that "violent media *can* play a role in such tragedies."[12] But Wilson did not choose to speculate about what that role might be. With so many pathological factors to choose among in the Columbine case — neglectful parents, taunting classmates, psychoactive medications, the availability of weapons — it would be difficult to credibly assign *the* cause of the killings.

U.S. District Judge Edward Johnstone of Kentucky, confronted by the suit against media producers brought by the grieving parents in his state, dismissed it on the grounds "that it was unreasonable to expect the defendants to have foreseen injuries from Michael Carneal's actions." He also asserted that Carneal's behavior was essentially a mystery: "This was a tragic situation, but tragedies such as this defy rational explanation."[13] Nevertheless, it is reasonable to declare that, however we interpret the riddle of the schoolhouse murders of the 1990s, the death-themed computer games play a haunting background melody to the tragedy. This is a prime example of what we have called the Werther effect, which functions in the cultural arena even though its liabilities cannot be adjudicated in the courts. The murderers Carneal, Harris, and Klebold gave ample evidence of having experienced the fantasy of video games and violent movies in such a way as to shape their sense of the real and desirable. They deliberately planned and took actions congruent with fantasies apparently shaped during the interaction with the games. Their murderous rampages — with their undercurrents of righteousness about their revenge — reflect the curious religious tinge within a nonreligious context visible in such episodes since the time of Goethe's novel. Yet no case can be made that the creators of the video games and films are solely and directly responsible.

Lt. Colonel Dave Grossman of the U.S. Army, who has studied soldiers' resistance to killing during military training,[14] has become a prominent crusader against video games because he believes that they employ the same conditioning techniques as combat training. Grossman felt confident that Michael Carneal's remarkably lethal performance as a first-time pistol shooter — eight head or upper torso hits with eight bullets — could be accounted for only by his training as a virtual killer in the games he played.[15] And Carneal himself confirms this assessment by reporting that he felt motivated by the destructive fantasy of *The Basketball Diaries* film.[16] Yet it is incontestable that tens of millions of adolescents have seen the same violent movies Carneal watched and played the same violence-themed games he played without becoming killers. Moreover, some teenagers do report that playing aggressive games dissipates their feelings of hostility.

The subtle question of when correlation amounts to causation burdens every effort to assess the influence of a culture's icons and symbolic stories. So, rather than trying to resolve such imponderables, we should look at games as another form of mythic socialization within world culture. The concept of the Werther effect should pose for us questions about the vision of community and individual responsibility conveyed by commercially available games that offer violent strategies for coping with problems. Is their vision of citizenship merely the sound of one hand killing in behalf of a righteous cause? While we may accept some of the skeptical disclaimers about the real-world impact of symbolic imagery, it still is relevant to ask whether the fantasy models of uninhibited destructive rage, rationalized by habitual exposure to myths of innocence, invite emulation by some deeply troubled souls. Reflecting on the religious garb in which so many games have begun to present themselves, it is also worth inquiring whether the games lend an air of sanctity and a sense of life's meaning to fantasies of deadly rage.

In a world awash with private, high-powered weapons, the question of Werther effects has become far more relevant than it was in Goethe's era. Whatever the countries of origin for producers of technology and software, the market for them is now international. And just as the American monomyth has become a dominant paradigm for world movie-goers, it permeates the current generation of fighting games. It is therefore important to understand how the technology of the computer became so firmly fused to our peculiarly American mythic tradition.

The Digital Transformation of the Toy World

Historically, children have received toys that reflect an adult sense of civilization's roles, challenges, and destiny. Typical playthings have been dolls and housekeeping tools for females, trucks, cars, weapons, and warriors for males. Generations of European boys got toy soldiers that introduced them to the fury of battles that so often swept through their lands. As Bruno Bettelheim put it, "Since ancient times children have played out war games in which *we* fight *them,* them being the enemy of the historical moment."[17] American boys during World War II received tanks, fighter planes, and destroyer ships so that they could simulate the wars fought in other lands. And during the early stages of the Vietnam War, the Hasbro company conceived of G.I. Joe with his "ten-inch bazooka that really works," a "beachhead flame thrower."[18] Joe was *not* a doll, because dolls were for girls. Joe was called an "action figure," masculine terminology for plastic warriors that has persisted to this day.[19] Games of violence mediated by the computer fit in with this older pattern, but they advance the style of play in revolutionary fashion.

As play spaces, the colorless appearance of early computer screens seemed unpromising. It was hard to imagine that a mere computer screen could become a stage for the enactment of mythic narratives. The primitive Etch-a-Sketch, which came to the toy market in 1960, was far more fluid and responsive by comparison. However, the limits of the computer screen were merely temporary. When the ripeness of technology permitted, elements of the video game had several independent births. One occurred in 1958 at the Brookhaven National Laboratory, where the physicist William Higinbotham created "Tennis for Two," a court with a net and a ball displayed on an oscilloscope.[20] The moving ball on the screen was used to entertain Brookhaven's visitors.

From the standpoint of myth, a more important genesis occurred in 1961 at MIT, where a young computer lab employee named Steve Russell used the Digital Equipment Corporation's PDP-1, an expensive business and scientific computer of the early 1960s, to develop "Spacewar."[21] This was a competitive game for two players, each of whom commanded a pair of control buttons for navigation and firing. Players could see their rudimentary spaceships, with dots representing loaded torpedo tubes, against the background of a starry heaven.

The game seemed to have no commercial potential because the PDP-1 minicomputer carried a price of $120,000. But the very costliness that blocked marketability doubtless contributed to the primitive Spacewar's addictive appeal for engineers and programmers. They were getting to play with a very expensive toy! Nonetheless, because the computer code could be shared with any other facility owning a PDP, a sizable noncommercial audience emerged for the game. Here is Stewart Brand's description of the fantasy war scene that had developed nationally for the PDP-1's successors by 1972:

> Reliably, at any nighttime moment (i.e., non-business hours) in North America hundreds of computer technicians are effectively out of their bodies, locked in life-or-death space combat computer-projected onto cathode ray tube display screens, for hours at a time, ruining their eyes, numbing their fingers in frenzied mashing of control buttons, joyously slaying their friend and wasting their employers' valuable computer time.[22]

In addition to the geeky fascination with what technology could do, the simple and equitable arithmetic of a successful kill (+1) or being killed (-1) challenged the adult male competitive sense. This widespread fascination with computer-simulated destruction eventually made possible an entertainment industry whose plots could parallel those of comics, cartoons, and films — while engaging the eyes and hands of the myth's consumers in a way surpassing any previous technology. It also fit in with the scientific-engineering community's emphasis on developing larger nuclear weapons and intercontinental ballistic missiles. The older skill-based pleasures of chess seemed coldly intellectual and deficient in strategic interest compared to the robust ecstasies of joystick-directed annihilation.

Playing to Save All Mankind

The profit-making potential for computer-based games finally became evident with the success of an arcade game called *Pong,* a two-dimensional simulated Ping-Pong game. The game's developer, Nolan Bushnell, first installed *Pong* in a bar, and the machine's overflowing box of quarters led him toward a larger market. By 1974, Bushnell's company, Atari, had delivered *Home Pong,* which could be played with a game console hooked up to a television set. The game's appeal lay in seeing the simple action on the screen as an extension of one's own hand. Other game companies followed with screen versions of badminton and tic-tac-toe. Ultimately, boredom with consoles restricted to a single spatial game greatly limited the market for them.

Atari achieved a technological milestone in 1977, when it introduced a cartridge software system for its model 2600, which opened the single console to a potentially unlimited number of games. The company made an important mythic breakthrough in 1978 with *Space Invaders,* whose animated squadrons of aliens "marched down like intergalactic redcoats firing laser bullets. The more you hit, the faster they advanced."[23] Like the science-fiction movies that inspired it, the game's premise was thoroughly paranoid. The instruction manual defines the scenario: "Each time you turn on *Space Invaders,* you will be at war with enemies from space who are threatening the earth. Your objective is to destroy these invaders by firing your 'laser cannon.'"[24] This game was followed by *Asteroids* (1980), whose innovation was adding the sort of scoreboard that pinball machines had displayed. *Battlezone* (Atari, 1980) brought the tank battle into the home and gave the U.S. Army one of its first game platforms for training real warriors.[25]

Missile Command (Atari, 1980), with its nuclear battles in space, emerged at a time when the film *Star Wars* (1977) had so triumphantly legitimated war as a children's pleasure. The Kenner Corporation was selling millions of *Star Wars* action figures in the late 1970s and early 1980s. Tom Engelhardt reminds us that "children's TV had become a *Star Wars*–like battle zone. Outnumbered rebels daily transformed themselves from teenagers into mighty robots loved by good, feared by evil *(Voltron),* or heroic teams of armed machines *(M.A.S.K).*"[26] *Missile Command* also came during a period of heightened national fear about nuclear exchange with the Soviet Union. This game expressed an appalling ambiguity about the consequences of undertaking a nuclear war.

Missile Command began its development with a scenario of attacking and defending the California coast. Dave Theurer, a game developer at Atari, recalled that the geographical identification made the game "too frightful"; so it was scrapped. There was also to be a scanning radar — part of the real world of nuclear warfare — but that would make it "too hard for the player to see what was going on."[27] Railroads and submarines, other real-world targets for missiles, also had to be eliminated, because "if you get too complicated, people won't play." The finished product was "a point-and-shoot game controlled with a trackball." The object was to defend six cities on the colony planet Zardon from nuclear attack. Although California had been eliminated from the game's geography, the Zardonian defenders were clearly stand-ins for the U.S. military. The game's box pictured a background rocket in its launch phase with a standing Caucasian officer in a Navy uniform and a seated Caucasian missile operator wearing a helmet.

The moral context of *Missile Command* was far more elaborate than the simplified paranoia of *Space Invaders.* According to the game instructions, the peaceful Zardonians are mining precious ores and they "go about their business with a sense of pride and well-being. They have actually built a uto-

The reissue of *Missile Command* in 1999 allowed players to experience the "classic" from the 1980s as well as the "ultimate." Both games allow you to "take command" and "execute a devastating counterattack against a massive alien invasion."

Credit: Box for re-released *Missile Command* © 1999 Hasbro Interactive, Inc.

pia for themselves."[28] However, these happy, innocent people are threatened by "the less fortunate Krytolians," who have received a good deal of "interplanetary aid" that they have not appreciated. They want the "Resource Planet" as their own. "At this very moment, the surprise attack is on its way."

The game, unlike the optimistic scenarios presented by the advocates of Reagan's Strategic Defense Initiative ("Star Wars"), could not be "won" in the sense of preventing the destruction of cities. As the game instructions warn, "Attacks come in waves lasting 30-45 seconds. Each wave is more difficult than the previous one. On the sixth wave, the enemy launches smart missiles that can evade your ABMs and 'home in' on your missile base and cities."[29] For those who developed this shimmering, two-dimensional screen with pointy blue pyramids as cities, the impact was enervating. Theurer reported that, for a long period, "I'd wake up in a cold sweat because I would have these dreams where I'd see the missile streak coming in and I'd see the impact. I would be up on top of a mountain and I'd see the missiles coming in, and I'd know it would be about 30 seconds until the blast hit and fried me to a crisp." Steve Calfee, an associate of Theurer at Atari, reported that "everybody I know who really got into the game had nightmares about nuclear war."[30]

When this game was sold to the public, fear moved to the background and was replaced by bright optimism based on the assumption of a controlled nuclear war. It was also clear that Atari's marketing division wanted its audience to believe in an earth-based setting. One television advertisement, repeatedly broadcast on national TV during the early 1980s, featured a boy in front of a television set attached to an Atari game console. *Missile Command's* missiles streak down the screen toward the six blue towers representing cities; the posted score is 103,665. A mother's whiny voice comes from off-screen: "Dear Atari Anonymous . . . My son Boris has *Missile Command* problems. . . ." Boris, the Atari Boy punching on his console, announces cheerfully: "My mission in life is to save all of mankind."[31]

Missile Command's savior premise, unusually explicit in Atari's advertisement, surfaces repeatedly in the world of shooter games that developed in the 1980s and 1990s. Nintendo's movie-derivative arcade game *RoboCop* takes its setting in a hopeless Detroit besieged by syndicate crime. The instruction manual intones the familiar monomythic perspective on the impotence of government: "The government has thrown up its hands in despair and turned over the police department to the O.C.P. — a private corporation that isn't as squeamish about individual rights as elected officials are."[32] The player gets to take on RoboCop's role as a brutal enforcer of law, confronting killers, the criminals' robot ED-209, and the evil mastermind Dick Jones. With such enemies, the prospects for regular law-enforcement powers are dim: "No flesh-and-blood cop has a chance against those odds. Once upon a time, you didn't either. But that was before you became ROBOCOP."[33] The notion that *you* become the superhero would become a familiar theme in the world of interactive games. Parker Brothers' *G.I. Joe: Cobra Strike* (1983) put it in a similar way: "You as G.I. Joe can protect the recruits with your atomic-powered energy shield. You as G.I. Joe can destroy the Cobra with your missile-firing guns. . . . It's a mission for only a highly trained commando like G.I. Joe — and you."[34]

The endangered-world scenario, with the innocent being politically unable to face down evil, became a dominant theme in the world of game consoles, arcades, and home computers. Provenzo's analysis of forty-seven top-rated Nintendo system games from the 1980s showed that forty used violence as the coping strategy and that "virtually all are based upon the principle of an autonomous individual acting on his or her own."[35] In games like *Platoon,* which takes its plot from Oliver Stone's 1986 film, the vulnerability to death is reduced in several ways, including that one can take "four hits" before dying; and in confronting the game's demand for strategic calculation, one can hit the "pause" button. Many Vietnam veterans felt that Oliver Stone's film accurately represented the terror and the unpredictability of war, but this game's "joystick" permits the restoration of a simpler world with cleaner, more heroic violence.[36] The "player" in this video Vietnam War moves in the direction of the serialized, immortal superhero who always lives again for another adventure in defending the innocent Us from the aggressive Other.

A similar mythic transmutation occurred when the plot of the popular film *Wargames* (1983) was licensed to ColecoVision for an identically titled video game (1984). *Wargames* the movie is a parable about the dangers of accidental nuclear war, and it recycles the *Dr. Strangelove* vision of a zealous, out-of-control military establishment. David, a teenage computer hacker, launches the countdown to Armageddon when he breaks into a Pentagon computer and plays a scenario mistaken as a real attack of the Soviet Union on the U.S. The drama turns on whether David and Professor Falken can "disarm" the strategic computer and dissuade the Pentagon warriors from launching an opportunistic first strike against the USSR. The capsule wisdom of the film emerges when David and Prof. Falken get the unlikely inspiration to make the computer play tic-tac-toe. The computer finally concedes: "A strange game. The only winning move is not to play." By transference, the computer concludes that nuclear exchange would end in a destructive draw.

The ColecoVision game reinstates the moral authority of the military by situating the player as the commander at North American Air Defense Command (NORAD). Somewhat more faithful to the film, this game's initial premise is: "*You* hold the fate of the United States — possibly the world — in your hands. Can you save the world from Doomsday?" And "if your defense is successful, you stop the NORAD computer from launching an ICBM counterstrike that will surely result in the destruction of all mankind." But beyond this starting point, the conventions of mythic innocence and the missile shooter genre seize the game's content. The film's emphasis on diplomatic efforts to prevent the ultimate mistake is replaced in the video game by "contact[ing] the incoming enemy to eliminate that enemy." Every U.S. weapon is construed as "defensive," and every incoming weapon is an "aggressor" — even though the whole affair was started by U.S. mistakes. And after enumerating the points awarded for destroying an "incoming missile" (10,000), "enemy sub" (50,000), and "enemy bomber" (50,000), the manual cheerily announces: "Good Guys Finish First."[37] Any shred of *Wargames* the movie's cautionary parable has been incinerated by the game's defensive blasts.

In parallel fashion, Atari's console version of *Defender* (1982) presents a contrast to the pessimism of *Missile Command*'s scenarios and the catastrophic realism of the arcade rendition. Consider these cheerful modifications to *Defender* announced to those who had first experienced its style of play at the arcade:

In the coin-operated DEFENDER game, two or more Alien Landers can kidnap humanoids simultaneously, whereas in the Atari version, Landers can abduct only one humanoid at a time. In the coin-operated game, you can accidentally kill a humanoid with your own missile fire while attempting a rescue, and even lose a life in Hyperspace. Such tragedies cannot happen in ATARI DEFENDER. ATARI humanoids are invulnerable to missile fire, and Universal Space Ship Defender will always emerge from the Hyperspace intact.[38]

In other words, children can play these nuclear games in the "God mode" of severely reduced vulnerability. The modified game enhances self-esteem and confidence in nuclear warfare through moral reassurance about winning because you are "the Defender."

Aided by the continuing popularity of *Star Wars* and *Star Trek*, games

Lucasarts Entertainment gives its users a comprehensive collection
of film clips, scripts, and background information about the *Star Wars*
universe. It also offers experiences of technology in the "Weapon Comparison
Test Bay." The user plays a simple variant of a shooter game, in which
the Imperial Storm Trooper can be alternately destroyed with a rock,
a Death Star ray, a light saber, etc.

Credit: *Star Wars: Behind the Magic* (2 CD-rom set) © Lucasfilm Ltd. and
Lucasarts Entertainment Company LLC n.d.

of space warfare have survived two decades. *Missile Command* has been identified as a "classic" and remains in circulation with slicker graphics and a rock-and-roll music track (Hasbro Interactive, 1999). The "Ultimate" version — issued on the same disk with the reissued classic — has been updated to reflect the realities of budget politics and high-tech military procurement. If you should succeed in defending the continent and destroying the mothership that brought the attacks, you receive money to use at the "purchasing screen"; there you can buy "Weapons Upgrades" and "Special Weapons" to assure your dominance over those who are hostile toward you. Team play is also possible via local-area network, modem, or the Internet. But the convention of earth's American innocence remains unaltered.[39]

Gunslinging with a Joystick

Although righteous pistols and rifles can be traced back to the Virginian and Buffalo Bill, realistic images of them arrived somewhat late on the video-game screen. The yearning for guns appeared in the themes of the earliest games offered by Atari, but their representations were awkward. Atari's *Outlaw* (1978), for example, featured "gunslingers" who used cumbersome joystick controls to aim and fire a weapon minimally represented on the screen. The instructions convey the remoteness of this experience from having a real handgun in hand: "Push the Joystick forward to move the gunslinger up the screen. Pull the Joystick towards you to move the gunslinger down the screen. . . . When you want to aim the gunslinger's gun, press the red Controller button. Hold the button down while you control the movement of the gunslinger's arm with your Joystick controller."[40]

The field of action for these outlaw guns was a television screen with large areas of solid color and jaggedly fringed human figures, obviously built out of geometrically regular shapes. The slow-moving bullet from the gun had the scale of a softball. These early console and joystick-mediated shooting experiences were feeble simulations of the magical .44 Magnum seen in the *Dirty Harry* movies or the legendary Colt .45 pistol, or even the Derringer pistols or Springfield and Winchester rifles of the Westerns.

Although the early joysticks offered less than visceral shooting pleasures, they sufficed to spur the development of elegantly realistic weapons. By the 1990s, the shooter peripherals included Logitech's complex joystick, the Wingman Force — advertised in a way that made it a target for moral critics:

Psychiatrists say it's important to feel something when you kill. When you kill without feeling, you're just another heartless sociopath. That's why you need Logitech's Wingman Force Joystick. . . . It uses high-precision steel cable drives to create a brutal force feedback experience. Jarring explosions. Shuddering recoils. Centrifugal force. Gravitational pull. Now you can feel them all, and feel them in every fiber of your being. Every sensation. Every vibration. Every mutilation. . . . Push the stick that pushes back. And feel your pain.[41]

Namco's arcade game *Time Pressure* featured a light gun, the Guncon, wired up with a light-beam-directed sight that seemed to have single-pixel accuracy in aiming at the screen and the feel of a gun recoil. But both arcade and home versions of the Sony Playstation gave the sense of shooting at others with precision. The gun-in-hand experience was enhanced by the increased graphic resolution, speed, and three-dimensional spaces for aiming. Most shooter games currently show the weapon to be used at the bottom of the screen. Through such games one learns to see the world framed by a gun sight — in which every object in the field of vision may conceal something that you should shoot at before it kills you.

The advertising for many video games suggests the appeal of audience identification with an immoral or completely amoral role. Eidos Interactive's *Revenant, One Lifetime Isn't Enough* (1999) shows the picture of a muscular, tattooed man carrying a cross-shaped sword with the emblem of a large skull. The caption is: "Jesus rose from the grave to forgive sins. This guy rose to commit them."[42] Interplay's *Carmageddon 2, Carpocalypse Now* pictures a sports car destroying a young girl in the street. A foot protrudes out of the frame with this label: "Carmageddon Victim No. 2,765. 25 points."[43] The central character of *Hitman: CodeName 47* is described as "the best *assassin* of his time, and he turned into a *perfect instrument* destined to fulfill the monstrous dreams of the physician that created him. He . . . performs his tasks with *remarkable precision* and zero remorse."[44] However, examining *The Hitman*'s scenarios for assassination, we find that they reflect traditional America-centric stereotypes of evil enemies who warrant destruction. For example, one "target" to select from a map is Pablo Belisario Ochoa, a drug criminal born in Cali, Colombia, who is dedicated to "the total control of heroin, cocaine, and marijuana production and export in Colombia." One must enter the jungle to kill him and yet avoid shooting the native people one encounters there. Another target is Frantz Fuchs from Linz, Austria, the home neighborhoods of Adolf Hitler and the Mauthausen concentration camp. He is one of the world's most dangerous mercenaries. Lee Hong is Chinese, the son of a man who formed a criminal group during the Boxer Rebellion. These bad guys, who are associated with

Colombian drugs, Hitler, and the Boxer Rebellion's attempt to eliminate foreign control, can surely be killed on assignment with "zero remorse."[45]

The scenarios for *Doom* and *Quake,* the games that claimed so much of the time and attention of Eric Harris and Dylan Klebold, embody plot elements familiar from the American monomyth. *Ultimate Doom* (Eidos Interactive, 1995) presents a heroic character whose moral credentials are that he has defied the command of his Marine unit to protect civilians. "You're a marine, one of the Earth's toughest, hardened in combat and trained for action. Three years ago, you assaulted a superior officer for ordering his soldiers to fire upon civilians. He and his body cast were shipped to Pearl Harbor while you were transferred to Mars, home of the Union Aerospace Corporation."[46] The game player's license to commit mayhem is further enhanced when his unit answers a distress call on Phobos, the site of secret projects. Every other member of his unit is destroyed with background sounds of screams and crunching bones. In this hopeless situation, the lone survivor — the player, of course — must use his fist, pistol, shotguns, chain-guns, rocket launchers, plasma rifles ("fry some demon butt"): "Your mission is to shoot your way through a monster-infested holocaust, living to tell the tale if possible."[47] The beauty of fluid movement through the screens and the technical challenges of doors, elevators, and teleporters can captivate players for hours at a time. But the story arc is invariable: you, the righteous one, are licensed to kill until you die yourself. And you can revive yourself to kill again.

In addition to creating a compelling shooter environment, *Doom* was a breakthrough product in building a worldwide community of players. In December 1993, Id Software's Jay Wilbur collaborated with the University of Wisconsin system operators in releasing a shareware version of the program to the Internet. According to the account of J. C. Herz, 15 million copies of the first two episodes were quickly downloaded; and Id Software quickly sold 150,000 copies of the full commercial version.[48] In addition to launching a software bestseller, Id achieved the innovation of opening its source code to the world of programming-proficient players. Within a few months, the Internet had an alt.doom.games discussion board with more than 10,000 messages. A 90-page FAQ (Frequently Answered Questions) appeared, as did three books on *Doom.*[49] Eric Harris was one of its committed players: *The New York Times* reported that he designed customized *Doom* scenarios that he allegedly made available to other players through the Web.[50] These scenes, including one that purports to be his rendition of Columbine High as a *Doom* setting, continue to circulate on the Web. If authentic, the scene permits the curious to see Columbine as an Eric Harris *Doom* "level," thus perpetuating the fame he sought in his own violent departure from life.

Quake's story has a similarly desperate survival theme that defines all of the player's aggressive behavior as defensive. Here the hero works on "the Slipgate device" at a secret installation: this technology permits instantaneous transport from one location to another. But "an enemy, code-named Quake, is using his own Slipgates to insert death squads inside our bases to kill, steal, and kidnap." You, the hero, get this charge: "You're our best man. This is Operation Counterstrike and you're in charge. Find Quake and stop him . . . or it. . . . You have full authority to requisition anything you need. If the egg-heads are right, all our lives are expendable."[51] What follows is a journey through doors, floor plates, and motion detectors. The enemies are steadily present in the shape of Rottweilers, grunts, death knights, rotfish, ogres, fiends, zombies. *You* get a formidable array of weapons — shotgun, nail gun, perforator, grenade launcher — for killing them. What follows is the righteous, ultimately sacrificial war of one against far too many others. The only reprieve is a "pause" or a "game-over" that permits the player to fight the battle again.

The *Duke Nukem* series, one of the oldest and most popular shooter titles, has deliberately cultivated a big-bad-boy image. One of his trademark slogans is "a babe, a stogie, and a bottle of Jack [Daniels]." He noisily urinates, uses a Microwave Expander to blow up animals, and explodes prostitutes, who turn into a shower of paper currency in *Duke Nukem 3D* (1997). But even Duke receives the warrant to kill through scenarios that define his murderous behavior as responses to the aggression of others. In *Duke Nukem 3D* the circumstance is that "murderous aliens have landed in Los Angeles, and the human race suddenly finds itself atop the endangered species list. Now it's up to Duke Nukem to stop the onslaught against Earth, by doing what he does best — KICKING ALIEN ASS."[52] In *Duke It Out in D.C.,* Duke dials up his patriotism to rescue the commander-in-chief: "After an alien ship crash-landed at the Capitol Building, aliens began a vicious assault destroying critical government buildings, invading national monuments and taking over key military installations. . . . Arriving in D.C., Duke is dropped off on the front lawn of the White House to begin his search for the President."[53] Duke "kicks alien ass" at the Oval Office, the Lincoln Memorial, and other sacred national sites.

Duke Nukem reminds us that government itself is at stake in these games, often the American government. But beyond the everyman-a-hero theme, which permits any player to rescue the world with a joystick, there is seldom any hint of democratic values as guidance for the conduct of war. Nor is there any alarm that those values might be in danger. There is no negotiation and no cooperation — except with other players who become part of the player's killing team. Fittingly for a gun-based genre, the political values reflect what

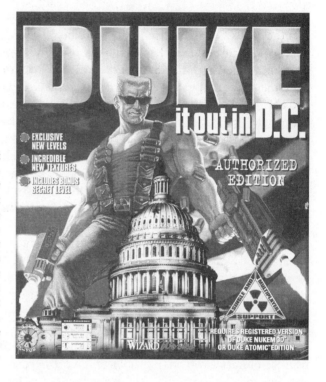

The premise is that Washington is under attack by aliens. Duke — or YOU as Duke — blast away at aliens in the White House, at the Lincoln Memorial, and other important sites in Washington. Since the President has been kidnapped, you must also carry out a rescue.

Credit: Box for *Duke it out in D.C.,* © 1997 Sunstorm Interactive Inc.

Richard Slotkin calls *The Virginian*'s "aristocracy of violence." He reminds us of the chapter in *The Virginian* that Wister entitled "The Game and the Nation," where the Virginian argues against Molly Wood's effeminate version of democracy. She, a mere genteel teacher, insists on equality before the law and abhors the practice of lynching. She cannot see the difference between racist lynching in the South and vigilante lynching on the frontier. For her, the ranch owners are the counterparts of Southern whites, while the cowboys and small farmers are proxy for the blacks. The Virginian answers these objections with a novel interpretation of the country's philosophical origins:

> All America is divided into two classes — the quality and the equality. . . . Both will be with us until women bear nothing but kings. . . .
>
> [T]he Declaration of Independence . . . acknowledged the *eternal inequality* of man. For by it we abolished a cut-and-dried aristocracy . . . [and] decreed that every man should find his own level. By this very decree we acknowledged and gave freedom to true aristocracy, saying 'Let the best man win, whoever he is.' That is true democracy. And true democracy and true aristocracy are the same thing.[54]

In the drama that plays out between the Virginian and Molly, the moral is that the needs of "civilization" transcend the procedural safeguards of a democratic political system. This is the view of the Virginian and his benevolent sponsor, Judge Henry. As Slotkin puts it, "Civilization . . . can be defended from the forces that menace it only by an armed and virile elite that is willing and able to take the law into its own hands and substitute itself for the will of the people." (p. 182) Molly intellectually loses out against this argument in the novel, emotionally accepting the man who believes that frontier social power grows out of the barrel of the gun and the lynch mob.

In the world of shooter games, after a full century of American crusading for democratic values, Molly's side of the argument has disappeared. The firmly established traditions of this genre presume that your finger must always be on the trigger, that you must be ready to kill easily defined enemies, and that you will hesitate only for tactical reasons. It is a world that is completely militarized, but without a command structure or any accountability to political authority. In such a world, the idea of judicial restraint on violence becomes laughable. It is a true aristocracy of violence that even the Virginian would find repellent.

To the extent that women have begun to appear in this shooter world, they do so as caricatures — with cartoonishly erotic bodies. The characteristic pose of Lara Croft from Eidos's *Tomb Raider* is a straight-on view of her scowling face, skinny waist, pneumatic breasts, and two huge guns that she's aiming directly at you. Like other female shooter games, such as *Perfect Dark* (Nintendo, 1999) and ONI (Bungie, 1999), the *Tomb Raider* series wants us to see the incredible buns and boobs, connected by a fragile Barbie waist, in motion. The series and the film *Lara Croft: Tomb Raider* (2001) eliminate the exclusively gunsight view of the world so that we can see hyperbolic female bodies. A woman like Lara does not take up the argument where Molly Wood left off with the Virginian. Instead, she has an arsenal of murderous weapons that allows her to triumph over the evil men unlucky enough to cross her path.

Monomythic Video Games

It is a dictum in the study of popular culture that genre, understood as a collection of character stereotypes and standard settings, largely determines dramatic content. Restating John Cawelti, we could say that convention trumps invention. Given the primitive representational tools of the earliest chip-based games, we can understand how the kinetic appeal of shooting would generate interest among boys and young men. Now the imagery of fighting games has matured to the point that some have inspired commercially successful creations in the older narrative technology of the film. Where the leap from arcade or console to big screen occurs, we see more complete embodiments of the American monomyth.

The phenomenon first occurred with the games *Tron* (1982), *Super Mario Brothers* (1993), *Street Fighter* (1994), *Mortal Kombat* (1995, 1997), and *Wing Commander* (1999). In the decade beginning in 2000, movies are actually being spun off from video games such as *Tomb Raider* and *Duke Nukem*. *Mortal Kombat* was one of the first to undergo this transition. As a story for the screen, it exhibits the full range of mythic premises characteristic of the monomyth. In addition, it is enveloped with an aura of spirituality that suggests religious commitment.

The plot of the *Mortal Kombat* series derives from a situation of danger for all mankind. The world as we know it is threatened by the forces of the Outworld, which is allied with the evil and wizardly master Shang Tsung. In the movie *Mortal Combat* (MK, 1995) we see him brutally beat and gratuitously kill the boy Chan, brother of the heroic Liu Kang, who will eventually confront Shang Tsung. We gradually learn that the masters of the Outworld have arranged ten intergalactic martial arts tournaments. They have imposed the condition that, if they win the tenth — and they have already won nine with an awesomely oversized warrior named Goro — a grim fate indeed will be assigned to the earth and the human race: all will die. As the hideous Shao-Khan evokes the situation in *Mortal Kombat: Annihilation* (MKII, 1997), "You are witness to the dawning of mankind's final days. . . . Bring Rayden and his pathetic mortals to bow at my feet."

Under the leadership of silver-haired Lord Rayden, a Caucasian before whom thousands of Asians bow, a redemptive team of martial artists assembles. Rayden is a Thunder God who commands extraordinary lethal phenomena, yet he cannot directly participate in the tournament's combat. To defend the earth, he has summoned Liu Kang (Taiwanese martial artist), Johnny Boyd (American Kung Fu film star), and Sonya Blade (American "special agent") — all of whom are reluctant and confused about their selection. Rayden defines the stakes by proclaiming that "the essence of mortal combat is not about death, but life. It's about defending the world. . . . The fate of billions will depend on you." This trinity of warriors has been chosen because of "their souls."

Emphasizing purity of character, Rayden exhorts these heroes to examine themselves and find their courage to defend humanity, a demand that is embodied several times in the resistance to the impulse for sexual intimacy. This is bluntly conveyed in two episodes of MKII. Liu Kang is sent on a mission with Princess Kitano, the beautiful 10,000-year-old princess whose kingdom has been ravaged. They must clutch one another as they travel through one of earth's wind tunnels. When they emerge, they realize that they want to kiss each other. Dropping their guard to do so, they are immediately attacked by the Ninja thugs of Outworld. Having failed to discipline his desire, Liu Kang must undergo an even more severe test. As he lies shivering in the snow at a site of his rescue, he is approached by Jade, who shows him her near-naked body. She blows his fingers and talks of her fear of dying alone. They kiss, but then he rejects her, saying, "My heart belongs to another." Jade, who is actually the evil Queen Sindel in disguise, replies, "You are even more pure and faithful than I thought."

Liu Kang and his team prevail in both MK and MKII. The movie is staged as a series of choreographed fight scenes, the counterparts of the game action that makes the computer-based game so engaging for young men. In order to gain a less restrictive rating for the film, producers omitted some of the "fatality moves" that have made the game a target of Senator Joseph Lieberman and other Congressional critics of fantasy violence. We do not see, for example, hearts ripped out or legs yanked off with a horrific splattering of blood. Nor do opponents explode to the accompaniment of cheerful musical riffs. We do witness relentless punching and kicking. The film, like the game, is an equal-opportunity fatality employer in that we witness Sonya Blade kicking an opponent to death in MK.

A significant feature of these movies is the religious symbolism they sometimes employ. It is as if the writers and producers are returning to the biblical origins of this redemptive mythology. Lord Rayden is a Christ figure in both films, a sacrificial figure who organizes the redemption of the world; and he seems intent on bonding together a holy family out of his warriors. After coming back from the dead once and leading the troops who save the world twice, he solemnly says to his team: "Be there for one another; you are family now." But this religious aura in the MK films is hardly unusual in this world of the fighting games. Producers have increasingly borrowed the language of the violent/sacred in developing and marketing their shooter products. Consider, for example, the advertisement for 3DO Company's *Requiem: Avenging Angel:* "You're an angel. Your name is 'Malachi.' That's ancient Hebrew for 'Bad Ass Mother.'" *Requiem: Avenging Angel* immerses you in the ultimate battle between good and evil, with three-dimensional first-person action so intense it transforms "fire and brimstone" into "fire and reload": "Turn enemies to salt, boil their blood, then unleash a flesh-eating plague. Get *Requiem: Avenging Angel*. Because you're a messenger of God. With a high-caliber message."[55]

Another game with a "messenger" theme is *Messiah* (Shiny, 1999), which features an angelic cherub named Bob, who floats to the earth as God's agent and begins to deal with assorted evildoers on earth. Because Bob is an angel, he is not permitted to do violence in his own person; but he may do so after "possessing" the body of someone who's authorized to act in a deadly way. His mission is to fight Satan, who appears in the form of pimps, prostitutes, bad cops, cannibalistic humanoids, and other evildoers.

The advertising pitch for *Populous, The Beginning* (Electronic Arts, 1998) invents its own retributive biblical verse from Populous 11:24: "Pity the mortal that trespasses against you for he shall be set adrift on rivers of fire and his dwellings laid waste." The theme of the game is: "The World is Yours . . . you are a deity. Control the elements and force the world's inhabitants to do your bidding. Build civilizations that revere you, and strike down the nonbelievers."[56] Evoking sanctity for its product, the company advertises a "divine transmission" from its Web site for additional information about the game.

With so many religious evocations, should we anticipate new forms of devotion that parallel the temples of Trekdom and the altars of Elvis? Are these games presenting themselves as guides for the development of life meanings? The mocking rejoinder to this earnest question is, of course, that we should "lighten up" and see that these are a parody of zealous, crusading religions. But the intent to ridicule implies some rejection of the values we are encouraged to laugh at. On the contrary, defenders of the games can be quite zealous about the ethos underlying the games' relentless attacks on evil. Jay Wilbur, one of the principals at Id Software, has helped create and market *Wolfenstein 3D,* a game of killing Nazis, in addition to the *Doom* and *Quake* titles. Asked in 1995 to respond to family-oriented criticisms of his products, he replied as follows:

> We have had our fair share of religious friends ask us about our imagery, which is satanic, but they overlook the object of the game. The player is the good guy in white whose job it is to stop demons, and you have to travel to Hell to do it. Do you have a problem with stopping Satan from his dirty work? Which side are you on?[57]

Assuming that Wilbur is sincere and a fair representative of his profession, this zeal for providing others with experiences of righteous destruction seems to be a motivating faith.

Computers and Democratic Hope

As computers have matured in their dramatic and interactive capabilities, they have become another way of singing the monomythic hymn to the younger generations. Computers stand proudly beside comic books, films, television series, and novels as purveyors of heroes who redeem threatened communities. By and large, the computer-borne forms of the monomyth are starkly simplistic: stories designed more for the quick hand than the thoughtful mind. In this regard, myth becomes a kinetic as well as an emotional experience. But, even though shooters and other forms of fighting games are intensely popular and energizing for the entertainment market, they do not define the limits of computer-based play. *Solitaire* in its myriad forms, Microsoft's *Flight Simulator, Tiger Woods Golf,* and hundreds of other widely experienced games offer mayhem-free challenges to our physical and intellectual skills. And some popular games directly engage the aptitudes required for civic participation and policy making.

An example of a beautifully designed, ecological game is *The Gungan Frontier* (1999), which is based on characters from *Star Wars: Episode I, The Phantom Menace.* Forsaking the blasters, light sabers, and fighter planes that drive the films and other game products from LucasArts Entertainments, *The Gungan Frontier* gives one a planet and a mission — "to successfully build and maintain a new ecosystem on the moon of Naboo."[58] You have responsibilities for creatures and the vegetation they feed on and an imperative to keep those populations in balance with the needs of the humanoids. As tools for tracking the progress, players use devices such as a "probe droid" with "biosensors," "the species indicator," and population graphs. The game creates contingencies such as disease, toxic clouds, moonquakes, and probe droid malfunctions that reinforce the sense of complexity and fragility within an ecosystem.

The best known of the "democratic" game titles are SIMCITY, introduced in 1989, and its many successors — SIMLIFE, SIMEARTH, SIMFARM, SIMCITY 2000, SIMCITY 3000, and, most recently, THE SIMS. These games give players some god-like planning responsibilities for the domains they govern.[59] There are policies to make, finances to raise, factions to placate, crises to solve. In SIMCITY 2000, players deal with the following situations: guiding Charleston through a hurricane and cleaning up afterward; experiencing a terrorist explosion at the Barcelona Games and then coping with the aftermath of calming and restoration; trying to reduce the pollution of Chicago while continuing to develop industry. In THE SIMS (2000), the suite of games evolved beyond public-policy-making scenarios into the creation of

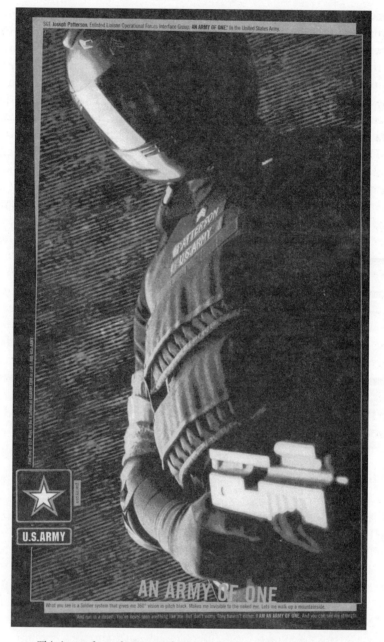

This image from the Army of One campaign presents the soldier, Sgt. Joseph Patterson, as a high-tech warrior with a disguised identity. The comics superhero Spiderman could comfortably wear this uniform.

Credit: Magazine advertisement, U.S. Army.

characters who develop their own personality and interact with one another in family settings. These games never let the player forget the complexities of the real world and the severe difficulty of finding a heroic solution that everyone will applaud. Tim Burke, a cultural historian at Swarthmore College who has studied the impact of THE SIMS, has observed that the issues in these games "can sometimes lead to profound forms of interaction. Even if two players are interacting through a crude medium and manipulating simple characters, sometimes that can spark conversation about life as it is lived."[60]

The SIM games have also developed a following as a successful instructional tool for young people and the basis for academic competitions in creative policy analysis. For example, the National Society of Professional Engineers holds a "Future City Competition" for seventh- and eighth-graders designed to promote interest in engineering and solving transportation problems.[61] The SIMCITY software was used as instructional preparation for the competitors. The games have also been used as discussion starters for real-world policy-makers and as a component in college-level instruction on planning issues.

Like many of the monomythic games, the SIM variants have created a large fan base in an international community of users. However, the SIM fans speak to one another about the problems of making worlds work with democratic methods.[62] When SIMCITY 3000 was released in 1999, it achieved sales of more than one million copies within a few months.[63] For cultures dedicated to intelligence, respect, and compromise, a life-match beats the death-match hands down. It is inspiring to know that a game based on the democratic ethos of debate and compromise can occupy such a prominent niche.

11 *Star Trek's* Humanistic Militarism

"The acquisition of wealth is no longer the driving force in our lives. We work to better ourselves and the rest of humanity."

Picard to Lily Sloan in *First Contact* (1996)

"On Earth there is no poverty, no crime, no war. You look out the window of Starfleet headquarters and you see . . . Paradise. Well, it's easy to be a saint in Paradise."

Sisko to Kira in "The Maquis, Part II," *Deep Space 9*

In popdom's frantic realm, lasting popularity is seldom achieved. But occasionally pop productions achieve a sliver of immortality that stretches into months, years, or even decades. These are the bronzed monuments that stand out amid mountains of evanescent cotton candy. Such artifacts offer significant clues to the human fears and yearnings of their time. Yet the source of their enduring popularity can be puzzling, even to the stars whose performances attract mass adulation. This issue confronts us nowhere more clearly than with the most durable artifact of the past three decades — *Star Trek*. A major source of *Star Trek's* appeal, we shall argue here, is rooted in its fidelity to the American monomythic archetype of plot, character, and communities in peril. *Star Trek* has given its selfless

Captain Jean-Luc Picard presents the demeanor of an obsessive old man in the final episode ("All Good Things") of *The Next Generation*. His intuitions, so puzzling to others, allow him to save all mankind from the very beginning of their existence.

Credit: © Paramount Pictures, 1994.

Star Trek's message of peaceful coexistence is frequently subverted in the films, video games, and comic books. In these frames from DC Comics' "The Tabukan Syndrome," the excitement is based on blowing things up.

Credit: © Paramount Pictures, 1992.

heroes an intergalactic scope of responsibility, benignly joining science with redemptive tasks.

The duty to act as wise and virtuous saviors is the role that spans all the television series and the films. And although *Star Trek* has considerable popularity in our militantly anti-socialistic democracy, its political values amount to a form of "military socialism" that we see operating in the family-oriented teams who guide the voyages. The inner circle of leaders on a starship and their living arrangements bear a clear resemblance to the philosophical "Guardian" class of Plato's *Republic,* a group deprived of private property and individual family relationships: thus freed from material temptations and the demanding distractions of an ordinary family life, the liberated Guardians were to rule society according to the principles of science.[1]

Gene Roddenberry, the visionary and principal creator who inspired all the series, initially produced seventy-nine episodes of *Star Trek* between 1966 and 1969. In a somewhat biblical manner, they have come to be called "The Original Series" (abbreviated to *TOS*). In 1967, NBC, the host network for the original series, was impatient with what it took to be the program's marginal audience. But when it first considered canceling the program, protest mail and a torch-light rally at their Burbank, California, studios in early 1968 forced the network to renew it for one more year.[2] The series evoked, in an unprecedented manner, the development of clubs, advocates from college campuses, and locally produced fan magazines dedicated to keeping the *Star Trek* programming and vision alive. William Shatner, who played the lead role of Captain Kirk, commented on the strange "fanaticism" of the first wave of these fans.

> I really don't understand it. . . . I recently attended two of the "Star Trek" conventions in New York — they have them all over the country, Chicago, Los Angeles, and San Diego. Frankly, it was an experience that was perhaps unique. I was asked to appear in an auditorium of some 8,000 to 10,000 people, there just because of "Star Trek." They were crazed. I don't know why the fanaticism has attached itself to the show. You wouldn't believe what they have at these conventions. . . . Why this is happening defies rational explanation.[3]

Despite these mysterious beginnings, *Star Trek* and its devoted followers went where no television series had ever dreamed of going. After its first death in 1969, the series eventually resurrected itself nearly twenty years later as the largest mythic franchise in the universe. A successor series, *Star Trek: The Next Generation* (*TNG*, 1987-1994), granted Roddenberry larger budgets for actors and special effects and greater authority over the content of program scripts. Following Roddenberry's death in 1991, *TNG* continued and *Star Trek: Deep Space 9* (*DS9*) spun off from 1993 to 1999, as did *Star Trek: Voyager* (*VOY*), from 1995 to 2001. The latest series, *Enterprise,* launched in 2001, is conceived as a prequel to *TOS* and works with many of its character and plot formulas. Paramount also released eight full-length feature films, beginning with *Star Trek: The Motion Picture* (1979), and extending through

Star Trek: Insurrection (1998). Paramount also created a permanent $70 million *Star Trek* theme exhibition called "The *Star Trek* Experience" at the Las Vegas Hilton in 1997. The merchandising of videos, comic books, toys, video games, and novels has meant that most human beings on the planet have likely had some sort of exposure to the characters and themes of *Star Trek*. Measured in television years, where series can be cancelled early in their first season, *Star Trek's* longevity has granted it a kind of Shakespearean permanence.

In addition to achieving mere survival, *Star Trek*, like the Disney productions, traversed the boundary of "mere entertainment" toward a zone of significant cultural influence. In 1976, NASA named its first shuttle the *Enterprise;* part of its strategy was to validate its exploration activities by demonstrating conformity to America's most popular space fiction.[4] The Smithsonian's National Air and Space Museum honored *Star Trek* — and presumably itself — by accepting a replica of the *Enterprise* from Paramount Studios for its permanent collection.[5] And in 1991, the U.S. Postal Service used an image of the *Enterprise* as a special cancellation mark for Space Exploration stamps.[6] Roddenberry received an additional honor when NASA posthumously conferred on him a Distinguished Public Service Medal in 1993. Its citation included this accolade: "For distinguished service to the Nation and the human race in presenting the exploration of space as an exciting frontier and a hope for the future."

In another gesture of appreciation, NASA placed a canister of Roddenberry's ashes on one of the space shuttles.[7] In digital-electronic space, one can now find Web sites constructed by fans in numbers beyond anyone's ability to count. Many of those contain finely detailed descriptions of programs and films, often accompanied by discerning commentaries on the plots, the technologies, the characters, and their relationships to the other creations within the *Star Trek* universe.

Why this dedication? It is widely reported and believed that many of the nation's scientific workers found inspiration for their careers in *Star Trek's* imaginary technologies and intergalactic mission.[8] Students from Cal Tech in Pasadena, one of the nation's premier science technology centers, were prominent among those who formed the "Save *Star Trek* Committee" and led the torch-light parade on January 8, 1968, representing twenty colleges, that marched on the NBC production center. A flummoxed NBC executive, perhaps fearing that the protestors would burn down the studio, denied that a decision had been made to cancel the series.[9] The students' loyalty stemmed in part from their perception that *Star Trek* validated scientific curiosity and made them feel less isolated in a culture that devalues intellectualism. It also created comrades who would share those interests and would engage in fascinating discussions.

From its very beginnings, *Star Trek* provocatively dramatized ideas about time, personal identity, emotion and reason, androids and their inner life, interspecies relationships, future technology, and alternative political forms. It even attracted older adult fans as sophisticated as Arthur C. Clarke, Isaac Asimov, and Stephen Hawking. For those who lacked such philosophical or scientific interests, but were concerned about the intractable conflicts in American life and the Cold War, the program swept several centuries forward, leapfrogging beyond the fears of nuclear or racial Armageddons, and showed a multicultural spectrum of "survivors," confident and happy in their life work together. The accounts of those who have been inspired by *Star Trek* have been legion since the mid-1970s. Fans of the program, including its creator, Gene Roddenberry, believe that the program had abandoned a destructive mythic past in order to affirm a far healthier vision of the future.

While we concede *Star Trek*'s unsurpassed creativity as a serialized program, the camaraderie and quality of its ensemble acting, and its frequently convincing displays of technology, we believe that its imagined ascent into the future is weighed down by its conformity to the conventions of the American monomyth. (We will discuss that continuity in this chapter and postpone until Chapter 12 our detailed discussion of the religious inspirations deriving from *Star Trek*.)

The Message of The Original Series

In identifying the prominent mythic elements that shape the *Star Trek* narratives, we must acknowledge the vastness of this corporate franchise. After the mythic core has been disseminated into so many series and types of merchandise, no one can say anything that applies to everything in *Star Trek*'s world. With the need for a limitless number of stories, *Star Trek* has become like many of the world's religions, except that there are far more candidates for the status of sacred text. Many scholars, modestly aiming for accuracy, have confronted the "essential message" issue in *Star Trek* and limited their gaze to *TOS*, or to *TNG*, or to some combination of television shows and theatrical films that Gene Roddenberry himself ruled over with a high degree of autonomy. Thomas Richards, for example, in his fine book *The Meaning of Star Trek*, announces that he will focus on *TNG*, not because of a particular preference for "its cast or stories, but because the second series represents Gene Roddenberry's vision of the Federation in its full maturity."[10]

Roddenberry's account of studio pressures on *TOS*, heavily documented by correspondence with his corporate managers, illustrates the studio's demands to compromise his vision and to render *TOS* through formulas of the cowboy Western that he no longer accepted. His background as a scriptwriter for cop shows such as *Shannon, The Detectives*, and *Highway Patrol*, and Westerns such as *Have Gun, Will Travel* gave him fluency in the reigning formulas of heroism and justice.[11] His efforts to break away from these stereotypes in *TOS* led to lost battles with his bosses. For example, "Cage," his first pilot program, was rejected because the script used Number One, a female commander of the spaceship. It was not until after his death in 1991 that women such as Katherine Janeway *(VOY)* and Dr. Beverly Crusher *(TNG)*[12] were shown commanding their own ships. These struggles persisted until the end of his life, the last relating to the *Star Trek* movies.[13] In addition to these compromises in the narrative vision, Paramount's aggressive licensing of toy weapons — video games that are nothing more than first-person shooters — adds another dimension of incoherence with Roddenberry's humanist vision of cooperative tolerance.

While we acknowledge all these complexities about what truly belongs to the Roddenberry–*Star Trek* corpus, we find significant American mono-mythic continuities extending from the older cowboy stories central to the archetype through each of the series and films, up to the final episode of *VOY* in 2001. Although there are important changes in the tone and message of the series, we believe that *Star Trek* has consistently remained true to mythic elements that originally "built the franchise." We accordingly devote more attention to *TOS* than to the successor shows.

Star Trek's American Mission in The Original Series

In *TOS*, the United Starship *Enterprise* is on a five-year mission to explore the galaxy. She is one of twelve starship-class spaceships under orders of the United Federation of Planet Earth, with a crew of 430 men and women and a gross weight of 190,000 tons. Since her speed on space-warp drive far exceeds that of light, the *Enterprise* explores and carries out her own assignments, making only infrequent contact with Federation authorities. Given this format, the episodes permit the *Enterprise* to intervene on her own initiative in the affairs of other planets, playing the role of cosmic sheriff, problem-solver, and plenipotentiary.

The leader of this semi-autonomous space probe is Captain James T. Kirk, the youngest man ever to be assigned a starship command, brilliant and irresistibly attractive to early female fans, and a hard-driving leader who pushes himself and his crew beyond human limits. He always leads the landing party on its perilous missions to unexplored planets, but, like a true superhero, regularly escapes after risking battle with monsters or enemy spaceships.

Kirk's main cohort, Mr. Spock, is cut even more clearly from superhero material. He is half-human and half-Vulcan, which gives him, in the well-chosen words of enthusiastic fans, "extra-keen senses, prodigious strength, an eidetic memory, the capacity to perform lightning calculations, telepathy, imperturbability, immunity to certain diseases and dangers, vast knowledge — especially of science."[14] As played by Leonard Nimoy, Spock is a strong, ascetic character of pure rationality, his emotions kept strictly under control by his Vulcan temperament. The emotional tension is hinted at by his slightly Satanic appearance, including pointed ears. A Spock feature that fascinated the early female "fanzine" writers of the stories is *pon farr*, the periodic rutting season which renders all Vulcan minds powerless and threatens death if union with an appropriate partner is not achieved. Nimoy reported that the question of Spock's extraordinary sex appeal emerged "almost any time I talked to somebody in the press. . . . I never give it a thought . . . to try to deal with the question of Mr. Spock as a sex symbol is silly."[15]

All the remarkable powers of Spock, Kirk, and their crew are required to deal with the adversaries of the good ship *Enterprise*. The original *Star Trek* universe includes two vicious races of bad guys: the "Romulans" are similar to the Vulcans in ability and technological development but are "highly militaristic, aggressive by nature, ruthless in warfare, and do not take captives"; the "Klingons" are even worse, though less intelligent. David Gerrold, an early scriptwriter for *TOS*, offered this delightful description: "Klingons are professional villains. They are nasty, vicious, brutal, and merciless. They don't bathe regularly, they don't use deodorants or brush their teeth. . . . A Klingon is a good person to invite to a rape — or even a murder, provided it's not your own. . . . Klingons build their battlecruisers without toilets . . . drop litter in the streets . . . pick their teeth in public. And those are their good points. . . ."[16] Clearly such villains are "more symbolic than individual," threatening the peace of the galaxy in a way that requires constant vigilance by the *Enterprise*. In the evolution of *Star Trek*, the Klingons eventually became more tolerable, particularly in the heroic characters of Worf *(TNG, DS9)* and the half-Klingon B'Elanna Torres *(VOY)*. Roddenberry had eventually concluded that the *TOS* Klingons were a convenient but crude mistake — favored by "writers who tended toward bad guys/good guys 'hack' scripting."[17] But despite Roddenberry's professed aversion to bipolar moral thinking, Klingons retained their tendency to relapse into wicked hostility; they nearly destroy the medical ship *Pasteur* in *TNG*'s final episode, "All Good Things." Their intractability in the expanding universe is matched by that of the Romulans, the Cardassians, and the most terrifying of all — the Borg, with their vicious Queen and pathetic hive mind.

To counter these threats and to cope with the weird and aggressive powers that seem to inhabit so many earth-like planets of the universe, the *Enterprise* of *TOS* acts as galactic redeemer in episode after episode. As Gerrold explains, "The *Enterprise* IS a cosmic 'Mary Worth,' meddling her way across the galaxy . . . to spread truth, justice, and the American Way to the far corners of the universe."[18] The format of *Star Trek* accentuates this role by keeping Kirk and his ship out of communication with Earth. The captain becomes "the sole arbiter of Federation law wherever he traveled . . . a law unto himself." The stories of *TOS* thus fit the genre of the isolated zealous hero or nation, answerable only to a higher law and fighting for right whenever called to do so, a theme America has tried to act out repeatedly. And like a sophisticated American, Captain Kirk does not allow himself to become "paranoid" about the enemies who are out to get him or the planets he must destroy in the fray. In the view of early, enthusiastic fans who took the U.S. Strategic Air Command's slogan[19] to heart, Kirk's "enemy is an adversary to be met with strength and even destroyed, if necessary, but not necessarily a villain with whom no reconciliation is possible. Peace really is his [Kirk's] profession. . . ."[20]

The moral vision of *Star Trek* in its original incarnation thus partook of *Pax Americana*'s spirit and rhetoric. Its basic moral principle is zeal for the mission.[21] This is in effect what the authors Lichtenberg, Marshak, and Winston celebrate in their early, comprehensive fan book *Star Trek Lives!* They affirm an admirable "equality of moral stature" on the parts of Spock and Kirk: "Each of them is that rarest of all things among men: a man of unbroken integrity . . . each remains dedicated to the striving, extravagantly willing to pay the price."[22] But when we measure this moral quality against standards forbidding deceit, adultery, and violence, we are struck by the lack of restraint. What we have here is moral zeal attached solely to the mission and to a particular vision of what amounts to "the American Way." It is a zeal transcending both due process and the moral code of the Federation's own "noninterference directive," which Kirk has sworn on pain of death to uphold. This directive is consistently broken in *Star Trek* episodes when it is "necessary" to do so for the fulfillment of the mission. It was thus an effective format for reinstating in the realm of fantasy some of the American values that floundered in the 1960s against ugly obstacles in Vietnam. Dedication to the ideals would alone suffice, in fantasy if not in reality: zeal for one's own value system justifies the intervention in someone else's. One episode that Gerrold claims is patterned after the *Pueblo* incident bears the message "that the ends justify the means; because if our ends are just, then no matter what means we choose, our means will be just too."[23] It is understandable that fans Lichtenberg, Marshak, and Winston would admire this kind of "fierce dedication, each to his own philosophy and vision of life, and the integrity of character that supports that dedication."[24]

The impact of this kind of uncompromising zeal on other cultures is worth noting. Gerrold writes that the cumulative message of the original *Star Trek* is that "if a local culture is tested and found wanting in the eyes of a starship captain, he may make such changes as he feels necessary."[25] This view was explicitly worked out as an apologetic for the Vietnam War in a backward time-travel episode entitled "The City on the Edge of Forever." McCoy has given himself an injection that results in his disoriented wandering around in the year 1930. Coming to his rescue, Kirk encounters and falls in love with a woman pacifist named Edith Keeler. When Spock looks into her background through newspaper research, he discovers that she will lead a peace movement that will delay U.S. entry into the war. The logical conclusion comes when Spock says, "Jim, Edith Keeler must die." Kirk performs the deed that ultimately allows for the twenty-third century of *Star Trek*'s world.

H. Bruce Franklin, who studied the production history of that episode, questioned the producer, Robert Justman, about it. Was it "consciously intended to have the contemporaneous anti-Vietnam-war movement as subtext?" he asked. Justman replied: "Of course we did."[26] And this episode was followed by "A Private Little War," where Kirk and McCoy have witnessed a war on the planet Neural between unequally armed participants and recall "twentieth-century brush wars on the Asian continent." Kirk comments: "Two giant powers were involved, much like the Klingons and ourselves. Neither side felt that they could pull out." They eventually decide that they must intervene with armaments for the weaker side so that the resulting parity will result in the preservation of both. This episode appeared to be a symbolic affirmation of Cold War power politics.[27]

The correlations between the *Star Trek* format and some tragedies in American history are troublesome and painful, especially for those who happen to enjoy the élan and imagination of this series and its successors. And in fairness to *TOS*, the stance of apologetics for the Vietnam war changed quickly after the Tet Offensive of 1968. With "Omega Glory" (March 1, 1968), written by Gene Roddenberry, we visit the planet Omega IV, where a war without end rages between the dark-skinned "Kohms" and the lighter-skinned "Yangs" — Commies and Yankees, as Kirk and Spock deduce. This becomes even clearer when we see that the Yangs carry a tattered flag, their "Omega glory." But, as H. Bruce Franklin puts it, "Forgetting all the principles for which they were fighting in their endless war against the Communists, these Yankees have become savage barbarians teetering on the edge of bestiality. All they have left of the great American ideals are their worship words, garbled versions of the Pledge of Allegiance and the Preamble to the Constitution of the United States, which they recite as mere sacred gibberish."[28] The episode ends when Kirk takes the Preamble, reads it with emphasis on "We the people," chastising them for their inhuman zeal that results in the denial of rights. *Star Trek*'s creators had quickly devised a clever putdown of what they had so recently defended.

Given such an episode, it would be absurd to label a series such as *Star Trek* as a mere apologetic for the debacle of Vietnam. What fascinates us is the peculiar commitment this series evoked from its earliest, most dedicated fans. Richard Slotkin's concept of "national mythology" provides an important clue. As we observed in our chapter on the American monomyth's birth, he shows how the historical experience of a nation provides metaphors and stories that assume mythic proportions in literature and art, so that the resulting myth exercises a reciprocal pressure on succeeding generations. It shapes the sense of reality and is itself reshaped by subsequent experience. Thus national mythologies may come to exercise the same unconscious appeal as the archetypal myths of which they are variants.[29]

Despite the quality and sophistication of much that was done in the original *Star Trek* and its successors, there is much that appears to be a reworking of traditional American ideology. However, as one might expect with creations of this sophistication, there is a hitch to linking any notion of myth with the original *Star Trek* series.

- -

Star Trek's Antimythic Bias and Its Own Mythic Ingredients

On the surface level, the *TOS* stories seem to defy interpretation as mythic. The series frequently takes a singularly dim view of myths, not to mention legends, fables, and their primitive religious accoutrements. *Star Trek* celebrates the freeing of the human spirit from superstition and narrow-mindedness. It wears the cloak of empirical science. It purports to be a future chapter in what Joseph Campbell called "the wonder story of mankind's coming to maturity." Campbell, the famous historian of world myths, argues that, with the coming of the scientific age, mankind has been set free from myths. "The spell of the past, the bondage of tradition, was shattered with sure and mighty strokes. The dream-web of myth fell away; the mind opened to full waking consciousness; and modern man emerged from ancient ignorance, like a butterfly from its cocoon, or like the sun at dawn from the womb of mother night."[30] Producer Gene Roddenberry surely agreed with Campbell in his moments of confidence in science. The antimythic bias in *TOS* is clearly visible in the following episode.

"Who Mourns for Adonais?"[31]

The U.S.S. *Enterprise* is approaching an unexplored M Class planet when an immense masculine face appears on the scanner screen and stops the ship in midspace with a tremendous exertion of energy. Captain Kirk leads the exploration party of Spock, Chekov, McCoy, Scott, and the ravishingly beautiful archaeologist Carolyn Palamas. They find themselves in a Greek-like temple complex. A magnificently muscular man, whose face they had seen on the scanner, rises to greet them with the words, "I am Apollo. . . . You are here to worship me as your fathers worshipped me before you." When Kirk asks what he requires, he insists that he is Apollo and demands "loyalty," "tribute," and "worship" in return for a "human life as simple and pleasureful as it was those thousands of years ago on our beautiful Earth so far away."

"We're not in the habit of bending our knees to everyone we meet with a bag of tricks," Kirk replies.

When they refuse obeisance, Apollo's wrath melts their phaser guns and injures Scott, who has attempted to protect Carolyn from Apollo's amorous advances. But Carolyn volunteers to go with Apollo, and she quickly falls in love with him. Captain Kirk theorizes that an unknown race capable of space travel had come to ancient Greece with the ability "to alter their shapes at will and command great energy." This theory is corroborated by Apollo's explanation to Carolyn:

"Your fathers turned away from us until we were only memories. A god cannot survive as a memory. We need awe, worship. We need love."

"You really consider yourself to be a god?" Carolyn asks.

He laughs: "In a real sense we were gods. The power of life and death was ours. When men turned from us, we could have struck down from Olympus and destroyed them. But we had no wish to destroy. So we came back to the stars again."

After making love to Carolyn, Apollo returns to the other members of the crew. The enraged Scott attacks him, only to be struck down with the blue-hot streak that lashes from Apollo's finger. This provokes Kirk to declare war on the god; but Apollo strikes him down as well. When Apollo disappears to recharge his power source, they decide to attack him in hopes of wearing him down. The *Enterprise* crew meanwhile prepares to fire phasers against Apollo's force field. When Carolyn appears again, Kirk tries to cope with her infatuation.

The lovely archaeologist relates Apollo's message: "He wants to guard . . . and provide for us the rest of our lives. He can do it."

"You've got work to do," Kirk reminds her.

"Work?" Carolyn replies.

Kirk insists: "He thrives on love, on worship. . . . We can't give him worship. None of us, especially you. . . . Reject him! You must!"

"I love him!"

"All our lives, here and on the ship, depend on you."

"No! Not on me."

"On you, Lieutenant. Accept him — and you condemn the crew of the *Enterprise* to slavery!"

She stares at him blankly.

Kirk pleads with her to remember "what you are! A bit of flesh and blood afloat in illimitable space. The only thing that is truly yours is this small moment of time you share with the rest of humanity. . . . That's where our duty lies. . . . Do you understand me?"

Carolyn comes to her senses when she discovers that Apollo will not accept her liberated intellectual interests. This time the god lashes out in fury at her. But the incandescing phaser beams from the *Enterprise* strike his power source just in time, reducing him to a "man-size being."

"I would have loved you as a father his children," Apollo says, in anguish. "Did I ask so much of you?"

Kirk's reply is gentle: "We have outgrown you. . . . You asked for what we can no longer give."

Denied the worship so necessary for his being, Apollo's body begins to lose substance, and for the first time he admits that the time of the gods "is gone. Take me home to the stars and the wind."

This episode bears the clear message that the era of myths is over, that retreating into slavery to the gods of the past would be terrible. Moreover, the episode suggests that the ancient myths can be scientifically explained by assuming that space travelers played the role of gods. The episode implies that meaning is purely of this world; it denies any threshold to mysterious, transcendent reality. In contrast to the illusive message of myths and religions, the meaning of Carolyn Palamas' life is simply her "duty" to the only reality of which she can be sure, the "humanity" she shares. This conviction of Captain Kirk fits the spirit of the entire series. It is unthinkable that he or his crew, not to mention the strictly scientific Spock, would give credence to myths for a moment.

Yet the story line of this and other episodes follows a mythic pattern. David Gerrold defined *Star Trek* as "a set of fables — morality plays, entertainments, and diversions about contemporary man, but set against a science-fiction background. *The background is subordinate to the fable.*"[32] This can be documented at those points in which dramatic coherence — that is, hewing to the mythic story line — caused scriptwriters to depart from the standards of scientific accuracy. For instance, the attractive young crew of the *Enterprise* never ages despite journeys through the light-year distances of outer space. Members of the bridge crew are regularly shaken off their seats by enemy torpedoes despite the fact that shock waves would not carry past a spaceship's artificial-gravity field. These scientific liberties are taken for dramatic effect, creating "action, adventure, fun, entertainment, and thought-provoking statements."[33] These are actually mythical elements that appeal to an audience schooled in a particular mythical tradition.

When we compare the themes of the *Star Trek* series with the content of classical myths, we immediately see similarities. Isolating such content from the genesis and function of myths, we point to three patterns that appear in "Who Mourns for Adonais?" The first is *saga,* which features a protagonist journeying to unknown and dangerous regions and undergoing trials to test his strength and wit. In the classical monomyth, delineated by Joseph Campbell, a human undertakes a journey in response to the requirement to move from childhood to maturity through "the crooked lanes of his own spiritual labyrinth."[34] But in materials embodying the American monomyth, the saga of maturation tends to be replaced by the defending of innocent communities against malevolent attacks.

Gene Roddenberry's original prospectus for *Star Trek,* featuring the format of "Wagon Train to the Stars," aims at saga. He planned the series to be "built around characters who travel to other worlds and meet the jeopardy and adventure which become our stories."[35] This correlates with the announcement at the beginning of *Star Trek* episodes that the mission of the *Enterprise* is "to explore strange new worlds, to seek out new civilizations, to boldly go where no man has gone before."[36] Thus in the episode about Apollo's planet, the *Enterprise* had to be mortally endangered by the gigantic face on its scanner, and it was essential for protagonists Kirk and Spock to leave their command posts and come face to face with the foe. It was obviously bad military and space-travel strategy, as many critics have pointed out.

No sensible commander would have sent himself and the key technical officers on a landing party like that. But it is essential to the saga format and thus is characteristic of almost every episode.

The final episode of *TNG*, "All Good Things," illustrates this characteristic in a delightful confrontation with the trickster figure Q, whose superiors have decreed the destruction of humanity. However, if Jean-Luc Picard can discover the puzzling phenomenon and figure out how to neutralize it, humanity can be spared a few more cosmic moments. For this prodigious feat, Picard must coordinate his actions through the Federation at three different time periods in his life history — past, present, and future. The "time-shifting" nature of his own puzzling affliction permits him this fantastic mobility through time and space.

The Mythic Call of Sexual Renunciation

The second mythic pattern visible in "Who Mourns for Adonais?" — and one very characteristic of the American monomyth — is sexual renunciation. The protagonists in some mythical sagas must renounce previous sexual ties for the sake of their trials. They must avoid entanglements and temptations that inevitably arise from satyrs, sirens, or Loreleis in the course of their travels. Thus Lt. Palamas is tested in the episode with Apollo: her sexual liaison endangers the survival of the *Enterprise*. After she renounces her passion, the saga can get back on course. In the classical monomyth this theme plays a subsidiary role in the initiation or testing phase. The protagonist may encounter sexual temptation symbolizing "that pushing, self-protective, malodorous, carnivorous, lecherous fever which is the very nature of the organic cell," as Campbell points out.[37] Yet the "ultimate adventure" is the "mystical marriage . . . of the triumphant hero-soul with the Queen Goddess" of knowledge.[38] In the current American embodiments of mythic renunciation there is a curious rejection of sexual union as a primary value.

In *Star Trek* each hero is locked into a renunciatory pattern closely related to the mission. On long expeditions in outer space, for example, there is no intrinsic reason why the captain would not be accompanied by his wife and family. In fact, it was a customary practice for the masters of some large sailing vessels in the era of extended voyages. But that would violate the mythic paradigm. So Roddenberry describes the renunciation pattern: "Long ago Captain Kirk consciously ruled out any possibility of any romantic interest while aboard the ship. It is an involvement he feels he simply could never risk. In a very real sense he is 'married' to his ship and his responsibilities as captain of her."[39] In numerous episodes Kirk is in the situation Carolyn Palamas faced, forced to choose between an attractive sexual partner and his sense of duty to his mission. The authors of *Star Trek Lives!* report that female fans

> . . . vicariously thrill to Kirk's sexual exploits with gorgeous females of every size, shape and type — from the stunning lady lawyers, biologists and doctors who have loved him, to the vicious and breathtaking Elaan of Troyius, who ruled a planet but was willing to risk destroying her entire solar system for him. . . . Many see Kirk's loves as having a tragic element. There is affection and warmth in his response, and evidently the capacity for deep love. But very often the situation is impossible. He loses not through his faults but through his virtues, because of the demanding life he has chosen.[40]

They go on to describe Kirk's renunciation of sexual bonds for the sake of loyalty to the *Enterprise* and its crew: "Time and again, he had to make a choice between a woman and his ship — and his ship always won" (p. 151).

One episode of *TNG*, "The Inner Light," works out this connection between redemption and renunciation in opposition to familial commitment with great explicitness. The *Enterprise* is minding its own business when an apparently primitive "probe" begins to shadow it, eventually sending a shower of nucleons that causes Captain Picard to faint. As the crew examines him and tries to find a way to break the "beam" that has seized him, Picard begins to have experiences on another planet, Kataan, in a community called Ressic. Initially disoriented, he gradually realizes that he is having the experience of another man, Kamin, an "ironweaver" who has had a wife, Eline, for three years. After initial hesitations about going to bed with her, Picard fully accepts his role as her husband, responds to her desire to have children, fathering a son and daughter, and becomes an accepted member of his new community. Reflecting on his several years of experiencing these new human riches, Picard says to Eline: "I always believed that I didn't need children to complete my life. . . . Now, I couldn't imagine life without them."

At that moment, the crew members caring for Picard on the *Enterprise* break the beam, causing his counterpart on Kataan to experience a tremor and collapse. Crew members attending Picard's "original" body on the *Enterprise* decide that the beam must be re-established to stabilize him. Years more pass and Picard becomes a grandfather. As a citizen of Kataan, he gradually discovers that the planet is dying — a secret that the authorities have hidden. The episode is resolved in a peculiar twist of time. At a rocket-launching on the planet, a deceased friend, Batai, and Picard/Kamin's dead wife reappear in the flush of health. Responding to Picard's puzzlement, Batai tells him: "We hoped that our probe would find someone in the future, someone who could be a teacher, someone who would tell the others about us." Picard acknowledges that "I'm the someone it finds. That's what this launching is, a probe that finds me in the future." Having saved Kataan and safely retreated back to the *Enterprise,* Picard awakes after a mere 20-25 minutes of coma and is led to the medical facility by Dr. Crusher. The symbolic message here is: Picard may experience some of the pleasures of family, but they are subordinate to his planet-saving mission. His place is on the bridge of the *Enterprise,* not sitting at hearth with family responsibilities.

This renunciation of sexual love for the sake of loyalty to one's comrades goes far beyond the classical monomyth. It is seen perhaps most clearly in the person of Spock. He is loyal to Kirk and his comrades to the point of risking his life for them again and again, but he persistently resists the temptation of entanglements with the opposite sex. Nurse Christine Chapel, a beautiful, talented crew member who is hopelessly in love with Spock, gets the cold shoulder from him in episode after episode. Here is a man who is "capable of the prodigious outpouring of passion triggered by the irresistible *pon farr* and yet incapable of lasting emotional ties" with women.[41] Sex is an autonomous force here, distinct from Spock's personality and capable of destroying his ability to reason. Since he cannot integrate it with his personality, he must rigidly repress it until it overpowers him in the rutting season. Spock bears within his person the temptation that threatens every saga with disaster: he must fiercely renounce the temptation for the mission to succeed. Such a motif may not be true to life, and it is certainly improbable that there are sophisticated planets with *pon farr* rites derived from Puritan fantasies. But it is true to the paradigm of the American monomyth.

As the series matured in the more sexually liberated 1980s and 1990s, *Star Trek's* writers kept finding ways to keep their leaders hermetically sealed from intimacy. The film *Star Trek VII: Generations* contains several moments in which both Kirk and Picard meditate on their value system that excludes permanent partnerships with women and the families that might result. Picard reveals to the counselor Troi that his brother's children have died and that he is depressed because he had always thought they would carry on the family name. Now the name will die with him. Somewhat later, Picard's *Enterprise* is threatened by the Nexus, a "temporal disturbance" that can generate pleasant illusions for those who fall within its field. Picard drifts into the fantasy that he's having Christmas with his own large family; but he snaps out of it, realizing that his duty is real and this family is not.

Back at the bridge, the *Enterprise* battles against the Klingons near the planet Veridian III; in an abandon maneuver, Picard's saucer section crashes on its surface. Safely landed, Picard is led by the spirit of the guide figure Guinan to find Captain Kirk, who did not die as presumed in an accident seventy-eight years earlier; rather, he is living as a contented farmer in Iowa with "Antonia" and some rather satisfying horses. Picard, intent on recruiting heroic assistance, hectors him about duty, about the need for his participation in a rescue operation. Eventually, Kirk concedes that "Antonia isn't real." And he confesses his longing for the call of the old duties on the bridge: "Maybe it's about the empty chairs on the bridge of the *Enterprise*." He leaves "Antonia" and helps Picard defeat Zoran, who is only moments away from killing 240 million people. After Zoran's defeat, the dying Kirk asks, "Did we make a difference?" Of course they did.

And so did Captain Kathryn Janeway, also married in a lonely way to her ship in the *Voyager* series. In an interview with Jeff Greenwald, Kate Mulgrew, who plays the Janeway character, fiercely defended the need of her character to resist sexual intimacy: "Janeway wouldn't risk it. She loves the crew too much. I love the ship too much. I simply couldn't jeopardize it."[42] Only Captain Benjamin Sisko, who commands a static space station in *DS9*, is permitted to have a family; but, predictably, his wife has been dead for several years.

All of these triumphs of renunciatory duty over sexuality in *Star Trek* reflect Gene Roddenberry's philosophical views about the possibilities of intimacy. In an extended interview with Yvonne Fern, he explained:

> Romance is a product of not knowing each other. Friendship develops when you know each other. . . . Sex is not germane to intimacy. . . . Two men can be more intimate than a man and his wife. Or two women. Or a man and a woman who understand one another, perhaps share one another's dreams, but have no wish to live together or to share their bodies with one another.[43]

Extending an essentially platonic notion of "true love" to the *Star Trek*–type settings, Roddenberry argues against marriage. When Fern asked, "So when do two people marry?" he responded:

> I think they don't, in a perfect world. I don't think there's that kind of mutual possession. Marriage in the form that it is now cannot possibly continue into the future. That's why we have so little of it in *Star Trek*.[44]

And then he added: "I think if we all lived in my *Star Trek* world, it would be pretty close to heaven." Thus the lonely duty of being married to the ship, in

Star Trek's ethos, is not a deprivation but a perfection. The duties of the bridge permit deeply satisfying friendships, unimpeded by the attractions and distractions of human desire and human bodies. As Batman might say, "Holy saintliness!"[45]

This skepticism about marriage as a possessiveness that works against military friendship is allied to the frequent sense that family authority must be rejected to permit Federation duty, that this duty is a higher calling than mere family can understand. When family members come into the vicinity of heroic crew members, they are disruptive and embarrassing. Deanna Troi's mother, Lwaxana, is domineering in the extreme. Deanna confronts her with these angry words in "Ménage à Troi" *(TNG):* "Mother, look. Perhaps some day I will marry. But you have to let me make my own choices, live my own life, and not the life that you would choose for me." Data, the positronic, humanoid-android officer of *TNG*, has an evil twin, "Lore." And in *Star Trek V: The Final Frontier* (1989), Spock has a wicked brother, "Sybok," a religious charlatan who almost destroys them.

We see enabling/crippling family dynamics worked out in some detail with the *VOY* episode "Tattoo," where Commander Chakotay explores his Native American roots as a descendant of Central American "Rubber Tree People." The background story shows him during a trip into the rain forest with his father. Chakotay expresses the idea that he is a "contrary" among his people since he believes that they "live in the past and myth." His father deeply disapproves of his decision to become a Starfleet cadet and predicts that he will be "caught between two worlds." This particular strand of the story emphasizes the idea that the Federation officer has the character to defy family authority to become a cadet. As the story works toward its resolution, Chakotay does use his native jungle lore to save his party from destruction when they encounter his ancestral people, initially hostile until they are reassured by his knowledge of them.

In this distancing from the threats that families pose to the spiritual perfection of the Federation military command, *Star Trek* stands with the Buddha, who abandoned his family in his search for enlightenment; it also stands with the spirit of Jesus' response to Peter, who has assured him that "we have left everything and followed you." Jesus replies that the disciples will receive much greater rewards than the bonds of family: "Truly I tell you, there is no one who has left house or brothers or sisters or mother or father or children or fields, for my sake and for the sake of the good news, who will not receive a hundredfold now in this age . . . and in the age to come eternal life" (Mark 10:29-30, NRSV). Those who leave behind their earthly attachments for the life of *Star Trek* will harvest the heavenly friendships that transcend the ordinary intimacies of sexual commitment and family.

Redemption

The third mythical pattern running through the episodes of *Star Trek* is *redemption*. In the classical monomyth, the beautiful maiden must be redeemed from the clutches of the sea monster, the endangered city spared from its peril, and the protagonist redeemed by fateful interventions in the nick of time. This pattern is much more diffuse in the classical monomyth than in the modern materials that lie closer to the American pattern. A classical hero may experience supernatural assistance as he crosses the threshold into the realm of initiatory adventure and then returns; and he may confront trials embodying the redemption of others. But his own redemption takes the form of gaining mature wisdom, achieving atonement with his father, enjoying union with the goddess, and returning home with benefits for his people. The redemption scheme in materials such as *Star Trek* has nothing to do with the maturation process; rather, it fits the pattern of selfless crusading to redeem others. This form of selfless idealism has been elaborated most extensively by Ernest Tuveson in *Redeemer Nation*.[46] As happens so frequently in American history, the *Enterprise*'s sense of high calling leads it to violate its own "noninterference directive." If Kirk and his crew encounter an endangered planet, their sense of duty impels them to intervene. It may not be legal, or right, or even sensible; but the zealous imperative to redeem is pervasive in *TOS*. While Gerrold overstates it in claiming that among the seventy-nine *Star Trek* episodes, "there never was a script in which the *Enterprise*'s mission or goals were questioned,"[47] he has accurately described the series as a whole.

This observation should be counterbalanced by the awareness that *Star Trek*'s selfless crew never interfered with a culture in the spirit of conquest. They always intervened merely to set things right before they flew away in their spacecraft. In the successor series, the writers became more self-conscious about violations of the Prime Directive and worked harder at maintaining the noninterventionist posture. But as Thomas Richards clearly explains, it is questionable whether nonintervention — apart from its dramatic undesirability — is even possible: "Behind the Prime Directive is the idea that it is possible to observe a society without affecting it."[48] *TNG* plays very self-consciously with this notion in its episode "Who Watches the Watchers?" The Federation has established a "duck blind" that permits it to observe a primitive society. When their presence is accidentally revealed, a chain of events compels them to realize that they have probably changed the society merely by making their presence known.

But the more usual role of the *Enterprise*, especially in *TOS*, is to intervene and to redeem some primitive society that has violated American norms of freedom and the challenge of self-development. Mr. Spock embodies the redemptive role in a particularly powerful way. His half-Vulcan origin makes him a godlike figure, peculiarly capable of effecting benevolent transformations. Spock consults his computer with superhuman speed to devise techniques for saving galaxies and men from prodigious threats, leading the audience to view him with a reverence that traditionally has been reserved for gods. Leonard Nimoy's interview, approvingly cited by the authors of *Star Trek Lives!*, points toward audience yearnings for an omniscient redeemer. The viewer sees Spock as someone

> . . . who knows something about me that nobody else knows. Here's a person that *understands* me in a way that nobody else understands me. Here's a person that I'd like to be able to spend time with and talk to because *he would know what I mean when I tell him how I feel*. He would have insight that nobody else seems to have. . . .[49]

In short, Spock is perceived as a god, which matches the requirements of the mythical pattern, namely that without a superhuman agency of some sort, there is no true redemption.

Captain Jean-Luc Picard carried the world-redemption theme to its fullest realization in the above-mentioned final episode of *TNG*, "All Good Things." But here it occurs with some irony, because the imminent destruction of the world was caused by an action of the *Enterprise* in bombarding an anomaly with "inverse tachyon beams" that set time rolling backward to destroy the primal soup that made all life possible. So, just as the future can be nullified by careless acts in the present, the past that made the present is pathetically susceptible to aggressively used tachyons. Q chastises Picard, who wants to hold *him* responsible: "I am not the one who causes the annihilation of mankind. You are!" Afflicted by his newly discovered anxiety that he alone is responsible for the whole world's past, present, and future — and that he alone can save it — Picard struggles and juggles his roles at three moments in history. Just when everything seems to crash into nullity despite his efforts, Q presents himself again to tell him that it's over — but only for the moment. Picard has survived this existential challenge, which Q defines for him in this way:

We wanted to see if you had the ability to expand your mind and your horizons, and for one brief moment you did. . . . For that one fraction of a second, you were open to options you'd never considered. That's the exploration that awaits you, not mapping stars and studying nebulae, but charting the unknown possibilities of existence.

In this moment of epiphany, when a god of chance reaffirms Picard's role as world redeemer, he seems to learn that he may have to save the world over and over again. A daunting task, but more prestigious than Sisyphus' job of endlessly pushing the boulder up a hill.

The Foreshortened Democracy of *Star Trek*

A final mythic feature to note in *Star Trek* is its utopianism. The escapist appeal to its fans is the presumption that in the distant past Earth somehow abandoned poverty, racism, and war. In "Time's Arrow, Part II" of *TNG*,[50] Deanna Troi explains to a skeptical Samuel Clemens/Mark Twain: "Poverty was eliminated on Earth a long time ago. And a lot of other things disappeared with it: hopelessness . . . despair . . . cruelty. . . ." And in the movie *First Contact*, Picard explains to the confused Lily, a person from the twentieth century: "In my century we don't succumb to . . . revenge. We have a more evolved sensibility." History's all-too-familiar conflicts regarding wealth, political power, and religious intolerance are all safely in the distant past. Life among humanoids affiliated with the United Federation of Planets has become abundant beyond our current imagination. The most evolved forms of the starships are outfitted like luxury hotels, with spacious personal quarters, magical food replicators, infinite entertainments on the fantastical Holodeck, and remarkable healing tools. The political and economic arrangements that make all this possible are vaguely democratic in the sense that occasionally there is a glimpse of elected Federation leaders.[51] But the focus of *Star Trek* is on the relationships among crew members and how they work as a redemptive team to save those communities that cannot save themselves. Does the *Enterprise*, in its organization and execution, exemplify the democratic ethos?

We could point to *Star Trek*'s well-known alignment with key values of recent democratic liberalism. Its pioneering efforts to include African-Americans in leading roles, albeit timidly at first, earned the praise of civil rights leaders such as Martin Luther King, Jr. Its expanding roles for women in commanding leadership positions have made *Star Trek* look far more egalitarian than the norm in American institutions. And the different series have

The hunger for *Star Trek* has led to comprehensive publications. *The Star Trek Encyclopedia*, here in its CD-rom version, offers Web-linked data about programs, films, anthropology, biology, chronology, etc.

Credit: Box, Simon & Schuster Interactive, and © Paramount Pictures, 1999.

The *Deep Space Nine Companion* provides episode summaries, video trailers, and the complete full-text shooting scripts for 176 episodes. The other series also have their "companions." These in-depth resources are comparable to the concordances and other aids to study in the religious traditions.

Credit: Box, Simon & Schuster Interactive, and © Paramount Pictures, 1999.

all had moments when the crew eschewed violence, even if it required acquiescence. Kirk, the most belligerent and interfering of the *Enterprise* captains, puts it colorfully in "Elaan of Troyius," where he comments on his refusal to blast a Klingon ship: "If I can accomplish my mission by turning tail and running, I'll gladly do that." Among the later captains, Janeway often takes perilous risks to preserve the sovereign autonomy of an alien adversary.

However, the political structure of all the *Enterprises* is hierarchical military command. This is especially clear in the "All Good Things"[52] episode, which trumps every other superhero tale in its redemption of human existence itself. As the story works out, the family team that usually works together in consultation is subordinated to Picard's disoriented, obsessive sense of responsibility and the stress of saving the world while so little time remains. At several points, he angrily snaps at others who don't understand: "I don't have time to explain. Do it!" This aspect of the story emphasizes that the Federation *Starfleet* is a military organization with a top-down command hierarchy. *Star Trek's* stories are not "militaristic" in the normal sense of that term: the members of the crew are not conscripts; they do not fondle and gloat over the destructive power of their weapons; they do not scheme to usurp civilian authority. This is a different kind of military: soldiers don't spend a lot of time shining their shoes, clicking their heels, snapping off stiff salutes against the brims of hats, and shouting "Sir!" to their superiors.

But in the end, what disappoints us about *Star Trek*, as a supremely successful series of mythic tales for a democratic nation, is that its vision of perfection seems limited to men, women, and assorted aliens under military command. They move rootlessly through the galaxies, as married to their starships as the Lone Ranger is to the great horse Silver — and most of them as subordinate as Tonto. They show no signs of civic responsibility or leadership as that would be normally understood in a democracy with rooted citizens. *Star Trek's* world is, of course, somewhat closer to democracy in spirit than the stories of hereditary rule and restoration that we get in other manifestations of the myth such as *The Lion King* or *Star Wars*. Yet, despite the years of programming opportunities to create mythic texts that embody the fullest range of democratic aspirations, there is something important missing here.

Star Trek's mythology, like other popular artifacts with weaker kinship to democratic values, is inspiring new forms of religious expression. In the next chapter, we shall consider the ritual lives of this new space-based spirituality.

12 *Star Trek* Faith as a Fan-Made Religion

"The anthropologist must . . . characterize our culture as profoundly irreligious."

Clyde Kluckhohn, *Mirror for Man*[1]

"At the death of Gene Roddenberry in 1991, boxes of mail from around the world were delivered for months to his widow, Majel Barrett Roddenberry. Every letter said the same thing: 'Star Trek changed my life.'"[2]

Visiting a Gothic cathedral, one encounters the popular art and religion of an earlier era. From the menacing gargoyles on the exterior to the stained glass and glittering altars within — all is emblematic of the religious and social order of an earlier time. Some of these cathedrals were under construction for hundreds of years, longer by far than the intended life span of most modern structures. They aroused powerful feelings in worshipers for centuries more. Historians, theologians, and philosophers have documented the gradual waning of the emotional energies that sustained the life of the great cathedrals. Their vaulted aisles will doubtless survive for years to come, but more as pilgrimage sites for secular tourists than as sustainers of the vital faith that inspired their construction. As Henry Adams said, "The art remained, but the energy was lost. . . ."[3]

This advertisement for the *Star Trek* Experience in Las Vegas invites the audience to break the fantasy barrier "on a mission." That mission turns out to be killing Klingons to save Las Vegas itself!

Credit: Magazine advertisement.

In a similar manner a popular belief has thus arisen — reinforced by death-of-God theologians and by cultural interpreters such as the anthropologist Clyde Kluckhohn — that religious impulses are dying. They will presumably lie entombed alongside pagan mythological consciousness, both victims of a patricidal, secular science. Phenomena like *Star Trek*'s popularity suggest an alternative hypothesis. Religion may have merely changed its theater and neglected to place its name on the marquee. The move from cathedral to the tube, silver screen, or computer display offers the faithful many of the values those in traditional religion always sought. Yet the pseudo-empirical sleight-of-hand, based on the realism of the film image and special effects, ensures that neither the new believers, the producers, nor even the sponsors could comprehend that a new sort of religious practice would emerge. With more than thirty years' hindsight, we can now recognize that the *Star Trek* franchise was an early leader in providing a commercial entertainment product that could inspire religious outpourings and rituals from satisfied consumers around the globe. For a person like Gene Roddenberry, who launched his series with the conviction that "religion was largely nonsense," such a prophetic role for his storytelling seems as miraculous as warp speed or the transporter.

Discerning the pop religion inspired by *Star Trek* requires us to first recognize The Original Series' thrust at discrediting traditional myths and faiths.[4] An antireligious bias lies close to the surface in *Star Trek* materials, and in several instances one finds overt smashing of idols. Given Gene Roddenberry's statements about his commitment to secular humanism, the only surprise is that network television would permit *Star Trek* to get away with frequent attacks on religious belief.[5] We can recognize Roddenberry's vintage iconoclasm in an early, instructive episode such as "The Apple." The narrative cleverly inverts the Garden of Eden premise and justifies a technologically motivated "Fall" — an eating of the mythical apple — as an advance from religious superstition toward human freedom. In fact, "The Apple" features Captain Kirk actually destroying the religion of a paradisiacal planet for the sake of a progressive, secular outlook.

Kirk as the Serpent in the Garden with "The Apple"[6]

A *Star Trek* landing party materializes in the lush garden of Gamma Trianguli VI, an unexplored planet that seems as close to an earthly paradise as they would ever see. When Chekov notes that it is "just like Russia," McCoy replies, "It's a lot more like the Garden of Eden, Ensign."

The idyll is destroyed when one of the security guards examines a thorn pod, which explodes and kills him. Spock picks up a unique rock specimen, which explodes when it is tossed to the ground. At this point Spock dramatically throws himself in front of Captain Kirk to save him from one of the thorn pods, because his Vulcan constitution proves immune to the lethal missiles. They decide to abandon this dangerous paradise when they discover that a mysterious power field is inhibiting the transporter. Within a few moments other security guards are killed.

Enraged by their deaths, Kirk and his landing party capture a humanoid, Akuta, who claims, "I am the Eyes of Vaal. He must see." Vaal turns out to be a great dragon god who requires periodic meals of explosive rocks to keep his underground power source humming. But the citizens of the planet are kept in a state of sexual and technological innocence by this god. These humanoids claim, however, that he makes "the rains fall, and the sun to shine. All good comes from Vaal." The planet lacks bacteria, and its inhabitants do not age, so they need no "replacements." It is truly a "paradise" like the mythical Eden, a "splendid example of reciprocity." But Dr. McCoy is appalled: "These are humanoids — intelligent! They've got to advance — progress! Don't you understand what my readings indicate? There's been no change here in perhaps thousands of years! This isn't life, it's stagnation!" In other words, a stable, primitive culture cannot be tolerated.

Kirk allows the young romantics Chekov and Martha Landon, who were previously warned against their "field experiments in human biology," to engage in public necking so that the citizens of Gamma T. will get subversive ideas. But Akuta, the leader of Gamma Trianguli, receives word from Vaal to kill the landing crew. The force that threatens the *Enterprise* and its crew must somehow be destroyed. Spock, however, responds to Kirk: "This may not be an ideal society, but it is a viable one. . . . If we are forced to do what it seems we must, in my opinion, we will be in direct violation of the noninterference directive."

"These people aren't living," Kirk says, "they're just existing. It's not a valid culture." He sees, in other words, a duty to interfere.

"Starfleet Command may think otherwise," Spock suggests.

"That's a risk I'll have to take," Kirk replies.

Moments after Akuta and his men attack the crew and are subdued, the *Enterprise* phasers are directed to destroy Vaal. There is a tremendous series of explosions.

Akuta comes forward, "But it was Vaal who put the fruit on the trees, who caused the rain to fall. Vaal cared for us."

"You'll find that putting fruit on the trees is a relatively simple matter. . . . You'll have to learn to take care of yourselves," replies Kirk. "You might even like it. . . . You will be able to think what you wish, say what you wish, do what you wish. You will learn many things that are strange, but they will be good. You will discover love; there will be children."

Back on the bridge of the regenerated *Enterprise,* the officers debate the correctness of smashing idols. Kirk insists, "We put those people back on a normal course of social evolution. I see nothing wrong with that." And he adds the moral: "It's a good object lesson, Mr. Spock, in what can happen when your machines become too efficient, do too much of your work for you."

Spock points out the analogy to the Garden of Eden story: "In a manner of speaking we have given Adam and Eve the apple, the awareness of good

and evil, if you will, and because of this they have been driven out of paradise."

That brings Kirk up short: "Mr. Spock, you seem to be casting me in the
role of Satan. Do I look like Satan?"

"No, sir. But —"

"Is there anyone on this ship who looks even remotely like Satan?"

There is a grin on McCoy's face as Spock replies in an even tone: "I am
not aware of anyone in that category, Captain."

"No, Mr. Spock. I didn't think you would be."

It may strike one as paradoxical that a series with seemingly enlightened episodes such as this one would produce a "crazed" following whose "fanaticism" appears thoroughly religious. To be sure, all of the now-familiar mythic
patterns are here: the saga of the *Enterprise's* dangerous mission; the sexual
renunciation of its leaders; and the redemption scheme through which the
inhabitants of Gamma Trianguli VI are freed from their superstitious captivity. Given the proximity of such mythic patterns to the perennial concerns of
religion, one wonders whether an unconscious process is taking place here
that the producers and audience neither intend nor understand. Could it be
that the myths, in their pseudo-empirical garb, are creating a new pop religion, capable of powerfully inspiring the thoughts and actions of fans?

The Ecstatic Trekkie Phase of Spiritual Formation

The evidence of such a pop religion, strewn throughout *Star Trek* fan literature, received its most extensive early formulation in *Star Trek Lives!* (1975).[7]
This book is written in the spirit of the bubbly religious devotion that it so
meticulously documents. In most religions, individual revelatory ecstasies
and redemptive experiences evoke a sense of wonder before a numinous, divine reality. Early fans as well as actors show this spirit in discussing *Star Trek*.
George Takei, who played the role of Sulu, admits, "I hate to deify any human
being, but Gene Roddenberry . . . really is like a god to us because he did bring
us together."[8] Lichtenberg, Marshak, and Winston, the authors of *Star Trek
Lives,* convey a numinous sense in describing Spock: "Spock is *utterly capable
of dealing with any sort of threat* . . . total master of any situation that technology can create."[9] A letter writer says that "in episode after episode we have
satisfied for us mankind's age-old yearning for a superman" (p. 112), that is,
Mr. Spock. Such attributes owe more to divinity than to humanity.

Both Spock and Kirk play the role of superhuman redeemer figures in *Star Trek* episodes, as we have seen. In "The Apple," Spock saves Kirk's life by throwing himself in the path of the exploding thorn pod, an act of selfless redemption on a superhuman scale. He evinces an

> ... aura of tightly leashed, restrained power ... enough power ... to destroy the *Enterprise* and take half the galaxy with it if he so chose. . . . But if power, personal efficacy, is the pure good, and it is the good in us which selects the goals toward which that good power will be used, then also Spock contains more good than any earthly human we are likely to meet. (p. 79)

In traditional theology God alone possesses unlimited power, and his goodness consists in using it responsibly. Within this frame of reference, Spock has definitely supplanted God in the pop religion of *Star Trek*.

If Spock has replaced God, it is Kirk who plays the role of a Christ without passion, and in this role he — even more than Spock — consistently appears as a superhuman redeemer. In "The Apple" he takes it upon himself to redeem a people even at the peril of his own life. Not only does he risk the missiles and explosive rocks of Gamma Trianguli VI, but he also voluntarily accepts the burden of violating the directive to avoid "interference with the normal development of a viable culture. It comes very close to forbidding *any* interference whatsoever, and it forbids it very strongly. A starship captain takes an oath to die rather than violate it."[10] Kirk thus risks his own life for the sake of redemption. This kind of willingness to "lay down his life for his friends" (John 15:13), to offer his "life as a ransom for many" (Matthew 20:28), is the mark of divine and semi-divine redeemer figures. But it is also characteristic that they are somehow able to inspire others with the same goals. Captain Kirk seems to be in view when the fan trio writes that "*Star Trek* is about one man's love for his goal . . . about that man's ability to communicate that goal to his co-workers, and to evoke in their hearts a similar love, a burning passion of total devotion to this image of how Man could and should be" (p. 149).

A special kind of discipleship arises from those who confess the pop religion of *Star Trek*. "Love" radiates from the redeemer figures and is transmitted in real life, primarily to other fans within the movement. The fans write: "Spock and Kirk and the whole realm of *Star Trek* speak to us eloquently of knowledge and efficacy and hope, of striving and prevailing, of seeing each other. And the sum of the message is love. Love of life. . . . Here is the supreme optimism of a primary kind of love which is *not* sexual and yet may find expression in sexual terms. . . . To experience the concrete sense of that love and that hope, people watch *Star Trek*" (pp. 120-121). In content, mood, and motifs, this is indistinguishable from what is commonly called "religion." Joan Winston, one of the organizers of the first *Star Trek* convention, describes the mood pervading the bedlam of unexpected throngs. "With all these people crushed into this too-small area, there were no incidents, no fights, just love. Miles and miles and tons and tons of love" (pp. 62-63). This seemed to be a Woodstock Nation for the straights, a *Star Trek* universe in which caring love replaces skinny-dipping, dope, and sexual show-and-tell.

Perhaps the ultimate proof of the religious nature of *Star Trek* fandom is in its outbursts of ecstasy. The authors of *Star Trek Lives!* claim, for example, that "the depth of William Shatner's Kirk leaves us speechless. But only figuratively, for throughout this book we have tried *heroically* to restrain the outpourings of boundless admiration that Mr. Shatner's achievement has aroused in us."[11] When Joan Winston received a phone call from Leonard Nimoy, she gave way to this kind of ecstasy: "Oh bliss, oh frabjous joy" (p. 212). It was beyond normal human joy, calling forth words and expressions from Lewis Carroll's *Jabberwocky,* a spontaneous effort to express the ineffable. This kind of ecstatic feeling is reflected in the title and mood of *Star Trek Lives!* To say that a program "lives" of its own accord seems patently absurd, especially one that had been out of production for years. But here the fans' convictions are decisive. Their yearning for a "resurrection" has produced a religious sleight-of-hand.

- -

Star Trek as the Private Redemption of Trekkers

Later groups of adherents to the *Star Trek* faith distanced themselves from such effervescent expressions and the condescending "Trekkie" label that conveyed an image of silly, costumed play. They became the more dignified sounding "Trekkers,"[12] living out their *Star Trek*-inspired revelations in less lighthearted fashion. But they too are convinced that there is something important in *Star Trek* that transcends mere entertainment values, something they may keep quietly to themselves most of the time.

Lichtenberg, Marshak, and Winston report hundreds of letters from secret fans who are "respectable, solid citizens who know their own family situations to be such that they dare not confess the depth of their feeling for *Star Trek*. They have tried, perhaps, and have run into such derision, teasing, or outright rage that they now feel compelled to hide their love like a secret vice" (p. 16). Many fans actually report personal redemptive experiences resulting from their encounters with the programs. A woman who is vice president of a fan club writes, "*Star Trek* has changed my life . . . opened my world to new thoughts and drained my pocketbook trying to keep up with everyone. . . . It's made me a much more real person, a lot easier to live with. I don't try to explain myself too much to outsiders" (p. 19). Another woman reports that after being hospitalized for depression she "started again to believe in the future of mankind"; her "mental outlook vastly improved." A man from Ohio writes, "*Star Trek* has been, and always will be, the biggest influence in my life" (p. 20).

These redemption experiences seem closely related to the "Goal Effect" of *Star Trek,* challenging a tired mankind to strive once again for goals that seem unreachable at a fatigued moment in American history. The series "gives us the energy and the fuel to make the effort. By its mere existence — by the kinds of things it is saying and the kind of effort it took to say them — it gives us the sense that great efforts are possible and can succeed. It gives us the courage to tackle goals of our own . . ." (p. 129). A form of inspiration is clearly evoking discipleship here. In explaining their faith, the authors cite approvingly Ayn Rand's theory of art: Art "answers the question why . . . why go on. The function of art, to me, is to give answers . . . to give reason to have courage" (p. 132). The creation of this kind of hopeful courage was evident in a letter Roddenberry received from a University of Wisconsin science student who was saved from being a high school dropout by seeing *Star Trek.* "For him it rekindled an interest in the future and in machinery" (pp. 190-191).

As decades of *Star Trek* fandom have passed, reports of life transformation have continued to flood in. Henry Jenkins, a leading scholar of the *Star Trek* fan movement, describes an early life with Republican parents in Cobb County, Georgia, where racially segregated schools and fervent anti-Communist indoctrination was the norm. He reports "*Star Trek* and its fandom offered . . . a 'utopian' vision of the world" that led him to progressive "commitments to feminism, homosexual rights, racial justice, and multicultural education."[13]

Jeff Greenwald, who traveled around the world in the mid-1990s searching for *Star Trek's* most serious fans, discovered people lauding it for its heroic view of science, the richness of its philosophical exploration of technological issues, and its vision of interplanetary cooperation — where "kindness, tolerance, and patience have superceded brutality and greed."[14] In Hungary he met Szolt Sàrközy ("Federation alias Lieutenant Commander Q"), who reflected on how his life would be different without *Star Trek:* "I think something would fail, would miss, in my life. I would be empty. . . . I'm happy that I'm a Trekker. It gives meaning to my life" (p. 95). Consistent with this sort of testimonial, Yvonne Fern, who lived with Gene Roddenberry's family during the last months of his life in 1991, reported constant references to altered visions and lives in the letters of condolences that flooded in when Roddenberry died.

More explicitly religious in a traditional sense are those who find in *Star Trek* a confirmation or extension of their Christian faith. Michael Jindra cites Jennifer Caprio's book *Star Trek: Good News in Modern Images* (1978), which "argues that *Star Trek* is essentially Christian in its outlook."[15] He also reports on teachers in the southern United States who "use Christian language to articulate their adherence to *Star Trek* beliefs" and that "many Bible Belt fans use *Star Trek* to speak of the values of duty, honor, and truth" (p. 225).

Professor Herbert J. Gans, a well-known 1970s interpreter of popular culture who adopted a "consumer" model, would undoubtedly discount the claims of personal religious transformation. Convinced that popular-culture materials do not really motivate people or alter their value systems, he argued that "content choice is affected by selective perception, so that people often choose content that agrees with their own values. . . . Thus the prime effect of the media is to reinforce already existing behavior and attitudes, rather than to create new ones."[16] The fundamentalist flirtation with the secular *Star Trek* seems to confirm Gans's consumerist framework. But given the total range of experiences reported by confessors of the *Star Trek* faith, the "user" model of popular reception has a rather hollow ring. To an extent, popular religion has always had a reciprocal relationship with human needs, momentary historical circumstances, and cultural values. Only in the rare instances of higher, prophetic religion do new values emerge. But this should not lead one to overlook the potent effect a particular pop religion may exert. Ordinarily, the more conformist and the less self-conscious a religion, the more powerful its hold. Gans's mistake is to view popular culture materials as mere entertainment rather than as influential, ritualistic forms of a pop religion.

Jeff Greenwald visited the Los Angeles laboratories and offices of the Jet Propulsion Lab corporation (JPL), which launched *Mars Pathfinder* and other interplanetary explorations. There he found "die-hard *Star Trek* fans. Some know the show backward, and unabashedly credit the series with launching their own careers in space exploration."[17] One engineer, Ralph Roncoli, reported that his circle of workers know the programs so well that they have "all the lines memorized," which they regularly interject into their work as comments on the nature of the technical problems they are trying to solve. He flatly says of *Star Trek* ways of thinking, "It's part of our personalities" (p. 24).

The Creation of a Fan-Made Religion

A popular religious movement usually produces an explicit theology over the course of time. At least this has been the pattern for religious groups in the Western world. It is not surprising, then, that a *pop theology* that elaborates and explains the assumptions and experience of the *Star Trek* faith has emerged. Much of this early material came in the form of fantasy literature, spinning out *Star Trek* episodes and characters to see what happened beyond the revelational scope of the original television series. This "fanzine" literature includes series such as *Eridani Triad, Star Trek Showcase, T-Negative, Grup, Impulse, Babel, Spockanalis, Alternative Universe, Tricorder Readings,* and *Tholian Web.* There are hundreds of different issues of these early magazines,[18] in a development strikingly similar to the growth of apocryphal literature in the biblical tradition. These creeds of the faith answer essentially theological questions, amplifying and illustrating a belief system.[19]

The authors of *Star Trek Lives!* ask why so many thousands of hours have been devoted to writing, editing, and publishing this fan literature. They ascribe it to "the sheer love of *Star Trek.* People have become so entranced with that world that they simply cannot bear to let it die and will re-create it themselves if they have to. . . ."[20] By writing stories, they produce the feeling that they in effect know the gods. Fanzine writers confess that "we want to know all about these *Star Trek* characters — their innermost thoughts, the most trivial details about them. They have become *friends* in a way that few flesh-and-blood people are, and almost no fictional characters are" (p. 256). There is a ritualistic, confessional quality to this writing. The writers' expression of their personal experience is largely subordinated to mythic conventions; in this ritual fashion they keep the fictional characters alive. The characters enter into personal relationships with their devotees. They live on in faith. It all sounds very much like the practice of dogmatic theology in a traditional religion.

A particularly good example of the theological activity in early fan magazines is *Kraith,* with its writers' guide and its collection of stories. It develops a "Demanding Fantasy" that is a "combination of the need for a demanding pleasure with the need to work out answers to certain fundamental human questions . . . 'Whither man?' and 'Why?' and 'What's it all about?' and 'What is the proper relationship of man to himself, to his group, to the universe?'"[21] Here, within premises of faith provided by the *Star Trek* format and characters, a kind of theology is set forth. Its scripture is embodied in the original seventy-nine television episodes; its task is to unfold the meaning of that revelation for the basic human questions.[22] The theological impulse in this kind of publishing program is unmistakable. *Kraith* claims that *Star Trek* is "a stag-geringly effective model for dealing with deep human questions,"[23] the kind of sentiment shared by many religious and occult groups in the current pe-riod.

The theological message of *Star Trek,* judging from these fan materials, relates to world redemption in general and redemption of individual audi-ence members in particular. The "Optimism Effect" referred to in *Star Trek Lives!* confirms the hope that, despite the present malaise, mankind "can overcome the problems of today" (p. 107). The television stories cultivate this hope by bringing into our living rooms imaginary cultures of the future, even on this planet Earth, that have transcended problems that look lethal today. George Takei (Sulu) attributes this redemptive effect in the television series to Gene Roddenberry: "I think he's the one who felt very seriously, and deeply believes, that we *can* overcome the problems of today." Fans extol with fervor "the optimism of *Star Trek* — its vision of a brighter future of man, and of a world characterized by hope, achievement and understanding . . ." (pp. 107-108).

The origin of this pop optimism is typically American, as betrayed by a peculiar competitive terminology. "But the deepest conviction of the creators of *Star Trek* was, and is, that triumph is possible, that we can *win.*"[24] This re-minds even the forgetful of Norman Vincent Peale's "power of positive think-ing" and his book *You Can Win.*[25] *Star Trek's* innocent optimism conceals the unexamined premise that the "American Way of Life" will somehow prevail in the universe. Here is a package designed to appeal to the innocent, a theol-ogy oblivious to its essentially religious premise, a philosophy sure that the fantasy values of a particular culture will appeal to galactic inhabitants every-where. The lack of critical principles, so essential to either theology or philos-ophy in the classical tradition, helps protect such convictions and values from the incursions of reality.[26]

There is also a profound appeal in the so-called Vulcan philosophy, which shaped Spock and presumably led that planet into centuries of peace. This philosophy adds up to an optimistic, nonviolent (except for holy causes), sexually renunciatory individualism. It urges the repression of sexual energies for the sake of larger causes, a renunciation of sexual commitments, an animalistic expression of sexual instincts at the appropriate rutting season, and in the meantime, a sublimation of sexual energies in the form of techno-logical zeal. Projecting traditional American values and repressions onto imaginary planets where their workability can be fantasized apparently en-hances believability. What has failed in American experience is nevertheless affirmed to be "true" because it is depicted operating successfully in outer space. Clearly this is uncritical religious faith rather than rational thought deriving its inspiration from science.

The Significance of Dress Up and Play

Among the evidences of *Star Trek* pop religion are voluntary behavior alterations. Some 1970s fans modeled their actions after those of the stars just as disciples in traditional Christianity imitate their Lord. A sixteen-year-old youth resembling Leonard Nimoy had his hair cut and his eyebrows shaped in slanted Vulcan style. He almost always wears a blue velour shirt and has taken on so many of Spock's mannerisms that he seems to be a second Spock.[27] Another young man, studying physics at the graduate level, "went to court and legally changed his name to 'Spock' — no last name, just 'Spock.'" A man in Los Angeles was reported to be constructing an *Enterprise* shuttlecraft, the small spacecraft used for short voyages. He has reproduced *Star Trek* equipment and uniforms and works at building the complicated *Enterprise* bridge seen on the television series.[28] Two men from Poughkeepsie, New York, have constructed their own bridge set and transporter room in order to make their own amateur movies.[29] The most widely publicized recent example of sartorial devotion to Trek religion came at the 1996 Whitewater trial in Little Rock, Arkansas. Barbara Adams, who worked at a printing company, served as an alternate juror wearing her "Next Generation" uniform. This was not a publicity stunt for the trial, since she normally wears it to work and refers to herself as "Commander." She reported that her demeanor reflected her commitment to the ideals of the program. Her service as a juror was perfectly satisfactory, except for an interview about her courtroom experience that led to her dismissal. Of her practice of wearing the uniform, she soberly declared, "I don't want my officers ever to feel ashamed of their uniform."[30]

The film *Trekkies* (1999) contains several anecdotes reflecting the theme of fans who bestow god-like attributes on the actors. James Doohan (Scotty/ *TOS*) tells of a suicidal woman who repeatedly wrote to him. He encouraged her to live on and she eventually regained her self-control. LeVar Burton tells of a dying young man, George LaForge, who felt that *Star Trek* had helped him continue living.[31] John DeLancie (Q/*TNG*) was making a celebrity appearance at a convention when he felt very ill. A fan bought his half-drunk glass of water at auction and drank it — telling others that he wanted to have the "Q-virus" and spread it. Such examples could be multiplied many times.

The motivations for these actions are probably as complex as those associated with the Christian imitation ethic. The desire to be like one's redeemer, to achieve union with him or her, or to gain self-identity by copying the redeemer's appearance or actions, often seems to coalesce in such mimicry.

The pattern of behavior alteration on the part of most female fans seems to be quite different. It is partially visible in the fanzine literature. The stories written about *Star Trek* characters, spinning out their life scenarios and debating whether the new fantasies correspond to the established patterns, seem to be written almost exclusively by women. While male fans write mainly about technological details, the early female storytellers wrote about Kirk and Spock. One genre of these stories came to be designated K/S and features the pair in a deeply satisfying homoerotic relationship.[32] Many of the stories featuring Spock remind one very much of the ancient mystery religions in which union with the god provides the ecstatic high point of the ritual. As in the mystery religions, one does not enter into a normal marriage with gods like Spock. *Star Trek Lives!* reports that a "favorite theme is the 'no strings attached' meeting of his peculiarly urgent need. Various females have volunteered for that with alacrity. (Practically everybody, it sometimes seems.)"[33] But unlike the mystery religions, the actual achievement of redemption through sexual union with the body of the god is available only in fantasy form because suitable temple rites are not available — yet! However, the rapid evolution of "virtual reality" technology makes it thinkable in our lifetime.

There are instances in which women actually attempted to carry out such rites of union with Star Trek actors. Gerrold reports that "one girl ran away from home to go to Hollywood and try to move in with Leonard Nimoy. She chased after him for months, in general making his life miserable. In the process she managed to interfere with shooting schedules . . . and the nerves of everyone she came in contact with."[34] An enterprising group of girls tried black-magic rituals to make their *Star Trek* heroes fall in love with them. They reportedly ceased their efforts in this direction when told that every hour of black magic takes away a year of one's personal beauty, for how could one ever hope to attract a god when one's beauty is gone? One little old lady from California achieved union with the god in an ingenious way. She tape-recorded the *Star Trek* programs "for the express purpose of later dubbing in her own voice over the leading lady's."[35]

Infatuation with celebrities and the desire to share their essence are hardly distinctive to *Star Trek*.[36] The crazy antics of fans of the movies and rock music have repeatedly been observed and parodied. What does seem culturally innovative are the bands of individuals, like those at Jet Propulsion Lab, who have taken the next step beyond imitative play to integrate *Star Trek* values in their lives as a kind of secular religion.

Star Trek's Corporate Version of Pilgrimage

The major world's religions have generally developed some form of pilgrimage as a means of reinforcing and revitalizing the faith. From early times Christians traveled to Jerusalem or Rome or visited some local site associated with sacredness or healing miracles. Muslims make their trips to the holy city of Mecca, where the prophet Muhammad was born. At such places the faithful can view the reliquaries containing objects of sacred significance; sometimes they purchase items that become a symbol allowing them to carry the holiness home. Pilgrimage may seem problematic for *Star Trek* since its world lies so far in the future. However, the Viacom/Paramount Corporation sensed an opportunity to call the faithful to Las Vegas, giving them a taste of the sacred future. In that scripted experience we discern a serious problem for the utopian-minded fans of *Star Trek*.

When the massive exhibit opened in 1997, the corporation framed its appeal in the hard-edged language of marketing. Jane Cooper, President and C.E.O. of Paramount Parks, said, "STAR TREK: *The Experience* will be the first, real 'branded' experience in town."[37] For corporations, the notion of the "real, branded" experience conveys their sense of confidence about knowing exactly what consumers want from their product — and confidence that they will deliver it in every aspect of every transaction. Reflecting his aspiration for the "branded experience," Rick Berman, Gene Roddenberry's successor, remarked that "the Experience" must "retain the essence of what *Star Trek* is all about." So what is this essence in Paramount's "branded *Star Trek* experience"?

On the basis of the exhibit's first years, one must conclude that *Star Trek* is "all about" the battle between good and evil, and Paramount is allowing you, the consumer, to play a role in that confrontation. The Klingons, those cardboard villains so detested by Gene Roddenberry, are back, and *you* can help destroy them! Spock's tolerant Vulcan philosophy of the IDIC hardly seems relevant when Las Vegas is under attack by Klingon birds of prey. The Experience is also about buying food and drink from those barely tolerable Ferengi, the skulking, money-loving creatures of the *DS9* series who still exhibit the acquisitive impulse in *Star Trek's* post-monetary world.

Paramount has structured the Experience in this way: one enters a darkened interior with ticket booths in a cavernous room where a model of the *Enterprise* hangs overhead.[38] Once past the gatekeepers, the pilgrim can see a fine exhibit of props — principally phaser guns and tricorders — and costumes worn in *Star Trek* productions. Interspersed among these handsomely presented artifacts are illustrated panels that indicate significant moments in the history of space exploration. Actual historical events in twentieth-century space flight, such as the flight of *Sputnik,* are integrated with *Star Trek* events, and the chronology marks no distinctions between the real and the imaginary.[39] Video monitors play dramatic moments from television shows or feature-length films. Progressing further, one finds anthropological exhibits that provide information about the cultures of the Vulcans, Klingons, Cardassians, Bajorans, Ferengi, and the most terrifying of them all, the Borg Collective, which flies in a box-shaped ship ruled by an evil, sexy Queen, whose semi-robotic monsters work at assimilating and destroying all conscious individuality in the universe. An oddity of the exhibition space is that no picture of Gene Roddenberry appears anywhere, nor any other sort of reference to the Great Bird of the Galaxy, as he was affectionately referred to by his fans. As a dramatic device, the Great Bird's omission may simply emphasize the early fans' notion that "*Star Trek* lives" in its own right — independent of its creators. But there is also an absence of any reference to Roddenberry's humanistic ideals for his crew and their work in the expanding universe. This becomes thematically significant in the engineered experience that follows the exhibition space.

Moving past the exhibit, one enters a zone of supervision by Paramount attendants. The corporation has designed a scenario that abruptly inserts the tourist into a redemptive mission with the *Star Trek* crew. After the pilgrims have viewed the bridge, with televised commentaries by Will Riker and Geordi La Forge, they are informed of an emergency: "You've all been abducted from the twentieth century by a hostile group of aliens known as Klingons." The channel to the twenty-fourth century is one of those "temporal rifts in the space-time continuum" that has opened so many dramatic possibilities for the series. The instigator in this case is a Klingon captain named Korath, who bears a grudge against Captain Picard because the latter bested him for top honors at the Starfleet Academy. Korath believes that one of the tourists in our group is Picard's ancestor. Since the Captain has disappeared from his chair, it is presumed that killing that tourist-ancestor will prevent Captain Picard from ever being born. Then Korath's snarling face appears: "There's no point in running away, *Enterprise.* Give me Picard's ancestor, and the others can return to the past." But Will Riker defies him: "Forget it, Korath. These people are under my protection." At this point Riker and LaForge direct the tourists to the transport shuttle *Valiant,* which they hope will locate the temporal rift so as to permit their return to Las Vegas.

Strapped into the *Valiant,* the pilgrims receive a harrowing, visceral ride through a nebula. Then a Klingon Bird of Prey is discovered pursuing the *Valiant,* quickly sucking its power and reducing its defensive shields. The ship goes into a free fall, "emergency induction manifolds" are activated, and the weakening system struggles to get power to the "Turbolift." Then the Klingons "decloak," indicating their readiness to fire at the *Valiant*. As the *Valiant* approaches the Klingon moon, we detect their "cloaking device beneath the surface." We swoop into one of their canyons, navigating like Luke Skywalker seeking the garbage hole of the Death Star. Then we fire on their generator, destroying it. Luckily we locate "the rift," fly into it, and suddenly hover above Las Vegas — but not necessarily safely because the Bird of Prey still seeks to kill all of us. Our shuttle trades fire with the Klingons and, with justice on our side, we "blast them to smithereens." Though our stomachs may be distressed by the maneuvers and the excitement of killing Klingons, it's a small price to pay for saving Picard, and as we know from the "All Good Things" *TNG* episode, all of humanity.

After this harrowing but redemptive experience, pilgrims are discharged to relax in Quark's Bar or to go to the Admiral Collection, Paramount's reliquary of branded merchandise. Every *Star Trek* video or novel, every CD-rom, every trinket from key chains and pens to mugs is available. For the true pilgrim of substance, there are the precious metals renditions of tricorders, phasers, and *Enterprises*. One can also purchase uniforms from the shows, plus life-size models of show characters. Lugging the items back out into the harsh sunlight and ravenous commercialism of Las Vegas, one feels the need for spiritual stimulation they may offer.

If one views the Hilton's "*Star Trek* Experience" as simply another part of Paramount's vast merchandising engine, it is perhaps not unusual in its indifference to aspects of the *Star Trek* narratives that have stimulated the utopian imagination of its fans. For example, Paramount regularly licenses video games that are little more than first-person shooters. *Star Trek: Invasion* (Activision/2000) is a war against the Borgs, fought principally with phasers and photon torpedoes. *Star Trek: Deep Space Nine Dominion Wars* (Gizmo/Simon Schuster Interactive, 2001) advertises itself with this slogan: "No base building, no gathering of resources — just glorious battles, and you're in command. . . . With unprecedented access to all phases of space combat . . . *Dominion Wars* asks YOU to decide who dies."[40] The movies often spin out of the Roddenberry orbit. Roddenberry was disgusted, for example, with the William Shatner–directed *The Final Frontier* (1989) because of its zealous mockery of religion. And the films, even with the supremely diplomatic Picard at the helm, typically feature explosive violence at some point.

This variety of *Star Trek* series, movies, video games, and fan movements should warn us that no simplistic analysis will suffice to explain what *Star Trek* "really means." We can respect those who describe their inspirations and transformations and find ourselves sympathetic to the values they promote. Who would want to declare their opposition to interplanetary cooperation, benevolent technologies, equal rights for humans and aliens? However, the routine celebration of violence, the idolization of characters as superhuman, and the lack of truly democratic institutions or processes give us pause. The deadly pursuit of the forces of Korath at Las Vegas hardly seems an appropriate model for responding to the attack on September 11, yet it resembles our campaign against Islamic fundamentalism in Afghanistan. Vulcan philosophy seems to provide no critical resources to confront the looming cultural conflict that threatens to destroy our planet. A pilgrimage to "The *Star Trek* Experience" at a Las Vegas hotel may simply reinforce the propensity to bomb another tribe of Klingons. We are also not sanguine about the future of beliefs that are administered by a global corporation whose goals are predominantly economic.

"The mission" at the Las Vegas Hilton's *Star Trek: The Experience* is to respond to the aggressive attack of the uncontrollably angry Korath, a Klingon. He demands the ancestor of Jean-Luc Picard, so that he can prevent Picard's potent personal rivalry. Your mission succeeds in thwarting him.

Credit: *Star Trek: The Experience* catalog © 1997 Paramount Pictures.

Moving Past "Poaching"

The phenomenon of Star Trek religion leads us to reflect on the theory of "textual poaching" in the field of popular culture scholarship. First developed by Michel DeCerteau in *The Practice of Everyday Life,*[41] this approach presents fans as creative meaning-makers for the products they consume. It alters the Herbert Gans "consumer" model of media experience in which popular products pass through one ear and out the other without having any effect on the user. Henry Jenkins, whose book entitled *Textual Poaching*[42] creates a sympathetic portrait of *Star Trek* fandom, opposes "media fostered stereotypes of fans as cultural dupes, social misfits, and mindless consumers." Instead, Jenkins sees "fans as readers who appropriate popular texts and reread them in a manner that serves different interests, as spectators who transform the experience of watching television into a rich and complex participatory culture." Asserting their independence from what they consume, they "borrow" and "inflect" "mass culture images, articulating concerns which often go unvoiced within the mass media."[43] Jenkins' discussion of the homoerotic Kirk/Spock fanzines (mentioned above) exemplifies this sort of creativity in moving *Star Trek* away from its muteness about homosexuality.[44] There is a democratic potential in this process that seems much more promising than corporate control of mythic imagination. What remains unrecognized, however, is that the content of both the *Star Trek* series and its fan religion remain significantly indebted to the American monomyth — with all of its narcissistic, violent, and undemocratic tendencies. This particular religion poaches from an already polluted stream that participatory activities have thus far done little to dispel. As in the case of all other religions, whether pop or traditional, there is an urgent need for critical examinations of *Star Trek*'s implications and its long-term effects on believers and their societies. But this can hardly occur when so many people continue to view fandom as nothing but an experience of consumption.

13 Fascist Faith in the *Star Wars* Universe

"The Church is similar to The Alliance of Star Wars. *It had a humble beginning, with only a few faithful followers. Just as the followers of the Force were set apart from the rest of the universe, so is the Church of Jesus Christ called out from the world to be true Jedi."*

Frank Allnutt, *Unlocking the Mystery of the Force*[1]

"With your permission, my Master, I have encountered a vergence in the Force. . . . A boy. His cells have the highest concentration of midi-chlorians I have seen in a life form. . . . Finding him was the will of the Force."

Qui-Gon to Jedi Master Yoda, discussing Anakin Skywalker[2]

"Who Will Save Your Soul?"

Scholars tracing the paths of American religion in recent decades have described a variety of interplays between corporate entertainment products and religious belief. Bruce David Forbes, who has provided one map, reminds us that religion can obviously be *in* popular culture when film creations like *The Ten Commandments* or *The Little Buddha* directly represent religious heritage or practice.[3] But he also suggests another possibility: that a television program can actually function *as* a religion for individuals — a phenomenon we

Star Wars gave its viewers an opportunity to feel ecstasy at the sight of nuclear destruction. This is the Death Star's explosion in the first film — an image that offered a rationale for Timothy McVeigh's indiscriminate killing in Oklahoma City.

Credit: Lucasfilms © 1977.

These action figures allow children ("4 & up") to handle the symbols of the Force. Emperor Palpatine, the Empire's Dictator, commands the "Dark Side Energy Bolts" that almost kill Luke Skywalker. Luke Skywalker comes with an "Electronic Commtech Reader" — a "Communication Output Memory Module" that speaks to the owner lines such as "We're going full throttle!" and "I got him!" The Luke Skywalker packaging conveys the excitement: "Now the power of the Force is YOURS."

Credit: Emperor © 1996 Hasbro, Inc.; Luke Skywalker © 1999 Hasbro, Inc.

encountered with *Star Trek.*[4] Other scholars have focused on individuals who accept film experiences as cultivators for what they call "spirituality," which they distinguish from "religion," a word whose associations they identify with institutional membership and group rituals. Wade C. Roof's study of "the spiritual marketplace"[5] characterizes 15 percent of Baby Boomers as "metaphysical seekers" who adopt a highly exploratory, positive attitude toward nontraditional sources of religious guidance. As a group, these seekers feel at ease with psychological self-help manuals, angels, the literature of near-death experiences, non-European religions, and narrative fictions such as *Star Trek.* They are far more comfortable with their self-constructed beliefs and practices than they are with supervised worship in bricks-and-mortar buildings.

As one of those "seekers" offering a rationale for this new quest, theologian Tom Beaudoin cites St. Ignatius' plea for Christians to "find God in all things." In Beaudoin's own confession, he reports: "I find that playing bass in a rock band is often as close as I get to God, in an experience that most churches can never match."[6] Endeavoring to speak for his generation of Gen-Xers, Beaudoin laments the hypocrisy, smug intolerance, and badgering of traditional churches as factors that help explain the new spirituality. He also notes that many popular artists, especially music groups, have taken on the task of posing religious challenges to their listeners. Here are just two musical lyrics that express what he calls "the new spiritual milieu of popular culture": "Jewel asks, 'Who will save your soul?' U2's Bono croons to Jesus: 'Wake up, dead man.'"[7]

In Beaudoin's view, such emerging expressions of faith reflect collaboration between a receptive audience and artists committed to giving them a spiritual stimulus. These recent recognitions of pop spirituality afford a frame for understanding the *Star Wars* religious phenomenon that emerged almost instantly after the release of the initial film, *Part IV: A New Hope,*[8] in 1977 and has continued with *The Empire Strikes Back* (1980), *The Return of the Jedi* (1983), and the so-called prequel, *Episode I: The Phantom Menace* (1999).

Star Wars resembles *Star Trek* in bearing a mantle of cultural honor. *A New Hope* was one of the first twenty-five films to be included in the Library of Congress's National Film Registry, which was created in 1989. George Lucas, the film's creator, has received the Irving G. Thalberg Memorial Award from the Academy of Motion Picture Arts and Sciences.[9] The movie series was featured in a major 1997 exhibition called *Star Wars: The Magic of Myth,* hosted at the National Air and Space Museum of the Smithsonian Institution.[10] The Lucas Learning Division of San Rafael, California, like the Disney and *Star Trek* franchises, has become an educator for the culture's children, dispensing numerous books, CDs, video games, and instructional materials.[11]

In addition, every release of a new *Star Wars* film provokes intensive press coverage, product merchandizing, and a new wave of committed expressions of loyalty. Each of these films has stimulated eccentric forms of fan dedication: camping out overnight to get the first tickets, attending the movie day after day, skipping school to watch the movie, and so forth. A 1999 Gallup poll revealed that 72 percent of all U.S. adults had seen *A New Hope* at least once in the theater, on television, or in video. Among adults who had seen it, the average number of times was more than eight; 17 percent had seen the film more than ten times.[12] Coinciding with *The Phantom Menace* release, a grade-school teacher from North Carolina, Jennifer Briggs, responded to a challenge from a radio station and officially changed her name to Obi-Wan Kenobi in exchange for a $1,000 promotional prize. Two other individuals changed their names without any inducement.[13] But beyond such goofy public stunts, there are those who, like Frank Allnut of this chapter's epigraph, find in *Star Wars* a vivid confirmation of their values or a new stimulus to spiritual development. Among our acquaintances at the time of *A New Hope*'s release were religiously conservative parents who were ecstatic about the film's messages and took their children for repeat viewings.

With public adulation of this kind, attendance at *Star Wars* films has become "critic-proof": commentators who lament comic-book characterizations and overt toy merchandising cannot impede the rising box-office records with each new film or reissue of the enhanced older titles.[14] *The Phantom Menace*, which evoked some harsh reactions even from dedicated fans, became the first film to exceed $400 million in U.S. box-office returns for its theatrical release.

From this resonant popularity, it becomes clear that the *Star Wars* franchise *could* make highly visible affirmations that deepen the symbolic supports for democratic values. But our judgment, defying our "new hope" to find here an exciting embodiment of the democratic ethos, is that *Star Wars* remains captive to the American monomyth — to which it has lent a new religious aura. Assuming that the classical monomyth has at least some potential to provide a new set of narratives and icons coherent with democratic faith, we find ourselves drumming our fingers while Lucasfilm, Ltd., cranks out more films about oppressed royalty, their loyal multicreatural retinue, and their serialized capers in hacking with magic swords or blasting their enemies with torpedoes and laser pistols. There is a sadly lost potential here for something more coherent with democratic values.

The Religious Aspirations of George Lucas

If we take George Lucas at his word, he was a man who brought a sense of religious mission to his *Star Wars* series. In addition to his fragmentary recycling of *Flash Gordon, The Wizard of Oz,* Edgar Rice Burroughs' pulps, and other youthful experiences, Lucas wanted to incorporate in his productions classical monomyth patterns set forth in Joseph Campbell's *The Hero with a Thousand Faces.* He found them attractive for the ways in which they seemed to highlight missing elements in contemporary culture. Lucas became the first notable filmmaker — but certainly not the last — to consciously use the archetype as a template for storytelling.[15] In the years following the first *Star Wars* release, Lucas conversed with Joseph Campbell at Lucas's Skywalker Ranch in Marin County, California, which became the location for the filming of segments of *The Power of Myth* series that featured Campbell and Bill Moyers in 1988.[16] Campbell himself became an enthusiastic advocate of Lucas's adaptations of his heroic archetypes. After Campbell's death, Lucas walked in his footsteps at the time of the release of *The Phantom Menace* (1999), collaborating with Moyers on a video entitled "The Mythology of *Star Wars*."[17]

The relevance of the heroic patterns of the monomyth lay especially with his perception of typical youth aspirations. As he bluntly put it in 1977, he wanted to get "children to believe there is more to life than garbage and killing and all that real stuff like stealing hubcaps — that you could still sit and dream about exotic lands and strange creatures."[18] Like Campbell, Lucas viewed these evidences of social breakdown as signs of corresponding decay in mythic consciousness: "[T]here was no longer a lot of mythology in our society — the kind of stories we tell ourselves and our children, which is the way our heritage is passed down. Westerns used to provide that, but there weren't Westerns anymore." He also saw his film as fulfilling a somewhat churchly moral role. "I wanted it to be traditional moral study, to have . . . palpable precepts . . . that children could understand. . . . Traditionally we get them from the church, the family, and in the modern world we get them from the media — from movies."

In a modest clarification for the Moyers interview, Lucas professed that his cultural disappointments were not to be mistaken for antagonism to institutional religion or a desire to replace it: "I would hate to find ourselves in a completely secular world where entertainment was passing for some kind of religion." His films were meant to be complementary rather than competitive. Whether they retain that intended status remains to be seen.

Luke Skywalker and Darth Vader as Monomythic Heroes

Because *Star Wars* has been released in episodes, the character of the story has changed through its elaboration over time. However, both the larger arc and the individual episodes have features pressed from the mold of the classical monomythic. In describing the series prior to *Phantom Menace*, John Seabrook identified important ingredients of the recipe for constructing the path of Luke Skywalker's life:

> One can go through *Star Wars* and almost pick out chapter headings from Campbell's *The Hero with a Thousand Faces:* the hero's call to adventure, the refusal of the call, the arrival of supernatural aid, the crossing of the first threshold, the belly of the whale, and the series of ordeals culminating in a showdown with the angry father, when, at last, as Campbell writes, "the hero . . . beholds the face of the father, understands — and the two are atoned — which is precisely what happens at the end of *Jedi.*[19]

The atoning moment in *Return of the Jedi* comes shortly after a laser-sword battle in which Luke refuses to kill his father, Darth Vader, then pleads with him to turn away from the Dark Side. The disgusted Emperor Palpatine, who had hoped to tempt Luke with a vision of unlimited power, begins to electrocute Luke with blue rays of energy. Darth finally turns and hurls Palpatine into the reactor of the Death Star II; but he absorbs fatal jolts of the dark force in killing the emperor. "I've got to save you!" Luke pleads with him; but Darth replies, "No, you already have." Then a miraculous bodily transfiguration occurs, linking Darth's redemption to the ascensions of Jesus and Mary. To quote words from the official *Star Wars* character databank: "He then died, his body disappearing into the light side of the Force."[20] The official character profile in *Star Wars: Behind the Magic* adds this poetic flourish in describing a vision Luke has after burning the armor of Anakin/Darth on Tatooine, further evoking biblical ascensions: "He saw that his father had joined Yoda and Obi-Wan Kenobi as a luminous being, basking in the light side of the Force."[21]

At this point, Luke has lost a great burden caused by his dual awareness of his father's evil and the possibility of redeeming rather than killing him. He is now an integrated, mature adult who can take a position of supreme leadership in his community. In this regard — and quite unlike the typical American monomythic tale — moral development does occur in the life of the hero. As he undergoes his training with Ben and with Yoda, we see him struggle with his impulsiveness. At times he rushes into gravely mistaken actions because he fails to heed warnings. Like a Christian or Buddhist saint, Yoda urges Luke not to surrender to hate in confronting evil, a message that Luke finally follows in the death scene with Darth Vader and the emperor. Han Solo also matures: beginning as a self-centered bootlegger, concerned only with getting full price for transportation in his Millennium Falcon spaceship, he becomes a loving companion who makes sacrifices for others.

When the back-flashing trilogy returned to the beginnings with the *Phantom Menace* in 1999, it restarted the monomythic story cycle with the young Anakin Skywalker, a child heroic figure who is to become in maturity the evil figure of Darth Vader by the time of the *New Hope* episode. Like his son, Luke, of that later episode, Anakin is discovered as a child on the planet of Tatooine by the young Obi-Wan Kenobi and Qui-Gon Jinn, Jedi knights searching for spare parts to fix the hyperdrive on the Queen of Naboo's royal starship. It has suffered damage in an attack by the forces of an illegal Trade Federation blockade, but the local repair shop refuses to accept monetary credits from the increasingly impotent Republic. Anakin, like his mother a mere slave, proves his generosity and remarkable talent by volunteering to compete in a pod race under a wager that will give over the prize for the repair of the royal starship. After his stunning victory in a competition in which other racers are destroyed, the older Jedis sense the presence of one who belongs among them. They arrange to purchase Anakin and persuade his mother to surrender her custody for his training as a Jedi knight.

In later meetings about his future, Yoda, supreme guru of the Jedis, feels skeptical about Anakin's worthiness, doubtless feeling a premonition that he will turn to the dark side of the Force. But Qui-Gon is equally insistent as Anakin's advocate, having conducted a blood test revealing that Anakin has an unprecedented "midi-chlorian count" — a hereditary marker for Jedi greatness. (The midi-chlorian cells in the blood seem to be a kind of biological interface that permits the Force to flow into one's body.) Using his characteristic syntactical inversion, Yoda says, "Clouded, this boy's future is." Despite Yoda's intuitions, Anakin is conditionally accepted for induction. By the end of the *Phantom Menace* episode, young Anakin has proved his redemptive potential for killing in a good cause: he pilots a Starfighter, facing down battle droids in the Trade Federation control ship hangar when it helps the much older knights in their battle. Reprising the moment that so endeared Luke Skywalker to fans in *A New Hope*, he fires torpedoes that disable the control ship's reactor room, causing a nuclear blast as he flies away in the nick of time.

Archetypally speaking, this has been his Jonah moment in the belly of the beast, but his escape is aided by firepower that no nine-year-old has ever commanded before — even in the realm of myth. This precocious violence, directed at the evil Trade Federation, prefigures Anakin/Darth's larger role as the redemptive killer who eventually rescues the Republic at the conclusion of *Return of the Jedi*. In the moment when Luke's mere love is impotent during the Emperor's attack on him, Darth Vader steps forward to smash the Emperor into the reactor core. This act both redeems himself and saves the Republic, finally confirming Qui-Gon's early judgment that Anakin was "the chosen one" who could save the Republic. Thus, even Darth Vader passes through the monomythic cycles of development that bring the hero home with the "elixir" that saves the community.

The Political Symbolisms of *Star Wars*

The political systems of *Star Wars* have never been articulated very clearly and reflect the same kind of pastiche as do the plot and characters of the movies. Not hesitant about the apparent contradictions, the creators obviously identify with those characters who combine features of both republican and monarchist government. In creating a dream world of individual heroism for the youth market, George Lucas had no compelling dramatic reason to clutter his plot with didactic expositions on the constitution of the Republic. We know from the first trilogy that Emperor Palpatine, assisted by the betrayal of Anakin Skywalker, strangled the old Republic, which had a chancellor and a senate; the Jedi knights played a prominent role in that government. Although we encounter queens, princesses, and knights, we do not know what powers derive from their status or how much of it is due to their heredity — social or genetic. Anakin/Darth, of course, gains his entry in part because of his midi-chlorian blood test.

Another factor in *Star Wars'* political vagueness is the steady emphasis on personal spirituality and morality. Lucas's mentor, Joseph Campbell, felt skepticism about both politics and economics, seeing both as inherently destructive. In late-life conversations with Michael Toms, Campbell flatly said: "In politics and economics, the mode inevitably is conflict. Politics is winning over somebody else. . . . But it's in the spiritual realm that there are constants." In answer to Toms's question of whether politics could ever get over its proclivity for in-group aggressions against out-groups, Campbell pessimistically responded: "I don't know what politics can do. . . . I'm a little bit discouraged by the people who are involved in the political life of this country. I begin to feel it has been betrayed. Its potentialities have been sold for values that are inscrutable to me."[22] And in his conversations with Bill Moyers, Campbell diagnosed Darth Vader's moral malady as failing to "listen to the demands of his own heart."[23] He also commented that it was irrelevant for Darth Vader to work at reshaping the tyrannical system he served; and he drew a contemporary political lesson as well: "How do you relate to the system so that you are not compulsively serving it? It doesn't help to try to change it to your own system of thought. The momentum of history behind is too great for anything really significant to evolve from that kind of action. The thing to do is learn to live in your period of history as a human being" (p. 144).

Joseph Campbell, the man who had made remarkably wide-ranging studies of world culture and mythology, ultimately found the politics of his native country mystifying, repugnant, and hopeless. The spirit of defeatism is quite unlike that of the monomythic heroes he extols, individuals who return from dangerous journeys with healing elixirs for their communities. George Lucas has expressed a similar despair about U.S. politics and the press. In his interview with Orville Schell for *The New York Times,* he showed his preference for the language of "rulers," as opposed to speaking of democracy as an opportunity for participation and shared responsibility. He offhandedly remarked that "a good despot" or "a benevolent despot who can really get things done" would be preferable.[24] He explains himself this way:

> There's no respect for the office of the Presidency. Not that we need a king, but there's a reason why kings built large palaces, sat on thrones and wore rubies all over. There's a whole social need for that, not to oppress the masses, but to impress the masses and make them proud and allow them to feel good about their culture, their government and their ruler so that they are left feeling that a ruler has the right to rule over them, so that they feel good rather than disgusted about being ruled. In the past, the media basically worked for the state and was there to build the culture. Now, obviously, in some cases it got used in a wrong way and you ended up with the whole balance of power out of whack. But there's probably no better form of government than a good despot.[25]

Given this preference for rulers who "wear rubies all over to impress the masses and make them proud," it's hardly surprising that Lucas drew from the well of the American monomyth for his vision of government.

Attuned to Campbell's pessimism about the power of politics to achieve social good, George Lucas excelled at the visual poetry of evil governments and its agents. *Star Wars'* bad political systems look Stalinist or German National Socialist in their dress, and their actions are dictatorial and harshly cruel.[26] Darth Vader routinely uses the dark side of the Force to strangle the throats of his own subordinates, sometimes killing them on the spot for their dismal performance against the rebel Alliance. The soldiers of the Empire wear reptilian or insect-like armors that efface their individuality; not one of them appears the least bit sympathetic or disobedient, and any of them can be killed without any hesitation. In contrast, Alliance members — despite their military roles — wear whatever they have, always looking more vulnerable, less uniform. In the final battles against the Empire in *Return of the Jedi*, General Han Solo appears to be dressed for "casual Friday" instead of a military Armageddon, while the forest's Ewoks wear thin, dirty canvas head coverings. Solo's dress and demeanor continue to fit his outlaw role as a smuggler who has gradually turned toward social commitment. Alliance members thus continue the sartorial tradition of Buffalo Bill, Dirty Harry, Buford Pusser, Martin Riggs, and other heroes whose opposition to authority is expressed by disdain for uniforms and badges.

Star Wars' cultural politics are just as explicit as the symbolic discourse about totalitarian (the Empire) versus monarcho-republican (the rebel Alliance) government. As Michael Ryan and Douglas Kellner point out in *Camera Politica, Star Wars* promotes individualism against the state, nature against technology . . . faith and feeling against science and rationality, agrarian values against urban modernity." Ryan and Kellner also note: "The rural family scenes are endowed with an aura of simple virtue, while the city is depicted as a site of vice where monsters gamble, kill, and listen to jazz."[27] And in the cantina scenes at Mos Eisly *(A New Hope)* and Jabba's Palace *(Return of the Jedi)*, the denizens drink and admire female flesh, giving off signs of moral decadence that distinguish them from heroic individuals such as Luke, Ben, and Leia, who come to such places with the discipline of their mission to save the Republic. In this valorization of the rural and stigmatization of the urban, *Star Wars* exemplifies the American monomyth's images of the innocent, peaceful community that is corrupted by aggressive outsiders with appetites for pleasure and power. It also betrays a yearning for a time past, when life was simpler and politics was less important than issues of public well-being.

Fascism, *Star Wars'* Spiritual Cousin

In evaluating *Star Wars* as popular faith, we cannot avoid the topic of European fascism, however unwelcome the thought may be to those who find *Star Wars* a source of spiritual enlightenment. Since the present authors have both lived for extended periods in Germany and Austria — Hitler's home country, which welcomed him back in 1938 — we may bring background experiences to this sequence of movies that are not shared by fellow audience members. We were quite startled by the final awards ceremony for Luke, Han, and Chewbacca in *A New Hope*, an image reprised at the beginning of *The Empire Strikes Back*. It seemed to "quote" the most famous of the Nazi propaganda films, *Triumph of the Will* (*Triumph des Willens*, 1935), which was made by Leni Riefenstahl as a celebration of the Nuremberg Nazi party rallies of 1934.[28] Our surprise over this emotion-stirring scene was heightened when S. Schoenbaum's review of *A New Hope* appeared in *Times Literary Supplement*. He too expressed surprise that the finale of *Star Wars* borrowed so liberally from the Nazi masterpiece: "The victorious heroes march through the massed throng and mount a dais to be decorated by the princess. Multitudes cheer; the orchestration is Wagnerian. . . . But what purpose does the reference to Nazi propaganda serve in *Star Wars?*"[29] Were our reactions and those of Schoenbaum merely an indication of over-sensitive academic excess? Hardly. The Lucas Entertainment Company's encyclopedic "Insider's Guide to *Star Wars*" frankly acknowledges it in its scene commentary: "The final ceremony scene emulates, almost shot-for-shot, a similar segment in *Triumph des Willens* (1934)."[30]

The fascist award ceremony may seem especially dissonant in light of the fact that the film uses Nazi stereotypes for the evil Darth Vader and his storm troopers. However, the ideas that provide dramatic unity in the film are in several ways harmonious with the spirit of fascist choreography and the massed voices rising in heroic acclaim at the end. Consider the convergent streams of ideology that bring *Star Wars* and European fascism to the same delta. The initial *Star Wars* story begins when the old Republic has already been corrupted by its vicious foes. Since Obi-Wan Kenobi is the last of the Jedi knights pledged to sustain the republican principles, a new generation of heroes must be trained before the galaxy can be saved. Thus the story centers not on public education but on Luke Skywalker's calling and training to be a fighting Jedi. He is an Everyman figure, a typical youth of the space age, adept at repairing robots but unhappy on his uncle's rural planet. When one thinks of earlier traditions of democratic reason in our society, the story of Luke's training is a curious one. He is assumed to be too thoughtful, too inhibited to be effective in mastering the powerful Force that he can turn to in crusading for the old Republic. Thus Obi-Wan Kenobi teaches Luke a value system that is basically irrational, one that represents a flat repudiation of Thomas Jefferson's democratic ideal of developing responsive, trustworthy institutions through widespread public learning.

Two crucial scenes in *A New Hope* embody a kind of militant irrationalism. When Obi-Wan Kenobi teaches young Luke to fight with the light saber, he places a helmet on his head with the light visor pulled down so that he cannot see the target. He says: "Remember, a true Jedi can feel 'the Force' flowing from him. Your eyes can deceive you. Don't trust them!" The young man swings at the target and misses again, but Kenobi encourages him to "stretch out with your feelings." Luke swings again and makes a perfect strike, confessing with amazement, "I . . . I did feel something! I could almost see the 'remote.'" Later in the climactic battle with the Death Star, the young Luke Skywalker uses his miraculous instincts to succeed where more experienced pilots had failed. He turns off his targeting computer and relies on manual control in response to his now-dead mentor. As the control officer protests the irrationality of Luke's decision, Ben Kenobi's words echo in Skywalker's mind while he fires the torpedo at precisely the right instant to blow up the nuclear reactors of the gigantic Death Star. It is a scene that brought audiences to their feet all over America, and its message is quite clear: trust your irrational feelings and trust "the Force" to destroy your enemies when you do. The role of "the Force" is consistent with the paradigm of the Main Street duel all the way from *The Virginian* to the present: it tells superheroes when to pull the trigger. The human mind in *A New Hope* simply becomes fate's vessel for pouring nuclear destruction on the enemy.

The heroic ideal in *Star Wars* is centered on the training of Luke Skywalker to be a Jedi knight. According to producer George Lucas's description in his novelized version of the original story, the Jedi had been "the most powerful, most respected force in the galaxy . . . the guarantors of peace and justice."[31] Their use of "the Force" allowed them to respond instinctively to danger and thus to become invincible. The idea of a natural aristocracy composed of martial heroes was, of course, central to fascism. Nations were to be led by heroes with triumphant wills, instinctively moving where their racial souls guided them.[32] The Italian fascist thinker Palmieri described such warriors as partaking of the divine to a measure impossible for ordinary mortals. Such persons are capable of "that magic flash of a moment of supreme intuition" that comes "to the hero and none other."[33] Just as the European heroes of the 1930s proclaimed, "We think with our blood,"[34] Skywalker is informed that his father was a Jedi who would never hesitate to embark on an "idealistic crusade" because his decisions came to him "instinctively."[35] The content of this "instinct" is heroic nationalism, a zealous willingness to crusade for the enactment of the national ideals through the destruction of their perceived enemies. Obi-Wan Kenobi plainly identifies "the Force" with such instinct when he describes Luke's father: "The Force . . . the instinct was strong in him."[36] One develops such instinct by learning to "stop thinking . . . to divorce your actions from conscious control" (p. 121).

The kinship of this idea of "the Force" to the metaphysical ethics of Fascism is unmistakable. Mussolini's dictum virtually provides the prooftext for *Star Wars:* "The Fascist state, the highest and most powerful form of personality, is a force, but a spiritual force, which takes over all the forms of the moral and intellectual life of man."[37] This is related to the fascist conception of the organic state, in which individuals find their identity in fighting for "Das Volk," also a prominent motif in *Star Wars.* George Lucas's novelization describes Skywalker's emotions when he joined the rebel airforce: "He was no longer an individual, functioning solely to satisfy his personal needs. Something now bound him to every other man and woman in this hangar" (p. 187). Palmieri had stated this ideal quite forcefully: "The true Fascist works not for himself alone, but for his nation as well; he believes not in a godless universe, but in a universe which exists by the will of God; worships this God not as a remote, abstract entity, but as something . . . to which he can confidently appeal in life and which he shall rejoin at death."[38]

Religious idealism of this kind is particularly appealing to a generation disillusioned by harsh events. Europe after World War I was similar to post-Vietnam America in this regard. Historian George L. Mosse summarizes the yearning that gave rise to European fascism: "Having survived the holocaust of a senseless war, they wanted to face the postwar world with purpose and direction. For these men, idealism, a purposeful world view, became of crucial importance."[39]

Another parallel that links fascism with *Star Wars* is a betrayal theory of political history. In *A New Hope's* fantasy, an old Republic is pictured as having been subverted and destroyed "by restless, power-hungry individuals within the government, and the massive organs of commerce."[40] Such language became commonplace in the Nazi tirades against the Weimar Republic: they attacked the institutions of a democratic society, including a free economic system, equal protection before the law, and the free exchange of ideas as the sources of subversion. The claim in *Star Wars* that the Jedi Knights had been exterminated through "treachery and deception" evokes the stab-in-the-back mentality arising in the wake of the Versailles Treaty that propelled Germany into a fascist approach to its problems. Brave German soldiers had allegedly been betrayed by democratic politicians lacking the will to sacrifice everything for the sake of victory.

If one accepts the moral simplisms of fascism, whether in its classic European or contemporary pop form, it becomes plausible to believe that good prevails only through violence. The glorification of violence lies at the very heart of the original *Star Wars* movie *(A New Hope)* and the concluding battles in *Return of the Jedi* and *Phantom Menace.* Violence resolves the political problem of the old Republic and the new Empire: the permanent subduing of evil with the killing of Emperor Palpatine and the destruction of Death Star II. Even the saintly Kenobi exhibits the cool savagery of "the Force" by slashing apart three humanoids in the Mos Eisley cantina scene. When Luke's torpedo strikes the vulnerable exhaust port of the Death Star, blowing it apart with an immense atomic blast, American audiences were elated. A grim destruction such as that of Hiroshima and Nagasaki was reaffirmed in fantasy. The ideal of Mussolini was thereby embodied in a new, atomically amplified form.

We are hardly suggesting that George Lucas is a European fascist or that the millions of Americans who flocked to *Star Wars* and its sequels are a new wave of Brown Shirts or *Hitlerjugend*. Instead, there is an indigenous American tradition of violent redemption that surfaces in this film, an undercurrent that runs parallel to European streams of idealistic crusading.[41] The notion that the Light Side must battle against the Dark Side is a hoary artifact of European- and American-style crusades against evil. Furthermore, the notion that all of life resolves into clear-cut battles between good and evil is itself antithetical to the democratic understanding of governance. Since the good cannot be identified with clarity, it must be debated and voted upon; the losers must reconcile themselves to live with a lesser good or with something they refuse to recognize as good at all. Americans must exercise this disciplined choice in every national election, living with what they regard as a tolerable alternative to a death struggle.

Showing the spiritual affinities of *Star Wars* with fascism suggests the profoundly anti-democratic spirit of this stream that continues to flow through the American imagination. These disturbing echoes indicate that, consciously or unconsciously, Americans are willing to relax and enthusiastically enjoy values contrary to those embodied in its religious and political institutions. Through the repeated celebration of creations such as *Star Wars,* the most destructive of our fantasies become mainstream even for children.

The history of our century suggests that widely applauded fantasies like this have an effect, though perhaps only in a few determined souls. George Sorel, who contributed to the formulation of modern totalitarianism, was more realistic than are media apologists who say it's all just entertainment. Popular myths provide emotional force for violent politics, according to Sorel: "Myths are not descriptions of things, but expressions of the determination to act." Their power is that those who accept the fantasy are "secure from all refutation."[42] People become convinced that if a violent war can restore some old Republic, it will surely bring virtue to the current era of corruption. Monomythic politics lives in the expectation of a superheroic explosion that will make all things new. Timothy McVeigh, who talked often of *Star Wars'* wisdom for action, has shown us just that.

Star Wars' Fascism and Pop Religion

A great religious disappointment during the years of fascist dominance in central Europe was the failure of the churches to recognize and oppose the destructive faiths growing in their midst. Despite notable acts of courage on the part of individuals such as Martin Niemoeller and Dietrich Bonhoeffer, most churches failed to muster the resources to be effective opponents of the smothering power that engulfed their societies. In Germany the majority of Protestants joined the "German Christian" movement that united fascism and anti-Semitism into the Christian faith. In Austria, the Catholic Church greeted its forceful annexation *(Anschluss)* by Germany and urged voters to ratify their fate as subjects by voting for unification in the "greater Germany."

However cloudy its relationship to democratic rationality or traditional religious values, the message of *Star Wars* captivated admirers within religious traditions. The idealized violence brought forth hosannas from strangely divergent disciples. The normally sober *Christian Century* film reviewer hailed *A New Hope* as "a breath of fresh fantasy" that "celebrates the possibility of a different and better world." The review concluded:

> *Star Wars* strikes so many of us as a breath of fresh air not only because we need to believe that the good can triumph but because lately we have had such difficulty in identifying the good . . . from the evil. . . . The alternative vision of *Star Wars* . . . strikes us with the force of stepping from the cave into bright sunlight.[43]

A Lutheran reviewer said the movie was "as old fashioned as a morality play," with "an undergirding religious premise that is theologically simplistic but nonetheless impressively reverent and sincerely introduced." He perceived the idea of "the Force" to be "a combination of the mysticism of ESP and the New Testament doctrine of the Holy Spirit."[44] Steven A. Galipeau, who had previously written *Transforming Body and Soul: Therapeutic Wisdom in the Gospel Healing Stories* (1990), found himself increasingly drawn to the life wisdom of the *Star Wars* films. As a tribute to the original trilogy, he wrote *The Journey of Luke Skywalker,* an extended psychological commentary from a Jungian perspective. Of Luke's trust in Ben's voice and the Force that allows him to instinctively release the torpedo that destroys the Death Star, he comments: "In psychological terms this moment represents the point in a person's development when the archetype of the Self is realized in a deeper and more conscious way."[45] Galipeau accepts without question the movie's stereotyped evil that offers Luke his moment of personal growth: "The Death Star was built as a vehicle of power that went beyond any humane purposes." With Luke's shot, "its destructive energy is turned back on itself" (p. 83). The notion that redemptive violence — driven by radically simplifying moral stereotypes — might itself be a dangerous precedent for spiritual formation does not lie within Galipeau's horizon. He mentions Yoda's counsel to Luke "that the Jedi knight seeks wisdom and knowledge but not violent action."[46] Galipeau appears to overlook the fact that in the plots of the films violence always trumps evil at the most crucial moments.

Some film reviewers for Christian publications have resembled Galipeau in suggesting that we sit back, admire the spectacle, and learn inspirational lessons. But when we turn to a commentator such as Frank Allnutt, we are back in the realm of *Left Behind* millennialism. Allnutt has probably been the most successful religious entrepreneur to spread the gospel of *Star Wars*. In his book *Unlocking the Mystery of the Force,* which has reached its fifth edition (more than 200,000 books in print), Allnutt describes a personal epiphany with *A New Hope*. As he stood in line to get his ticket, he wondered why he felt "a tinge of excitement. . . . But I sensed that I was destined for some special reason to see *Star Wars*."[47] After he saw the movie, Allnutt, who had worked as a publicist for Walt Disney Productions, realized that he had seen "the greatest contribution to the art and science of motion pictures since Walt Disney's *Snow White and the Seven Dwarfs*." Back in his hotel, he began writing his commentary on the movie because he "began to see the depth of eternal truths in *Star Wars*." For him, the movie offered the answers to all the big questions about who he was, where the world came from, and where it's going (pp. 7-8). This he encapsulates in his conclusion:

> My premise is that long before the *Star Wars* movies, in a place far, far away, there were *real* Star Wars, a *true* Force, and *real* Jedi. The ancient Star Wars erupted when the evil Fallen Star (Satan) rebelled against the True Force (God) and later waged war against the Son of the True Force, the Bright Morning Star (Jesus Christ) and His faithful followers, who, in my way of thinking, can be seen as true Jedi for Jesus, or *JEsus DIsciples*. (p. 9)

In *Star Wars,* Allnutt also perceived a stirring prefiguration of the apocalyptic battle that the universe requires for its moral purification:

The galactic wars in the movies are really religious wars. The people of the Alliance, who believe in and follow the ways of the Force, are pitted against the satanic emperor Palpatine, Darth Vader and all the other "fallen stars" of the Old Republic. The Bible tells us that there is a bitter conflict raging throughout the spiritual universe, and it's no secret to anyone that a fierce battle between the forces of good and the forces of evil is being fought on planet earth today. (p. 90)

As Allnutt warms to his elaborate allegory, he likens the church to that "small band of Rebel forces led by Luke, Han, and Princess Leia on a mission to restore the former glory of the Alliance" (p. 143). In the real, spiritual "star wars" that Allnutt sees today, "Jesus has an even deadlier sword" than the light sabers, and he will use it "to strike down all the ungodly nations of the world" (p. 169). This strong identification with the apocalyptic ideology of *Star Wars* is widely shared in conservative religious circles, as our own lectures and conversations over the past couple of decades have revealed.

It is easy for those who do not share Allnutt's millennialist theology to scoff at his literal-minded effort to map *Star Wars* as the rewritten drama of the end-times. But he is representative of many who come to *Star Wars* to find an exciting, commercial confirmation of religious biases. Yet even more scholarly minds have responded ecstatically to *Star Wars'* vision of clear-cut good and evil followed by heroic destruction. Robert G. Collins, writing in

The surprising turn of plot in *Return of the Jedi* makes Darth Vader part of the redemption scheme for the Old Republic. At film's end, we see the ghostly trinity — Darth, Yoda, and Ben — who contributed to the victory of the rebel Alliance.

Credit: *Return of the Jedi* © 1983 Lucasfilms.

The Journal of Popular Culture, remarks that the film handles "the moral distinction . . . so well . . . that a freshness and innocence is achieved which virtually makes credible the call for a renewed faith in the underlying truth of things ('The Force') of which Ben Kenobi is the spokesman. . . . The simplicity and beauty of the total experience yields a warm sense of delight . . . tied to no specific place or time but founded on the most familiar as well as the deepest of our mythic instincts, there is a glory about it."[48]

That such sentiments are widely shared among well-read Americans is confirmed by the numerous hostile comments after the authors of this book have given public lectures on college and university campuses, hostilities that are consistently directed against any effort to evaluate the film's ideology. Colleagues have also reported to us that some students are so emotionally committed to *Star Wars* that classroom discussions become awkward because these students feel that the core of their belief system is being undermined. The continued popularity of the now multi-sequeled movies accounts for the virtually universal acceptance of the expression "Star Wars" for the Strategic Defense Initiative during the past two decades. It is also allied to the naïve notion that other countries would see orbiting U.S. weapons platforms in their sky as "purely defensive" — to be used only against "rogue nations" with evil leaders.

Few seem aware of *Star War's* profound disparities with democratic ideals or with religious traditions of peace and reconciliation. The physical beauty of the movies and the charming qualities of their invented worlds are the candy coating that renders their spirit of idealized destructiveness invisible to those enthralled by it. This is the same phenomenon that we shall see prevailing among fans of The *Matrix* (discussed in the next chapter). The cultural reception of the *Star Wars* series illustrates a kind of "mythic dissonance." Whereas popular myths often sustain the leading values and institutions of a culture, the American monomyth consistently undermines the democratic ethos and the democratic components of religious faiths. Given its elitism, irrationalism, stereotyping, and appetite for total solutions instead of compromise, it is difficult to find any comparably emphatic democratic sentiment in the myth, except perhaps in its convention of Everyman as the redemptive hope. Although American superheroes consistently strive to redeem corrupted republics, the definition of their roles and the means of their triumphs reflect fascist values that ultimately undermine democratic processes and hollow out the religious faith of the enchanted.

14 Monomythic Credotainment

"The boundary-crossing, barrier-breaking tendencies . . . intrinsic to both hypertext and computer networks are a . . . happy conjunction of theology and technology. And there is every reason to believe that world-shaking forces of similar proportions and power to those . . . of the Protestant Reformation are being set loose once again, and shall have equally profound effects upon the way . . . people practice faith, as well as communicate with each other and with God."[1]

Charles Henderson, a Presbyterian and organizing pastor
of the First Church of Cyberspace (www.godweb.org)

"On several occasions I had considered seeking help for being so affected by a children's movie. . . . It actually feels good to be telling this to people who understand what I've gone through. As already stated, I feel alone here as none of my friends, parents, brothers or sisters seems to understand what a profound impact this movie has had on my life."

Jasons Ahrens' message to alt.fan.lion-king,
an electronic forum for Disney's *The Lion King*[2]

As we have seen in the foregoing chapters on *Star Trek* and *Star Wars*, admiration for the American monomyth's stories can take on qualities of religious

In a place far, far away, and long before the movie, there were

REAL STAR WARS!

5th EDITION With "Menace"!

UNLOCKING THE MYSTERY OF THE FORCE

The Best-Seller By FRANK ALLNUTT

Updated & Expanded
More than 200,000 in Print!

Frank Allnutt's book celebrates *Star Wars* as a powerful retelling of Jesus' story — as the apocalyptic destroyer in the Book of Revelation. This interpretation is apparently shared by a large audience.

Credit: © 1999 Allnutt Publishing Co.

devotion. For Frank Allnutt, who transformed his stirring exegesis of *Star Wars* through five editions, the films continue to revitalize his faith in the Christ of the book of Revelation, an apocalyptic general who crushes the enemies of God.[3] For *Star Trek*'s more peace-loving fans, the program's messages provide steady guidance as they steer toward an optimistic world of expanding technology and galactic exploration. This chapter tours past some other gatherings of monomythic faith and celebration that have come to the Internet in the last decade, first as text-based discussion forums for e-mail exchanges and then as graphics-enhanced Web sites that are attracting global participants. These electronic communities of faith are increasingly assisted by the great corporate mythic franchises, attracted to develop their financial interests on the Web by steadily expanding their market for products from which fans derive spiritual inspiration — corporate-copyrighted books, music, licensed toys and video games, as well as information about programs and celebrities. Disney.com, Starwars.com, Startrek.com service their Web sites almost daily with fresh material; other sites are creations of unpaid individuals, sometimes working alone and sometimes linking with other sites that share the same appreciations and spiritual stances. Situating these digital faith communities within a broader evolutionary vision of American popular culture and religion, we describe a few significant sites, their objectives, the voices of celebration, and their impact in reaching an electronic congregation. Toward the end of the chapter we speculate on the implications of electronic fan sites for the democratic ethos. But first we need to describe the changing status of entertainment and its symbiotic interactions with religion.

Credotainment Culture

In the 1980s, Neil Postman wrote a popular jeremiad about American culture entitled *Amusing Ourselves to Death: Public Discourse in the Age of Show Business.*[4] He contended that the glitzy production values of entertainments and their celebrities were reshaping the news industry, education, politics, and religion. Lamenting Americans' sound-byte attention spans for discussions of public policy, he harkened back to the spell-binding, hours-long Lincoln-Douglas debates on slavery from more than a century ago. So persuasive was Postman's perception of the realm of television that his coinage "infotainment," a blend of "information" and "entertainment" came to be widely used. As the trends to which Postman referred spread, we also began to hear the term "edutainment," which described a comparable fusion in the field of education.[5] The implication of using such language is that the blended product's entertainment portion dominates and trivializes the education or informational content that it supposedly enhances.

Postman's critical assessment included a recognition that religious faiths could walk along this same amusing path. Focusing on television, he put it this way: "[O]n television, religion, like everything else, is presented . . . as an entertainment. Everything that makes religion an historic, profound, and sacred activity is stripped away; there is no ritual, no dogma, no tradition, and above all, no sense of spiritual transcendence. On these shows, the preacher is tops. God comes out as second banana."[6] Postman's view was influenced by figures such as Jim and Tammy Faye Bakker, with their Hollywood game-show broadcast arena, their puppets, and their Heritage USA religious theme park.[7] Robert Schuller, Oral Roberts, and Jimmy Swaggart were also part of

This cover from *Newsweek* seems to share in celebrating the mixture of secular entertainment forms with Christianity. We call this merger "credotainment."

Credit: Newsweek, Inc. © 2001.

the televangelist spectacles of that era. Now that new forms of spirituality are emerging in the electronic spaces of the Internet, we can see that the 1980s blend of showmanship and religious piety represented just one way to graft televisual show biz values to the spiritual enterprise.

Nearly two decades after the Bakkers' decline and fall, it has become even more timely to talk broadly about "religiotainment" or "credotainment," entertainment products that play a role in the religious life — sometimes by design, but often by accident. The character of these new religious fusions with the higher amusements is also conveyed by the category "recreational religion," a term coined by John Strausbaugh in his book about "Elvism," the developing religious practices focusing on the life of Elvis Presley. Clarifying this new kind of devotion, Strausbaugh points out that churches traditionally used strategies of separating the sacred and the profane, but that "recreational religions are more holistic, more integrated . . . the infusion of religious fervor and faith into the pursuit of an avocation one intensely *enjoys*."[8] We believe that it is more historically accurate to acknowledge that religion and entertainment have had symbiotic relationships, often demanded by the artistic patronage or the social power of the church. But we do find something new in the recreational religion phenomenon: the independence of these religious expressions from institutional churches, creedal systems, and ritual-specified ways of expressing religious faith. For this reason, we prefer our term, *credotainment,* because it illustrates the personal designer-faith character of the phenomenon with its stronger emphasis on inner states rather than acts in the community.

This realignment of historical relationships between church authority and member behavior evokes for us John Dewey's progressive theories of education. Perhaps we should be talking about the "progressive religion" that takes its cues from the entertainments aimed at the young. Dewey was a proponent of effective, attention-engaging schools that espoused the values of democracy in both instruction and administration. He had an animus against the schools' emphasis on authority external to the pupil: he believed that such an emphasis led to undemocratic attitudes of subservience that later resurfaced in political life. It was also striking to him that schools in nondemocratic countries showed educational styles similar to those of America. Shouldn't a country that calls itself a democracy have a distinctive democratic style of education?

Rejecting the schooling patterns he had come to know in the United States, Dewey wrote: "Since the subject-matter as well as the standards of proper conduct are handed down from the past, the attitude of the pupils must, upon the whole, be one of docility, receptivity, and obedience."[9] Dewey's plan for democratic classrooms lay in the analysis of children's experiences and their own perspectives on what is important to know. He leaned toward allowing curricula to grow out of the children's own interests, with the teacher functioning as a more experienced guide and partner. Dewey envisioned a series of new emphases that would become the progressive ideal: "To imposition from above is opposed expression and cultivation of individuality; to external discipline is opposed free activity; to learning from texts and teachers, learning through experience" (p. 19).

Dewey's ideas never had smooth sailing when they flew under his own rebellious flag; their head-on collision with traditionalism aroused immediate opposition. And even his progressive sympathizers often lacked the skills to make his ideas operative in their own classrooms, not to mention achieving reform on a large scale. As an idea that had its moment in history, progressivism was succeeded by B. F. Skinner's behaviorism, then by humanistic psychology's emphasis on self-esteem, by the home-schooling trend led by distrusting parents, by political calls for standardized testing — and many other kinds of reformist inspiration. However, in a surprising way that Dewey never could have anticipated, several of his progressive principles for reaching youthful minds would eventually filter into American life. For example, popular culture itself has delivered hilarious elaborations of Dewey's attack on the stern custom of teaching respect for adult authority. Searching for profitable markets among those very teens needing civilization, popular entertainers have mocked schools ruthlessly, and with irresistible humor. It has given us fuming, fumbling principals such as Mr. Rooney in the film *Ferris Bueller's Day Off* (1986), who never catches Ferris at his outrageous pranks and fibs. *Mad Magazine*, the comic-book satire of culture, and television series such as *The Simpsons* and *Beavis and Butthead* regularly deflate serious adult pretenses to authority based on competence or superior knowledge.

Generally speaking, the amusements for children such as television, music, video games, comic books, and computers offer informal curricula that claim far more of young people's attention than the schoolhouse and its old-fashioned books. So captivating are youth entertainments that a recurring cultural question has become: "How can traditional institutions such as family, church, and school compete with popular culture?" The twentieth century brought us a variety of answers to this question, ranging from censorious opposition to a kind of surrender in the form of syncretism.

An early suppressive strategy was simply to denounce and to forbid amusements. North America has seen moralistic campaigns against Sunday morning bicycle rides, films, comic books, ball-room waltzing, rock and roll, video arcades, and many other activities. This pattern is so strong that almost every form of popular diversion has been attacked in its emergent stages. When such assaults failed, opponents of the new entertainment experiences regrouped for strategies of cooperative reform that worked with the noxious industries. Out of those impulses came the Motion Picture Code of 1934 and the Comics Code Authority of 1954: both were attempts at industry self-regulation designed to ward off officially exercised government censorship. The former came in response to the late 1920s suspicion that movies were causing a breakdown in sexual codes, while the latter was linked to the 1950s suspicion that comic books caused juvenile criminal behavior.[10] Such regulative tactics tended to weaken over time because commercial forces tenaciously prove the marketability of their wares and manage to skate along the wavering boundaries separating the acceptable and the forbidden. The producers have also made effective appeals to American culture's twin ideals of a free market and free speech.

Another strategy, used so often in history, has been syncretism: the blending of the traditional with the popular so as to revitalize the former. We currently live in an age of marketing-based syncretism. Examples of such strategies (discussed in earlier chapters) include NASA's adoption of *Star Trek* themes/names and the Smithsonian's major exhibit for *Star Wars'* imaginary world. These hoary institutions, by honoring cultural artifacts that have a wide audience, seem to legitimate themselves culturally with youthful fans

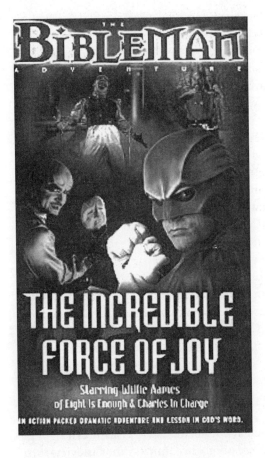

This video box for Pamplin Entertainment's *Bibleman* title, *The Incredible Force of Joy,* is explicit in its fusion of Batman and *Star Wars* with Christian teaching.

Credit: *Bibleman* video box cover. Pamplin Entertainment © 1996.

and hold out the promise of building new constituencies among the succeeding generations.

Within Christian evangelical culture, some of the syncretistic accommodations with amusement culture are so overt as to hide any embarrassment about straying from tradition. A bold example of this is afforded by the *Bibleman* Christian videos for the grade school set, promoted at www.bibleman.com and other Web sites. The Bibleman character is taken straight from the Batman template — and without apology. The character has a dual life as Miles Peterson, a rich, handsome person who has a hunger for something more. In one of his moments of despair, the Bible has given Miles the inspiration to fight evil. He does so in a costume that has the hard-shell body articulation of the recent *Batman* films. With a nod to Luke Skywalker and Darth Vader, he carries a laser sword for his confrontations with evil foes such as the Gossip Queen, the Fibbler, and Dr. Fear. In another nod to *Star Wars*, one full-length episode is entitled "The Incredible Force of Joy" and features an R2-D2 modeled sidekick U.N.I.C.E (Universal Intelligence Computing Entity). If there is one departure from the Batman model, it is the downplay of physical violence: Bibleman overcomes his foes by quoting appropriate scriptural passages.

As the advertisement for the Bibleman action figure tells us, his sword is merely "the Sword of the Spirit," his body armor "the Breastplate of Righteousness," and his helmet "the Helmet of Salvation."[11] Willie Aames, the actor who has played Bibleman for several years, declares the syncretic strategy for children with clarity: "We need to go after them in such a way that we get their attention so that we can bring them to the point where they connect with Jesus Christ."[12] The appropriation of superheroic garb and story lines — however watered down in their violence — suggests the constant dilemma of syncretism. How well can the comic-book-style narrative lead to understanding the Prince of Peace when the signposts are laser swords, action figures, and rigid stereotypes of the righteous Hero and the evil Other? How compatible are superheroic disciples with a biblical religion that insists that God alone is super? This is not, to use the optimistic phrase of Rev. Charles Henderson of the First Church of Cyberspace, "a happy conjunction of technology and theology," even when Bibleman has his own Web site.

Smash-Face Buddhism: The "Ballistic Mystic"

Tom Beaudoin, in discussing the Gen-X embracing of cyberspace as a form of community, says that "the net is increasingly becoming a monastery for the spiritually disposed. As in 'real' monasteries, a user may seek community at specific times or in particular sites, and there are myriad opportunities for self-reflection, prayer, meditation, and scripture studies."[13] Perhaps the most prominent monomythic actor/filmmaker to project himself into the spiritual surfing scene is Steven Seagal, the renowned practitioner of Aikido martial arts in movie roles and an advocate of Buddhism. His Web site (stevenseagal.com) reaches out to those who have come to know him through his successful fantasy movie career in protecting the weak and avenging the wronged. But unlike any other actor who has played such roles, Seagal presents himself in an evangelical role for spiritual enlightenment. Through stories conveyed to the press, Seagal has described searching out several masters for personal religious instruction over several decades. And in 1997, Seagal was widely reported to be recognized as a reincarnation of the eighth-century Tibetan lama Chung-rag Dorje by Lama Penor Rinpoche, "the eleventh throneholder of Palyul tradition from Eastern Tibet and the Supreme head of Nyingma lineage of Tibetan Buddhism," in the account by Orville Schell.[14]

Seagal, who has lived in Japan and studied there with Buddhist priests and with Japanese masters of Aikido, feels comfortable with such standing as a religious teacher, although he did report that he fled from Japan because "people tried to deify me, and the reason I left there was that deification is a death trap."[15] He does accept a role, however, as spiritual leader: "There are many great lamas who recognize me as someone strange and from another time, who refer to me as one of them. . . . People all over the world come up and recognize me as a great spiritual leader. I'd like to spread any kind of light I can and lead people into the dharma. I do films because I can put little seeds in them that can become spirituality."[16] Seagal offers financial support to Tibetan Buddhism, spending time raising money for the cause, and he gives public instruction in Aikido and meditation topics such as "Awakening Compassion Through the Martial Arts."[17] He also sells his video *The Path Beyond Thought*, which features his own martial arts wizardry.

What is the foundation of Seagal's guru life? As an actor he made his career in cultivating American monomythic narratives that mirror a life trajectory he has offered to the press in the following account: he discovered a Japanese martial arts instructor in Fullerton, California, when he was a teenager and then traveled to Japan for an extended period of study and eventually the management of a martial arts studio in Tokyo. He reports that his fighting mastery earned him respect from the Japanese and also attracted the attention of CIA officials, who invited him to become a consultant during the period of the Vietnam War. He has also reported giving security advice to Anwar Sadat of Egypt, to Bishop Desmond Tutu of South Africa, and to the Shah of Iran. No one in any official position of responsibility will confirm or deny these claims by Seagal.[18]

Trading on his background story as master of secrecy, security, weapons, and hand-to-hand fighting, Seagal has made movies that incorporate his preferred spooky version of his past self in his characters. He has reaped great box-office success, even when the films received poor critical reviews — especially for his acting ability. His tales of righteous revenge incorporate themes of secrecy and out-of-control governments that attack powerless victims; against that background, he is the barely audible man of peace who speaks most effectively in his destructive rampages that protect the weak. Unlike other action heroes, such as Sylvester Stallone, Chuck Norris, and Bruce Willis, who act out fantasy themes of the political right in America, Seagal uses plots in which his character defends such causes as environmentalism and the sanctuary movement of the Christian churches, intervenes in domestic abuse situations, and other liberal causes. His heroic roles sometimes include a spiritual aspect, for example, defending a church, calling upon a church official to have courage, or receiving spiritual enlightenment himself.

Seagal's first film, *Above the Law* (1988), reprised his early life story and enunciated the "liberal" violence that would become easily recognizable in his subsequent productions. The hero, Nico Toscani, is a young Sicilian immigrant to Chicago who develops an interest in martial arts, travels to Japan as an adult, learns the language, and astounds the fighters there with his ability to teach and to easily defeat entire groups of students simultaneously. From there Nico goes to a CIA assignment in Cambodia, where he witnesses the torture and murder of captured natives by vicious Americans and develops a knowledge of their involvement in illegal drugs. Rather than participating further in such crimes, he resigns his CIA role. Later, working as a drug enforcement cop in Chicago, he discovers a basement sanctuary for Salvadoran refugees in his own neighborhood church. These refugees are being terrorized by his own former CIA bosses, who are now engaged in the drug trade and are also plotting to kill a U.S. Senator who threatens to expose them and their corrupt government defenders. An explosion in his church, while Nico is there for mass, kills the parish priest. Because Nico himself engages in so many illegal and usually violent law-enforcement actions, he is always in trouble with his Chicago police superiors. He saves his own skin only by stopping the assassination plot against the senator. This paradox of illegal methods used against those who consider themselves "above the law" is utterly transparent to filmgoers. Seagal's dramatic mask for this contradiction lies in the convention that every scene of mayhem begins with his gentle, almost whispered requests to comply with his wishes. The limited acting range that critics complain about actually helps to build his persona as the man of peace who is always pushed to violence by others who are more aggressive. Nancy Griffin captured this contradictory combination when she referred to him as "an action lama" and the "ballistic mystic."[19] The producer of Seagal's film *The Patriot* (1998) put it this way: "His character is pushed to become violent when all else fails. . . . He has to save the world."[20]

Seagal has re-enacted the basic elements of his monomythic debut story in most of the movies that have followed, changing only the specific cause from film to film. Because Aikido is his special superhero power, he must inevitably resort to violence. *Glimmer Man* (1996) exhibits Seagal's favored mixtures of Eastern spirituality and brutal defensive violence. There he plays Lt. Jack Cole of the Los Angeles police, a former special-forces jungle fighter in Vietnam who "went native, disappeared," and then was saved by a holy man.[21] His dress reflects his time of learning in the jungle with the master and his deep daily spirituality. He wears, even at his police workplace, Tibetan prayer beads and a gold brocade jacket. This bizarre get-up marks his outsider status and invites constant ridicule from others, but Cole is completely unaffected by their scorn; his own deep spirituality is conveyed by scenes in which he meditates with incense.

The Glimmer Man's investigative assignment in Los Angeles is a series of ritual killings: all the victims are Catholics and all have been crucified, a circumstance that takes him into church, where he prevents the murder of a priest by a serial killer. At one point, even Cole's ex-wife is murdered, which points suspicion squarely back at him. The film's beginning gives us immediate mythic cues that Jack Cole is a man of extraordinary compassion and super powers. While out on assignment, a suicide call comes over the radio, and Cole's partner says, "That's not our call." Cole replies: "We gotta have compassion for the dead, the dying, and the about-to-be-dead." He prevents a schoolhouse shooting and suicide, and in the process accidentally discovers clues that will eventually allow him to solve the case. Cole has deductive powers of Sherlock Holmes' caliber: while viewing the corpse of one of the crucified Catholics, a naked woman on a morgue slab, he announces that she is a Russian from Georgia. Staring at her naked breasts, he takes a knife and — while others gasp — deftly slices a piece of contraband from her breast. The bad guys in this film, importers of biological warfare material that they plan to sell to Serbian terrorists, are sensualists who work in posh offices and enjoy wine and women at poolside. When Cole finally faces one of the key suspects in his case, he demonstrates his contempt by forcing a confession out of him with a shot through the foot and then through the hand, finally leaving the man to drag himself to a hospital.

In *Fire Down Below* (1997), Seagal plays an undercover Environmental Protection Agency agent, Jack Taggart, who is assigned to investigate toxic dumping. But he goes under spiritual cover to carry out this government duty: he pretends to be an Appalachian Relief Mission worker volunteering to do carpentry for poor people. He wears a clerical collar, which he explains to the suspicious by saying that he's "just doing God's work" and "it makes me feel good to help people." He quickly discovers that everybody in town who might exercise leadership in fighting the environmentally induced illnesses has been bought off by a wicked chemical tycoon, Orin Hanner, a man who acts brutally toward his pathetic son. Hanner also loves fine suits, female flesh, alcohol, and gambling; in fact, he is so morally dissolute that he has a bedroom at his office — with a lingering playmate at the ready. Even the pastor of the local church has been bought off by this Mr. Big, and he consents to give his pollution-related testimony in court only after Jack pleads with him.

But he has turned too late, and he dies in his burning church, which has been torched by the tycoon.

Seagal also pursued the environmental theme in *On Deadly Ground* (1994), where he plays the firefighter Forrest Taft, who discovers major pollution at Aegis Oil Company in Alaska. At one moment in the plot, an explosion blows him unconscious and into the care of Alaskan Indians. While recovering from this injury, he has a series of spirit encounters that tell him of threats to Mother Earth. After he has predictably defeated all the corporate foes, Seagal appends a lecture to the end of the movie in which he lambastes corporate environmental values as the route to mankind's death. This didactic plea, tacked onto the end of *On Deadly Ground* with his usual Aikido-styled ultraviolence, prefigured Seagal's role in world culture as an aspiring spiritual leader.

After Seagal's recognition as the reincarnated lama Chung-rag Dorje in 1997, it must have seemed timely to launch an electronic worship space where his fans could congregate and have a regular venue for his messages and his aids to spirituality: his Aikido martial-arts video, incenses, and essential oils. It fits in with the larger goal that Seagal claimed in his interview with *Shambhala Sun Magazine:* "What I want to do in this life is only important if I can ease the suffering of others, if I can somehow make the world a better place, if I somehow serve Buddha and mankind."[22]

Does the Seagal Web site further those aims? As a place for fans who have taken an interest in Seagal and his brand of spirituality, there is little evidence that his face-smashing Aikido style of the monomyth has done much more than further trivialize or popularize such violence as a cultural amusement. The "Message Board" section of the site has organized topics of discussion for differing interests and offers a barometer of interests in the Seagal franchise. By mid-July 2001, more than 25,000 messages had been posted, with the following posting categories and numbers of comments:

Movies	18,490
Aikido	6,143
Dharma[23]	960
Music	486
Ask Steven Seagal — Top 5 Questions	171

Reading through the messages, one's strongest impression is that the martial arts are the principal magnet drawing people to the films and to the electronic message boards. One posting in the "Aikido" section that drew several comments involved a situation in which a man described himself as contemplating the use of his deadly Aikido skills against an abusive partner of one of his female friends. "I may have to hurt him severely in the course of defending her, but he's a professional bouncer so it might be difficult. It looks like after years of forging a killer instinct I might have a life-or-death opportunity to test it. I do have one thing in my favor — nobody treats my friends that way and gets away with it."[24] The response to this public musing was not enthusiastic: one respondent urged calling the police instead of using his "killer instinct." Such a response demonstrates that some fans may see Aikido as a way of settling disputes, while others are not completely gripped by the myth of righteous violence regularly acted out by Steven Seagal.

On the whole, the official Seagal Web site does not advance the flowering of compassionate Buddhism so much as it provides an aromatic coating for the familiar myth of the hero who defies almost all laws and authorities to redeem the innocent. Seagal's own good intentions, presuming their sincerity, seem overpowered by the mythic acts of revenge that he continues to portray. Superheroic innocence is no less lethal when clothed in Buddhist garb.

Superheroic Bullet Time in *The Matrix*

Like Steven Seagal, the creators of *The Matrix*, Andy and Larry Wachowski, have endeavored to place "spiritual seeds" in their work. They have created an entertainment product that touches people emotionally and evokes their admiration for a technomythic allegory about spiritual development. "Bullet time," one of the film's most dazzling special effects (for which it received Academy Awards),[25] gives faith an invincible armor. The hero Neo, transformed from his doubting Thomas self, flies like an angel and possesses the vision, speed, and body hardness to deflect oncoming bullets. We witness this miracle as a sort of floating, time-delayed motion. Just as *Star Wars* seems to flirt with Taoism in its notion of The Force, *The Matrix*, despite its startling violence, seems most obviously to be "about" Christianity,[26] while scattering hints of other spiritual credos as well. The appropriate semantic term for such flirtation is *polysemy*, which describes ambiguities that prevent interpreters from assigning a determinate meaning to a symbol. *The Matrix* seems to exist in a state of "cultivated polysemy," in which both creators and fans collaborate in making the most of its suggestive indeterminacies. Philosopher Slavoj Zizek has sagely commented on the eagerness of fans to control the "ownership" of *The Matrix* for their own preferred vision and attendant messages:

My Lacanian friends tell me that the writers must have read Lacan; Frankfurt School partisans see in *The Matrix* the extrapolated embodiment of Kulturindustrie, the alienated-reified social Substance (of Capital) directly taking over, colonizing our inner life itself, using us as a source of energy; New Agers see in it a source of speculations on how our world is just a mirage generated by a global Mind embodied in the World Wide Web.[27]

This listing is only a hint of the diverse credotainment communities who have found "their" message colorfully brought to life in *The Matrix*. Zizek wonders whether the movie "function[s] as a kind of Rorschach test, setting in motion a . . . process of recognition, like the eye of God which always seems to stare directly at you, from wherever you look at it." The diversity of communities excited by *The Matrix* is not purely an accidental product of fan projection. Interviewed about the film's symbols, the Wachowskis were asked whether "the religious symbolism and doctrine throughout this movie [are] intentional." They responded that "most of it is intentional." When asked specifically about the Judaeo-Christian, Egyptian, Arthurian, and Platonic allusions, they responded that "all of it" was intentional.[28] The Wachowskis, former comic-book artists, have a wry sense of humor and may be playing along in a game that heightens interest in the film and its sequels. But the fans have supplied sufficient commentaries and testimonials to confirm their polysemic willingness to look behind the film's surrealistic veil and to celebrate what they find there.

Because the movie is sprinkled with religious references ("The One," "Trinity," "303,"[29] etc.) and biblical names ("Zion," "Nebuchadnezzar," etc.), some Christian fans stepped forward early to applaud the film's powerful affirmation of favored spiritual implications. Canadian clerics were among the first to announce their epiphanies. One of the first public conversion experiences occurred with Joel Crouse, a Lutheran pastor serving in Pembroke, Ontario. Interviewed shortly after the film's release, he revealed that he had already seen it three times and planned to give sermons on it — in addition to showing it in youth confirmation classes at his church. Crouse believes the film to be "based on one of the world's most profound narratives, which is the Passion story . . . the elements [are] there: the Messiah, the betrayer [Cypher — the Judas], Mary Magdalene [Trinity]."[30] Rather than taking offense at the appropriation of the passion as "heresy," Crouse sees the hero of the film as a symbol of the oppressed whom Christians should lift up from their misery: "I'm seeing battered women saying no to being battered, gay and lesbian persons saying no to being persecuted, and the poor and oppressed saying no to oppression." Echoing this focus on Christian youth work, the Canadian Conference of Mennonite Brethren Churches posted on the Web guidance for "*The Matrix* Discussion and Bible Study." Al Rempel, a youth pastor from Chilliwack, British Columbia, watched the film with his charges and then mapped the characters and moments of dialogue against biblical correlates.[31] The sympathetic adoption of the film's perspective was suggested by questions such as, "How can we be released from the imprisonment of the matrix we live in?"

At conservative Asbury College in Wilmore, Kentucky, where permission to see an R-rated film had been a recent innovation, student editorialists remarked on President Gyertson's repeated references to the film in his chapel talks, the first occasion causing "a titter of surprise from the students."[32] But his emphasis on the dead hero resurrected through love led to a campus screening of the film and a discussion of how to reconcile its violence with the Christian symbolism. The Asbury College editorialist came to the conclusion so common among Christians celebrating the power of The Force in *Star Wars.* "We may accept the violent acts on one ground: that they represent a symbolic metaphor of the battle 'not against flesh and blood,' but against evil — and evil loses." Complimenting the movie for its transcendence of "the popular dualistic heresy that the battle between good and evil is a close fight," the editorialist came to a comforting conclusion: "Surprisingly, in the midst of the machine-gun massacres, the producers of *The Matrix* got it right."

In a far more sophisticated way, Paul Fontana, a student at Harvard Divinity School, confronted the film's conjunction of Christian symbolism with "high speed ultraviolence" and found his explanation in the notion that the Wachowski brothers "knew their audience."[33] Fontana writes:

> The excessive violence is included in the film for the same reason that farmers have to annually increase the strength of pesticides: young people have become so anaesthetized by violence and irreverence that the only way to speak to the young movie-going public today is to up those standards by using cooler effects to make things sexier and faster or else nobody cares. . . . [T]he blistering pace of the action scenes is something one *has* to include to reach such a wide audience; innocuous films do not command much publicity.[34]

Fontana argues that the attention-grabbing instrumental violence of the plot, speaking to a generation that feels itself "in exile," fulfills that generation's "eschatological hope" for a restoration of spiritual meaning. He also reminds us that the film's violent savior is faithful to one strand of early Christian messianic expectations, represented by the Jesus of the book of Revelation, who "returns in glory, destroys all the enemies of God, and establishes a New Heaven and a New Earth" (p. 23). In this respect, the "film is surprisingly true to Biblical theology — despite its unorthodox appearance" (p. 1). This is the same sword-wielding Jesus so thrilling to fans of *Star Wars* such as Frank Allnutt.

As Kelly J. Triezenberg and Annalee R. Ward have shown in their survey of religiously inspired fans of *The Matrix,* there are also Buddhist believers and Gnostics eager to stake out the film for their faith. For certain Buddhists, "Neo represents a Buddha or bodhisattva who begins his journey, ignorant of the false reality around him, only to come to full consciousness . . . discovering that all he has seen as real was simply his lack of knowledge."[35] The adherents of Gnosticism, a heresy in early Christianity that has been revived in contemporary variants of New Age wisdom, hold that knowledge rather than faith is the key to salvation. W. T. Jones describes the ancient movement: "Not all men are saved — only those who have a divine spark that enables them to understand the knowledge given them."[36] According to those *Matrix* fans of the Gnostic persuasion, the special knowledge that relieves suffering mankind is mirrored in Neo's passage from the illusion of his ordinary experience to his awareness that the world is a manipulative projection of artificial intelligence. Neo's liberation comes when he finally knows the false reality and develops the courage to know himself fully as a potential savior of mankind. This is the symbolic message of hope about our human journey out of oppression. Jake Horsley, a Gnostic *Matrix* fan on the Web with an oft-linked treatise, gives these words of extravagant praise, despite his reservations about the wooden acting of Keanu Reeves:

> *The Matrix* is a reality map for potential artists and dreamers and would-be shamans to mull over for hours. The possibility that everything in it is exactly and precisely true — if metaphorically stated — and that the film itself is a breakthrough work in the propaganda-illumination program of the hidden rebel forces of "the future" . . . is a possibility . . . that invites our most serious consideration.[37]

In addition to hinting at this "exactly and precisely true" form of enlightenment for future rebels, Horsley also bathes in the mythic massage of redemption that *The Matrix* gives him:

> [I]t is a potential balm for the weary . . . soul of the cinemagoer. Maybe even it is a blessing. It brings the sort of exhilaration, anticipation, and joy (to this viewer at least) that may be more associated with childhood than

anything. Or dreams. To see *The Matrix* and believe can make you feel like every day is Christmas. Watching it frees the mind.

To our skeptical and undoubtedly too-weary souls, the prospect of salvation with heroes magically acting in bullet time does not stir childlike feelings of warm Christmases pasts. Our more gloomy memory makes us think of an earlier messiah figure, Wovoka (Jack Wilson), a Paiute Indian of the nineteenth century who was a prophetic creator of the Ghost Dance religion that was taken up by many Native American tribes, most notably the Western Sioux. His dream visions pointed toward the resurrection of the dead on a renewed earth in a time of peace and "establishe[d] a moral code . . . teaching the Indians to abandon all forms of glorified violence" and called for ritual dancing and washing.[38] He also had a reputation as a wizard with the power to withstand being shot by guns, a gift to which others testified. Without making a threat, he told Lt. Nat Phister, a soldier who came to investigate his religion, that "he was invulnerable and if anyone tried to kill him, the soldier would be killed."[39] But transformed within the more war-oriented culture of the Sioux in South Dakota, the Ghost Dance developed a flavor of hostility to whites and adopted the decorated "Ghost shirts," which the Sioux chief Short Bull reported to be "impervious to bullets."[40] Short Bull also believed that singing a song while wearing such a shirt would cause white soldiers to fall dead.

The tragic limitations of these beliefs became known at the Wounded Knee Massacre of 1890, when U.S. troops took pre-emptive action against what they perceived to be an incipient rebellion. Black Elk, a spiritual leader among the Lakotah Sioux who wore his Ghost shirt in these skirmishes, experienced a few moments of miraculous bullet time, in which he held his "sacred bow" and deflected the oncoming shots from the cavalry. He describes the scene: "All this time the bullets were buzzing around me and I was not touched. I was not even afraid. It was just like being in a dream about shooting."[41] But then he awakened and he suddenly felt as if he had been struck on his belt by an axe; his guts were coming out and he was falling from his horse. The protective Ghost shirts had not transported their wearers into the bullet time of invulnerability and redemption. More than two hundred men, women, and children were slaughtered by the soldiers. Black Elk was haunted forever by his memory:

> [F]rom this high hill of my old age, I can still see the butchered women and children lying heaped and scattered all along the crooked gulch. . . . And I can see that something else died there in the bloody mud, and was buried

in the blizzard. A people's dreams died there. It was a beautiful dream. . . .
And I, to whom so great a vision was given in my youth, — you see me now
a pitiful old man who has done nothing, for the nation's hoop is broken
and scattered. There is no center any longer, and the sacred tree is dead.
(p. 276)

There are numerous Web sites that celebrate Black Elk's life and the sad wisdom he attained. But the ecstatic *Matrix* fans have not yet linked their sites to
tragic visions of bullet time.

Touched by . . . Whatever You Need

Other forms of credotainment rely on less violent means of redemption, although the monomythic plot remains the same. An example is the *Touched by
an Angel* program series launched in the fall of 1994 after several years of ascending public interest in guardian angels. It has typically enjoyed very large
audiences, and the program entered its eighth year in the 2001-2002 broadcast
season. The opportunity for such a program had been revealed by best-selling
books such as Billy Graham's *Angels: God's Secret Agents* (1975), Sophy
Burnham's *Book of Angels* (1990), and Frank Peretti's novels of "spiritual warfare" between good and bad angels.[42] Feature-length films such as *Michael*
(1996) tell stories about the earthly adventures of angels. The narratives have
been accompanied by a torrent of commercial products — pins, calendars,
datebooks, prints, CDs, and other items that maintain the angelic presence
for consumers.

Touched by an Angel bears the mythic stamp of the Heidi-redemption
scheme we discussed in Chapter 4. The angelic squad of Andrew, Monica, and
Tess — always in disguise — inevitably succeed in pumping up a soul shriveled by some kind of self-imposed limit. Then, like the Lone Ranger, they disappear while a dove flutters its wings in the background. Violence never figures as a means of redemption for Tess, Andrew, or Monica. The scope of
their work is seldom more than a pinpointed individual in a small circle,
someone who must be redeemed to permit that person to re-establish a relationship with the others in the circle. In "Sign of a Dove,"[43] for example, a financially embarrassed printer plans to commit suicide by blowing up his
shop, hoping that his family will benefit more from his death than from his
straitened life. Monica and Andrew struggle with him mightily, almost surrendering to his stubborn desire for death. But, finally, at the last moment,
they pull him back.

According to the show's producers, viewers regularly report miracles from assimilating the show's weekly message about God's unconditional love for every human being. A 1997 *Good Housekeeping* article recounted numerous anecdotes from letters testifying about the program's personal impact. A Tennessee inmate described the quiet calm that characterized viewing sessions by prisoners who feel alienated because many "go for years without hearing an I love you." Individuals report retreating from the brink of suicide or calming down about a medical crisis they're experiencing, situations frequently depicted in the show with happy outcomes.[44] The CBS-maintained Web site for *Touched by an Angel* reinforces its reputation for such effects on audiences by maintaining an e-mail address and publishing the "TBAA Fan Quote-Of-The-Week."[45] Independent of the corporate site, which vends angel-wares and accurate information about all the episodes in the history of the show, fans have created their own Web sites. In comparison with the apocalyptically hued ecstasy of fans for world-redemptive violence that we see among Trekkers, Star Warriors, and *Matrix* devotees, the fan celebrations of these modest stories about individuals redeemed by gentle words from angels seem muted. Yet the monomythic certainties remain intact.

The flavor of much mail-list chat is conveyed by an expanding discussion thread entitled "You Know TBAA Has Taken Over Your Life When. . . ." For example, one finds references to complex devotional transcription: "You have the episodes written in chronological AND alphabetical order, with the ones that you've seen checked off." There are references to writing efforts inspired by the show ("you have eight pages of titles and summaries of your past, present, and future fanfic[46] stories"); collecting activities ("you have three folders — one for miscellaneous stuff, one for articles about TBAA, and one for your favorite stories on the Creative Connection");[47] experience with the show's spin-off products ("you listen to the Christmas album year round"); and, of course, youthful efforts to put the knowledge of the show to work at school ("you manage to work TBAA into multiple homework assignments this year").[48] At a higher level of effort are the fan fiction stories, which, like other so-called Ezines[49] on the Internet, are projections of plot and character formulas into new situations of the writer's own invention.

Unlike *Star Trek, Star Wars,* and *The Matrix, Touched by an Angel* has provoked relatively little philosophical discussion among its fans. The personally therapeutic experiences or the sentiments of shared joy at seeing others redeemed seem sufficient. Since the show has had tens of millions of viewers weekly for several years,[50] we know that it has plenty of adult viewers who could speak in electronic forums about how they understand the show's theology in relation to their own religious faith. The muted discussion in cyberspace includes impatience with the show's lack of reference to Jesus or to Scripture. There are also voices of suspicion about the show's connection with feminism and with New Age trends that fuzz off into complacent relativism. Della Reese, who plays the role of the boss angel Tess, invites skepticism from more traditional Christians because of her weekly pastoral duties in the Understanding Principles for Better Living Church[51] in Los Angeles. As advertised by the nondenominational church's home page on the Web — its icon a rising hot-air balloon — its ministry flatly declares, "We are the religion for the New Age," which consists of helping the human discover that "through his God-nature, [he] can be the victor of circumstances rather than a victim of circumstances."[52]

The soothing effect of angelic redemption seems consistent with the optimism and anthropocentrism of New Age religion. For example, Sophie Burnham's book *Angel Letters* declares that our guardian angels "pour their blessings on us overwhelmingly. They play with us. They heal us, comfort us with invisible warm hands, and always try to give us what we want."[53] Enlisting these creatures is easier than hiring a reliable employee. Burnham told one reporter that you look "inside yourself. . . . Then ask for what you need, you sit back, and wait. It will come."[54] Advocates like Burnham make easy targets for Bible-based critics of the New Age, who can also point to scriptural cautions about angels. Timothy Jones and Andrew J. Bandstra explored the angel trend in a 1993 *Christianity Today* article, quoting Paul's warning from Colossians: "Do not let anyone who delights in false humility and the worship of angels disqualify you for the prize. . . . Such a person goes into great detail about what he has seen. . . . He has lost connection with the Head" (Col. 2:18-19).[55] Della Reese is quite sensitive about being linked with New Age sentimentality about angels as personal comfort pals. In her book *Angels Along the Way* she makes the following strong affirmation of the show's emphasis on a traditional view of personal responsibility:

> The angels on the show don't come to fix people in trouble. They come to teach them how to fix themselves. And to reassure them that they are never alone, that God loves them unconditionally and forever. God wants only the best fix for them, but God can't make them do anything. Human beings have been given free will, and the choice is always ours.[56]

True to this characterization of the show, the angels are never called and manipulated by the magic of persuasive prayer. The afflicted are chosen by the grace of God to receive ministry from these angels.

Despite this age-old feature in the theology of *Touched,* conservative voices of opposition to its soft-edged theology pop up occasionally on the Web. Berit Kjos has written *A Twist of Faith*,[57] which is highly critical of feminism as a diversion from the path of Christian truth. A segment of the book criticizing the unbiblical theology of *Touched by an Angel* appears on the Internet at several sites that host conservative Christian critiques of popular culture. Kjos evokes "the holy angels of the Bible who brought people to their knees in fearful humility" and contrasts this tradition with the remarks of Martha Williamson, the producer of *Touched*, who finds that the "wonderful thing about angels is that they are non-judgmental."[58] Echoing the fears of so many on the Christian right about the dangers of world government, Kjos rejects universalistic statements by Della Reese that "proper models for the new global spirituality are needed to unify the world." In the last analysis, according to Kjos, *Touched* is a dangerous "spiritual substitute" that has grown out of the feminist movement.

A more appreciative Probe Ministries commentary on the Web by Don Closson, while pleased that "the audience gets a reasonable picture of what life might be like if a spiritual reality is taken seriously," deplores the omission of the 'J' word (Jesus) in the program. His overall judgment is that *Touched* "might be a useful springboard from which to present the biblical plan of salvation, but its message is too shallow to . . . evangelize the viewing public."[59]

As we take into consideration the range of electronic murmuring about *Touched*, it seems to us that the speakers seem easily classified as excited fans or skeptical analysts. And the two communities do not link up or try to enrich each other's perspectives. They are simply different sides of the same row in cyberspace's spiritual supermarket, neither of which shows any awareness of the monomythic structure of the series. Another gap in this electronic Babel is the absence of talk about the image of the church and its functions for ordinary parish members. In its market-sensitive avoidance of denominationalism and creeds, *Touched* never shows us a working church, complete with a nursery, church school, meals-on-wheels for elderly members, soup kitchens for the poor, rousing sermons on social justice, or the other activities that allow churches to function vitally for ordinary people. That Tess's red Cadillac does not brake for churches is a symptom of the American monomyth's deeper aversion to institutions.

Credotainment and Redemptive Expectations

In this book, we are sharply critical of the monomyth in both its violent and nonviolent forms. It may seem logical, then, that we should also be critical of

Once he finally believes in his world-redemptive status as "The One," Neo
can see and stop individual bullets — a miracle rendered through the film's
technological breakthrough of "bullet time."

Credit: *The Matrix* © 1999 Warner Brothers Studios.

the new monomythic credotainments in cyberspace. But this is a place where
we should temper our stance. We see a paradox in these cyberspatial communities of faith: the behavior of the congregants is potentially far more democratic than the myths they log on to celebrate. We can begin to see how democratic these fans are by comparing them to some recent deadly utopian
groups, such as Heaven's Gate and Aum Shinrikyo in Japan. Thirty-nine
members of Heaven's Gate committed group suicide in March 1997 in San
Diego, apparently believing that they could accelerate their transition to the
next level of existence.[60] In March 1995, Aum Shinrikyo released the highly
poisonous sarin gas into five Tokyo subways, hoping to trigger mass deaths
that would lead to world redemption.[61] Both groups accepted bizarre beliefs
and authoritarian leaders who demanded group discipline and shielded their
followers from contacts with others who might inspire skepticism.

Fan discussions or skeptical analyses in electronic gathering places are
carried out by free citizens. When participants reason out their perspectives
on the stories that they find gripping — as opposed to just sharing their delights — the atmosphere generally involves the spirit of give-and-take as participants elaborate or qualify their perceptions. And even though fans may be

very favorably disposed to a series as a whole, they can be quite dismissive about particular episodes or characters. Moreover, since the Web is a worldwide vehicle, fans can encounter voices from other cultures. As to Charles Henderson's statement that cyberspace "shall have equally profound effects upon the way . . . people practice faith, as well as communicate with each other and with God," it is not clear that digital faith communities will reduce the influence of the American monomyth on our religious or political horizons. Since the space has become available for all to speak their minds, there are an increasing number of perspectives for those who seek intelligent alternatives. Perhaps an awareness will dawn that assuming normal human responsibilities is more congruent with both democracy and religion than helplessly waiting for superheroic intervention. Our larger hope is that among the "profound effects" Charles Henderson perceived of the new media "upon the way . . . people practice faith, as well as communicate with each other and with God," will emerge an awareness of the theological and ethical challenge of credotainment itself.

V CADENZA: SEARCHING FOR DEMOCRATIC MELODIES

The great mythic arc of the twentieth century has been the redemption of impotent communities by superheroes who rise above institutions and laws. Disaster films regularly present scenes of selective punishment, failed authority, and superheroic rescues. We suggest in Chapter 15, "The Discordant Music of Catastrophes," that the events of September 11 suggest new perspectives on disaster that defy these spectacles-by-formula. The real heroes of those tragic events show us both the power and the limits of democratic citizens. Turning to the larger political scene in the United States, Chapter 16, "Deceptive Fugues, Democratic Dances" poses a paradox: Can democracy create materials that reflect its official ethos of trust in average individuals who live within the rule of law? Oliver North, Jr.'s behavior in the Iran-Contra affair has given us a case study in the deceptive enactment of the *Rambo* myth. Despite the fact that North received a depressing amount of applause for his bold, private crusade, we also see mythic countercurrents in America generated by films such as *Glory* and *The Straight Story*. We are especially encouraged by the success of *Dead Man Walking* — first as popular book, then as a film, and finally as an opera — and the new platform it has offered for serious democratic debate about capital punishment. We have a spirit of hope that other materials — surely inspired by the real world heroic behavior at the World Trade Center and on Flight 93, where passengers overcame the hijackers and prevented it from reaching an even deadlier destination — will help to change our national tastes in entertainment. Perhaps new and compelling stories can emerge that celebrate and reinforce the myths and faiths of democracy.

15 The Discordant Music of Catastrophes

"The sight of hell-torments will exalt the happiness of the saints forever."

Jonathan Edwards, *The Eternity of Hell Torments* (1739)[1]

"This city is finally paying for its arrogance."

a line from the disaster film *Volcano* (1997)

"Stupidity is an elemental force for which no earthquake is a match."

Karl Kraus, "The Earthquake"[2]

As recently as the nineteenth century, American reformers could still nourish millennial hopes for their country. Bronson Alcott, the prominent abolitionist, educational reformer, and advocate of women's rights, proclaimed: "Our freer . . . land is the asylum, if asylum there be, for the hope of man; and there, if anywhere, is the second Eden to be planted in which the divine seed is to bruise the head of evil and restore Man to his rightful communion with God in the Paradise of Good."[3] The contemporary mood shows few traces of such optimism about our "second Eden." Our news industry, with satellite links permitting instant broadcast from most locations on the globe, repeatedly shows us images of hurricanes, blizzards, floods, forest fires, earthquakes, volcanic eruptions — along with their disrupting effects on aircraft, ships, trains, and freeway traffic. Myth has always provided interpretations of natural catastrophe, recasting the surface physical appearances so that we discern moral forces that trigger the disturbing events. Given our tendency to gawk at physical spectacles, disasters were always a promising theme for filmmakers, ambitious set-builders, and stunt artists. The collective creators of the American monomyth have answered the philosophical and religious challenge to interpret the natural forces that constantly affect life.

A golden age for the disaster film came in the 1970s, when a group of films perfected and reiterated a formula that defined the hero, the community, and the benevolently destructive forces that punished the wicked — who were usually marked by their desire for sex or wealth — while preserving the innocent. The heroic conventions that developed in the cowboy Western and the caped superhero comics were adapted to the task of saving the community. *Airport* (1970) launched the era with a story about the effects of a blizzard on a metropolitan air center. *The Poseidon Adventure* (1972) followed with the story of a tsunami wave, a sinking ship, and a courageous minister who defies the ship's crew to rescue a mere six of the more than one thousand passengers. *Towering Inferno*, a technological parable about a 135-story building in San Francisco, and *Earthquake*, a tale of a Los Angeles too big to govern itself, appeared in 1974.

But the greatest artistic and box-office success of them all came in 1975 with *Jaws*. Like the other disaster epics of the era, it gambled on its production budget but broke box-office records. Along with *Airport*, it proved that feature-length films, like comics and television, could be serialized into successors that delivered the same characters and patterns of moralized nature. *Jaws* was succeeded by *Jaws 2* (1978), *Jaws 3-D* (1983), and *Jaws the Revenge* (1987). The *Airport* successors were *Airport 1975*, *Airport '77*, and *The Concorde — Airport '79*.[4] *Beyond the Poseidon Adventure* surfaced in 1979.

Cable channels and video rentals have kept these older films alive into a new period of mythically rendered disasters for the 1990s. *The Great Los Angeles Earthquake* (1990) and *Volcano* (1997) both retrashed Hollywood's home ground. *Twister* (1996) gave us an outsized tornado in the Midwest, and *Dante's Peak* (1997) portrayed a major eruption in an Edenic small town in Washington state. *Titanic* (1995) produced one more remake of the great ship's collision with an iceberg. *Asteroid* (1997) fantasized about a large asteroid threatening to destroy the earth, as did the more imaginatively titled *Deep Impact* (1998) and *Armageddon* (1998). In an explicitly biblical vein, the blockbuster *Left Behind* series of books is being translated into a series of Rapture/

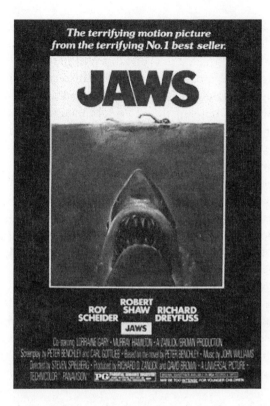

In the film poster for *Jaws*, the shark displays the punishment pattern of the film. Like other disaster films, it suggests that disaster begins with female sexuality and demands retribution. This righteous shark instantly punishes the woman's overt eroticism with a rapish attack.

end-times films. *Left Behind: The Movie* (2001), which transports a selection of naked adult Christians and innocent children to heaven, leaves the survivors to face seven years of rule by the Antichrist during a period of natural tribulations. To the extent that it mirrors popular attitudes, the *Left Behind* phenomenon suggests total despair about human leadership as the basis for a good community. The best hope is to be delivered physically from the problems of this world — literally leaving everything behind.

Collectively, these films have achieved staggering box-office success with their pessimistic images of feeble human leadership, authority-defying heroes, and corrupt civilization, combined with ferocious and morally selective punishments doled out by nature itself. A somber mythic consciousness seems to be at work here, shaping a grisly image of the future as strangely attractive to fantasy as the mythically reshaped past. To an extent unparalleled by any other pop genre, the technomythic miracles wrought by increasingly skilled special effects create believable images of natural annihilation and heroic redemption.

Like most popular disaster films, *Left Behind*'s trigger for the catastrophe is violation of a conservative sexual norm. At the very moment that Captain Rayford Steele and Flight Attendant Hattie Durham are clutching and smooching in the galley of their plane, their innocent and faithful passengers are raptured away.

Credit: *Left Behind* © 2000, Cloud Ten Pictures.

Nature as Ferocious Moralist

Catastrophe films range through the spectrum of the natural and social crises with encyclopedic thoroughness, alert always to potential messages about civilization's failure. *Earthquake* (1974) projects a destruction of the Los Angeles basin with explicitly mythic formulas and technomythic manipulations. *Earthquake* is particularly suited to analysis because its writer, George Fox, explains the way the earthquake's punishment of decadence is made "believable."

The story line of *Earthquake* features a series of personal vignettes framed by a cataclysmic event. As the film opens, we learn that seismologists have developed new techniques by which to prophesy the destruction of Los Angeles in the near future. Working independently of the scientists, a talented architectural engineer, Graff, leads an unsuccessful one-man crusade against buildings with insufficient resistance to earthquake damage. He even refuses to carry out a project until its specifications are upgraded, a financially distressing piece of personal integrity in the eyes of the company he works for. Graff's annoying wife, Remy, is destroying their marriage through deception and self-imposed childlessness. Slade, a good but bitter cop, has been suspended from the force for damaging a movie star's hedge while chasing criminals. Denise is an attractive young widow who is taking up a career as an actress; her sexual readiness proves to be important for the seismic activity of the Los Angeles basin. Miles Quade is a motorcycle stunt performer; his sister, Rosa, has a lovely body that stimulates male interest. A sinister character, Jody, is a supermarket clerk and a National Guardsman who wears a blond wig and inspires taunts about his masculinity from the men who know him.

The actions of these characters symbolically trigger the destruction of Los Angeles. Discovering that his wife has aborted her pregnancy, Graff angrily leaves her and makes love to Denise for the first time. The screenwriter candidly describes his intent to establish a relationship between such personal events and the natural forces that destroy Los Angeles:

> An earthquake is a release of seismic energy. Our people ought to be as pent-up and ready for release as the ground under their feet. Without slamming them over the head with the fact, we ought to make the audience feel — unconsciously, in their nerve ends — that the quake is somehow generated by the characters they're watching, not the San Andreas fault alone.[5]

Precisely what screenwriter Fox intends is illustrated by the lovemaking of Graff and Denise on the day their orgasms trigger the earthquake. "They have made love with a desperate urgency, giving way to a need neither had acknowledged until today" (p. 27). Fox similarly describes nature's own urgency for release: "For years, in these areas, the land has been compressed and warped, storing energy like a colossal spring" (p. 9).

A parallel connection between catastrophe and the behavior of the characters is visible in the motorcycle episode. The earthquake strikes at the precise moment Miles Quade is prepared to perform his stunt. The timing is more than coincidental, because Fox admits that as he studied Los Angeles, he "gradually developed the impression of a community unconsciously dedicated to a state of endless peril" (p. 79). The death of Miles Quade is a symbolic comment on the power of foolhardy entertainment to precipitate catastrophes. Such moralistic "causes" of the natural disaster are strewn throughout the script, each one precipitating an apocalyptic punishment for the offender.

All the sinful characters in *Earthquake* receive physical punishment. Charlton Heston, who plays the role of Graff, suffers a rare screen death. Despite his efforts to rescue others, his infidelity with Denise apparently seals his fate. His dragon-like wife, who precipitated Graff's infidelity and caused her father's heart attack by meddling in company affairs, drowns along with him. Miles Quade dies during his stunt performance. Slade kills Jody after the latter has threatened Rosa with rape to prove his masculinity. Since Slade had earlier suppressed his desire for Rosa, he is morally qualified to play the redeemer role and finally gets her as compensation after the rubble has settled. Among the moral offenders in *Earthquake,* Denise is spared; but she has a son to take care of and is likewise chastened by the loss of Graff. In general, though, nature is portrayed as responding in a neatly retributive fashion to the community's need for moral cleansing.

This precisely calibrated relationship between violation of sexual mores and punishment by the forces of nature is characteristic of the disaster-film genre. In *Towering Inferno,* a publicist for the building and his beautiful secretary have a fling in the bedroom adjoining his office; both die in the flames as the camera lingers over their agony. At the same time, the faithful mayor and his unattractive wife are spared. In *Tidal Wave,* the first volcanic eruptions are stimulated by the lovemaking of an unmarried couple on the beach. They are permanently separated by the tidal wave in spite of the young man's heroism in saving others. As was evident in the death of *Earthquake's* motorcycle performer Quade, the moralized forces of nature take special displeasure in frivolity or revelry: *The Poseidon Adventure* begins its deathly upside-down voyage during a New Year's Eve ballroom party; *Tidal Wave* opens with scenes of huge crowds amusing themselves at the beach; *Towering Inferno* begins with a party celebrating the opening of the building, and the fire develops while the celebration progresses.

These contemporary images of disaster obviously parallel those biblical stories in which the pattern of retribution for sexual infidelity and frivolity is deeply embedded. The flood story in Genesis is placed immediately after the so-called "Second Fall" account, in which the angels fall from heaven to take their pleasure with the seductive daughters of Eve. The dismayed and angry Lord resolves to flood the earth after seeing "that the wickedness of man was great in the earth, and that every imagination of the thoughts of his heart was evil continually" (Gen. 6:5). The announcement of the flood catastrophe to Noah is expressed in terms that support the view that "flesh" in its sensual manifestations is punished: "And God said to Noah, 'I have determined to make an end of all flesh; for the earth is filled with violence through them . . .'" (Gen. 6:13). In the Sodom and Gomorrah account, which features earthquake, brimstone, and fire, it is the lewd demand of riotous homosexuals to violate the angelic guests of Lot that provokes the retribution. As in the flood account, the only ones to escape are Lot and his family when they heed the demand, "Flee for your life; do not look back or stop anywhere in the valley; flee to the hills lest you be consumed" (Gen. 19:17). The paradigm was thus established for posterity: sexual improprieties provoke natural disasters, from which only the pure and faithful will escape. The retributive principle is Deuteronomic: sin brings disaster, while virtue brings success and escape from disaster. The most prominent advocates of this scheme in American life have been the evangelists Pat Robertson and Jerry Falwell. After the September 11 attacks at the Pentagon and the World Trade Center, they used "The 700 Club" forum of Robertson's network to assign responsibility to the American Civil Liberties Union, abortion practitioners, and gay rights advocates. God had "lifted the curtain of protection" and would permit "more tragedies" if America did not repent, in the words of Falwell.[6]

It is paradoxical that the secular disaster-film genre struggles so hard for the modern illusion of visual realism while retaining these archaic biblical conventions of retribution. George Fox speaks with pride of how accurately his film *Earthquake* depicts disaster: "Every moment of fictional destruction was checked out for what someone — I forget who — called 'the reality quotient.'" He argues that "today's sophisticated audience wouldn't accept the scene if process photography and other obvious special effect tricks were used. It would look incredibly phony" (p. 70). To avoid this, Fox studied earthquakes of the past, interviewed earthquake victims, studied the San Andreas fault system, and interviewed seismologists. He further enhanced the "scientific accuracy" with the use of Sensurround, a sound system that created tremor sensations in the audience. The system "has been refined to the point where, at will, it can affect specific parts of the human body." The producers of the movie also considered but rejected "bouncing huge chunks of Styrofoam debris off the audience's heads during the tremor scenes" (p. 123). They made rocking platforms for the sets and cameras to simulate earthquake motions; they used thousands of special garments to simulate the deterioration of clothing during the progress of an earthquake. And they employed 141 stuntmen during the filming, some of whom were seriously injured.

While the high-budget special effects provide the believability of the modern disaster film, the archaic biblical fantasy of selective and moralistic destruction remains as the central dramatic convention. In point of historical fact, this sort of plot was almost required by the now-defunct Motion Picture Production Code, whose moral strictures for films are so perfectly satisfied by this genre. Geoffrey Shurlock, administrator of the code, stated that "details of sin have to be balanced against details of compensation. There would be no sense in too much retribution for too little sin. This, of course, is not our problem. Ours is the other extreme of too much sin and too little retribution."[7] In 1966, the Production Code was replaced by the Motion Picture Rating System, but the disaster genre retained the retributive scheme.

Cues for Impending Punishment

Untangling the way the punishment scheme gains credibility is crucial to understanding the attractions of catastrophe films. We suggest that such materials feature a kind of *mythic cuing*. The visual cues convey the message symbolically without the verbal articulation of religion or ideology. The technique juxtaposes visual fragments with conversational fragments as the story progresses; the selective focus of the camera forces the eye of the audience into stereotypical judgments essential to the development of the retribution scheme. Traditional evidences of depravity are rapidly flashed before one's eyes so that one is mythically prepared for the punishment that inevitably follows. Having seen the sin, viewers are moved by the sight of the punishment to the acceptance of an archaic idea that would likely arouse jeers if articulated verbally as a biblical threat against sinners. Just as Mark Twain uncritically accepted a mythic presentation of western history in the Buffalo Bill shows that he would have scorned if they were stated verbally, so the modern audience is swayed by mythic cuing of disaster films and television programs.

The context for mythic cuing in the catastrophe genre is the sense of dread about the forthcoming suffering. Unlike historical catastrophes, which usually come when least expected, the horror of the film is anticipated with a combination of yearning and dread. From the safe distance of the theater seat, the audience vicariously undergoes the experience of escaping a horrible fate. The dread of being caught up in the cycle of annihilation is relieved by a double identification pattern: the personal identification with the superhero, who will inevitably escape death if he remains true to the faith; and the marking of those fated for destruction. To use the commonly accepted sense of the term, it is as if the "mark of Cain" has been placed upon sinners so that the audience can be sure of their annihilation and thus not identify positively with them while watching the movie. Mythic cuing relieves the audience of its sense of dread to the extent that it helps to eliminate painful elements of sympathy and identification with the doomed. It also offers a moral confirmation of the audience's righteousness, since only the virtuous survive.

Moralistic *Jaws*

Both in its novel and film versions, *Jaws* has been one of the great commercial successes of our time. It has been praised as "taut adventure" and "superb entertainment." So successful is its use of mythic cuing, which operates at times with subliminal subtlety, that it thoroughly disarmed critics at the time of its initial release. For instance, Hollis Alpert of *The Saturday Review* concluded that *Jaws'* story content is insignificant. "Does the film have any real meaning, other than a warning about where to swim? Probably not. It's a tale designed to thrill, and this is what it does."[8] *The New Yorker,* famed for its reviews of even trashy movies when they possess social significance, allowed a timid and condescending "Don't bite" to stand beside *Jaws* for months in its weekly movie listing.

In contrast to these nonchalant denials of meaning, we suggest that *Jaws,* an early Steven Spielberg film, is a very skillful embodiment of the American monomyth and offers an excellent opportunity to apply technomythic critical insights, for the following reasons:

- The American monomyth typically begins and ends in an Edenic setting. In *Jaws* the very name of the setting, Amity Island, suggests paradisiacal qualities. Just as Heidi left the evil Frankfurt to return to her Edenic Alps, Martin Brody has escaped from Manhattan, where there are "so many problems you never feel you're accomplishing anything. Violence, ripoffs, muggings, kids can't leave the house — you gotta walk 'em to school. But in Amity one man can make a difference. In twenty-five years there's never been a shooting or a murder in this town." The movie portrays the island as an unproblematic arena for children's play — that is, until the malevolent shark arrives. And it is the one man, Martin Brody, who indeed makes the difference for the community in saving it from this threat. In the final scene, Brody swims back to a broad, deserted, paradise-like beach on Amity Island, from whence evil has been expelled.
- The monomyth features a disruption of paradise. In the case of Amity Island, evil comes in many forms, but it arrives most conspicuously as the great white shark. Its arrival is precipitated by a provocative display of female sexuality. The movie begins on a beach with a party of young people smoking and drinking around a campfire. One woman sits at the edge of the group, clearly differentiated as an outsider. Approached by one of the young men, she proposes a swim, tossing off her clothing with abandon as she runs toward the water. Her shouts of "Come on in" are fol-

lowed by his drunken collapse on the beach. She swims alone with voluptuous yearning, symbolically reminiscent of *Playboy*'s eager playmates. With her companion proving incapable of fulfilling her need, the males in the audience are cued to a *Playboy* fantasy, reinforced when the camera allows them to see her lovely, undulating form from the perspective of the shark below. This erotic display is provocative; and the censor's Deuteronomic code, demanding the punishment of sexual depravity, lives on in the present by rationalizing the fate of the beautiful temptress: she is attacked by the shark.

The advertising for *Jaws* used the phallic symbol of a shark streaking up toward the naked woman. Both visually and aurally, the attack scene carries out the sexual theme implicit in the ads: the music throbs to a climax as the shark approaches, and the initial rhythmic gasps of the woman after she has been nudged by the shark are orgasmic. This striking detail provides a subliminal reinforcement to the sexual power of the scene. The woman then clings to a phallic-shaped buoy in the water to protect herself until she is attacked and torn away. In later scenes that show the remaining portion of her body, the audience sees long and red-polished fingernails and multiple rings — symbols of former seductive conquests.

Just as in the Garden of Eden story, the corruption of Amity's inhabitants justifies the shark's disruption. The mayor and city selectmen are portrayed as fatally corrupt: because of their own economic interests, they refuse to call for help or close the beaches. The predatory campaign of the shark thus lasts so long that it shatters the safe reputation of the island and reduces the mayor to babbling.

- In monomythic materials, citizens are unwilling to face evil and thus unable to act intelligently in its presence. Amity is Eden compared to New York, but its inhabitants and summer guests are bent on the festivals and entertainments that catastrophe films love to punish. Various scenes of the film represent these people as utterly stupid and obsessed with pleasure. When Chief Brody experiences his first sense of urgency about the shark attack, he must force his way through the preparations for a silly parade. The citizens seem dumbly intent on pursuing their routines and ignoring the danger. When the town posts a large reward for anyone who might catch the shark, floods of incompetent fishermen descend on the island, overloading their boats and menacing everyone's safety. When someone does catch a large shark (though not *the* shark), people assume that the danger is past and crowd onto the island aboard every kind of conveyance. The camera cues the audience to view the public as lambs dumbly led to slaughter, a stock mythic background for the emergence of the redeemer figure.

• The democratic institutions in monomythic stories are invariably pictured as incapable of coping with evil. They are as helpless as the stupid public before the appalling threat from the mythic depths. The Board of Selectmen is in the mayor's pocket, agreeing with his statement about the overriding need to keep the tourist trade: "I'm only trying to say that Amity is a summer town. We need summer dollars. If people can't swim here, they'll be glad to swim at Cape Cod. . . ." The mayor forces the coroner to falsify his report on the cause of the first death — changing "shark attack" to "boating accident." Later the mayor coerces one of the selectmen to lead his family into the water as the crowd of bathers clings fearfully to the beach. The crowd immediately follows them into the risky waters, and true to the quick-draw justice of the catastrophe genre, the selectman is trampled by the retreating crowd when a prankster shark fin is sighted.

Thus far the plot of *Jaws* fits the template for the American monomyth with the need for redemption by a superhero apparent. But at this point the film seems to break out of the paradigm. There is rescue through violence, but where is the superhero? Surely Brody, the ineffectual police chief of Amity Island, who in the end fires the shot that blows up the shark, is far from Superman!

Brody as a Neurotic Spiderman

In some ways Martin Brody fits the antiheroic tradition of high culture rather than the superheroic tradition of American pop culture. For instance, he is so fearful of water that the very thought of a boat ride throws him into panic: "On the water? But not drunk enough to go out in the boat! I can't do that!" Carl Gottlieb describes the producer's aim of creating such a flawed, indecisive protagonist: Chief Brody "would have to begin as a man who lets others shape his decisions, even to the point where those decisions cost people their lives; he would have to discover his flaw, struggle to correct it, and emerge at the end of the picture as a man who has faced up to the demons inside him and conquered them while at the same time subjecting himself to the gruesomest sort of physical danger."[9] If such features were consistently developed in a story with a tragic structure, one would surely place Brody in the tradition of realism. But the story of *Jaws*, as we have seen, is monomythic down to the happy restoration of paradise at the end. Within the context of this story Brody clearly carries out the function of the violent redeemer.

Other distinguishing traits coincide with the redemption formulas. The monomythic superhero usually renounces sexuality because redemptive obligations cannot be integrated with normal sexual responsibilities. Although Chief Brody is married, his lovely and understanding wife poses the typical barriers to his redemptive task and thus, in pop heroic fashion, Brody achieves sexual renunciation within marriage. In one of the movie's early scenes, she lies temptingly on their bed as he rises to perform his police work; her beautiful body is framed through the door, but he renounces temptation. In subsequent scenes Brody is repeatedly indifferent to his wife, who clearly loves him and desires more intimacy than he grants. At one point she hands him a drink while he studies shark books, and says, "Want to get drunk and fool around?" He responds to her proposition with indifference. But when he sees his son playing on the sailboat, he shouts a harsh warning. The need to clear the beach of its threat to innocent children seems to eliminate the possibility of sexual gratification.

In another scene, Brody's wife explicitly tempts him to forsake his redemptive task. On the day when their son is taken to the hospital for shock treatment after a narrow escape from the shark, Brody tells his wife, "You go on back home now." She replies, "Do you mean . . . New York?" Her inclination is clearly to return to Babylon and take Martin away from the dangerous island, where "one man can make a difference." In a final comment on sexual renunciation, the film closes with Brody and Hooper paddling back toward an empty beach — together in male camaraderie. It would seem to indicate that Brody's reunion with his loving wife is subordinate to the lonely mastery of superheroes over evil. One cannot avoid the impression that Brody has gained his redemptive power through a renunciation of sexuality.

The theme of sexual temptation as the source of the shark attacks is one of the strongest continuing elements in the *Jaws* successor films. In *Jaws 2*, the great white shark warms up for his attack on Amity by swallowing a female water skier and the boat that pulls her. With that the shark really becomes aroused and attacks an entire group of teenagers after Ed and Tina grope each other in her drifting boat, "Tina's Joy." They have brought along some wine and a blanket so that she won't "get bruises on her butt." In *Jaws 3-D* the first to be eaten is a worker whose girlfriend accuses him of "messing around with that bitch at the refreshment stand." The fearful Sean Brody, son of the now-deceased police chief of Amity, is lured into the water by a water-ski performer who strips down to her bra and panties. She is later eaten by the shark, while the more cautious Sean is spared.

The monomythic superhero is frequently aided by fate — just in the nick of time. Chief Brody's incredible destruction of the shark conveys a sense that the powers of destiny are at work. Up until the moment when Quint, the monomaniacal Ahab of a shark hunter, is devoured by Jaws, Brody has been a bumbling crew member. He could not learn to tie a proper knot or keep from stumbling over the equipment. He was constantly afraid and eager for the help of other government agencies. But in the decisive duel with the shark, Brody's character suddenly changes. He straps on his gun belt and begins to fire at the shark. In one dramatic image, his gun-holstered silhouette is flared against the horizon in the style of a cowboy superhero. And strangely, as if he were Clark Kent, his glasses are no longer present as he takes up the superhero role. Yet he is able to accurately fire at the tank of oxygen he had kicked into the shark's mouth in a moment of fate-controlled bumbling. One is reminded of the last-minute precision of the white-hatted gun fighters, which allows them to kill black-hatted marauders who have drawn their weapons first.

The hero in a monomythic story rarely originates in the community he is called to redeem. He is an outsider, either in fact or in attitude. Thus it is established early in *Jaws* that Brody is a newcomer who cannot be fully integrated into Amity. His wife, more eager to establish community than her isolated husband, says to a neighbor, "I just wanna know one simple thing. . . . When do I get to become an islander?" The neighbor's answer is: "Ellen . . . never . . . never. . . . You're not born here, you're not an islander, and that's it." This does not seem to bother Chief Brody in the least, because his redemptive task is a sufficient *raison d'etre*. Just as he does not join his wife in glad reunion at the end of the movie, there is no hint that he returns to a community that acclaims his membership. He returns in monomythic fashion to the uninhabited beach with his fellow outsider, Hooper, privately celebrating their victory over a fearful adversary.

Given the congruity of Brody's actions with the monomythic paradigm, one might look around in popular culture for a figure who would provide a suitable model for this antihero who plays the superhero role. Although Brody is far from Superman or Buffalo Bill, he fits so neatly into the mold of Spiderman that one suspects a little cribbing. Spiderman, very popular in the 1960s and '70s and still a favorite among fans of the comics, was "the first superhero to wear his neuroses on his sleeve." Stan Lee, who created the Spiderman figure, wanted a new kind of "strip in which the main character would lose out as often as he'd win — in fact, more often." He wanted Spiderman to be "an ordinary guy . . . not too handsome, not too graceful, not too muscular. . . ."[10] Spiderman's alter ego, Peter Parker, is a striking match for Roy Scheider, who played Brody. Both have slender builds and narrow shoulders, wire-rimmed glasses, worried expressions on faces with relatively small mouths, chins, and noses. Even Parker's hair color and style is similar to that of the modest police chief of Amity Island.

Who can say whether Steven Spielberg and the other creators of *Jaws* were actually influenced by Spiderman? The sources of the creative process are notoriously elusive. It suffices here to suggest that Brody is indeed cut from the same pattern as a highly popular contemporaneous comic-book hero.

As a redemption drama with a sexually segmented redeemer, whose miraculous action is performed against a background of communal stupidity and institutional impotence, *Jaws* and its sequels are at home with *Death Wish, Walking Tall,* and other popular artifacts. In addition, however, *Jaws* and other disaster films emphasize blood, suffering, and sacrifice in ways that take us to even deeper mythical roots. When exposed, they raise disturbing questions about the state of mind that enjoys moralized destruction as entertainment while pretending to be unaffected by it.

The Redemptive Function of Women's Blood

Jaws drips with blood. Pools of blood spread ominously in the water after each attack by the horrendous shark. The fishermen constantly throw blood into the water to lure the shark, and after Quint has been devoured, Brody must walk through his blood on the deck of the sinking fishing boat. Bloody water drips from Brody's face after he destroys the shark, and when the oxygen tank explodes, a sea of blood showers downward into the ocean. The camera cues the audience to the decisive significance of this scene. The sequel films are equally drenched in the blood of bait used to attract the shark and the blood of the numerous victims. The precedents for redemption through blood reach back to the archaic ceremonies of atonement. A passage from the Bible summarizes the matter: "Without the shedding of blood there is no remission of sins" (Heb. 9:22). In an ancient myth that sounds quite a bit like the plot of *Jaws*, the Babylonian god Marduk conquers the sea monster Tiamat. He forces "evil wind" into the dragon's mouth and then shoots her with his arrows:

> They marched to war, they drew near to give battle.
> The Lord [Marduk] spread out his net and caught her in it.
> The evil wind which followed him, he loosed it in her face.

> She opened her mouth, Tiamat, to swallow him.
> He drove in the evil wind so that she could not close her lips. . . .
> He let fly an arrow, it pierced her belly.
> Her inner parts he clove, he split her heart;
> He rendered her powerless and destroyed her life.[11]

This episode plays a decisive role in the Babylonian myth of the creation of paradise by Marduk. Its premise is that chaotic, female sources of evil must be ripped apart for the sake of an orderly Eden. The writers of Genesis demythologized such material by having the monsters of the deep created on the fifth day of creation rather than sacrificially offering their bodies as the raw material of creation.

In effect, the producers of *Jaws* remythologize this material, reverting back to the bloody and archaic myths of the ancient Near East that require female destruction as the cost of creation. This is not to suggest that writers in Hollywood spend their valuable time poring over books on ancient religion. Popular creative processes are seldom so deliberate. But the fact remains that they enlarge the shark by a third over the size of any known shark, thereby making it into a chaotic and mythic source of malevolence. As one of the film previews puts it, "It is as if nature had concentrated all of its forces of evil in a single being." The blood of the supernatural shark has restored nature for human purposes and re-created Martin Brody in the process, while freeing the community from the threat of chaos. The priests of the Marduk cult could scarcely have done better in creating an artifact that embodied their archaic view that creation requires bloody destruction.

It is not so much the use of this bloody material but its magnetic attractiveness to its continuing audiences that raises questions about its motivational appeal. It parallels religious materials that delight in picturing the bloody destruction of evildoers. Psalm 58 proclaims:

> The righteous will rejoice when he sees the vengeance;
>   he will bathe his feet in the blood of the wicked.
> Men will say, "Surely there is a reward for the righteous;
>   surely there is a God who judges on earth."[12]

A similar audience appeal of moralized destruction is implicit in the biblical tale of the wicked Queen Jezebel seeking to dissuade Jehu from vengeance by sitting in the upper window at Jezreel with her beautiful makeup and ornate coiffure. He demands that she be thrown to the ground, where her blood spatters the building and the trampling horses. Just as crabs come to pick at the remainder of the temptress's body in *Jaws*, the dogs of Jezreel feast on Jezebel's bloody remains. In a parallel incident, wicked King Ahab is slain and brought to Samaria, where the prostitutes of the city wash themselves in the blood flushed from his chariot, while the stray dogs lap up the rest.[13]

What does the retelling of such tales of violent and bloody cleansings reveal about the state of a culture? What are the outlooks and motivations of those who enjoy moralized suffering and bloody redemption? What is the relationship of such themes to a discomfort with the facts of human sexuality that threads through these artifacts?

Tertullian Ecstasy

In reflecting on these elusive questions, our attention fell upon the early church father Tertullian. In a well-known passage, he argued that the spectator pleasures offered by the Christian faith are immeasurably superior to popular Roman diversions. The faithful are promised the opportunity to witness the eternal suffering of sinful pagans. When the day of judgment comes, the Roman poets, tragedians, philosophers, charioteers, and wrestlers would be seen with flames billowing around their agonized bodies. Tertullian poses the following to his readers:

> What quaestor or priest in his munificence will bestow on you the favor of seeing and exulting in such things as these? And yet even now we in a measure have them by faith in the picturings of imagination . . . they are nobler, I believe, than circus, and . . . theaters, and every race course.[14]

Tertullian's argument was repeated centuries later by the American divine Jonathan Edwards, who promised that "the sight of hell-torments will exalt the happiness of the saints forever."

In these citations from Edwards and Tertullian there is a strange exulting in the painful punishment of others. It is particularly striking in thinkers who harbor profound suspicions of ecstasy, especially sexual ecstasy, as they did. It is as if sexual ecstasy were replaced with *Tertullian ecstasy* — the enjoyment in seeing the punishment of the wicked. In any event, this is what seems to be involved in the audience response to catastrophe films. Unlike sexual ecstasy, which is potentially communal and creative, at its best involving love and mutual respect, Tertullian ecstasy can be achieved privately. It demands no creative effort, only that someone suffer for the pleasure of others. Tertullian ecstasy works toward its climactic visceral gratification by a kind of inverted foreplay. Whereas sexual love begins with attraction, the preparation for re-tributive ecstasy requires revulsion triggered by negative stereotypes. The camera cues the audience to recognize targets of retribution by scenes of evil behavior and exclusion from the community. This de-identification of inter-est, an inversion of mutual respect and attraction, blocks any sympathetic re-sponse that the audience might have when the wicked suffer their punish-ment.

At the moment the evil of the marked ones becomes unbearable, and the desire for punishment reaches its climax, the moralized forces of catastrophe provide a kind of retributive coitus with an ecstatic release. The cheering of audiences in such scenes is evidence of a ritual release from tension. Tertullian ecstasy therefore provides one of the few publicly acceptable forms of visceral gratification or ecstatic release in American popular culture. The reward for the audience conforms to a Deuteronomic pattern of compensat-ing every virtue and punishing every vice. The ecstasy of violent punishment is thus provided to those who identify with the pure superhero and his renun-ciation of sexual gratification. In the subtlest version of this tradeoff, we are allowed a faint and vicarious taste of sexual excitement in the almost sublimi-nal orgasmic cries of the temptress Chrissie in *Jaws:* the sounds of her being devoured suggest the need for sexual release at the very moment that she — a symbol of yearning — is destroyed.

A somewhat cruder celebration of ecstatic, sexually displaced retribution occurs in Mickey Spillane's *One Lonely Night.* In this 1951 novel, Mike Ham-mer is granted the opportunity to punish a socialite, Ethel, who had helped the Communist Party. He forces her to remove her clothes and then takes off his belt:

> A naked woman and a leather belt. I looked at her, so bare and so pretty, hands pressing for support against the paneling, legs spread apart to hold a precarious balance, a flat stomach hollowed under a fear that burned her body a faint pink, lovely smooth breasts, firm with terrible excitement, ris-ing and falling with every gasping breath. A gorgeous woman who had been touched by the hand of the devil.
>
> I raised the belt and heard the sharp crack of the leather against her thighs and her scream. . . .[15]

There is a deliberate effort in this passage to build sexual tension, while at the same time constructing a rationale for its denial. In spite of the spread legs and sensuous breasts, Hammer resists sexual temptation. With the judgment of her devilish betrayal pronounced, prepared in the reader's mind by the inverted foreplay of details about her traitorous actions, the release of "orgiastic sadism"[16] is provided by the blows directed toward the center of her sexuality.

The victims of sexually focused disaster films seem to be objects for audience pleasure whose destruction provides ecstatic release. The unlimited and impersonal scale of punishment in this genre apparently heightens audience pleasure. However, it is a mistake to believe that such pleasures are restricted to the realm of entertainment. In the wake of September 11 we have witnessed similar forms of Tertullian delight in the annihilation of those perceived to be wicked. Religion, entertainment, and politics seem to be blending in an ominous manner that reveals the flaw in mythicizing disaster. At the same time, we can see an awareness that those lives destroyed were not markedly sinful — thus calling into question the precise moralistic punishments portrayed in the catastrophe film.

Disaster Politics in *Armageddon* and *Left Behind*

In the disaster film's recent resurgence, the monomyth's formulas remain intact. Natural crises attack as incompetent and corrupted institutions regularly wilt. Unattached men, often abandoned by unloving women, must step in to provide superheroic solutions that elude government agencies and elected leaders. What has changed most since the 1970s is the scale of redemption. The earlier scenarios focused on smaller communities such as *Jaws'* Amity Island, the occupants of a hotel floor in *Towering Inferno*, or the passengers of a single plane or ship in the *Airport* series and *The Poseidon Adventure*. While recent disaster movies show us city- or town-sized salvation in films such as *The Great Los Angeles Earthquake*, *Volcano*, and *Dante's Peak*, the stakes are raised even higher when all human life is at stake in the movies *Armageddon*, *Deep Impact*, and *Left Behind: The Movie*. While women's sexuality remains a provocative distraction from men's redemptive work, the newer disaster scenarios reflect furious new grievances over women's lack of loyalty to men or their presence in professional career roles. This anger is most blatant in *Armageddon*, where an amateur astronomer named Karl, a former Navy man who flies the U.S. flag at his observatory, tells NASA that he wants naming rights for the world-threatening asteroid he has discovered. As he stares hatefully at his wife, who sits quietly playing cards alone, this dialogue ensues:

KARL: The person who finds her gets to name her, right?
NASA DIRECTOR: That's right . . . that's right.
KARL: Well, I want to name her Dottie, after my wife. (Overhearing this,

Dottie begins to smile in surprised appreciation.) She's a vicious, life-sucking bitch from which there's no escape.

NASA DIRECTOR: Yeah, that's sweet, Karl.

As we will see, men not only "save the world for all mankind" — to echo the words of Boris the Atari video boy — they must save it despite "vicious, life-sucking bitches" who make their work more troublesome. The antidemocratic bias of the monomyth in such films is thus expressed in part by symbolic affirmations of why women must return to subordinate roles within a heroic, patriarchal system of leadership. We can best see the fierce antigovernmental and antifeminist politics of the latest films in *Armageddon* and *Left Behind: The Movie*.

Preventing the End Times in *Armageddon*

The man who does most to save the world in *Armageddon* is Harry Stamper (Bruce Willis), a Texas oil producer who is the world's best driller. NASA needs his skill because of its hope that astronauts can land on the approaching asteroid, drill an 800-foot hole, and place a nuclear explosive that will fragment it before it reaches earth's atmosphere. Early in the movie, smaller meteors are beginning to fall on the earth, causing fires in major cities and ominously smashing New York City's Chrysler Building to the streets below. The monomyth's typically stupid public is symbolized by a dopey black man who saunters through the streets of New York with his dog, gapes at the meteor shower ripping through the crowds, and eventually climbs out of a smoking crater.

As the film draws character backgrounds for the principals, we quickly learn that Harry has contempt for Greenpeace demonstrators and that he is raising his daughter, Grace, on an offshore drilling platform because her mother has inexplicably deserted them years ago. When NASA comes for help, Harry insists that his own group of ragged roughnecks be trained as astronauts in twelve days, a process that begins to establish how out of touch NASA's bureaucracy and the entire military are with the kind of manhood needed to save the world. Harry says to his crew of misfits: "The U.S. government just asked us to save the world." But the Pentagon's scheming General Kimsey comments: "The fate of the planet is in the hands of a bunch of rejects I wouldn't trust with a potato gun." While training, Harry's group confirms the notion that strict procedures will not entirely restrain their anarchic impulses. The mission almost falls apart at several points because of the explosive wizard Rockhound's manic disregard for prudence.

Once Harry and his crew have landed on the asteroid, *Armageddon's* tale reveals depravity all the way into the U.S. government. When the drilling rig initially breaks down and the men cannot place their explosives at the proper depth, President Stanley Anderson and his advisors panic and decide to blow up the nuclear device on the surface. This futile gesture will obviously take the lives of the men and, in turn, destroy any hope for human survival. Colonel Sharp, who has piloted the shuttle, accepts this wicked and stupid order, but Harry Stamper threatens to kill him — finally coercing him with just one second left. However, Col. Sharp's disarming of the device by cutting its wires has disabled its capability for remote detonation. Facing this crisis, Harry contrives to take his future son-in-law's place as the person to sacrificially descend the 800-foot shaft to trigger the explosion manually.

When the shuttlecraft cannot take off, the female copilot, Jennifer Watts, fumbles with the propulsion system, trying to follow the standard procedures. But Lev Andropov, the Russian cosmonaut who has joined the team after his fueling station caught fire, seizes control of the situation by taking a huge wrench and bashing a critical propulsion assembly: "This is how we do in Russian program." This manly abuse of the system immediately brings the power up; the surviving crew members escape while Stamper detonates the nuke, splits the asteroid, and saves humanity. The final scenes of the film shuffle through villages, mosques, churches, and synagogues around the world. As in the sister disaster films *Deep Impact* and *Independence Day,* a grateful world lifts its eyes to the heavens and expresses relief at being saved by the heroes from the United States. In *Armageddon,* the U.S. government gets national glory, though every viewer knows that the success must be credited to that singular man Harry Stamper, who courageously disobeyed an evil president who was willing to betray him and his men.

The End Times for All Politics in *Left Behind*

The *Left Behind* series of Tim LaHaye and Jerry Jenkins takes natural terror into an explicitly theological frame. Despite the fact that we in North America have become increasingly secular in some ways, this biblical/apocalyptic stream of stories has been one of the world's most successful publishing ventures. By 2001, Tyndale House Publishing was reporting sales of more than 39 million copies of *Left Behind* materials, including audiotapes and children's versions.[17] The plots of the *Left Behind* books derive from certain verses in the biblical books of Ezekiel, Daniel, Thessalonians, and Revelation. This inspiration is not merely presupposed but lies especially close to the dramatic surface when the knowing characters in the novels quote the verses with the didactic intent to guide others to salvation. The original novel, *Left Behind* (1995), is based on the highly contested notion of the Rapture, which was first formulated by the Irish preacher John Darby in the nineteenth century and later popularized in America by Hal Lindsey in his book *The Late Great Planet Earth* (1970), for which he has recently claimed sales of some 40 million copies worldwide.[18]

The initial *Left Behind* story was such a commercial success that the authors conceived a series of twelve books, quickly producing *Tribulation Force* (1996), *Nicolae* (1997), *Soul Harvest* (1998), *Apollyon* (1999), *Assassins* (1999), *The Indwelling* (2000), *The Mark* (2000), and *Desecration* (2001). *Left Behind: The Movie* was released in 2001, and its momentum has generated plans for other films and television programs, including children's versions. The *Left Behind* movie represented a major investment ($17.4 million)[19] in the evangelistic attempt to reach a wider audience.

The original novel *Left Behind* should be seen as the beginning of a grand story arc that stretches toward a dramatic conclusion to be revealed in Book 12. The series as a whole will eventually show us the world's final, sad face for the unsaved after they have experienced seven years of "tribulations," including the last battle between Jesus and his enemies at Armageddon. Although *Left Behind: The Movie* radically condenses a much larger book, what the movie shares with the book is the stunning moment of Rapture before the time of tribulation. This Rapture appears to be a blessing for the few who experience the painless ride into eternity; but it becomes an immediate disaster for those who must cope with the physical disappearance of motorists, airline pilots, and others who are performing critical services at the moment of their personal lift-off, not to mention the emotional trauma of losing loved ones.

Two converging plot lines of the first installment of *Left Behind* draw us into the drama about the struggling souls of the survivors. In one strand we encounter Buck Williams, a journalist who frequently appears on GNN television. On assignment in Israel, he reports on the biologist Chaim Rosenzweig's miraculous "Eden Formula," a fertilizer that gives wheat fields in the desert an appearance that prompts Buck to say, "It looks like Iowa." As Buck and Chaim stand in Rosenzweig's lush desert field, speculating about the end of world hunger, Israel's enemies choose that moment for an all-out attack with swarms of planes, helicopters, and tanks. And even though Israel — well known for its sophisticated defense systems — mysteriously cannot send its own fighter planes or missiles into the sky in self-defense, the invad-

The post-Rapture world of *Left Behind* creates a chaos that civil authorities
cannot master. Planes fall out of the sky, driverless cars and trucks crash,
while the miserable survivors face chaos.

Credit: *Left Behind* © 2000 Cloud Ten Pictures.

ing planes explode and fall from the sky. The secular Buck has no scriptural
background with which to frame the malevolent attack and miraculous survival; so he is merely dumbfounded by what he witnesses and conveys that to
his TV audience. When he first encounters the interpretation according to
biblical prophecy, he responds skeptically.

Equally clueless in the other stream of events is Rayford Steele, an airline
pilot who flies international routes. Troubled at home by an evangelical wife
whose beliefs and insistence on family participation he prefers to ignore, he
leaves home in anger after yet another confrontation with her and flies to
London. A professional companion is the flirtatious Hattie Durham, a flight
attendant who has been waiting for him to decide about "us." Because he has
not raised the heat of their affair to the level she wants, she has decided to
leave airline work for a position at the United Nations, which Buck Williams
— who just happens to be aboard this London flight — has helped her acquire. As Rayford clutches and kisses her in the galley, anxiously hoping that
they can continue their relationship, the moment of Rapture comes for the
saved and the innocent on that plane. The first to go is an elderly gentleman
who has been reading his Bible during the flight. He and many other passengers, mostly children, disappear into invisible nakedness, leaving neat piles of

clothing and jewelry on their seats. As in *Tidal Wave, Earthquake,* and other disaster stories, this moment of cosmic distress has come when a man has surrendered to the embrace of Eve's sister tempter.

The disturbing flight leads Rayford back home to a chaotic Chicago, where disappearing people have caused both physical and emotional chaos. At his luxurious house he finds his sassy daughter, Chloe, alive — but only empty garments where his wife and son once were. Meanwhile, Buck Williams also shows up at Rayford's home, wishing to interview the confused captain of the aircraft. From this moment forward, Buck and Rayford begin a quest in which they frequently collaborate. Rayford wants to understand his own spiritual situation, and Buck wants the big story that lies behind his startling personal experiences. Rayford quickly figures out that he has sinned, but he develops a sense of hope that in the time of Tribulation he may yet experience salvation. He passes his first Tribulation test when Hattie comes to visit, wondering whether he's more fully available now that his wife has "raptured" out of the household. Rayford's first spiritual triumph, witnessed by his cynical daughter, is his refusal to yield to Hattie's temptation.

Buck's investigations, on the other hand, take us directly toward the politics of retributive extinction so common among the Revelation-based end-time scenarios. The political truth about the world comes to light when Buck pursues information provided by an agitated conspiracy theorist who has been murdered by an agent of a pair of bankers who are collaborating with the United Nations. The bankers, Cothran and Stonagal, have arranged to have the smooth-talking young Nicolae Carpathia, a Romanian, installed as the Secretary-General of the United Nations. Although Carpathia preaches a message of peace, disarmament, and feeding the hungry children of the world, it becomes obvious that these gospel-like sentiments are a ruse, since he is actually the Antichrist. Once installed as Secretary-General, he demonstrates unlimited powers of mind control over almost everyone who enters his charming presence.

As his first "object lesson in leadership," as he puts it, Carpathia openly assassinates the very bankers who have secured his position, using their words of disagreement with him as a pretext. He announces: "From this day forward, no one can stand against me." Nicolae then hypnotically imparts a version of the event to those present that assigns complete responsibility for their shootings to the bankers themselves.

The former flight attendant and new U.N. employee Hattie Durham, who later becomes Nicolae's lover and bears his child, is one of these gullible witnesses who repeats his version as though she were an automaton. And as a sign of her degenerate perception, she says, "The U.N. is the only source that offers any hope." Only Buck retains any independent judgment about what he has seen. His insight into this radical evil allows him to join up with Rayford Steele and others who are left behind but have a chance of improving their eternal prospects in the organization Tribulation Force, a militia-type venture that is dedicated to resisting "one-world government" and fighting the regime of the Antichrist.

The *Left Behind* story as worked out in subsequent books focuses on world-domination by the United Nations and its corollary, the perversity and special powers of the Antichrist.[20] Carpathia, for example, dramatically exhibits his capacity for resurrection after Chaim Rosenzweig appears to have killed him: he comes back to life during his own funeral.

All political institutions become symbolically devalued during this prolonged struggle. The President of the United States, a member of the Democratic party, surrenders to Carpathia's mind control and cheerfully gives up U.S. military power. Carpathia demands that the rest of the world destroy 90 percent of its military resources and donate the remaining 10 percent to his new world government. The United Nations itself is scrapped; after being reconstituted as the new Global Community (GC), it abandons New York City to reseat itself at the New Babylon in Iraq. Carpathia creates the required religion of the New World Order, and in one of the later novels, *The Mark*, he imposes the mark of the beast (tattoo and identity chip) on everyone, as well as demanding personal worship of him as a kind of Roman emperor. Whoever resists this worship will be executed. In a world so structured, the only honorable path, of course, is secret resistance.

In these ways *Left Behind* leaves democracy itself behind. Given its world-scale apocalyptic conditions, focused in the unconditionally evil United Nations/Global Community, pragmatic democratic politics has no place. The only hope is that resistance will earn some credits toward salvation at the moment of Jesus' reappearance. And it is a peculiar form of opposition: Buck accepts Carpathia's invitation to manage a major publishing enterprise, while Rayford Steele becomes the pilot of his plane. They devote much of their effort to private devotions — and hiding their true beliefs from the Antichrist. As many critics of apocalypticism have pointed out — many with Bible-based beliefs of their own — the short-term end-time perspective has no patience for working with institutions or working on social justice as a way of improving the world. True believers are promised that they will not have to experience the worldwide destruction of nuclear or biological holocaust because they will be raptured out of their homes, cars, and offices.

There is a kind of double reinvention of the fundamentalist impulse here. First, the authority of selected words in the Bible takes precedence over any

kind of institutional authority of church or government.[21] Further, apoca-
lypticists use those selected words to condemn every existing institution as irrelevant in the light of both the Rapture and Armageddon. With Christ as the
violent superhero who will cleanse the world, there is no place for peacemak-
ing, for international institutions, or even for law enforcement. But it is clear
that apocalyptic fantasies can erupt into human-made disasters either by human scheming or by fatal passivity. As we have seen in Chapter 8, the evidences of Tim McVeigh and *The Turner Diaries,* of David Koresh and the
Waco conflagration, of Ted Kaczynski in his role as the Unabomber — all tell
us that fantasies can translate into tragic actions. Religious systems are particularly prone to such tragic consequences because they lend certainty to mythical visions, as recent events have demonstrated. What we know about the
participants in the September 11 attack on the World Trade Center and the
Pentagon indicates that they shared a parallel version of fundamentalism,
with a similarly mythic assumption about the need to annihilate governmental institutions perceived to be evil. Like McVeigh and Kaczynski, they were
motivated by suicidal fanaticism to produce what they believed to be a redemptive catastrophe. Now that Americans have become the target of such
cleansing actions by internal as well as external enemies, we have an opportunity to recognize their adherence to the myths we ourselves have espoused
and popularized. There is now a need for a global participation in evaluating
such destructive mythical forms, even when they derive from hoary religious
traditions or from recent popular entertainments.

Karl Kraus and the Acoustics of Disaster

The American public's mood of anxiety and dread about the future, so faithfully expressed in the catastrophe films, cannot be dismissed. Yet it is clear that
the focus of these films does not really fall on natural forces so much as on the
ways of life that seem to invite correction. These attempts to predict the consequences of present lifestyles, and the quest for the moral structure of human experience, stand in the best traditions of social responsibility. Yet monomythic
materials are so preoccupied with moral stereotypes and repressed sexuality
that they divert attention from aspects of social life and current behavior that
promise greater damage to the human prospect. We turn here to Karl Kraus,
whose drama *The Last Days of Mankind* may help us understand the impact of
catastrophes and the role of human responsibility in causing them.

Karl Kraus was a Viennese writer and social critic who spent the greater
part of his life pondering the nature of the disasters that had befallen the

Austro-Hungarian Empire. He felt that his fellow Viennese unduly magnified the significance of sexual irregularities at the expense of ignoring practices that had a more ominous social character. He wrote: "Corruption is worse than prostitution: the latter might endanger the morals of an individual; the former invariably endangers the morals of an entire community."[22] Kraus traced this corruption with shocking objectivity, revealing terrors that do not fit the stereotypical form of sea monsters, sexually provocative females, retributive earthquakes, or burning skyscrapers. He portrays an entire community in the process of destroying itself, clinging festively to the very idols that corrupt it until all is lost, while the victims deny responsibility for the doom they have ensured.

Kraus wrote *The Last Days of Mankind* in 1918-19 as an 800-page satirical tragedy with nearly 500 characters in hundreds of scenes spread over Europe during World War I. The play opens with the voice of a newsboy and ends with the voice of God, ironically echoing the words used by Kaiser Franz Joseph as he contemplated the destruction wrought by the war: "I didn't want it to happen."[23] The tragedy is that of a people who unconsciously will their own destruction, who perform their daily patriotic duties in fostering the war that destroys them, deceiving themselves to the very end. Every group in European society is implicated in the catastrophe, yet the scenes are consistently banal: an angry crowd threatens an old woman who protests the use of underfed dogs to pull a cart; a priest fires an artillery weapon at the battlefront to bless it; a patriotic sermon proclaims that killing the enemy is a religious duty; a soldier berates his angry son for asking for a hot breakfast; a display of Italian shrapnel, barbed wire, and grenades is seen at a pilgrimage chapel; children play at war games; a manufacturer markets a "Hero's Grave for the Home"; leading literary figures Rilke and Werfel write martial poetry for public propaganda; a psychiatrist classifies a "patient" as a "madman" for expressing pacifist convictions; and a man is arrested for stating the truth that 800,000 people have starved.

These scenes of frightful inertia and festive martial celebration dangle over the catastrophic abyss much like Jonathan Edwards' sinners dancing on a string over the fires of hell, yet nowhere is there an admission of human responsibility. The play portrays Emperor Franz Joseph not as an evil conspirator but as an ineffective mediocrity: "Never before in history has a more powerful nonentity placed his stamp on all things and forms. In everything that blocks our path, in every failure to communicate, every misery, we detected his imperial beard. . . . A demon of mediocrity has decided our fate" (Vol II, p. 79). Evil here is the banal vacuum that stifles the vigor of every institution at the time of crisis.

Kraus rejects the neat moralistic formulas guaranteeing that catastrophes would punish the wicked and selectively spare the righteous. His play presents scenes of indiscriminate destruction such as hungry children poking through a pile of garbage adjacent to a factory, finding an unexploded shell, and being killed by it. He avoids the petty moralism that envisions mere frivolity as triggering disasters. For instance, during the drunken revelry at a love feast attended by officers and prostitutes, the general makes grandiose speeches extolling the heroism of his unit: "Steeled through battle, our heroic soldiers — these brave men — will march into new victories — we will not flinch. . . . I expect every one of you to fulfill your duty with complete disregard — to the last breath of man and beast" (Vol. II, p. 235). At that moment the message of the enemy's breakthrough arrives, and he flees rather than directing the resistance. Stopping near a field hospital, he pulls the tarp off a wounded soldier to protect his staff car from the rain. Kraus's point is not that the stupid orgy precipitates the release of a moralized catastrophe, but that it reveals a more pervasive moral depravity that brings disaster on the culture as a whole. He uses the ironic juxtaposition of idealistic rhetoric and unconscionable behavior to point to the moral reality: the innocent are harmed, and their loss is nonredemptive. Eden cannot be regained the day after the catastrophe is over, even though the powerful will strive to protect themselves from the consequences (Vol. II, pp. 262, 235).

Kraus predicted that when the great catastrophe of World War I was over, no one would feel responsible. His "Grumbler" says: "They weren't really conscious of their actions. Austria can't be blamed for it! She merely let herself be encouraged by Germany to drag Germany into the war. And Germany drove Austria into a war she did not want. . . . Neither could really do anything about it" (Vol. I, p. 325). Kraus uses this evasive doubletalk to show how language itself had become corrupt. In his own voice, Kraus expresses the judgment that the press had played a major role in sustaining the catastrophic delusions by repeating the corrupted words of public propaganda:

In the end was the word. For the word that killed the spirit, nothing remained but to bring the deed to birth. Weaklings grew strong enough to shove us under the wheel of progress. And that was the press's achievement. . . . Not that the press set the machines of death in motion — but that it hollowed out our hearts, so that we could no longer imagine our future: that is its war guilt! And all peoples have drunk the lascivious wine of its debauchery, the kings of the earth have joined in the fornication. (Vol. II, p. 230)

Kraus developed a kind of "acoustic empiricism" to trace this corruption of language. He listened carefully to everyday speech for evidences of decay and self-deception, gleaning hundreds of authentic artifacts from articles, documents, and conversations. He saw in popular culture the evidence that "a world . . . talks its way to perdition," as Max Spalter observed.[24]

Karl Kraus would be amused at the mythic empiricism of Hollywood's disaster films. He would likely point out that the contrived King Kong or asteroid terrors are less menacing than the corruption hidden in our daily routines. He would remind us of the terrible possibility that we may enjoy and even worship what has the power to destroy us, and probably not even realize why the catastrophe occurs. His "Grumbler" concludes:

> Far greater than all the outrage of the war itself is that of people who wish to know nothing more about it. . . . For the survivors of the war, the war simply went out of fashion. . . . How easy it is to comprehend the sobering up of an epoch that never had valid experiences nor any grasp of what it had undergone — an epoch unshaken even by its own collapse! It perceived its atonement as dimly as its crime and possesses just enough self-preserving instinct to plug its ears to the heroic tunes on the phonograph, but sufficient self-sacrifice to sing along again whenever the occasion arises. (Vol. 1, p. 6)

The "occasion" arose, of course, within two decades of his writing those words, leading the Germanic peoples into the next disastrous crusade. Unlike the catastrophe films, which assume that the violent destruction of evil restores a lasting peace, Kraus accurately foresaw what the survivors of World War I would bring upon themselves. The "Grumbler" predicts:

> That the war will turn the entire surrounding world into a huge hinterland of deceit, of debility, and of the most inhuman betrayal of God, while evil sustains itself through and beyond the war, prospering behind pretended ideals and fattening on sacrifice! That in this war, this modern war, culture is not regenerated but rather rescues itself from the hangman by committing suicide. (Vol. 1, p. 171)

This rejection of renewal through catastrophe was vindicated by later events, whose nature Kraus continued to document until the time of his death in 1936. His vision passes the test of time and warns us that to seek the nature of evil requires a painful look into ourselves, our institutions, and the popular language of our time. In the light of the American catastrophe of September

11, 2001 — which could become as ominous a date as August 1914 — such honest introspection is required for each of our crusading traditions, whether Christian, Jewish, Islamic, secular, or whatever. Evil is not a set of apocalyptic jaws that neatly punish the wicked and spare the virtuous before being driven away by heroes. It is rather the perpetual tendency to deceive ourselves and to blunder even when we most sincerely attempt to avoid the catastrophes our present actions are bringing. If we fail to grasp how our own policies sometimes encourage others to consider us as enemies, and how our mythic conformity in mounting military crusades is ill suited in response to terrorism, then our situation will likely become ever more vulnerable. It is time to break free from the violent mythology and to create and sustain appropriately democratic international institutions of justice to cope with the evils that will always continue to arise, even the catastrophes that we ourselves sometimes cause.

16 Deceptive Fugues, Democratic Dances

"This is going to make a great movie one day."

> Ronald Reagan, in appreciation of Oliver North
> on the day of his firing from the National
> Security Council staff in 1987[1]

"John Bolton is the kind of man with whom I would want to stand at Armageddon, or what the Bible describes as the final battle between good and evil in this world. . . . John is a patriot."

> Senator Jesse Helms (R-NC), introducing President
> George W. Bush's nominee for Undersecretary of State
> for Arms Control and International Security[2]

The patterns we have established in discussing popular materials show that there is a kind of "mythic dissonance" in the United States. Whereas popular myths might be expected to sustain the leading ideals and institutions of a culture, the American monomyth consistently undermines the democratic ethos. Given its elitism, irrationalism, zealous stereotyping, and appetite for total solutions instead of compromise, it is difficult to find any democratic emphasis in the myth, except perhaps in its convention of the ordinary person who develops extraordinary powers.

338

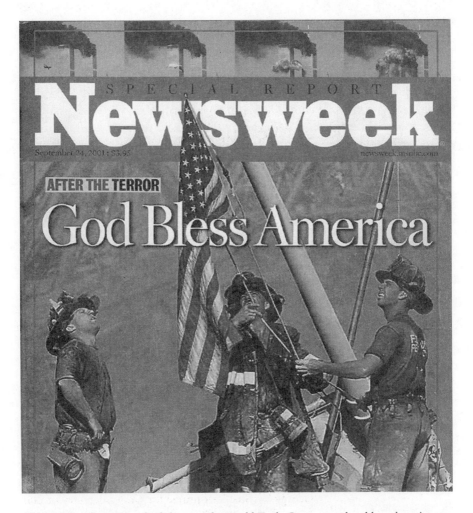

This picture of surviving firefighters at the World Trade Center — echoed by other pictures in U.S. media — may signal a shift in American heroic tastes. Perhaps we can now applaud more often citizens without weapons who work for the government.

Credit: Newsweek, Inc. © 2001.

When the nation itself is conceived in those superheroic terms, we can see how the tendency toward total, violent solutions so easily slips into public discourse, as, for example, in the above statement by Senator Helms. His somewhat Manichean linkage of arms control and Armageddon can be traced in part to an American ambivalence about whether it is to be a "light to the nations" — guided by laws and treaties — or "a rod of iron" that terrorizes them with overwhelming force. The latter tradition, while sitting comfortably with the latest apocalyptic versions of the American monomyth, certainly emerged before the twentieth century.[3] But there are cases in which the monomyth seems to leap straight off the screen into the highest reaches of government.

We think that this happened, for example, during the 1980s when Oliver North, Jr., a White House National Security Council adviser under President Ronald Reagan, became embroiled as an operative in the trade of arms to Iran for American hostages held in Lebanon. North used the proceeds from these covert arms sales, which violated U.S. policies on negotiating for hostages, to help finance a war in Nicaragua, where financial assistance had been severely restricted by acts of the U.S. Congress. The deviations from U.S. declared policy became so brazen that these operations finally came under public scrutiny, and they were eventually shown to involve several key policy-makers in the U.S. government. However, what we learned from the North case is that the enacted myth can win public applause, even when its performers walk a fine line separating criminality from constitutional policy-making. Oliver North — or "Ollie" as he came to be known by so many of those who affectionately lionized him — had a program that echoed the foreign-policy imperatives of the hulking, sweaty, bare-skinned John Rambo. This policy's underlying vision of the public is also embedded in an enormously popular film of the era, *Close Encounters of the Third Kind* (1977).

"Rambo Goes to Washington"

In the summer of 1987 — the bicentennial year of the U.S. Constitution — the American public found itself enthralled by a strange television spectacle. After months of investigations into the confusing Iran-arms-for-hostages deal, with its leitmotif of diverted profits for the Contra rebels of Nicaragua, the moment came when a reluctant witness, Lt. Col. Oliver North, would appear before the joint congressional committee. From the very first day of his appearance, he testified openly about his secret missions, including "Project Democracy," to assist the Nicaraguan Contras. He punctuated his testimony with references to the betrayal of America in Vietnam. He seemed proud as he described his bold shredding of documents that he knew the Congress would want to seize in its efforts to discover the activities of the National Security Council. Just as changing congressional sentiment had eventually led to disengagement in Vietnam, he feared that his activities, if discovered, would be terminated. So zealous was he in protecting the nation by disguising his actions that he reported destroying documents virtually in the presence of Justice Department officials who had come to investigate.

Admitting that many of his activities were known to agents and officials in Iran, Israel, and the Soviet Union, and to private citizens in the United States, North nonetheless alleged that it would be dangerous to the nation's security if these facts were disclosed to the elected leaders with formal oversight of the actions in question. Although he spoke frequently of the nation's enemies in foreign lands, it was utterly clear that he regarded the American government as equally menacing to the nation's future. It was a message that we would hear a decade later from another proudly defiant soldier — Timothy McVeigh. North's message was a resounding success with several members of Congress and with millions of viewers, some of whom immediately began a "North for President" movement. Walking along a path toward national leadership, Oliver North did indeed run for Senator from Virginia in 1994, and he almost defeated the incumbent Chuck Robb. He remains politically active today as a radio show talk host, newspaper editorialist, and leader in the Freedom Alliance.[4]

Oliver North's message and values were hardly new; we had seen and heard it all before — at the movies. During the 1970s and 1980s a popular new genre of action-adventure, foreign-policy film emerged. One of the things the stirring tales of this genre sought to do was resuscitate and win the lost war of Vietnam. In *Rambo: First Blood — Part II*, the disillusioned and rejected Vietnam veteran John Rambo is told that he is wanted for a secret mission: to investigate reports of American POWs in Vietnam. When he asks whether "we get to win this time," the recruiting officer replies, "It's up to you." Rambo does win his own private war, but not without fighting a bureaucracy that wants to restrain his activities behind the lines. After a miraculous and successful mission, he expresses his contempt for his government by spraying automatic weapons fire into the machinery of the communications center of his operation.

In a similar way, the Chuck Norris films *Missing in Action* (1984) and *Delta Force* (1986) refight other lost conflicts. The latter begins with a reprise of the bungled "Operation Blue Light" of the Carter administration, in which the rescue of American hostages in Iran was aborted in the desert because of poor planning and equipment malfunctions. From that point forward, the episode of TWA Flight 847 is woven into the plot. But rather than ending in negotiations and release — the way the situation was actually resolved — Major McCoy (Chuck Norris) succeeds in fighting a private war with Shiite Moslems, killing them one by one in hand-to-hand combat or with the incredible arsenal of weapons that he packs onto his magic military motorcycle. Private initiative thus resolves the conflicts of the Middle East with a minimum of munitions and casualties; it is merely a matter of allowing righteous, heroic zeal do its work.

Like other savior figures, the heroes of both *Rambo* and *Delta Force* are presented as lonely, selfless, and sexless beings whose sole interest resides in their zeal for the mission. Thus they join mythic hands with the John Wayne characters of the past and with Luke Skywalker, Neo and Trinity of *The Matrix,* and the array of Mel Gibson characters who shoot and slash their way into our captive hearts. Their thrilling feats help cultivate the habit of redemptive expectation, which leaves us ready — in fantasy and too often in real life — to surrender our common fate to a hero who arises above all our laws and institutions to save us. The Oliver North episode in American politics illustrates how easily these values of outsized fantasy can be transferred to the conduct of the real world, earning the applause of mythically receptive voters.

The appearance of Ollie North before the joint House-Senate hearings on the Iran-Contra affair was a remarkable case study in monomythic politics. The country virtually halted in front of television sets as millions of enthralled Americans responded to "Jimmy Stewart cast in 'Rambo Goes to Washington.'"[5] This is an apt allusion to the classic 1939 film *Mr. Smith Goes to Washington,* starring Jimmy Stewart as the selfless hero who kept his integrity in the wicked capital. Jonathan Alter observed:

> North has Stewart's cracking voice and patriotic gaze down pat; the nobility of the common man shines through, particularly when set off against big-city lawyers. . . . The difference, for those who have trouble discerning it, is that Jimmy Stewart triumphed in the end by telling the truth. Oliver North has triumphed by defiantly admitting lies. Somehow these two quite distinct reels of American morality have been spliced together in the public mind.[6]

In our view, this curious splice joins Mr. Smith and Rambo: it fuses Jimmy Stewart with Clint Eastwood and Sylvester Stallone, whose character fights the CIA to save forgotten POWs. More than once Oliver North incorporated *The Good, The Bad and The Ugly,* the title of one of Eastwood's tough Westerns, into his testimony: "I came here to tell you the truth — the good, the bad and the ugly."[7] "Ugly" actions never contemplated by Mr. Smith were now required for the noble cause. Like Rambo, North played the role of the persecuted superhero with aplomb. The political system for whose integrity Mr. Smith struggled is now perceived as the source of corruption, with congressional lawyers playing the malevolent role that Claude Raines played in *Mr. Smith Goes to Washington.*

The fusion of these heroic images into the new Rambo persona was evident in North's military garb. Although he had not worn the uniform at the White House — indeed, was a civilian there — North displayed it proudly at the hearings; the rows of medals reminded the audience of his prowess and bravery in Vietnam. At one point in the hearings he virtually cited Rambo's line about that war they were not "allowed to win."[8] Like Rambo, his soldierly exploits were reportedly on the superheroic level. A fellow officer said admiringly that "Ollie could fight his way through a regiment of North Vietnamese regulars armed with nothing but a plastic fork."[9] But the exploits that most captivated the public were, like Rambo's, efforts to gain the release of American hostages in Beirut, Lebanon. The accounts of North's risky journeys, the threats against his life, and his willingness to die rather than reveal secrets under torture led one writer to gush freely about his film-heroic qualities:

> He came across as a hero. Not a phony Hollywood hero. A real hero. In his first week as a witness, North was dazzling. . . . This wasn't Sylvester Stallone or Arnold Schwarzenegger fighting a play war with catsup blood. This man fought real wars. He dripped real blood. His war didn't end when the cameras stopped turning. His enemies pursue him into his home. Right this minute they're after him. And face to face with the scariest terrorist in the world, he doesn't blink. Any time, any place, he told Abu Nidal. Man to man. One on one. You and me. The country watched transfixed.[10]

It was as if a more real, more perfect Rambo had suddenly emerged, live on television! A wave of merchandising followed, including Ollie North t-shirts, dolls, bumper stickers, and political buttons.

Although he was a career officer and an efficient bureaucrat, Oliver North felt Rambo's contempt for the constitutional process. The orders and sentiments of a zealous commander-in-chief, President Reagan with his policies of strident anti-communism, were the standard of obedience. North's code name for the State Department was "Wimp"; he blamed Congress for being "fickle, vacillating, unpredictable" in its policy toward the Nicaraguan Contras, thus justifying his illegal and secret operations. He repeatedly expressed scorn for the Boland Amendment and other Congressional attempts to act as a check and balance against executive power in foreign policy. He was contemptuous of the lack of public support for the Contra cause, while he repeatedly affirmed the anti-Communist imperative as the key to the national interest. He set up dummy companies and bank accounts to move the money needed for the Contras, and he traveled with a fake "black diplomatic passport" as a businessman, "Mr. William B. Goode," on his secret deal-making trips.[11]

North admitted, but never apologized for, the phalanx of lies with which he had shielded his activities. Years later, in his memoir, he said, "What I did was wrong" (p. 322). But he retained his larger, self-justifying perspective: "I continue to feel that saving a life — or trying to — is more important than preserving a policy" (p. 406). He remained unrepentant about shredding vital documents in the very presence of his investigators and creating false governmental records. Feisty and tough, proud and humble at the same time, loyal to God and country, he embodied the persona of a mythically tailored hero. R. W. Apple, Jr., put it this way: "The marine spoke in the language of the zealot. Those allied with him in his cause were 'patriots,' 'freedom fighters,' people who could cut through the niggling concerns of the bureaucracy. Those who opposed him were dupes or incompetents or worse. His world view and that of his colleagues, as he pictured it, allowed no room for honest differences of opinion on strategy, on tactics, on honor or propriety. He described a . . . world of demons and angels. . . ."[12]

That the public admired North's stance is rather explicit evidence of the appeal of monomythic politics. As Jonathan Alter observed, "The instant North resolutely admitted to having lied and falsified documents, many viewers thought it unfair to hold him accountable for it. Confession became salvation before the hearings broke for lunch."[13] The idea of lawless exploits restoring national honor and winning a lost war, the mark of the Rambo paradigm, surfaced in the outpouring of public support for Ollie North. Among the 120,000 supportive telegrams North received during the course of his testimony, there were many that referred to the restoration of patriotism and pride. *USA Today* ran an Ollie hot line and received 58,863 calls advocating another medal for his efforts; 1,756 calls said he deserved a jail sentence instead.[14] A woman from Beaver Island, Michigan, reported to David Broder that people "would like to elect Ollie president, just as soon as he's out of jail." By this line of reasoning, if North were forced to suffer even more for his righteous cause, his qualifications for office would be complete. Senator Robert Dole made a similar comment to the Young Republicans during the course of the hearings, suggesting North as an excellent possibility for Vice President.[15] David Broder concluded that North's popularity revealed the kind of a political leader Americans now preferred: "He will be someone, in short, quite unlike those now regarded as the best bets in either party. Not someone adorned with political-governmental credentials, but someone who believes enough to make us, at least for a moment, suspend our massive disbelief."[16] What many Americans really wanted at that moment in history, it appears, was a Rambo as their supreme political leader.

The congressional hearings left no doubt about the serious tensions between the Rambo style of heroism and the requirements of a constitutional democracy. Yet in the final two days of North's testimony, members of the congressional committee reasserted these traditional values in a powerful series of appeals to the American public. For those Americans who had not succumbed to the myths they saw on the movie screen, this intense and sustained civics lesson reminded them of the issues that had been raised by the Iran-Contra episode. The thousands of telegrams and phone calls that flooded congressional offices to indicate support for these constitutional values suggest that America surely had a divided mind about the activities of Lt. Col. North. Since these impassioned statements stand in such strong counterbalance to monomythic politics, they are worth examining in some detail.

- That the nation was defeated in Vietnam by a cowardly acceptance of limited, compromising goals was repudiated by Senator Warren B. Rudman: "The American people have the constitutional right to be wrong. And what Ronald Reagan thinks or what Oliver North thinks or what I think or what anybody else thinks makes not a whit if the American people say 'Enough!' There comes a point that the views of the American people have to be heard."[17] The essential democratic principle is that the majority must rule in matters of war and peace; self-appointed zealots who assume the responsibility of conducting private foreign policy on their own are the ones who truly betray it.
- That patriotism is expressed through dissent rather than zealous adherence to stereotypical ideals was affirmed by Senator George J. Mitchell, who told North that "it is possible for an American to disagree with you on aid to the Contras and still love God and still love this country just as much as you do. . . . In America, disagreement with the policies of the Government is not evidence of lack of patriotism. Although he's regularly asked to do so, God does not take sides in American politics."[18]
- That some super-agency or super-warrior, acting beyond the bounds of lawful authority, should be encouraged to carry out the task of rescuing the innocent and saving American democracy was rejected by Congressman Louis Stokes. He found North's testimony to be "more than ugly. It has been chilling and in fact frightening. I'm not talking just about your part in this but the entire scenario — about government officials who plotted and conspired . . . lied, misrepresented and deceived, officials who planned to superimpose upon our government a layer outside of our government shrouded in secrecy and only accountable to the conspirators."[19] Stokes added that reliance on the rule of law had permitted him, a

formerly segregated, black serviceman, to become chairman of the House Intelligence Committee.

- Finally, Congressman Dante Fascell contended that the National Security Council had "adopted the methods of a totalitarian government in pursuing democratic goals." When North sharply disagreed, Fascell backed off from this penetrating and accurate observation with the admission that he was not talking about a "substitution of values." But the swap was there for all to see. This theme was reiterated at a dramatic highpoint of the hearings, from the perspective of democratic principles. Senator Daniel K. Inouye was rudely interrupted during his statement at the close of North's testimony while arguing that the military personnel have "an obligation to disobey unlawful orders. This principle was considered so important that we, we the Government of the United States proposed that it be internationally applied in the Nuremberg trials. And so in the Nuremberg trials we said that the fact that the defendant —" At this point, defense attorney Brendan V. Sullivan shouted: "I find this offensive. I find you're engaging in a personal attack on Colonel North and you're far removed from the issues of this case. To make reference to the Nuremberg trials I find personally, professionally distasteful and I can no longer sit here and listen to this. . . . Why don't you listen to the American people and what they've said as a result of the last week? There are 20,000 telegrams in our room outside the corridor here that came in this morning. The American people have spoken. . . ."[20] This impassioned exchange revealed the profound disparity between what some of the telegrams favored and the American principle of lawful obedience. The reference to Nuremberg infuriated Sullivan because it indicated a similarity between his client's behavior and the politics of willful disobedience.[21] What the public was allowed to glimpse in this exchange was that *Rambo*-style patriotic heroism cannot be indulged without grave threats to a constitutional democracy.

The Premise of a Spectator Democracy

Fantasy-style heroism presupposes an audience of spectators that can appreciate the great deed. *Close Encounters of the Third Kind* (1977), a successful film that remains in wide circulation,[22] opens with an archetypal scene of the American public as so incompetent and its government so corrupt that the sole alternative is to wait for its salvation. Concerned citizens from Muncie, Indiana, who have traveled to a nearby Air Force base to describe their UFO experiences, are presented as so witless that they could never fumble their way to a sound judgment about a genuine threat. The movie's hero, Roy Neary (Richard Dreyfuss), truthfully claims that he saw a gigantic spaceship; but the briefing officer replies with condescension that the government had no such evidence and Neary and all the other witnesses must be mistaken. "We are the evidence . . . and we want to be taken seriously," Roy shouts back.

"I think there are all sorts of things that would be great fun to believe in," the hostile officer replies. "Time travel and Santa Claus, for instance. . . . We seem to want proof that there is something that can solve our problems for us."

A farmer interjects: "I saw Bigfoot once. . . . It was up in Sequoia National Park."

"What about the little star of Bethlehem . . . ?" an addled lady interrupts.

"Sir, is there any truth at all to this Loch Ness monster crap?" another voice intrudes.[23]

This meeting of citizens with their Air Force protectors ends in chaos, a scene paralleled in *Jaws, Death Wish, Rambo: First Blood, Part II, Armageddon, Deep Impact,* and most other disaster films. Democratic institutions are typically depicted as chaotic, irrational, and dishonest, incapable of coping with reality. The stupid spectator-citizens cannot communicate with one another rationally, cannot form an intelligent plan, and hence could never act effectively. These widely popular films are symptoms of the death of the dream of a government responsive to the collective interests and insights of average citizens. The contrast with some traditional American ideals of collective intelligence is striking. Thomas Jefferson wrote, for example:

> I know of no safe depository of the ultimate powers of the society but the people themselves, and if we think them not enlightened enough to exercise their control with a wholesome discretion, the remedy is not to take it away from them but to inform their discretion by education.[24]

It is wholly apt that Oliver North's own campaign for the U.S. Senate would betray a cynical disavowal of such ideals. The 1996 documentary film *The Perfect Candidate*[25] offers an unusually frank exploration of the perceptions of voters and the corresponding strategies for enlisting their support. Mark Goodin, North's key campaign strategist, reflected: "We provide daily entertainment. What we are not providing is serious solutions to what's going on in the country. Not us, not Chuck [Robb, North's Democratic opponent], not Clinton, not Bush.[26] Not anybody." He also conceded that the charismatic appeal of North as candidate was "the triumph of anger over politics." This scale of manipulative cynicism makes one yearn for a redeemer from another planet, which is exactly what *Close Encounters* provides.

The repository of political wisdom in *Close Encounters* is not the public but the invaders from outer space, who recruit a typical American to become a future superhero. Roy Neary, an electrical engineer, is the nondescript Everyman-as-outsider mysteriously selected for this role. He goes off on a quest, finally intruding at the Devil's Tower UFO site because of an inner compulsion. He has no special qualifications for his implied redemptive task. But he is selected by the benign invaders to join the mysterious spaceship and must forgo the usual temptations of sex, family responsibilities, and job security to achieve his calling. The film provides one-half of the typical superheroic tale of the Heidi type. But the movie ends in mid-myth, so to speak. At the tale's conclusion, the Everyman figure is about to be enlightened and transformed by his encounter with the space creatures from a realm of mysterious light and power. Until he returns as the earth's savior in some future episode, the mythic plot will not be completed.

This helps explain why audiences were observed to remain seated through the credits of *Close Encounters of the Third Kind*, watching the fading starship blink off into space. They had the impression, as Stanley Kaufmann observed, that the story was not really finished. Martin Gardner stated the premise of the film accurately in suggesting that Roy "will be brought back later . . . stuffed with transcendent wisdom. The Age of Aquarius has dawned."[27] The French scientist Lacombe, one of the outsider figures who assists in mediating the world's salvation, is described in Steven Spielberg's novelization of the screenplay as knowing that Neary is crucial to this historic turning point. At stake is Roy's imminent ascension into "all the wisdom, all the superintelligence, the experience that it had to take to build these vehicles" from outer space.[28] Since he alone is receptive, Roy is chosen to lead twelve anonymous apostles into the spaceship to absorb the insights necessary for world salvation. Jefferson's dream of universal enlightenment has devolved upon a tiny and select "depository of the ultimate powers of the society. . . ."[29]

The Heidi-redemption scheme implicit in *Close Encounters* is particularly clear in the words of Spielberg's novel: the music and lyrics of Disney's *Pinocchio* echo inside Neary's head as he enters the blinding light of the godship. Though they were cut after evoking snickers at an early screening of the film, the lyrics remain in the novel and evoke the nonviolent redemption scheme implicit in the entire film.[30] In the story of *Pinocchio*, the Blue Fairy plays the role anticipated for the space creatures of *Close Encounters*. She grants the wooden Pinocchio the opportunity to become a real, live redeemer figure, capable of saving Gepetto from the giant Monstro. "When you wish upon a star, your dream . . . comes true" is her happy message. Similarly, the miracle of happy endings is promised in *Close Encounters,* now that the future superhero has penetrated the radiant womb of cosmic wish-fulfillment. The Heidi-redeemer will return as the millennial Christ followed by twelve astronaut-apostles, setting things right at the end of time. The public in this final scene, as in most monomythic entertainments, is in the spectator position, "silently watching."

The political implications of this final scene are obvious when placed in the context of the film as a whole. American political institutions and traditions are depicted as basically ineffectual and dishonest, standing in need of regeneration by the Everyman Neary and the godlike figures from outer space who have elected him. The film's conclusion is, in effect, an epiphany of that future redemption. Special effects director Douglas Trumbull described the gargantuan spaceship as "a very religious kind of thing. For a filmmaker, it's like trying to show Jesus Christ or God. It's very hard to meet people's expectations. We went for a vision."[31]

Judging from the public's ecstatic response to one of the more commercially successful films in history, the effort to depict an epiphany of future enlightenment was a cinematic triumph. A reviewer for *Today's Student,* a fundamentalist Christian publication for university students, was ecstatic: "Nothing has ever approached the rapture and enchantment of the closing scenes. . . . The grand scale they're working on suggests a magnitude that only approaches God." The entire film, this reviewer insisted, conveyed "man's smallness, helplessness and need of a Savior."[32] In other words, the democratic public is so helpless that only superhuman powers of rubber-armed humanoids can save it. To state the political theme in terms of imperial ideology, the only hope for the bumbling fools on this planet is a selfless redeemer figure who possesses the wisdom, power, and love to solve the problems of democracy in their behalf. This monomythic political vision requires a philosopher-king-as-Everyman, equipped with super power and wisdom from a superior world. It needs an Oliver North, Junior, who is much better at not getting caught.

How could *Close Encounters,* a movie with such a dim view of average human capability, achieve such popularity in a democratic society? Perhaps it mirrors a self-conception of the American public as the spectator democracy that is so frequently depicted in our films. Running parallel to this negative picture of public capability is the often remarked decline of American voting in national elections (discussed in Chapter 7). As Robert D. Putnam has shown in his widely discussed *Bowling Alone: The Collapse and Revival of*

American Community, America's "social capital" — manifested positively as "mutual support, cooperation, trust, institutional effectiveness" — is dropping as well.[33] Putnam has documented a significant withdrawal from what he calls "civic engagement" with both private and public institutions that do the work of responding to communal needs. In accounting for this decline, he mentions several factors, including the "pressures of time and money"; "suburbanization, commuting and sprawl"; "generational change" as an older generation fails to transmit its civic values to the younger; and finally, "the effect of electronic entertainment — above all, television — in privatizing our leisure time" (p. 283).

Since almost everyone in America watches television, Putnam distinguishes between the minimalists and maximalists among the watchers, confirming that those who watch the most TV do the smallest number of community projects and "give other drivers the finger" the most, while the minimalists reported the highest number of projects — and the smallest number of "fingers" (pp. 231-232). Speaking directly to the content of television programming, he suggests that television regularly presents characters and ways of life "that weaken group attachments and social/political commitment."[34] Putnam does not categorically condemn TV as the antithesis of community life, since "at its civic best, [it] can be a gathering place, a powerful force for bridging social differences, nurturing solidarity, and communicating essential civic information" (p. 243). We agree and believe that popular culture has a far greater potential to affirm the complexities of the democratic ethos than it has shown in recent decades. We discuss some significant examples below.

Help Wanted: Democratic Dancers

A significant pressure for entertainment media has been the formation of advocacy groups who press for favorable, or at least neutral, depictions in public narratives. The National Association for the Advancement of Colored Peoples (NAACP) launched one of the earliest campaigns in attacking the racial stereotypes in D. W. Griffith's *Birth of a Nation.*[35] Since that time, groups of Latinos, Native Americans, gays and lesbians, and others have sought to foster images that represent them more fairly. It is similarly appropriate to ask that democratic entertainments should, with significant frequency, create stories expressing a strong democratic ethos, stories of ordinary heroes and heroines rather than of superheroic redeemers who employ fascist methods in a futile effort to redeem a democratic society.

Some premier products of the major franchises for the American monomyth examined in this book — *Star Trek, Star Wars,* and Disney's *Lion King* — have yielded, respectively, the following:

- Multicultural crews under military command in outer space;
- Jedi royalty and warrior priests seeking to restore a monarchy;
- One restored Lion King — acclaimed cheerfully even by lion prey.

These narratives seem democratic in their spirit of multiculturalism (or multi-speciesism) and some acceptance of group judgment. But these democratic flavors are overpowered by themes of individual superheroism, the celebration of instinct, the employment of extralegal means of redemption, and the vision of an impotent public. Below the level of these mythic behemoths, the individual heroes such as Rambo, Batman, Superman, and Mel Gibson's characters similarly disappoint our hope for democratic representations. American superheroes, in their striving to redeem corrupted republics or instantly adjust psychological problems, typically reflect values that are antithetical to democratic processes. Superheroic figures are never elected to public office, never submit to the restraints of law or constitution, and never contribute to the discussion that is the very stuff of democracy. The behavior of the macho heroes is typically fascist, despite all claims to redeem democracy. Yet despite the bleakness of this democratically impoverished landscape, we still notice recurrent traces of promise in the realm of popular entertainment.[36]

One of the important Hollywood figures of recent decades was Stanley Kramer, a film director who created several decades' worth of work. He was particularly well known for his films about racial intolerance: *Home of the Brave* (1949) focused on racial tensions in the armed forces; *The Defiant Ones* (1958) looked at the ramifications of a black and a white prisoner chained together in an escape situation; *Guess Who's Coming to Dinner* (1967) explored liberal white racism. Kramer's *On the Beach* (1959) was one of the first movies to present characters meditating on the concrete consequences of nuclear warfare. His *Inherit the Wind* (1962) depicts the courtroom battle over evolution in Tennessee (the "Scopes trial") that pitted Clarence Darrow against William Jennings Bryan. *Judgment at Nuremberg* (1961) recasts the post–World War II war crimes trials in Germany as a story of locating and accepting responsibility. Kramer's films tend toward the melodramatic, probably a requirement for meeting the tastes of the wide audience he aimed for; but they depict people grappling with serious issues, using the tools of law or reasoned discussion. The resolutions we see in these pictures do not come out of physical, moral, or psychological superheroics. Instead, rather limited people grapple with complexities to reach some kind of accommodation.

Another film with a democratic stream running through it is *Glory* (1989), which explored the creation of the 54th Regiment of the Massachusetts Volunteer Infantry, a group of blacks formed during the Civil War and led by Robert Gould Shaw, a member of a prominent abolitionist family in Boston.[37] Although most of the characters and incidents are fictional, it offers historical substance that opens many pathways for those who look through the screen to the events represented. In the view of Civil War historian James M. McPherson, *Glory* is "one of the most powerful and historically accurate movies ever made about that war."[38] In the segment of the Civil War that this film re-creates, the task of the 54th Regiment is to capture Fort Wagner in South Carolina. It fought valiantly in this effort in 1863, but it lost half of its fighting force, including Shaw. The movie ends with this defeat, even though surviving members of the unit went on to fight other battles. The successful struggles within the film occur among the men themselves, over whom hangs the question, "Will the black soldier fight?" According to McPherson, the success of this unit "not only advanced the liberation of the slaves but also helped liberate President Lincoln from certain constitutional and political restraints" that had made it impossible to make war against the institution of slavery, as opposed to merely quelling the rebellious states.

The men of *Glory* are shown fighting for a democratic cause — the equality of whites and blacks and the preservation of a constitutional system — but they do so without any superhuman or remarkable moral or physical powers. Racism among the Northern troops is very evident. The men are not escaping from women who seek to turn them into wimps. None of them can hack away in a wild Rambo/Mel Gibson-style frenzy that mows down whole squads of enemies. They are shown as the kind of limited but tenacious people who are required to change history. Their limits are conveyed in one of the film's most striking scenes: the leading pair, Rawlins and Forbes, ascend the ramparts at Fort Wagner with the rest of the men behind them. There they meet head-on the rifles that will surely destroy most of them. No Gnostic confidence or magic bullet time is invoked to save them from their death, though the movie mercifully does not show their slaughter. The scale of heroism on the part of Robert Gould Shaw is conveyed in part by his moral willingness to be identified with his men at a time of scorn for them — and to fight for their uniforms, shoes, and right to participate in combat. It was significant for a democratic society that *Glory* stimulated popular interest in the role of African-American military history. It probably opened the door for another film, *The Tuskegee Airmen* (1995), which sympathetically explored the role played by African-Americans in some European air campaigns of World War II.

The Straight Story

Vengeance is one of the most durable themes of the American monomyth. But very few movies can examine the impulse critically and with complexity while surviving at the box office. We examine two significant films of the last decade that have done so in noteworthy fashion. On the plane of personal relationships, we found the movie *The Straight Story* (1999) to be a serious investigation of family conflict and its crippling effects. The book *Dead Man Walking* (1993), and the 1995 movie inspired by it, deal with the issue of vengeance by expressing some wholly new ways of looking at the death penalty in America. In both movies we see ordinary heroes at work, persons lacking superheroic capacities, yet nevertheless bringing to bear some of the moral resources needed by a democracy to counter its bias toward destructive Armageddons.

The Straight Story[39] is based on factual incidents. Alvin Straight of Laurens, Iowa, is a retired 73-year-old security guard who lives with a daughter whose mental limitations have led to the loss of her children. The dramatic point of departure for this story is that Alvin has for years been alienated from his brother, who lives in Mt. Zion, Wisconsin.[40] In the movie's portrayal of his life, Alvin has poor vision, bad hips, and many regrets, which include accidentally killing one of his own squad members while serving as a sniper in World War II, in addition to a number of "moon-faced" German adolescent boys. He has experienced a prolonged period of alcoholism, and perhaps has some responsibility for the death of his daughter Rose's child in a fire. This tragedy has led to confrontations with social workers, who may be overly alarmed by Rose's stammering speech pattern and have taken public custody of her other four children. Alvin has had fourteen children, but only one of them, Rose, still lives near. She lives with him and helps to look after him in his weakened condition.

Alvin wants to visit his brother; but because he is legally blind and can't drive a car — and rather than taking a bus or a train — he rigs up a riding lawn mower to pull a trailer that carries his survival needs for the 325-mile journey. His first attempt at the trip fails, resulting in a quick return and his rigging of a better mower for a second try. His journey, we gradually learn, is a kind of pilgrimage for atonement at a moment that he feels is surely close to the end of his life. He meets people along the way and shares such life wisdom as he has; but he makes no pretensions about being a healer of other people's souls. When he gives a runaway, pregnant teenage girl a "bundle of sticks" homily about "the unbreakability of family bonds," we know that he is talking about a quality that he has not achieved himself. He carries the memory of many guilts, some of which he acknowledges to a sympathetic priest who finds him camping in the parish cemetery. After many delays and encounters with people, he finally reaches the home of his brother in Wisconsin. They laconically acknowledge one another and are reconciled to the degree conveyed by their mutual presence.

Thematically, *The Straight Story* presents us with a version of the Everyman-as-hero myth. Alvin Straight is a dying man (which has been confirmed by his doctor), and he is averse to any procedures that might prolong his existence. He is a person who finally understands himself: he knows his weaknesses, and he mourns his troubled past. He is thus finally enabled to reach out to a brother, suffering in the aftermath of a stroke, whom he has probably dealt with in a hateful way. Here an ordinary person, confronting an injustice for which he bears some responsibility, tries to undo a past retribution he has inflicted. Ultimately, it is a story of pride reduced, self-knowledge increased, and the exercise of courage to rectify an old wrong. These are the personal qualities that people have to muster in quelling their impulse for vengeance. They are precisely the qualities they need in their efforts to make a common life together in a democratic society, despite the antagonisms and struggles that inevitably arise therein.

The Straight Story was immediately recognized for its wisdom. It received the Lloyd C. Douglas Spiritual Quest Award for the best film featuring "Judeo Christian values of care, compassion, and transforming love."[41] And the late Richard Farnsworth, the actor who portrayed Alvin Straight, was nominated for an Academy Award in the Best Actor category.

Dead Man Walking

At the level of a public-policy issue, perhaps the most significant portrayal of democratic discourse of the past decade — as well as being a contribution to that discourse in its own right — came in the form of Sister Helen Prejean's best-selling book *Dead Man Walking: An Eyewitness Account of the Death Penalty in the United States* (1993), which was followed by the Hollywood movie in 1995. Susan Sarandon, who portrayed Sister Helen in the film, received a Best Actress Academy Award for the role. In addition, the story was retold in the musical form of opera, in a well-received production that debuted in

2000.[42] Although the United States is one of the few countries in the world where there is still strong support for the death penalty, the book, and especially the film, gave the crusading Sister Helen a platform and opened many doors for her testimony.

Prejean's prison ministry "conscripted" her, as she put it, when a bishop assigned her the task of counseling a death-row prisoner in 1981. After counseling him and his family, and then watching his execution, she began a ministry of commitment against capital punishment, which led to the publication of her best-selling book in 1993. She collaborated with Tim Robbins in developing a screenplay about her experiences,[43] and she described the impact of the film on her outreach in this way: "[M]y mission was born to begin to speak about the death penalty to anybody. Believe me, before the movie 'Dead Man Walking,' that whole Susan Sarandon thing, the audiences were pitifully small. . . . Three people here, five people there."[44] The movie, like the book, had concretized and dramatized the issue of capital punishment in a way that reached new groups of citizens, not just in the United States but in other countries as well. It has been the subject of discussion for countless reading groups and has stimulated several study guides found on the Web. What was particularly democratic about the story of Sister Helen's opposition to the death penalty?

What is immediately striking is that she describes a journey of her own learning as she tries to find her way through the thicket of moral issues involved in capital punishment. She lacks the infallible moral instincts of the superheroine that would allow her to make quick decisions about the good and evil characters in her landscape. She hesitates to take her first assignment, the condemned rapist-murderer Mathew Poncelet,[45] because she cannot imagine how to carry out her mission. When she meets with her prisoner, she senses his self-destructive rage and self-pity; yet she is partly conned by his plea that he is innocent of murder and thus offers some assistance to his last-minute appeals for a stay. By the time she has witnessed his execution, she has seen through some of his scams. She has not converted him, but at least she has managed to bring him to the point of a choked apology to the parents of the victims in the rape-murders he perpetrated. This element of redemption, however, is not a point of closure for either the book or the movie, which strive to create a panoramic view of the human chain unwillingly linked to one another at executions: the condemned and their families, the families of the victims, and the officials whose job it is to administer death.

What Sister Helen learns from her first execution is not only the pain of the condemned and his family but also the anger of the victims' parents — the Leblancs and Bourques — directed at her. As Lloyd Leblanc confronts her (in the book's account), he says, "How can you present Elmo Patrick Sonnier's[46] side without ever coming to visit with me or the Bourques to hear our side?"[47] So she does begin to meet with these families, uncomfortably at first, but eventually establishing a continuing relationship of counseling with Lloyd. This is reflected in the final scene of the movie, when she meets with him at a church for prayer together. In addition, she begins to meet with support groups for victims' families; she also encounters prison officials in distress over their work, some of whom find themselves pressured and sleepless. Just as Sister Helen strove to avoid stereotyping or excluding anyone's concerns, the film avoids presenting the condemned as an innocent victim of circumstances. At the moment of Sonnier's execution, audiences also view a reprise of the moment when he was killing his terrified victims. Marc Bruno generalizes about the film: "*Dead Man Walking* is a kind of ethical laboratory. Those who oppose capital punishment are forced to watch the crimes, while those who support it are forced to look into the killer's soul."[48]

Neither the book nor the film has any simple solution to the issue of the death penalty. What they both show is the commitment of a determined woman, Sister Helen, who is optimistic about the power of public discussion to find a less humanly destructive policy for capital crimes than the death penalty. Just as Harriet Beecher Stowe used *Uncle Tom's Cabin* as an ethical prod on the issue of slavery, Prejean has used her experience and her ability to communicate through popular culture to bring an intense light to a subject so often buried in darkness.

On the role of the church in Sister Helen's story, there is one additional noteworthy difference from the American monomyth. She does her work within the framework of an institution that offers support for her conception of her ministry. But as is typical for work by subordinates within large organizations, there are awkward moments when Sister Helen feels that some of her superiors share the very public attitudes she is fighting against. As with other adversaries against whom she wages her gentle war, she pleads and persuades rather than rejecting or sidestepping the issue. In providing this mixed picture of the church, *Dead Man Walking* goes against decades of monomythic tradition that depicts the church as a collection of fools who must inevitably allow the superhero gunman to compensate for their timid pacifism. The church's role also recalls one of Robert D. Putnam's interpretations in *Bowling Alone* — that "faith communities in which people worship together are arguably the single most important repository of social capital in America" (p. 66). As evidence, he cites the fact that "churches provide important incubator grounds for civic skills, civic norms, community interests, and civic recruitment." He also mentions surveys indicating that "membership in religious groups . . . [is] most closely associated with other forms of civic involvement, like voting, jury service, community projects, talking with neighbors, and giving to charity" (pp. 66-67). All of these ordinary forms of civic commitment,[49] incidentally, are what we find missing in the "church-less," miraculous interventions of the team in *Touched by an Angel*, for example. Because she is anchored within her institutions, Sister Helen does not disappear in a red Cadillac or fly away into the heavens as does Neo in *The Matrix*.

Concessions to the Monomyth

Part of the challenge of dealing with the American myth system is that it contains some elements of truth. For example, one of our principal objections to the American monomyth has related to its peculiar form of sexual segmentation, usually presented as the need for the male hero to reject the experience of intimacy lest he lose his redemptive potency. The appeal of such intimacy is that in sexual love the "two become one flesh," overcoming their lonely separateness. The mutual responsiveness, trust, and sharing that can grow out of permanent sexual relationships — values that have their counterparts in the democratic political process — are among the most commonly sought human experiences. That the institution of marriage, a permanent covenant to secure such values, proves durable in spite of its current pressures is evidence of the persistent yearning for such experiences. The successful channeling of sexuality is undoubtedly the key to creativity in the lives of many persons. We are sympathetic to Rollo May's suggestion: "Eros is the drive toward union with what we belong to — union with our own possibilities, union with significant other persons . . . in relation to whom we discover our own self-fulfillment."[50]

Monomythic heroes suppress their needs in order to achieve a selfless perfection that requires no personal fulfillment. They display a static personality structure, lacking the need for development and thus transcending the nurturing values of sexuality. Furthermore, the achievement of redemption through destruction or manipulation sidesteps procreative and companioning dimensions that usually accompany the attainment of realistic goals. Monomythic heroism is marked by nullification rather than creation. The murderer Charles Manson, who styled himself in the heroic mold of an exterminating angel, felt that sexual gratification was subordinate to his mission. If one can believe his words, he said that his sexual relationships became a means of cultivating the loyalty of disciples: "I don't need broads. Every woman I ever had, *she* asked *me* to make love to her. I never asked them. I can do without them." Manson had internalized the monomythic ideal of sexual segmentation, providing some justification for his accusation against American culture that "I am what you have made of me."[51]

Despite the distortions of the monomyth, its vision may contain important insights. Its hostility toward human sexuality conveys the awareness — on the flipside of the above discussion — that love often takes tragic and destructive forms. As Rollo May puts it, "Sexual love has the power to propel human beings into situations which can destroy not only themselves but . . . other people. . . ." He mentions the mythic figures of Helen and Paris and Tristan and Iseult as embodiments of the insight that sexual love can "seize man and woman and lift them up into a whirlwind which defies and destroys rational control."[52] In forcing our attention to the danger of neglecting responsibilities for gratification and of sexual exploitation, the monomyth's partial insights deserve to be taken with some seriousness. At a time when the story of President Clinton's prodigious sexual appetites and proclivity for destructive affairs remains fresh in our memory, it is all too obvious that several decades of sexual liberation have hardly erased the potential for disrupting the nation's business.[53]

The monomythic concern about human evil must also be incorporated into any realistic grappling with the problems of community. But the monomyth's failures lie in the stereotypical identification of who is evil, its melodramatic exaggeration of evil traits, its facile belief in selective punishment, and the assignment of a retributive role to nature and to superheroes. Monomythic materials overplay the role of conspiracy in accounting for evil, overlooking the propensities for evil within each member of the chosen community.

The yearning for larger-than-life figures mirrors the eternal need for leaders who will stand forth and assume lonely and unpopular tasks. The monomyth smudges this point by depicting heroes who win acclamation at the completion of their work. The anti-elitist bias, expressed through the hint that anyone can become a superhero, embodies a respect for widely distributed human potential, a worthy democratic theme. However, the kind of leadership a democracy requires does not promise total solutions but undertakes the more limited human task of coping with life as it needs to be lived. As Reinhold Niebuhr suggested, democracy is a system offering "proximate solutions for insoluble problems."[54] Basic human dilemmas and conflicts cannot be eliminated by a process of destructive purgation.

The monomythic convention of allowing the redeemer to disappear from the redeemed community is perhaps a sad recognition that "no prophet is acceptable in his own country" (Luke 4:24). The deaths by assassination of so many American leaders and the constant effort by some to torture those who attain distinction suggest that heroic stature is an affront to the impotent few whose sense of significance stems from destructive urges. The classical monomyth is more promising at this point because it so often features the re-integration of the heroic person back into the community at the conclusion of the adventure.

Finally, the Edenic inclinations of the monomyth point toward the human need for intimate relationships with the forces of nature, requiring a balance between the demands of urban, industrial life and the sustenance of the physical environment. The difficulty again lies in the lack of realism in the American monomythic vision. In an essay entitled "Nature Nostalgia and the City," John McDermott shows that the mixture of the urban, the pastoral, and the primitive in America's yearning for paradise results in falsifying the essential qualities of each:

> We lament the city as being without nature. On the other hand, the nature . . . about which we are nostalgic *is* stripped of its most forbidding qualities: loneliness, unpredictability, and the terrors of the uninhabitable. . . . For the most part, the nature envisioned by urban and suburban man *is* one that has been domesticated by the very qualities of the city which we take to be unnatural. . . . Under the press of nostalgia, however, we strip both nature and city of ambivalence, in a bizarre reversal of the wilderness and paradise theme.[55]

McDermott forcefully reminds us that the American monomyth blocks the celebration of experiences that make urban life attractive and locks its adherents into a nostalgic yearning that can never be satisfied.

Reviewing these elements of truth in the monomyth compels us to recognize that it has valid roots in experience, however selective or partial its interpretation. It is unlikely that a powerful fantasy could otherwise arise and be sustained through generations as the American monomyth has since the axial decade of 1929-1941. Even slender shreds of evidence confer credibility when shaped by the wish of the faithful and the eloquence of technomythic presentation. So believable does the monomythic creed remain that its mere recital renders most improbable statements credible. It seems to immunize its audiences to any sort of critical response.

Censorship or . . . ????

Gazing at the American monomyth and its potential for enactment in national life is admittedly a disturbing experience. Once its electronic radiance has been dimmed through critical short-circuitry, the mood of entertainment passes, and one feels a sinister presence. It is therefore tempting to embark on a zapping crusade such as Frederick Wertham's campaign against comic books during the 1950s.[56] The result of that crusade, in fact, was the codification of monomythic values in the Comics Code Authority (CCA), whose conventions paralleled those of the Motion Picture Production Code launched in the 1930s. The CCA's "Seal of Approval" on a comic book dealing with serious themes guaranteed that tales of miraculous victories over powers of pure evil were to be found within. The belief that "badness" could be purged from comic books by a single stroke was thoroughly monomythic. But the American mythic system is not the result of a conspiracy localized in a guilty few whose behavior can be controlled by law. Most Americans, including the present authors, have resonated to the articulation of the monomyth and have felt the pull of its assumptions even when attempting to reject them. The seductive appeal, even after one discounts its escapist elements, is rooted in a form of moral idealism that has been developed through generations of popular creation and restatement. It is foolish to believe that monomythic values can be dispelled quickly.

The American monomyth is one of those vexing issues that calls for the virtues of democratic coping rather than redemptive crusading or "problem solving." It requires a public examination of popular materials with all the critical intelligence that can be mustered. There is sufficient common sense even among those indoctrinated by the monomyth to make a careful diagnosis possible. New forms of technomythic criticism are needed to discern and evaluate the messages so glamorously displayed in popular materials, sensitizing audiences to the new forms of mythic eloquence, and providing rabbit tests for the gestation of Werther effects. In carrying out this task, we should be aware that other nations and cultures have crucial insights to contribute and a vital stake in the outcome. The tempering of the American monomyth will be easier if we can escape the provincialism to which we are prone and begin to look into the mirror others can hold up for us.

It is sobering to think that America spreads its monomyth to the rest of the planet through the powerful new technomythic media. In many lands there is a paralysis of political responsibility accompanied by curiously passive and nostalgic publics. Violent redemption is often promised by secretly placed explosives or by masked gunmen. This was observable long before the

September 11 attack traumatized much of the "free world." In 1973, Friedrich Hacker, an Austrian who practiced psychiatry in Los Angeles and served as negotiator with terrorists, made this observation about international patterns in manufacturing justifications for acts of violent aggression:

> Never before was mankind so inventive in preparing and refining symbols of its enemies and in producing and intensifying its feelings of clear conscience. . . . Everywhere and always, everyone is fully justified, whether in the ruling palaces or underground, whether in seats of power or in the slums, on every continent, the First, Second, and Third Worlds.[57]

Hacker believes that the mass media have popularized this verbal weaponry that now ranks among the dangers to the world. Hacker concludes that this "secret message of the mass media" — that violent deeds can always be justified — inspires some of the heroically destructive acts around the world.[58] It is as if Joseph Campbell's "hero" has become an anonymous killer in search of an enemy "with a thousand faces."

Sifting through monomythic materials, one encounters the traditional notion that America somehow has a responsibility to the rest of the world. This is not the time to discard that belief, though we would insist that the attempt to act on it should take democratic forms. The critical evaluation of America's role as an international purveyor of mythic fantasies recalls for us an important statement by Alfred North Whitehead about cultural criticism: "The art of a free society consists first in the maintenance of the symbolic code; and secondly in fearlessness of revision . . . to secure that the code serves . . . purposes which satisfy an enlightened reason."[59] The spirit of criticism calls for the "fearlessness of revision" that Whitehead refers to; but it should be combined with "a reverence for symbols" recognizing that the monomyth has roots in centuries of creative American dreaming.

Ultimately, the monomyth will have to be temperately reshaped by those who have enjoyed and fully understood its appeals. We must discard its skepticism about merely human agencies and its preference for final solutions. Above all, coping with the monomyth demands creators and performers who understand its political implications and resolve to give their work a greater resonance with the democratic ethos. The same technomythic means that have given the monomythic premises their credibility can be turned to the celebration of democratic and sexually integrated alternatives. But we should avoid the illusion that we shall ever live entirely without myths or transcend the human condition of "seeing through a glass darkly."

September 11 and Democratic Heroism

A potential resource for the development of healthy democratic myths may lie in the tragic events of September 11, 2001, which gave the lie to every monomythic expectation. Neither New York City nor Washington, D.C., fit the images of peaceful Edens whose endangerment should have led to a superheroic rescue. No caped superheroes flew through the air to divert the flight of the doomed airplanes, and no superheroic president was on board who, like Harrison Ford in *Air Force One,* could dispatch the terrorists before their evil mission could be completed. No Atari Boy used his joystick on a *Missile Command* video screen to stop the planes before they reached their target. None of the Ingalls family was present who, along with Heidi or Mary Poppins, should have been able to convince the terrorists that their scheme was unwise and unfair. No angelic team provided a tinkling shower of light to divert the hijackers from their mission of destruction.

The monomythic expectation about a passive, incompetent, spectator public also proved to be mistaken. The behavior of Americans as they coped with the terrorist attacks could have a greater impact in popularizing forms of democratic heroism than any work of imagination could achieve. The scenes at the World Trade Center in New York, the Pentagon in Washington, and on United Airlines Flight 93, which crashed in Pennsylvania, each present a different visage but all have implications for the heroic ideals that Americans should still find resonant. At the disaster sites in New York and Washington, uniformed police, firefighters, and medical personnel, serving under command, acted courageously to save citizens trapped in the buildings. In fulfilling their mandate to serve the community, they took risks that they might have avoided. Hundreds died in the collapse of the two towers that comprised the World Trade Center. To our knowledge, there are no stories of actions taken by individuals who defied rules or commanders to carry out a rescue. Instead of the panic and passivity depicted in monomythic entertainments, thousands of office workers exited and at times led each other out of burning buildings. Leaders were competent, workers were audacious, and many lives were saved. When it became clear that the disaster overwhelmed the resources of the governmental workers, many citizens from other areas volunteered to help with the rescue efforts. These were all people who cared about the welfare of their community and took risks for it.

The ability of citizens to respond heroically to crises, despite their lack of superheroic powers or insights, was particularly clear on Flight 93. Cell phone communication allowed some passengers to know of events at the World Trade Center and to infer that they had likely become one of the flying bombs. Recognizing their dilemma, a group of passengers consulted among themselves about how to divert the airliner from a strategic target. They decided to rush the hijackers on a signal. Todd Beamer, one of the passengers who had developed the plan to seize the plane, asked a GTE telephone operator to recite the Lord's Prayer and then said to his companions, "Let's roll." None of them had a gun like Buffalo Bill's .50-caliber rifle, or a satchel of weapons like that employed by Neo and Trinity in *The Matrix*. Neither John Wayne nor Charles Bronson was present to deal with the situation by magic fists or six-guns. Unable to move at "bullet speed," these citizens used ordinary muscles in diverting the plane from its mission of destruction, but were unable to save their own lives, as superheroes always can. The plane crashed in a Pennsylvanian field.[60] Historian Jack Rakove, reflecting on political responsibility in this situation, made this observation: "The passengers deliberated, and then voted, as democratic citizens are supposed to do, and apparently decided to storm the cabin. The resulting crash was presumably the result of that decision — a tribute to their bravery, but also to their ability to reach a decision that was at bottom a matter of common sense. For what other alternative did they have?"[61] The democratic ideal latent in this act, according to Rakove, is "not a conception of citizenship that expects heroism or even exalts extraordinary acts." Instead, he sees a readiness to act and to do "the right thing when the moment comes." Such a sense of responsibility, widely diffused in our citizens, is surely an antidote to the superheroic ideal — and the best hope that ordinary people can sustain the lives of their communities.

The mythic expectation that the wicked will be punished while the righteous are saved was also invalidated by the events of September 11. While the *Left Behind* novels and films promise that the pious who belong to the right sect will be raptured out of airplanes and buildings at the time of the great disaster, not a single person appears to have escaped in this manner. The disaster films depict the deaths of sinners whose promiscuities provoke earthquakes, tidal waves, and flaming skyscrapers, but no one can make a credible case that those who escaped were more righteous than those who died. Despite the hopes of the terrorists that their violence would re-create a righteous world, just as the violence of American superheroes allegedly restores Eden in story after story, the ashes of the just and unjust lie intermixed at the end of Manhattan Island. Among the more than eighty nations whose citizens died in the World Trade Center were in all probability representatives of every major religion in the world. The powdered ashes of Christians, Jews, Muslims, and Hindus of many varied persuasions lie next to the nonreligious in such confusion that no monomythic separation remains credible. The hope to restore Eden through superheroic violence must now give way to sober honesty in the face of the ghastly smoldering ruins at the foot of Wall Street. Such a hope must now be recognized as inappropriate for a democratic society, indeed as a threat to civilized life anywhere on the planet. However, it is unreasonable to expect that the hope of regeneration through violence can be quenched by one more campaign against foreign terrorism when our own myths have glorified it for the past seventy years. The events of September 11 that inaugurate a new millennium call for a reconstruction of the American myth system by the creation of genuinely democratic entertainments.

Democracy has its own necessary myths concerning the need for personal responsibility, the wisdom of the majority, the efficacy of individual reason, the enhancement of due process, and the advancement of equality. Even these hallowed myths of democracy must be subject to public scrutiny. Rather than yearning for a final vision that contains the whole truth, we must move forward through mythic sifting and renewal toward insights capable of sustaining life and love on a planet that seems to spin ever more fatefully. It is not too late in history to hope for an abundance of entertainments worthy of a free society, which may enter our experience — as Plato so grandly put it — "like a breeze bearing health from happy regions."[62]

A Comment on Sources

Evolving information formats have made full-text electronic databases, the Internet, and the World Wide Web important for this book. For post-1980 periodicals, we have relied on the following sources: the Lexis-Nexis database (University of California at Berkeley), the Gale Group collections (the Berkeley Public Library), and the Personal Edition of the Electric Library (http://www.elibrary.com). While knowing that cited material and URL addresses can be ephemeral, we also make numerous references to Web sites. We indicate the "view dates" for such references.

Some citations from *The New York Times* were affected by the Supreme Court decision in *New York Times* vs. *Tasini*, rendered June 25, 2001. The ruling held that the newspaper had violated the copyrights of freelance writers in reselling content to electronic full-text aggregators such as Lexis-Nexis. The newspaper responded to its legal defeat by purging from electronic archives 115,000 articles written by 27,000 authors between 1980 and 1995. (See "Freelance group files suits against *New York Times*," *Reuters Business Report*, July 5, 2001.) Temporarily such articles will no longer be available online; they will remain in paper collections and indexes and in microfilm. Other publishers have also withdrawn articles that we have cited.

We also mention here the absence of pagination in electronic full-source texts. When we cite from such sources we simply indicate the page range for the article in its original print format (or the beginning page along with the number of pages when the latter is available).

Endnotes

Chapter 1: The American Monomyth in a New Century

1. Cindy Crosby, "*Left Behind* fuels growth at Tyndale House," *Publishers Weekly* (May 7, 2001), p. 18. The fiction series had released ten of its projected twelve titles by 2001.

2. *The Matrix.* Dirs. Andy and Larry Wachowski. Time Warner Entertainment, 1999.

3. John G. Cawelti, *The Six-Gun Mystique* (Bowling Green: Bowling Green State University Press, 1971), pp. 12, 28.

4. Joseph Campbell, *The Hero with a Thousand Faces* (New York: Meridian, 1956), p. 30.

5. Herbert J. Gans, *Popular Culture and High Culture: An Analysis and Evaluation of Taste* (New York: Basic Books, 1974), pp. ix, 35, 32.

6. William G. Doty, *Mythography: The Study of Myths and Rituals*, 2nd ed. (Tuscaloosa: University of Alabama Press, 2000), p. 26 (italics in original).

7. Stuart Pratt Atkins, *The Testament of Werther in Poetry and Drama* (Cambridge: Harvard University Press, 1949), p. 2.

8. Walter Kaufmann, *Without Guilt and Justice: From Decidophobia to Autonomy* (New York: Delta, 1975), p. 161.

9. Atkins, *Testament*, p. 2.

10. *Ibid.*, p. 64; it is also revealing that Goethe assigned the date of his own birthday to that of his character Werther. Cf. the foreword by Herman Weigand in *The Sorrows of Young Werther* (New York: New American Library, Signet Classics, 1962), p. viii.

11. *Chicken Run.* Dirs. Peter Lord and Nick Park. Aardman Animations; Dreamworks SKG; Pathe, 2000.

12. "President Bush's address to the nation in response to terrorist attacks," *San Francisco Chronicle* (Sept. 12, 2001), p. A4.

13. Marc Sandalow, "Bush promises to conquer a new kind of enemy," *San Francisco Chronicle* (Sept. 13, 2001), p. A7.

14. John McCain, "Yes, war is hell — so let's get on with it," *San Francisco Chronicle* (Nov. 4, 2001), p. C6.

Chapter 2: The Birth of a National Monomyth

1. J. H. Plumb, "Disappearing Heroes," *Horizon,* Vol. 16, No. 4 (Autumn 1974), pp. 50-51.

2. Sanford, *Quest for Paradise* (Urbana: University of Illinois Press, 1961), p. vi.

3. Cf. William Haller, *The Rise of Puritanism* (New York: Columbia University Press, 1938), pp. 174-75, 269 ff.; Conrad Cherry, *God's New Israel: Religious Interpretations of American Destiny* (Englewood Cliffs, N.J.: Prentice-Hall, 1971), pp. 25-30; Winthrop S. Hudson, *Religion in America: An Historical Account of the Development of American Religious Life* (New York: Charles Scribner's Sons, 1973, 2nd ed.), pp. 18-22.

4. Sanford, *Quest,* pp. 82-83, italics omitted.

5. Roderick Nash, *Wilderness in the American Mind* (New Haven: Yale University Press, 1967), p. 26.

6. Daniel J. Boorstin, *The Americans: The Colonial Experience* (New York: Random House, 1958), p. 29.

7. Sanford, p. 117.

8. Cited by Nash, *Wilderness in the American Mind,* p. 97.

9. Henry Nash Smith, *Virgin Land: The American West as Symbol and Myth* (Cambridge: Harvard University Press, 1950), p. 107.

10. David M. Emmons, *Garden in the Grasslands: Boomer Literature of the Central Great Plains* (Lincoln: University of Nebraska Press, 1971), pp. 34-36.

11. John Seelye, "The Mouse in the Machine," review of Christopher Finch's *The Art of Walt Disney, The New Republic* (Dec. 22, 1973), p. 24.

12. Richard Slotkin, *Regeneration Through Violence: The Mythology of the American Frontier, 1600-1860* (Middletown: Wesleyan University Press, 1973), p. 104.

13. Ibid., p. 95.

14. Smith, *Virgin Land,* p. 95.

15. *Birth of a Nation.* Dir. D. W. Griffith. Epic, 1915.

16. Gerald Mast, *A Short History of the Movies* (New York: Pegasus, 1971), p. 85.

17. Marsha Kinder and Beverle Houston, *Close-Up: A Critical Perspective on Film* (New York: Harcourt Brace Jovanovich, 1972), p. 20.

18. Fred Silva, *Focus on the Birth of a Nation* (Englewood Cliffs: Prentice-Hall, 1971), p. 11; cf. Lewis Jacobs' compilation of Griffith's shots in this concluding scene, "D. W. Griffith: *The Birth of a Nation,*" in *Focus on the Birth of a Nation,* ed. F. Silva, p. 166; Marshall McLuhan overlooks these technomythic advances of early filmmakers when he claims that movies ". . . would prove unacceptable as mass audience films if the audience had not been preconditioned by television commercials to abrupt zooms, elliptical editing, no story lines, flash cuts." *The Medium Is the Massage* (New York: Random House, 1967), p. 128.

19. Cf. Jonathan Rosenbaum's chapter "The AFI's Contribution to Movie Hell . . . ," in *Movie Wars: How Hollywood and the Media Conspire to Limit What Films We Can See* (Chicago: A Capella Press, 2000), pp. 91-106.

20. Arthur Knight, *The Liveliest Art: A Panoramic History of the Movies* (New York: New American Library, 1957), p. 34.

21. Mast, *Short History of the Movies,* p. 86.

22. Sanford, *Quest for Paradise,* p. 14.

23. Robert Jewett, *The Captain America Complex: The Dilemma of Zealous National-ism* (Philadelphia: Westminster, 1973), pp. 176-214.

24. Knight, *Liveliest Art,* p. 35.

25. Cited in Leon Litwack, "Birth of a Nation," in *Past Imperfect: History According to the Movies,* ed. Mark C. Carnes (New York: Henry Holt, 1995), p. 141.

26. *Independence Day.* Dir. Roland Emmerich. 20th Century Fox, 1996.

27. Smith, *Virgin Land,* p. 188.

28. Daniel J. Boorstin, *The Americans: The Democratic Experience* (New York: Random House, 1973), pp. 34-41.

29. Owen Wister, *The Virginian: A Horseman of the Plains* (New York: Grosset & Dunlap, 1911, 3rd ed.), pp. x-xi.

30. Boorstin, *Democratic Experience,* p. 27.

31. W. Eugene Hollon, *Frontier Violence: Another Look* (New York: Oxford University Press, 1974), p. 152.

32. Harry Sinclair Drago, *The Great Range Wars: Violence on the Grasslands* (New York: Dodd, Mead, 1970), p. 275.

33. Hollon, p. 161; Neal Lambert, "Owen Wister's Virginian: The Genesis of a Cultural Hero," *Western American Literature,* Vol. 6 (1975), p. 101.

34. Wister, p. 414; for an extensive discussion of the relation between the novel and Wister's life, cf. Sanford E. Marowitz, "Testament of a Patriot: The Virginian, the Tender-foot, and Owen Wister," *Texas Studies in Literature and Language,* Vol. 15, No. 3 (1973), pp. 551-75.

35. Max J. Herzberg, *Reader's Encyclopedia of American Literature* (New York: Crowell, 1962), p. 1183.

36. Robert V. Hine, *The American West: An Interpretive History* (Boston: Little, Brown, 1973), p. 270; on the genre see Roy W. Meyer, "B. M. Bower: The Poor Man's Wister," *The Popular Western,* ed. R. W. Etulain and M. T. Marsden (Bowling Green: Bowling Green State University Popular Press, 1974), pp. 25-37; Leslie A. Fiedler, *Love and Death in the American Novel* (New York: Criterion, 1960), p. 255.

37. *The Virginian.* Dir. Victor Fleming. Paramount Famous Lasky Corp., 1929; cf. Robert Warshow, "Movie Chronicle: The Westerner," *Focus on the Western,* ed. J. Nachbar (Englewood Cliffs: Prentice-Hall, 1974), p. 49.

38. Hine, *American West,* p. 270.

39. Peter Homans, "Puritanism Revisited: An Analysis of the Contemporary Screen-Image Western," *Focus on the Western,* p. 84.

40. Burne Hogarth, *Tarzan of the Apes* (New York: Watson-Guptil, 1972), p. 22.

41. James Steranko, *History of Comics* (Reading, Pa.: Supergraphics, 1970-), Vol. I, p. 19.

42. Ibid., Vol. 1, p. 37.

43. Cf. Daryl R. Coats, "Comic Book Superheroes," in *The Guide to United States Popular Culture,* ed. Ray V. Browne and Pat Browne (Bowling Green, Ohio: Bowling Green State University Popular Press, 2000), pp. 190-91.

44. Jim Harmon, *The Great Radio Heroes* (Garden City: Doubleday, 1967), p. 202.

45. Cf. Gary Yoggy, *"The Lone Ranger"* in *The Guide to United States Popular Culture*, pp. 494-495.

46. "The Adventures of the Lone Ranger," Decca Records (DL 75125).

47. Ibid.

48. Harmon, pp. 196-97.

49. Cf. Hollon, *Frontier Violence*, pp. 42ff.

50. "The Adventures of the Lone Ranger," Decca Records.

51. Cf. Jewett, *Captain America Complex*, pp. 90-98; John G. Cawelti, *The Six-Gun Mystique* (Bowling Green: Bowling Green University Popular Press, 1971), pp. 60-61.

52. "The Adventures of the Lone Ranger," Decca Records.

53. Harmon, pp. 212-13.

54. Les Daniels, *Comix: A History of Comic Books in America* (New York: Bonanza Books, 1971), p. 11.

55. Ted White, "The Spawn of M. C. Gaines," *All in Color for a Dime*, ed. R. A. Lupoff and D. Thompson (New York: Ace, 1970), p. 27.

56. Jules Feiffer, *The Great Comic Book Heroes* (New York: Bonanza Books, 1965), p. 18.

57. Ibid., p. 26; italics omitted.

58. Ibid., p. 68; some caps omitted.

59. "Shazam-Isis," CBS (Nov. 1975).

60. *Flash Comics* (Aug. 1971).

61. E. E. Smith, "What Does This Convention Mean?" in *All Our Yesterdays: An Informal History of Science Fiction Fandom in the Forties*, ed. H. Warner, Jr. (Chicago: Advent, 1969), p. 96.

62. See note 1 above.

63. H. L. Nieburg comes to similar conclusions in *Culture Storm: Politics and the Ritual Order* (New York: St. Martin's Press, 1973), p. 15: "But modern man is immersed in a universe of magic and ritual that he ethnocentrically considers 'scientific' and 'rational.' He thinks himself the most advanced product of human history standing at a pinnacle of self-understanding, mastery of his environment, and free from delusion and superstition. This pose has always been characteristic of man whatever his condition. Advanced civilization is greatly augmented by technology and large-scale organization, but it remains as saturated with ritual as any primitive society. Magic, faith, and arbitrary mental constructs encompass the needs of modern man."

Chapter 3: Buffalo Bill: Staging World Redemption

1. Cited by Henry Nash Smith, *Virgin Land: The American West as Symbol and Myth* (Cambridge: Harvard University Press, 1950), p. 107.

2. John Burke, *Buffalo Bill: The Noblest Whiteskin* (New York: G. P. Putnam's Sons, Capricorn Books, 1973), p. 95.

3. Burke, *Buffalo Bill*, pp. 23-35.

4. Ibid., p. 48.

5. Smith, *Virgin Land*, pp. 106-107.

6. Burke, *Buffalo Bill*, p. 45.

7. Dixon Wecter, *The Hero in America* (Ann Arbor: University of Michigan Press, 1963), p. 355.

8. Burke, *Buffalo Bill*, pp. 289-92.

9. Cited by Wecter, *The Hero in America*, p. 357.

10. Cf. Don Russell, *The Lives and Legends of Buffalo Bill* (Norman: University of Oklahoma Press, 1960), pp. 88-89, for a cautious evaluation of Buffalo Bill's claim.

11. Excerpt from *Buffalo Bill: Story of the Wild West*, reprinted in W. A. Wilbur, *The Western Hero: A Study in Myth and American Values* (Menlo Park, Calif.: Addison-Wesley, 1973), p. 31.

12. Cf. Russell, *Buffalo Bill*, pp. 185-87.

13. Ibid., p. 188; Russell notes that Cody associated his wound with this expedition, but that he probably confused it with a verified graze wound in 1869.

14. Ibid., p. 230.

15. Cf. ibid., pp. 221-35, for a discussion of the varying accounts.

16. Smith, *Virgin Land*, p. 108.

17. Cf. Burke, *Buffalo Bill*, pp. 120-21.

18. Ibid., p. 11.

19. Ibid., p. 143.

20. Ibid., p. 195.

21. Cf. Russell's reprinting of the 1893 program, pp. 376-77.

22. Robert V. Hine, *The American West: An Interpretive History* (Boston: Little, Brown, 1973), pp. 277-78.

23. Wecter, *Hero in America*, p. 359.

24. Burke, *Buffalo Bill*, p. 164.

25. Ibid., pp. 12-13.

26. Cf. Robert Jewett, *The Captain America Complex* (Philadelphia: Westminster, 1973), pp. 42-45.

27. See Joy S. Kasson, "Performing National Identity," in her *Buffalo Bill's Wild West: Celebrity, Memory, and Popular History* (New York: Hill and Wang, 2000), pp. 265-273. She suggests that Cody's legacy is visible in the Boy Scouts, the Girl Scouts, and in the mythic persona of John Wayne.

28. Burke, *Buffalo Bill*, p. 231.

29. Kent Ladd Steckmesser, *The Western Hero in History and Legend* (Norman: University of Oklahoma Press, 1965), p. 241; cf. John G. Cawelti, *The Six-Gun Mystique* (Bowling Green: Bowling Green University Popular Press, 1971), p. 78: "With such a hero, the creators of Westerns were able to express some sense of ambiguity about these ideals and yet at the same time to reaffirm the essential benevolence of American progress."

30. Don Russell, "Cody, Kings and Coronets," *The American West*, Vol. VII, No. 4 (1970), p. 62.

31. Cited in Warren Zimmerman, "Jingoes, Goo-Goos, and the Rise of America's Empire," *The Wilson Quarterly* (Spring 1998), p. 42 (24).

32. Ibid.

33. Ibid.

34. Richard Slotkin, *Gunfighter Nation* (New York: Harper, 1993), pp. 82-83.

35. Michael Straight, *Carrington* (New York: Knopf, 1960).

36. Citation from John R. Milton, *Three West: Conversations with Vardis Fisher, Max Evans, Michael Straight* (Vermillion: University of South Dakota Press, 1970), pp. 130-31; details about Straight's research methods are provided on pp. 113 ff.

37. Ibid., pp. 159-60.

38. *Buffalo Bill and the Indians; or, Sitting Bull's History Lesson.* Dir. Robert Altman. De Laurentiis/Talent Associates Ltd, 1976. Some of the film's incidents derive from Arthur Kopit's play *Indians* (1968).

39. The film was not commercially or critically successful.

40. Paul A. Hutton has provided a careful documentation of this point in his examination of the Custer legends in recent films: "Thus from a symbol of courage and sacrifice in the winning of the West, Custer's image was gradually altered into a symbol of the arrogance and brutality in the white exploitation of the West. The only constant factor in this reversed legend is a remarkable disregard for historical fact." "From Little Big Horn to Little Big Man: The Changing Image of Western Hero in Popular Culture," *Western Historical Quarterly* (Jan. 1976), p. 45.

41. Straight, *Carrington*, pp. 373-74.

42. "RIPOFF Boosting Nebraska," *Sioux City Journal* (Jan. 23, 1976).

43. Milton, *Three West*, p. 138.

Chapter 4: Heidi Visits a *Little House on the Prairie*

1. Johanna Spyri, *Heidi* (Racine: Western Publishing/Whitman Book, 1970; original German, 1884), p. 210.

2. "Highway to Heaven," *People Weekly* (Sept. 24, 1984), p. 4.

3. The conformity of this film to our mythic paradigm has been worked out in Robert Alan Brookey and Robert Westerfelhaus, "Pistols and Petticoats, Piety and Purity: *To Wong Foo,* the Queering of the American Monomyth, and the Marginalizing Discourse of Deification," *Critical Studies in Communication,* Vol. 1, No. 2 (June 2001), pp. 141-156. The authors point out that the male drag queens remake the Western tradition by using their wiles to confront male aggression.

4. Steven Marcus, *Dickens: From Pickwick to Dombey* (New York: Basic Books, 1965), p. 142.

5. Charles Dickens, *The Old Curiosity Shop* (Boston: Houghton Mifflin, 1894), p. 329.

6. Dickens, *Old Curiosity Shop*, p. 536.

7. A. E. Dyson, *The Inimitable Dickens: A Reading of the Novels* (London: Macmillan and St. Martin's Press, 1970), p. 173.

8. J. Hillis Miller, *Charles Dickens: The World of His Novels* (Bloomington: Indiana University Press, 1969), p. 240.

9. Charles Dickens, *Hard Times* (New York: Signet, New American Library, 1961), p. 94.

10. According to H. R. Hays, *The Dangerous Sex: The Myth of Feminine Evil* (New York: Pocket Book, 1966), p. 213.

11. Ibid., p. 219.

12. Cf. May Hill Arbuthnot, Zena Sutherland, *Children and Books*, 4th ed. (Glenview: Scott, Foresman, 1972), p. 96.

13. *Heidi*. Dir. Alan Dwan. 20th Century Fox, 1937; a child-star, Shirley Temple appeared in numerous films as the abandoned girl who charms the adults around — frequently charming their problems into disappearance. In *The Littlest Rebel* (1935, 20th Century Fox) she cares for her sick mother during the Civil War — and then confronts Abe Lincoln himself in the White House to get her prisoner-of-war father released. In *Susannah of the Mounties* (1939), she quells conflict between Indians and the railroad.

14. *Heidi's Song*. Dirs. Joseph Barbera and William Hanna. Paramount, 1982; *Heidi*. Dir. Michael Ray Rhodes. Walt Disney TV, 1993.

15. Spyri, *Heidi*, p. 33.

16. "Plague" (Episode 18), *Little House on the Prairie*, NBC (Jan. 24, 1975).

17. "Money Crop" (Episode 20), *Little House on the Prairie*, NBC (Feb. 19, 1975).

18. "Ebenezer Sprague" (Episode 22), *Little House on the Prairie*, NBC (Nov. 19, 1975).

19. Laura Ingalls Wilder, *On the Way Home* (New York: Harper & Row, 1962), p. 1.

20. Lewis K. Parker, "Big Hearts, Big Hit: In a 'Little House,'" *Read: The Magazine for Reading and English* (Sept. 3, 1975), p. 13.

21. "I'll Be Waving as You Drive Away" (Episode 87, 88), Mar. 6 and 13, 1978.

22. Ruth Shalit, "Angels Speak: Inspiration from 'Touched by an Angel,'" *New Republic* (July 20, 1998), p. 24 (7).

23. CBS, April 8, 2001.

24. Shalit, "Angels Speak."

Chapter 5: John Wayne and Friends Redeem the Village

1. Garry Wills, *John Wayne's America: The Politics of Celebrity* (New York: Simon and Schuster, 1997), p. 302.

2. Dialogue from the film *Walking Tall*.

3. Zane Grey, *Riders of the Purple Sage* (Lincoln: University of Nebraska Press, 1994), p. 157.

4. *The Shootist*, directed by Don Siegel, was released by Paramount Pictures.

5. W. R. Morris made a career of writing books about Pusser. His titles were *The Twelfth of August: The Story of Buford Pusser* (Nashville: Aurora Pub., 1971); *Buford: True Story of "Walking Tall" Sheriff Buford Pusser* (Shiloh, Miss.: Popular Books, 1983); *The State-Line Mob: A True Story of Murder & Intrigue* (Nashville: Rutledge Hill Press, 1990); *The Legacy of Buford Pusser: A Pictorial History of the "Walking Tall" Sheriff* (Paducah, Ky.: Turner Pub., 1994).

6. *Sands of Iwo Jima*. Dir. Alan Dwan. Republic Pictures, 1949.

7. *The Cowboys*. Dir. Mark Rydell. Sanford/Warner, 1972.

8. *The Man Who Shot Liberty Valance*. Dir. John Ford. Paramount, 1962.

9. "A Medal for Big John," *New York Times* (May 27, 1979), p. D5, and "Medal for John Wayne Approved by Congress," p. D22.

10. Bruce Wetterau, *The Presidential Medal of Freedom: Winners and Their Achievements* (Washington, D.C.: Congressional Quarterly, 1996), p. 274.

11. "Myth as Man Realized Our Dreams," *New York Times* (June 13, 1979), p. B10.

12. Charles John Kieskalt, *The Official John Wayne Reference Book* (Secaucus, N.J.: Citadel Press, 1985), pp. 208-11.

13. Pauline Kael, "The Street Western," *The New Yorker* (Feb. 25, 1974), p. 100.

14. The films were all the creations of Bing Crosby Productions. The television series was produced by NBC; see Tom Shales, "'Tall' Toils," *Washington Post* (Jan. 17, 1981), p. F9.

15. Bill Torpy, "Tupelo sheriff to be honored for standing tough against drugs," *Atlanta Journal and Constitution* (May 27, 1995), p. B7.

16. Dwana Pusser Garrison is the proprietor of several Pusser-related enterprises in Adamsville described at <http://www.sheriffbufordpusser.com>, viewed July 2001.

17. House Bill 205 (Rinks), Feb. 4, 1999.

18. Details gathered from W. R. Morris, *The Twelfth of August* (New York: Bantam Books, 1974), pp. 45-50, 88; Charles Thompson, "The Saga of the Hem Stitched Sheriff," *Nashville Tennessean* (Aug. 24, 1969), and Kathy Sawyer, "Everybody's Out to Get Buford Now," *Nashville Tennessean: Sunday Magazine* (Aug. 12, 1973).

19. Details from Charles Thompson, "The Slowest Gun in the West," *Nashville Tennessean* (Aug. 31, 1969); Morris, *Twelfth of August*, p. 102.

20. Charles Thompson, "The Slowest Gun in the West," *Nashville Tennessean* (Aug. 31, 1969).

21. Kael, "The Street Western," p. 105.

22. Evidence regarding the crash is discussed by John Pope, "Crash Kills Buford," *Nashville Banner* (Aug. 21, 1974).

23. "Pusser Film Stood Too Tall to Let It Die," *Nashville Tennessean* (Dec. 1, 1973).

24. Citation from *Nashville Banner,* printed on the jacket of Morris, *Twelfth of August.*

25. Morris, *Twelfth of August*, pp. 163-64.

26. The sermon is cited by Bill Hance, "His Action Was Fast, Hard," *Nashville Tennessean* (Aug. 21, 1974).

Chapter 6: Cleansing Perilous Cities with Golden Violence

1. Cited by Arthur Schlesinger, Jr., *Violence: America in the Sixties* (New York: Signet Books, 1968), p. 52.

2. Adam Nossiter, "Race is dominant theme as 2nd Goetz trial begins," *New York Times* (Apr. 12, 1996), p. B3.

3. Ezra Bowen, "Getting Tough New Jersey Principal Joe Clark kicks up a storm about discipline in city schools," *Time* (Feb. 1, 1988), p. 52 (7).

4. *Lean on Me.* Dir. John Avildsen. Warner Bros., 1989.

5. Cf. Rollo May, *Power and Innocence: A Search for the Sources of Violence* (New York: W. W. Norton, 1972), for the thesis related to the problem of mythic coherence in his presentation of March 14, 1975, at the Symposium on Violence at Kearney State College, Kearney, Nebraska.

6. *Death Wish II.* Dir. Michael Winner. Menahem Golan and Goran Globus for Columbia, 1982; *Death Wish 3.* Dir. Michael Winner. M. Golan and G. Globus, 1985; *Death*

Wish 4: The Crackdown. Dir. J. Lee Thompson. Pancho Kohner, 1987; *Death Wish V: The Face of Death.* Dir. Allan A. Goldstein. 21st Century Film Corp., 1994.

7. Jackson's character brought cynical brutality to the role of Shaft. For example, he uses the infamous phrase, "It's Giuliani time!" in attacking a suspect — the words allegedly used by the New York police when they nearly killed the Haitian immigrant Abner Louima as they sodomized him with a broom.

8. Brian Garfield, *Death Wish* (New York: David McKay, 1972).

9. *Death Wish.* Dir. Michael Winner. Dino de Laurentiis, 1974.

10. Brian Garfield, *Death Sentence* (New York: M. Evans and Company, 1975).

11. Cf. Henry Tudor, *Political Myth* (New York: Praeger, 1972), p. 35.

12. Richard Slotkin, *Regeneration Through Violence* (Middletown, Conn.: Wesleyan University Press, 1973), pp. 6-7.

13. Victor Turner, "Myth and Symbol," *Encyclopedia of the Social Sciences,* Vol. 10, pp. 576-77.

14. Ernest Becker, *Angel in Armor: A Post-Freudian Perspective on the Nature of Man* (New York: Braziller, 1969), p. 183.

15. John G. Cawelti, *The Six-Gun Mystique* (Bowling Green: Bowling Green University Popular Press, 1971), p. 60.

16. George P. Fletcher, *A Crime of Self Defense: Bernard Goetz and the Law on Trial* (New York: Free Press, 1988), p. 1.

17. Michael Brooks, "Stories and Verdicts: Bernard Goetz and New York in Crisis," *College Literature* (Jan. 1, 1998), p. 77 (17).

18. Fletcher, *A Crime,* p. 17.

19. Details compiled from Lillian B. Rubin, *Quiet Rage: Bernie Goetz in a Time of Madness* (New York: Farrar, Straus, Giroux, 1986). Richard Stengel, "A Troubled and Troubling Life; who is Bernard Goetz and why did he do what he did?" *Time* (Apr. 8, 1985), pp. 38-39.

20. Ibid.

21. Charles Krauthammer, "Toasting Mr. Goetz," *Time* (Jan. 21, 1985), p. 76.

22. "Jury Says Bernard Goetz Must Pay $43 Million," Morning Edition (NPR), Apr. 24, 1996; Adam Nossiter, "Bronx jury orders Goetz to pay man he paralyzed $43 million," *New York Times* (Apr. 24, 1996), p. A1.

23. In the year of the film's release, the State Department of Education revealed "that only 30 percent of Eastside students passed all three parts of the state proficiency test" in the prior year. See Stephen Barr, "New Jersey Q&A: John G. Avildsen; Directing the Movie on Joe Clark," *New York Times* (Apr. 23, 1989), 12NJ, p. 3.

24. See for example, Michele L. Norris, "The Movie Meets Reality; Washington Principal's Critique of Joe Clark's Methods," *Washington Post* (Mar. 3, 1989), p. D1.

25. Ibid.

26. "Principal to be suspended over strippers," *New York Times* (Mar. 11, 1989), p. 32.

Chapter 7: Superheroic Presidents Redeem the Nation

1. From the Director's commentary, DVD edition of *Air Force One*. Dir. Wolfgang Peterson. Sony Pictures, 1997.

2. *Independence Day*. Dir. Roland Emmerich. 20th Century Fox, 1996.

3. *Gabriel Over the White House*. Dir. Gregory LaCava. Cosmopolitan Productions, 1933.

4. *The Young Mr. Lincoln*. Dir. John Ford. 20th Century Fox, 1939.

5. Stephen Skowronek, *The Politics Presidents Make* (Cambridge: Harvard University Press, 1993), p. 20.

6. Michael A. Genovese, *The Power of the American Presidency* (New York: Oxford University Press, 2001), p. 7.

7. See Garry Wills, *Cincinnatus: George Washington and the Enlightenment* (New York: Doubleday, 1984).

8. A. J. Langguth, *Patriots: The Men Who Started the Revolution* (New York: Simon & Schuster, 1988), p. 291.

9. Genovese, p. 30.

10. Clinton Rossiter, "Our Two Greatest Presidents," in *A Sense of History: The Best Writing from the Pages of American Heritage* (New York: American Heritage Press, 1985), p. 107.

11. Thomas Jefferson to Walter Jones, January 2, 1814; from Paul Leicester Ford, *Writings of Thomas Jefferson*, Vol. 9 (New York: G. P. Putnam's Sons, 1898), p. 448.

12. Genovese, p. 77.

13. Quoted in ibid., p. 81.

14. "The Great Depression," *Encyclopaedia Britannica* CD-Rom, 1999.

15. Walton Bean, *California: An Interpretive History*, 2nd ed. (New York: McGraw-Hill, 1973), p. 417.

16. David Nasaw, *The Chief* (Boston: Houghton-Mifflin, 2000), p. 470.

17. Ibid., pp. 472-73.

18. Ibid., p. 474.

19. John Kreuckeberg, "The Limits and Extremes of Imaging a Fascist Presidency: *Gabriel Over the White House* and the 'Strong Leader' Films of 1933," unpublished paper from "The President on Film" conference of the Film and History League, Nov. 10-14, 2000, Westlake Hills, Calif., pp. 7-9.

20. Kreuckeberg's citation of the America Film Institute's figures, p. 10.

21. See Giuliana Musco, *Hollywood's New Deal* (Philadelphia: Temple University Press, 1997), p. 92, for a summary of the correspondence shaping the film's content in directions desired by Roosevelt; similar details, also based upon a reading of the Roosevelt correspondence archives, are contained in Kreuckeberg's paper.

22. Nasaw, *Chief*, p. 460.

23. From the *Gabriel Over the White House* film dialogue.

24. Ibid.

25. Matthew Bernstein, *Walter Wanger: Independent* (Berkeley: University of California Press), p. 83.

26. See Nasaw, *Chief,* p. 466, for Hearst's complaints about the film's tendency to re-write and moderate texts he provided for the script.

27. Ibid.

28. Cited in Kreuckeberg, p. 23.

29. Mordaunt Hall, "Walter Huston as a President of the United States Who Pro-claims Himself a Dictator," *New York Times* (Apr. 1, 1933), p. 18.

30. Lippmann quoted in Nasaw, *Chief,* p. 466.

31. Quoted in Kreuckeberg, p. 22.

32. Frank Thompson, *Abraham Lincoln: Twentieth-Century Popular Portrayals* (Dal-las: Taylor Publishing, 1999), p. 278.

33. Ibid., p. 14.

34. Norman Rosenberg, "Young Mr. Lincoln: The Lawyer as Super-Hero," *Legal Studies Forum,* Vol. 15, No. 3 (1991), p. 217.

35. Ibid., p. 217.

36. Ibid., p. 225.

37. Cited in Skowronek, *The Politics Presidents Make,* p. 216.

38. John Orman, "Covering the American Presidency: Balanced Reporting in the Presidential Press," *Presidential Studies Quarterly* (Vol. 14, 1984), pp. 381-82. Cited in Mi-chael A. Genovese, "The President as Icon and Straw Man: Hollywood, Pop Culture, and the Presidential Image," unpublished paper at "The President on Film Conference," of the Film and History League, Nov. 10-14, 2000, Westlake Hills, Calif.

39. Norman Ornstein and Michael Robinson, "The Case of Our Disappearing Con-gress," *TV Guide* (Jan. 11, 1986), pp. 4-10, cited by Genovese.

40. *Independence Day.* Dir. Roland Emmerich. 20th Century Fox, 1996.

41. Wendell S. Broadwell of Georgia Perimeter College worked these points out in "The President as Superman: The Idealization of the Presidency in the Movie, *Indepen-dence Day*" presented at the Film and History League conference, "The President on Film," Nov. 10-14, 2000, Westlake Hills, Calif.

42. Details provided in Michael Rogin, *Independence Day; or, How I Learned to Stop Worrying and Love the Enola Gay* (London: British Film Institute, 1998), p. 9.

43. Source: U.S. Department of Census figures posted at <http://www.census.gov/population/socdemo/voting/history/voto2.txt)>.

44. As of this writing in 2001, national statistics had not been compiled.

45. George W. Bush, "National Day of Prayer and Remembrance for the Victims of the Terrorist Attacks on September 11, 2001," spoken at Washington (D.C.) National Cathe-dral service on Sept. 14, 2001.

Chapter 8: Lethal Patriots Break the Rhythm

1. Lou Michel and Dan Herbeck, *American Terrorist: Timothy McVeigh and the Oklahoma City Bombing* (New York: HarperCollins, 2001), p. 154. His seething letter sug-gested that Steve Hodge deserved punishment for his failure to join McVeigh's conspiracy. "Those who betray or subvert the Constitution are guilty of sedition and/or treason, are domestic enemies and should and will be punished accordingly," he threatened (p. 153).

2. *The Patriot.* Dir. Roland Emmerich. Centropolis Effects, 2000.

3. Kate Connally, "Terrorist's Legacy: U.S. Agents Discover Will of Hijack's Leader," *The Observer* (Sept. 30, 2001), p. 4; see also Peter Finn and Charles Lane, "Will Gives Window into Suspect's Mind," *Washington Post* (Oct. 6, 2001), p. A16.

4. These notions were popularized in Robert Bly's *Iron John* (1990) and ritualized in men-only retreat experiences. Bly did not advocate the sort of heroics seen in the action-adventure genre film.

5. Mark Juergensmeyer, *Terror in the Mind of God: The Global Rise of Religious Violence* (Berkeley: University of California Press, 2000). Robin Morgan has pursued the theme of dominating male violence and its connection with contemporary terrorist movements in *The Demon Lover: On the Sexuality of Terrorism* (New York: W. W. Norton, 1989).

6. The title was apparently borrowed from a collection of stories by Ernest Hemingway (1927), but the script itself was devised by the filmmakers. Wayne was an extra in this film.

7. Warren Farrell, *The Myth of Male Power* (New York: Simon and Schuster, 1993).

8. Without denying that men victimize women, he suggests that "Men's victimizer status camouflages men's victim status. . . . The practical result is not only that women live longer, but that white women live the longest, black women second, white men third, black men fourth. In the industrialized world, men are the new 'niggers'; black men are niggers' niggers" (p. 357).

9. James William Gibson, *Warrior Dreams* (New York: Hill and Wang, 1994), p. 52.

10. *First Blood.* Dir. Ted Kotcheff. Anabasis N.V./Carolco Pictures, 1982; *Rambo: First Blood Part II.* Dir. George Cosmatos. Anabasis N.V./Carolco Entertainment, 1985; *Rambo III.* Dir. Peter McDonald. Tri-Star Pictures, 1988.

11. *Braveheart.* Dir. Mel Gibson. 20th Century Fox, 1995.

12. *The Unforgiven.* Dir. Clint Eastwood. Malposo Productions/Warner Bros., 1992.

13. William Pierce, *The Turner Diaries,* 2nd ed. (Hillsboro, W.V.: National Vanguard Books, 1978), p. 42. Like the successor novel, *Hunter* (1989), the book appeared under the pseudonym "Andrew Macdonald." The author was a physicist who had taught at Oregon State University. Pierce's career has been profiled several times since the 1980s. Cf. Eric Sciliano, "Aryan World Congress: America's Down-Home Racists," *The Nation* (Aug. 30, 1986), p. 129 (5).

14. Michel, *American Terrorist,* p. 50.

15. McVeigh apparently saw this movie for the first time in prison.

16. See *Magill's Survey of Cinema,* 1993, for a complete listing of honors.

17. For a fuller exposition on the theme of shame in this film from a Pauline theological perspective, see "Shame and the Other Gospel in *The Unforgiven,*" in Robert Jewett, *St. Paul Returns to the Movies: Triumph Over Shame* (Grand Rapids: William B. Eerdmans Publishing, 1999), pp. 147-161.

18. Ina Jaffe's interview with Clint Eastwood, National Public Radio, March 30, 1993.

19. See "Wallace, Sir William," in *Encyclopedia Britannica,* CD Edition of 1997. For a scholarly discussion of the film's legendary and historical elements, see Matt Ewart's online essay, "MacBraveheart," <hhtp://www.bravehart.co.uk/history/Wallace/ewart.htm>, viewed 5/25/01, which originally appeared in the *Herald* newspaper of Scotland, Nov. 15th, 1997.

20. The Mechling essay, "American Cultural Criticism in the Pragmatic Attitude" appears in *At the Intersection: Cultural Studies and Rhetorical Studies,* ed. Thomas Rosteck (New York: Guilford Press, 1999), pp. 137-167; details about transformations in the film are worked out at pp. 156-160. The Mechlings drew upon James MacKay's recent biography *William Wallace: Braveheart* (Edinburgh: Mainstream Publishing Company Ltd., 1997).

21. Kacznyski was also called "Unabomber."

22. Mark S. Hamm, *Apocalypse in Oklahoma: Waco and Ruby Ridge Revenged* (Boston: Northeastern University Press, 1997), reports McVeigh's liking for the 1990 album *Pretty Hate Machine* with its "Head Like a Hole" containing these words: "I'd rather die than give you control./Bow down before the one you serve./You're going to get what you deserve" (p. 178).

23. Unless otherwise indicated, McVeigh's biographical details are derived from Michel and Herbeck's *American Terrorist;* information about his first encounter with *The Turner Diaries* at pp. 38-39.

24. Phil Bacharach, "The Prisoner Letters of Timothy McVeigh," *Esquire* (May 1, 2001), p. 130.

25. Hamm, *Apocalypse in Oklahoma,* p. 170.

26. In the Ruby Ridge situation, FBI agents came to Randy Weaver's cabin after he had failed to appear in court on charges of selling an illegal sawed-off shotgun. In the ensuing battle, the FBI killed Sammy, aged 14, and Randy's wife, Vicki, as she stood in a door with her infant daughter. A U.S. Marshall was also killed in the gunfire. Randy Weaver surrendered after a siege of eleven days. Michel and Herbeck, pp. 108-109.

27. On February 28, 1993, the Bureau of Alcohol, Tobacco and Firearms arrived at David Koresh's Mount Carmel religious compound in Waco, Texas, to retrieve illegal weapons. In the ensuing shootout four agents were killed, as well as six of Koresh's Branch Davidian followers (Michel and Herbeck, 118-119). After a prolonged standoff that lasted until April 19, BATF and the FBI launched a military-style attack whose outcome was the burning of the compound along with the deaths of 80 Branch Davidians, including Koresh and 17 children. Joseph L. Galloway, "The woe outsiders brought to Waco," *U.S. News and World Report,* October 4, 1993, p. 73.

28. This was a phrase he used in a letter to his Kingman, Arizona, friends, Michael and Lori Fortier, according to Michel, *American Terrorist,* p. 184.

29. See Pierce, *Turner Diaries,* pp. 35-37, for Earl's truck bomb recipe and the strategies of maximizing its destructive power.

30. Pierce, *Turner Diaries,* p. iv.

31. See Michael Barkun, *Religion and the Racist Right* (Chapel Hill: University of North Carolina Press, 1994), pp. 225-228, for an account of *The Turner Diaries'* importance to the Christian militia groups.

32. Michel, *American Terrorist,* p. 88.

33. Quoted in ibid., p. 228.

34. See James Coates, *Armed and Dangerous: The Rise of the Survivalist Right* (New York: Hill and Wang, 1987), especially the chapter, "The Order," pp. 41-76.

35. Gibson, *Warrior Dreams,* p. 225.

36. Cf. ADL: Law Enforcement Agency Resource Network, "The Turner Diaries,"

<http://www.adl.org/learn/Ext_US/Turner_Diaries.html>, viewed August 10, 2001; see also "Supremacist pleads guilty in robberies," *The New York Times* (Feb. 19, 1997), p. A11.

37. Paul Duggan, "First Trial Opens in Dragging Death," *Washington Post* (Feb. 16, 1999), p. A5.

38. *Millenarian Movements from the Far Right to the Children of Noah* (Syracuse, N.Y.: Syracuse University Press, 1997), p. 170.

39. Osama bin Laden's taped interview is quoted in "Centuries of Pious Combat Have Made the Middle East History's Graveyard," *The Washington Spectator* (Oct. 15, 2001), p. 2.

40. Details about the life of Kacznyski are taken from Robert Graysmith, *Unabomber: A Desire to Kill* (Washington, D.C.: Regnery, 1997).

41. The linguistic and ideological clues led to Kaczynski's arrest on April 4, 1996, on the basis of suspicions expressed by members of his family. The "Manifesto" was organized by section numbers that follow the quoted material.

42. Kaczynski had dug a cave under his Montana cabin, probably to protect himself from the winter's severest cold.

43. The manifesto, titled "Industrial Society and Its Future, by FC," appears in its original typescript form as Appendix D in Graysmith. It is also available from several Internet sites.

44. Michael Mello, *The United States of America versus Theodore John Kaczynski* (New York: Context Books, 1999), sets forth the issues in the legal proceedings.

45. The full text of the letter, sent on April 25, 2000, appears as Appendix B in Michel, *American Terrorist*, pp. 398-402.

46. *Fight Club.* Dir. David Fincher. Art Linson Productions, 1999.

47. Faludi, "It's '*Thelma and Louise*' for Guys," *Newsweek* (Oct. 25, 1999), p. 89.

48. Roger Ebert, of the *Chicago Sun-Times*, for example, commented that "'Fight Club' is the most frankly and cheerfully fascist big-star movie since "Death Wish," a celebration of violence in which the heroes write themselves a license to drink, smoke, screw and beat one another up." <http://www.suntimes.com/ebert/ebert_reviews/1999/10/101502.html>, viewed Aug. 10, 2001.

Chapter 9: Cheerful Saints and Melodious Lions

1. Mortimer J. Adler, *Art and Prudence: A Study in Practical Philosophy* (New York: Longmans, Green, 1937), p. 581; the citation is critically evaluated by Max Horkheimer in his essay "Art and Mass Culture," *Critical Theory* (New York: Herder and Herder, 1972), p. 281.

2. Mildred Houghton Comfort, *Walt Disney: Master of Fantasy* (Minneapolis: T. S. Denison, 1968), p. 123.

3. Hortense Powdermaker, *Hollywood: The Dream Factory* (Boston: Little, Brown, 1950), p. 58.

4. Murray Schumach, *The Face on the Cutting Room Floor* (New York: Da Capo Press, 1974), pp. 280, 282-83.

5. Christopher Finch, *The Art of Walt Disney: From Mickey Mouse to the Magic Kingdoms* (New York: Harry N. Abrams, New Concise Edition, 1975), p. 52.

6. Ibid., p. 53.

7. Cited by Leonard Maltin, *The Disney Films* (New York: Crown, 1973), p. 5.

8. Fritz Moellenhoff, "The Remarkable Popularity of Mickey Mouse," *The History of Popular Culture*, ed. N. F. Cantor and M. S. Werthman (New York: Macmillan, 1968), p. 611.

9. Richard Schickel, *The Disney Version* (New York: Avon, 1969), p. 75.

10. Ibid., p. 204; one realizes how thoroughly Disney banished sex by comparing his work with that of the Warner Brothers' "Looney Tunes" cartoons. Cf. Joe Adamson, *Tex Avery: King of Cartoons* (New York: Popular Library, 1975), who discusses the sexual content of "Red Hot Riding Hood" (1943), "Swing Shift Cinderella" (1945), "Wild and Wolfy" (1945), and "Uncle Tom's Cabana" (1947).

11. *Snow White and the Seven Dwarfs.* Dir. David Hand. Walt Disney, 1937.

12. *Halliwell's Film Guide,* ed. John Walker (New York: Harper, 1994), p. 1098.

13. *Kinder- and Hausmärchen, Gesammelt durch die Brüder Grimm* (Munich: Bardtenschlager, n.d.), pp. 195-96, in our translation. Cf. the similar version in the Marian Edwardes translation, "Snow-Drop," *Anthology of Children's Literature*, ed. E. Johnson, C. E. Scott, and E. R. Sickels (Cambridge: Houghton Mifflin, 1948, 2nd ed.), pp. 86-89.

14. *The Wonderful Worlds of Walt Disney: Fantasyland* (New York: Golden Press, 1965), p. 113.

15. *Bambi.* Dir. David Hand and Perce Pearce. Walt Disney, 1942.

16. Maltin, *Disney Films,* p. 56.

17. Ibid., p. 55.

18. Ibid., p. 7.

19. Ibid.

20. Burne Hogarth, *Tarzan of the Apes* (New York: Watson-Guptil, 1972), pp. 27-28.

21. Robert D. Feild, *The Art of Walt Disney* (New York: Macmillan, 1942), p. 31.

22. *Mary Poppins.* Dir. Robert Stevenson. Walt Disney Productions, 1964.

23. Pamela L. Travers, *Mary Poppins* (New York: Harcourt, Brace & World, 1962); *Mary Poppins Comes Back* (New York: Harcourt, Brace & World, 1963); *Mary Poppins Opens the Door* (New York: Harcourt, Brace & World, 1943); *Mary Poppins in the Park* (New York: Harcourt, Brace & World, 1952); *Mary Poppins from A to Z* (New York: Harcourt, Brace & World, 1962).

24. Judith Crist of the *New York Times* as cited by Leonard Maltin, *Disney Films,* p. 230.

25. *Walt Disney's Stories from Other Lands* (New York: Golden Press, 1965), p. 6.

26. International Movie Data Database <http://imdb.com/Charts/USAtopmovies.html> viewed July 30, 2001.

27. J. Glenn Gray, *The Warriors: Reflections on Men in Battle* (New York: Harper & Row, Torchbook, 1967), p. 31.

28. Cited by Feild, *Art of Walt Disney,* p. 122.

29. Bob Thomas, *Walt Disney: The Art of Animation* (New York: Simon & Schuster, 1958), p. 56.

30. Finch, *Art of Walt Disney,* p. 66.

31. *Victory Through Air Power.* Dirs. James Agar, H. C. Potter, et al. Walt Disney Pictures, 1943.

32. Maltin, *Disney Films,* p. 61.

33. Cited by Schickel, *Disney Version*, p. 233.

34. Cited by Robert Batchelder, *The Irreversible Decision, 1939-50* (Boston: Houghton Mifflin, 1962), p. 172; Batchelder also reports the results of the U.S. Strategic Bombing Survey, undertaken by the Department of Defense after the end of the war. It showed that bombing of civilian populations was of minimal and even negative military value (p. 186).

35. Maltin, *Disney Films*, p. 70.

36. Siegfried Kracauer, *From Caligari to Hitler* (Princeton: Princeton University Press, 1947), p. 300.

37. An analysis of the social effects of Disney's work in Latin American culture has been written by scholars Ariel Dorfman and Armand Mattelart, *How to Read Donald Duck: Imperialist Ideology in the Disney Comic* (New York: International General, 1975).

38. Cited by Schickel, *Disney Version*, p. v.

39. Cited ibid., p. 187.

40. Cited in Schumach, *Face on the Cutting Room Floor*, p. 285.

41. Douglas Gomery, "ABC Television Network," in Ray V. Browne and Pat Browne, eds., *The Guide to United States Popular Culture* (Bowling Green, Ohio: Bowling Green State University Popular Press, 2000), p. 5.

42. Disney, Inc. "Capsule," Hoovers Online <http://www.hoovers.com>, March 2001.

43. *The Lion King*. Dirs. Roger Allers and Robert Minkoff. Walt Disney Productions, 1994.

44. Matt Roth, "A Short History of Disney-Fascism: The Lion King," *Jump-Cut: A Review of Contemporary Media* 40 (1996): 15-20.

45. *Pocahontas*. Dirs. Mike Gabriel and Eric Goldberg. Walt Disney Productions, 1995.

46. From Disney's *Pocahontas* Press Kit, cited in Gary Edgerton and Kathy Merlock Jackson, "Redesigning Pocahontas: Disney, the 'White Man's Indian,' and the Marketing of Dreams," *Journal of Popular Film and Television* 24, no. 2 (1996): 90-99.

47. Ibid.

48. <http://Disney.go.com/educational/classroom.html> visited on April 4, 2001.

Chapter 10: The Sound of One Hand Killing: Monomythic Video Games

1. Caption for Sgt. Joseph Patterson's picture in a Spiderman-like combat uniform that appeared in national magazines; also at <http://www.GoArmy.com> viewed April 4, 2001.

2. *Braveheart Manual* (San Francisco: Eidos Interactive, 1999), p. 2. The EPILEPSY WARNING appears in manuals for many video games; caps in original.

3. Kelly Zito, "The Waiting Game: Fans camp outside the Metreon for chance to score scarce PlayStation 2," *San Francisco Chronicle* (October 26, 2000), p. B1.

4. See Geoffrey R. and Elizabeth Loftus, *Mind at Play: The Psychology of Video Games* (New York: Basic Books, 1983).

5. See Terry Toles, "Video Games and American Military Ideology," in *The Critical Communications Review*, ed. Vincent Mosco and Janet Wasko, Vol. III, *Popular Culture and Media Events* (Norwood, N.J.: Ablex Publishing, 1983), pp. 207-23, for some community controversies in the late 70s and early 80s.

6. Loftus, *Mind at Play*, p. 182.

7. Sherry Turkle, *The Second Self: Computers and the Human Spirit* (New York: Simon & Schuster, 1984), p. 79.

8. See Justine Cassell and Henry Jenkins, *From Barbie to Mortal Combat: Gender and Computer Games* (Boston: MIT Press, 1997), for discussions of the gendered character of game development and markets.

9. "Media companies are sued in Kentucky shooting," *New York Times* (Apr. 13, 1999), p. A19.

10. The victims of the massacre are listed in Matt Bai, "Death at Columbine High," *Newsweek* (May 3, 1999), pp. 22-23.

11. "The Columbine Tapes," *Time* (Dec. 20, 1999), pp. 40ff.; letters omitted in the original.

12. *Computer Gaming World* (July 1999), p. 21.

13. James Malone, "Media Suit in Carneal slayings dismissed: Judge rules makers of movie, games, Web site not liable," *The Courier-Journal* (Apr. 7, 2000), <http://www.courier-journal.com/localnews/2000/0004/07/000407carneal.html>, viewed July 10, 2001.

14. Dave Grossman, *On Killing: The Psychological Cost of Learning to Kill in War and Society* (Little, Brown and Co., 1995). Lt. Colonel Grossman and others collaborate in maintaining the "killology" Website (www.killology.org).

15. Dave Grossman and Gloria DeGaetano, *Stop Teaching Our Kids to Kill: A Call to Action Against TV, Movie, and Video Game Violence* (New York: Crown Publishers, 1999), pp. 75-76.

16. "Film May Have Fueled Kentucky Rampage," Reuters (Dec. 5, 1997), <http://www.reuters.com>, viewed Sept. 5, 2001.

17. Bruno Bettelheim, "The Importance of Play," *Atlantic Monthly* (Mar. 1987), p. 46.

18. Detail from Tom Engelhardt, *The End of Victory Culture: Cold War America and the Disillusioning of a Generation* (New York: Basic Books, 1995), p. 176.

19. Ibid., p. 177.

20. Frederic D. Schwarz, "The Patriarch of Pong," *Invention and Technology* (Fall 1990), p. 64.

21. J. C. Herz, *Joystick Nation: How Videogames Ate Our Quarters, Won Our Hearts, and Rewired Our Minds* (Boston: Little, Brown, 1997), pp. 5-8.

22. Stewart Brand, "SPACEWAR: Fanatic Life and Symbolic Death Among the Computer Bums," *Rolling Stone* (Dec. 7, 1972), posted at <http://www.wheels.org/spacewar/stone/rolling_stone.html>, viewed July 12, 2001.

23. Herz, *Joystick Nation*, p. 15.

24. Instruction Manual, *Space Invaders* (Atari, 1980), n.p.

25. Herz, *Joystick Nation*, p. 16.

26. Engelhardt, *End of Victory Culture*, p. 269.

27. Dave Theurer, "The Atari Library — Atari *Missile Command*" <http://markn.netlink.co.uk/Arcade/missile.html>, viewed Sept. 25, 2000.

28. Instructions, *Missile Command* (5200 cartridge) (Atari, 1982), n.p.

29. Ibid.

30. Theurer, "The Atari Library — Atari *Missile Command.*"

31. Sean Kelly, *Digital Press CD-Rom* (Vol. I, 11/1997); television ads played from the file Atari4.avi.

32. Cited in Eugene F. Provenzo, Jr., *The Video Kids: Making Sense of Nintendo* (Cambridge: Harvard University Press, 1991), p. 86.

33. Ibid.

34. Instruction Manual, *G.I. Joe: Cobra Strike* (Parker Brothers, 1983), n.p.

35. Provenzo, *The Video Kids*, p. 127.

36. Ibid., pp. 121-124.

37. Instruction Book, *Wargames* (ColecoVision, 1984), n.p.

38. Instruction Book, *Defender* 2600 (Atari, 1982), n.p.

39. Instruction Book, *Missile Command* (Atari/Hasbro, 1999).

40. Instruction Book, *Outlaw* (Atari, 1978), n.p.

41. *Computer Gaming World* (Nov. 1998), pp. 220-21.

42. *Computer Gaming World* (Aug. 1999), pp. 38-39.

43. *Computer Gaming World* (Nov. 1998), p. 115.

44. Eidos Interactive ad in *Computer Gaming World* (Nov. 2000), p. 162; boldface in original.

45. Sample scenarios played at <http://www2.eidosinteractive/games/hitman.html>, Oct. 2000.

46. Instruction Manual, *The Ultimate Doom* (Id Software, 1995), p. 1.

47. Ibid., p. 2.

48. Herz, *Joystick Nation*, p. 84.

49. Neil J. Rubenking, "The DOOM Phenomenon," *PC Magazine* (Nov. 8, 1994), p. 314 (4).

50. Dirk Johnson and James Brooke, "Terror in Littleton: The Suspects," *New York Times* (Apr. 22, 1999), p. A1.

51. *Quake* Instruction Manual (Id Software, 1997), n.p.

52. User Guide, *Duke Nukem* (3D Realms Entertainment, 1996), n.p.

53. User Guide, *Duke It Out in D.C.* (Sunstorm Interactive Inc., 1997), n.p.

54. Cited in Richard Slotkin, *Gunfighter Nation* (New York: HarperCollins, 1993), p. 178.

55. *Computer Gaming World* (Jan. 1999), pp. 136-37.

56. Ibid., pp. 256-57.

57. Joe Nick Patoski, "Jay Wilbur: A High Tech Pioneer," *Texas Monthly* (Sept. 1995), pp. 133f.

58. Manual for *The Gungan Frontier* (San Rafael, Calif.: Lucas Learning, 1999), p. 10.

59. The generic title for games of this type is "god games."

60. Quoted in Mary Wiltenberg, "Playing at Life," *The Christian Science Monitor* (Apr. 4, 2001), p. 14.

61. Cf. the Web sites <http://www.futurecity.org>, viewed Feb. 20, 2000.

62. A list of SIMCITY fan sites can be seen at <http://simcity.ea.com/us/guide/chat/fansites/index.phtml>, viewed July 2001.

63. "EA (Electronic Arts) ships more than one million copies of 'SIM CITY 3000,'" *Multimedia Publisher* (July 1, 1999).

Chapter 11: *Star Trek's* Humanistic Militarism

1. See Book 3 (416-418), *The Republic,* ed. G. R. F. Ferrari (Cambridge: Cambridge University Press, 2000), pp. 109-110.

2. Details of the program history have been retold often. For the earliest account, consult David Gerrold, *The World of Star Trek* (New York: Ballantine, 1973), p. 222.

3. Interview with Joseph Thesken, *The Press Democrat* (Santa Rosa, Calif.), (July 30, 1975); in a similar vein, Gene Roddenberry discussed ". . . the near fanatical cult that continues to follow the series. . . ." He described his reactions to the *Star Trek* conventions: "It is scary to be surrounded by a thousand people asking questions as if the events in the series actually happened" (*Sioux City Journal,* March 31, 1976).

4. See Constance Penley's book *NASA/Trek: Popular Science and Sex in America* (London & New York: Verso, 1997) for a discussion of the agency's *Star Trek* strategy in justifying its existence.

5. Michael Okuda and Denise Okuda, "Smithsonian Institution," *The Star Trek Encyclopedia: A Reference Guide to the Future,* Version 3.0 CD-Rom (New York: Simon and Schuster Interactive, 1999).

6. April Selley, "*Star Trek,*" in *The Guide to United States Popular Culture,* ed. Ray Browne and Pat Browne (Bowling Green Ohio: Bowling Green State University Popular Press), p. 783.

7. David Alexander, *Star Trek Creator: The Authorized Biography of Gene Roddenberry* (New York: ROC/Dutton Signet, 1994), p. 556.

8. Cf. Larry Lange, "Series boldly went where science is just starting to go — EEs celebrate the tech of Trek," *Electronic Engineering Times* (Sept. 16, 1996), p. 1.

9. Alexander, pp. 302-303.

10. Thomas Richards, *The Meaning of Star Trek* (New York: Doubleday, 1997), p. 5.

11. See Roddenberry's script credits in Alexander, pp. 557-66.

12. Crusher is shown commanding her own ship in *TNG's* final episode "All Good Things."

13. See Alexander's account and the furious Roddenberry correspondence with Paramount, Isaac Asimov and Arthur C. Clarke about the Shatner-directed *Star Trek V: The Final Frontier,* pp. 519-33.

14. Jacqueline Lichtenberg, Sondra Marshak, and Joan Winston, *Star Trek Lives!* (New York: Bantam, 1975), p. 50.

15. Ibid., pp. 78-79.

16. Stephen E. Whitfield and Gene Roddenberry, *The Making of Star Trek* (New York: Ballantine, 1968), p. 256.

17. Alexander, pp. 516-17.

18. Gerrold, *The World of Star Trek,* p. 32.

19. SAC adopted this slogan in the late 1950s and posted it at its bases. General Jack Ripper has the sign on the wall of his office in the film *Dr. Strangelove* (1964).

20. Lichtenberg, *Star Trek Lives!,* p. 40.

21. Cf. Robert Jewett, *The Captain America Complex: The Dilemma of Zealous Nationalism* (Philadelphia: Westminster, 1973).

22. Lichtenberg, *Star Trek Lives!,* pp. 99-100.

23. Gerrold, *The World of Star Trek*, p. 256.

24. Lichtenberg, *Star Trek Lives!*, p. 100.

25. Gerrold, *The World of Star Trek*, p. 256.

26. H. Bruce Franklin, "*Star Trek* in the Vietnam Era," *Film and History* (Nos. 1 & 2, 1994), p. 38.

27. Ibid., pp. 40-42.

28. Ibid., p. 43.

29. Richard Slotkin, *Regeneration Through Violence: The Mythology of the American Frontier, 1600-1860* (Middletown: Wesleyan University Press, 1973), pp. 14-24.

30. Joseph Campbell, *The Hero with a Thousand Faces* (New York: Meridian, 1956), p. 387.

31. Cf. James Blish, *Star Trek 7* (New York: Bantam Books, 1972), pp. 1-27; story by Gilbert A. Ralston and Gene L. Coon. The narrative of Blish's adaptation of this *Star Trek* episode has been summarized. Blish's dialogue is based upon the show's shooting script and differs only in minor details from the broadcast version.

32. Gerrold, *The World of Star Trek*, p. 48; italics in original.

33. Whitfield and Roddenberry, *The Making of Star Trek*, p. 213.

34. Campbell, *The Hero with a Thousand Faces*, p. 101.

35. Whitfield and Roddenberry, *The Making of Star Trek*, p. 23.

36. Ibid., p. 202.

37. Campbell, *The Hero with a Thousand Faces*, p. 121.

38. Ibid., p. 109.

39. Whitfield and Roddenberry, *The Making of Star Trek*, p. 217.

40. Lichtenberg, *Star Trek Lives!*, p. 41.

41. Ibid., p. 80.

42. Jeff Greenwald, *Future Perfect: How Star Trek Conquered Planet Earth* (New York: Viking, 1998), p. 226.

43. Yvonne Fern, *Gene Roddenberry: The Last Conversation* (Berkeley: University of California Press, 1994), p. 100.

44. Ibid.

45. A rare instance of sex among officers occurs in the film *Insurrection* (1998), when the "regenerative metaphasic particles" of the Ba'Ku people's planet stimulate good times between Commander Riker and Counselor Troi, who observes, "My boobs are beginning to feel firm again." Even Captain Picard feels randy with the beautiful Anij, a several-hundred-years-old woman, but chastely begs off because of pressing Starfleet business once he finally gets his chance to relax with her.

46. Ernest Lee Tuveson, *Redeemer Nation: The Idea of America's Millennial Role* (Chicago: The University of Chicago Press, 1968).

47. Gerrold, *The World of Star Trek*, p. 251.

48. Richards, *The Meaning of Star Trek*, p. 15.

49. Lichtenberg, *Star Trek Lives!*, p. 74.

50. "Time's Arrow, Part II," *TNG*, Oct. 4, 1992.

51. As in the films, *Star Trek IV: The Voyage Home* and *Star Trek VI: The Undiscovered Country*.

52. "All Good Things," *TNG*, June 5, 1994.

Chapter 12: *Star Trek* Faith as a Fan-Made Religion

1. Clyde Kluckhohn, *Mirror for Man* (New York: McGraw-Hill, 1949), p. 247.

2. Yvonne Fern, *Gene Roddenberry: The Last Conversation* (Berkeley: University of California Press, 1994), p. 215.

3. *The Education of Henry Adams* (Boston: Houghton Mifflin, 1961), p. 387.

4. As the *Star Trek* franchise aged and diversified, *TNG* and especially *DS9* and *VOY* presented more exploratory and tolerant views of religious belief and practice.

5. Roddenberry was raised as a Southern Baptist, but rebelled against its philosophical assumptions as a teenager. He reports that in listening for the first time to a sermon at his church, he felt "complete astonishment because the things they were talking about were just crazy." Later in life, he formally affiliated himself with the American Humanist Society. See David Alexander, "Interview of Gene Roddenberry: Writer, Producer, Philosopher, Humanist," *The Humanist,* Mar. 1991, pp. 5-30.

6. The narrative of Blish's adaptation of "The Apple," which appeared in the second season, has been summarized. James Blish, *Star Trek 6* (New York: Bantam Books, 1972), pp. 49-68; story by Max Erlich and Gene L. Coon. Blish's dialogue differs only in minor details from the actual television program.

7. Jacqueline Lichtenberg, Sondra Marshak, and Joan Winston, *Star Trek Lives!* (New York: Bantam, 1975).

8. Ibid., p. 149.

9. Ibid., p. 87; italics in the original.

10. Ibid., p. 43.

11. Ibid., pp. 144-45, italics in original.

12. The documentary film *Trekkies* (1999) shows the continuing appeal of wearing costumes and pretending to be part of *Star Trek*'s imaginary world. The term "Trekker" is freighted with South African history: it names the white settlers who took guns, horses, and wagons to the task of subjugating the native people — a clear violation of the Prime Directive.

13. John Tulloch and Henry Jenkins, *Science Fiction Audiences* (New York: Routledge, 1995), p. 21.

14. Jeff Greenwald, *Future Perfect: How Star Trek Conquered Planet Earth* (New York: Viking, 1998), p. 99. Among the most prominent fans are the scientist Steven Hawking and the science fiction writer, Arthur C. Clarke, who receives a chapter in the book.

15. Michael Jindra, "'*Star Trek* to Me Is a Way of Life': Fan Expressions of *Star Trek* Philosophy," in *Star Trek and Sacred Ground: Explorations of Star Trek, Religion, and American Culture*, ed. Jennifer E. Porter and Darcee L. McLaren (Albany: State University of New York Press, 1999), p. 224.

16. Herbert J. Gans, *Popular Culture and High Culture: An Analysis and Evaluation of Taste* (New York: Basic Books, 1974), p. 32.

17. Greenwald, *Future Perfect*, pp. 18-19.

18. The World Wide Web has multiplied opportunities for fan creative expression and interaction exponentially. Informal *Star Trek* forums can no longer be counted because of their large numbers and ephemeral character.

19. Sondra Marshak and Myrna Culbreath, *Star Trek: The New Voyages* (New York:

Bantam Books, 1976), presented a collection of stories of the fanzine type. Gene Roddenberry lifted up the devotional quality of this writing in his "Introduction," p. x: "Eventually we realized that there is no more profound way in which people could express what *Star Trek* has meant to them than by creating their own very personal *Star Trek* things . . . it was their *Star Trek* stories that especially gratified me . . . all of it was plainly done with love."

20. Lichtenberg, *Star Trek Lives!*, p. 222.

21. Ibid., p. 269.

22. Gene Roddenberry confirmed this "scriptural" aura in an interview: "I'm not a guru and I don't want to be. . . . It frightens me when I learn of 10,000 people reading a 'Star Trek' script as if it were scripture. I certainly didn't write scripture . . ." *Sioux City Journal* (Mar. 31, 1976).

23. Lichtenberg, *Star Trek Lives!*, p. 273.

24. Ibid., p. 7.

25. Norman Vincent Peale, *You Can Win* (New York: Abingdon, 1938).

26. One of the paradoxes of Jacqueline Lichtenberg's overflowing enthusiasm is that she published in 1976 a fan novel called *Centennial*, in which Captain Kirk stands before a tribunal that cross-examines him with critical subtlety about his numerous violations of the Prime Directive. See Tulloch and Jenkins, *Science Fiction Audiences*, pp. 175-177.

27. David Gerrold, *The World of Star Trek* (New York: Ballantine, 1973), p. 182.

28. Lichtenberg, *Star Trek Lives!*, p. 78.

29. Gerrold, *The World of Star Trek*, p. 184.

30. "Where no juror has gone before," *Entertainment Weekly* (Mar. 29, 1996), p. 7; Adams was also featured in the Paramount Films documentary *Trekkies*, which is the source for the quotation.

31. In one of his characteristically kind gestures towards a fan, Gene Roddenberry had named the Geordi La Forge character, who has a severe vision disability, for the dying young fan.

32. This story genre has been studied in Henry Jenkins, "'Welcome to Bisexuality, Captain Kirk': Slash and the Fan-Writing Community," in *Textual Poachers: Television Fans and Participatory Culture* (New York: Routledge, 1992), pp. 185-222, and in Camille Bacon-Smith, *Enterprising Women: Television Fandom and the Creation of Popular Myth* (Philadelphia: Temple University Press), 1992.

33. Lichtenberg, p. 238; parenthesis in the original. The stories in Marshak and Culbreath, *Star Trek: The New Voyages*, are all written by females but are introduced by the stars of the television programs whose presence is used to prove that the gods are real, so to speak. The editors claim, p. xvi, "Here are not merely bold knights and fair damsels, but flesh-and-blood men and women of courage and achievement . . . if this be our new Camelot, even more shining — make the most of it." An excellent example of the Spock sexual fantasy in the volume is "The Enchanted Pool" by Marcia Ericson, pp. 66-79.

34. Gerrold, *The World of Star Trek*, p. 184.

35. Ibid., pp. 182-83.

36. David Letterman, for example, who makes no pretense to heroism, was stalked for years by Margaret Ray, who several times broke into his house, drove his car, and referred to herself as "Mrs. Letterman" when arrested by the police. She also stalked astronaut Story

Musgrave and ended her life by placing herself in the path of an approaching train. Tom Gliatto et al., "Tragedy: Fade to Black Margaret Ray, the woman who stalked Letterman," *People,* Oct. 20, 1998, pp. 133ff.

37. "*STAR TREK: The Experience* at the Las Vegas Hilton" (catalog), Paramount Pictures, 1997, n.p.

38. John Lawrence visited the exhibition in April, 2001.

39. Details in the exhibit are compiled from Michael and Denise Okuda's *Star Trek Chronology: The History of the Future* and Debbie Mirek's *The Star Trek Encyclopedia,* both from Pocket Books.

40. Advertising at <http://www.simonsays.com/dominionwars_site/Main.htm>, June 23, 2001.

41. Michel DeCerteau in *The Practice of Everyday Life* (Berkeley: University of California Press, 1984).

42. Henry Jenkins, *Textual Poaching* (New York: Routledge, 1992).

43. Jenkins, *Science Fiction Audiences,* p. 23.

44. Jenkins has been eloquent in defending the rights of fans — contrary to the copyright wishes of corporations — to appropriate images and texts so that they can be displayed, discussed, and reshaped according to their personal vision. See Henry Jenkins, "Digital Land Grab," *Technology Review* (Mar. 2000), pp. 103-105.

Chapter 13: Fascist Faith in the *Star Wars* Universe

1. (Denver: Allnutt Publishing Co., 1999), p. 131. The first edition was initially published as *The Force of Star Wars* in 1977; with the "Menace" 5th edition of 1999, Allnutt reported sales of more than 200,000.

2. This dialogue is reproduced in the official story book and screenplay. George Lucas, *Star Wars: Episode I: The Phantom Menace* (New York: Random House/Lucas Books, 1999), p. 40. Qui-Gon has faith that Anakin is "the chosen one" who will rescue The Republic.

3. See "Finding Religion in Unexpected Places," in *Religion and Popular Culture in America,* ed. Bruce David Forbes and Jeffrey Mahan (Berkeley: University of California Press, 2000), pp. 10-12.

4. See Forbes' section "Popular Culture as Religion," pp. 14-15.

5. *The Spiritual Marketplace: Baby Boomers and the Remaking of American Religion* (Princeton: Princeton University Press, 1999).

6. "Virtual Faith: The Gen-X Quest for Meaning," *Christian Science Monitor* (Aug. 6, 1998), p. 11. Beaudoin has written the book *Virtual Faith: The Irreverent Spiritual Quest of Generation X* (San Francisco: Jossey-Bass/Simon & Schuster, 1998).

7. Beaudoin, *Christian Science Monitor,* p. 11.

8. This full and less frequently used title for the first film reflects the larger serial vision of George Lucas and seems to be a jesting nod to the *Flash Gordon* movies produced by Republic Pictures that Lucas acknowledges as one of his inspirations.

9. Library of Congress inclusion and Thalberg Award listed in *George Lucas: Interviews,* ed. Sally Kline (Jackson: University Press of Mississippi, 1999), p. xix. The award also reflected the great success of *American Graffiti* and the *Indiana Jones* trilogy — *Raiders of*

the Lost Ark (1981), *Indiana Jones and the Temple of Doom* (1984), and *Indiana Jones and the Last Crusade* (1989) — for which he acted as executive producer.

10. The content of the exhibition is liberally illustrated and interpreted in Mary Henderson, *Star Wars: The Magic of Myth* (New York: Bantam Books, 1997).

11. The materials are on display at the Lucas Learning web site (<http://www.lucaslearning.com>.

12. " 'The Phantom Menace' — A Force to Be Reckoned With," The Gallup Organization, May 7, 1999, <http://www.gallup.com/poll/releases/pr990507.asp>, viewed on June 30, 2001. The poll surveyed 1,014 adults. Attendance figures were highest among adults who had been children in 1977. Despite the overwhelming popularity of the films, there are individuals who view the films with distaste or feel that they have outgrown them; see the chapter *"Star Wars"* in Tom Stempel, *American Audiences on Movies and Moviegoing* (Lexington: University Press of Kentucky), pp. 110-127.

13. Tricia Johnson, "News and Notes: Go Figure," *Entertainment Weekly* (June 4, 1999), p. 9.

14. The four *Star Wars* films released through 1999 regularly rank among the most profitable films ever released. In the International Movie Data Base listing for June, 2001, *SW: A New Hope* ranked #2, *Phantom Menace* #3, *Return of the Jedi* #7, and *The Empire Strikes Back* #11, http://www.imdb.com. Among children's films (rated G or PG), the films all rank in the top six films <http://www.infoplease.com/ipea/A0776504.html>.

15. Cf. Christopher Vogler, *The Writer's Journey: Mythic Structure for Storytellers and Screenwriters* (Studio City, Calif.: M. Wiese Productions, 1992), a set of prescriptions aimed at helping screenwriters adapt Joseph Campbell's models of mythic heroism.

16. Joseph Campbell and Bill Moyers, *The Power of Myth* (New York: Mystic Fire Video, 1988). The book version carried the same title (New York: Doubleday, 1988).

17. George Lucas and Bill Moyers, *The Mythology of Star Wars* (Princeton, N.J.: Films for the Humanities, 2000); the transcript of the conversations appeared as "Of Myth and Men: A Conversation between Bill Moyers and George Lucas on the Meaning of the Force and the True Theology of Star Wars," *Time* (Apr. 26, 1999), p. 90.

18. Stephen Zito, "George Lucas Goes Far Out" (Interview/1977), in Kline, *Interviews*, p. 53.

19. John Seabrook, "Letter from Skywalker Ranch: Why Is the Force Still With Us?," in Kline, p. 205.

20. "Darth Vader," character information from the official *Star Wars* web site <http://www.starwars.com/databank/character/darthvader>, viewed Aug. 5, 2000.

21. Darth Vader biography in *Star Wars: Behind the Magic* (CD-rom), (San Rafael, Calif.: LucasArts Entertainment, 1999).

22. Joseph Campbell (in conversation with Michael Toms), *An Open Life* (New York: Larson Publications, 1988), pp. 100-101.

23. Joseph Campbell and Bill Moyers, *The Power of Myth* (New York: Doubleday, 1988), p. 147.

24. Lucas qualifies this praise for the despot by remarking, "The idea that power corrupts is very true and it's a big human who can get past that."

25. "I'm a Cynic Who Has Hope for the Human Race" (Interview with Orville Schell), *New York Times* (Mar. 21, 1999), sec. 2, p. 28.

26. In this regard, *Star Wars* resembles Lucas's stirringly successful *Indiana Jones* trilogy, which features vicious Nazi conspirators or evil Thuggee blood cultists as a foil for the heroic derring-do of Indiana Jones, played by Harrison Ford, the same actor who portrays the Han Solo character.

27. Michael Ryan and Douglas Kellner, *Camera Politica: The Politics and Ideology of Contemporary Hollywood Film* (Bloomington, Ind.: Indiana University Press, 1988), pp. 229-31.

28. On a personal commission from Hitler himself, she had also made a film for the German Ministry of Propaganda called *Victory of Faith* (*Sieg des Glaubens,* 1933). See the entry "Leni Riefenstahl," *Encyclopaedia Britannica* CD, 1999.

29. S. Schoenbaum, "Another Part of the Galaxy," *Times Literary Supplement* (Aug. 5, 1977), p. 961.

30. *Star Wars: Behind the Magic,* "Scenes," Disk 2. An incorrect year (1934) is assigned to the 1935 film.

31. George Lucas, *Star Wars: From the Adventures of Luke Skywalker* (New York: Ballantine, 1976), pp. 79-80.

32. *Star Wars'* universe contains plenty of ordinary helpers for the heroes, ranging from the roguish Han Solo, who becomes a General, to the fish-like Admiral Ackbar of *Return,* to the indigenous teddy-bear Ewoks of the forest moon Endor. All are loyal and subordinate to leaders composed of the natural Jedi elite.

33. Cited by Carl Cohen, ed., *Communism, Fascism and Democracy: The Theoretical Foundations,* 2nd ed. (New York: Random House, 1972), p. 346.

34. The slogan is Mussolini's, cited by Cohen, *Communism,* p. 314.

35. Lucas, *Star Wars,* p. 21.

36. Ibid., p. 71; elision in the original.

37. Cohen, *Communism,* p. 332.

38. Ibid., p. 348.

39. George L. Mosse, *The Culture of Western Europe: The Nineteenth and Twentieth Centuries* (Chicago: Rand, McNally, 1961), p. 368.

40. Lucas, *Star Wars,* p. 1.

41. For those who downplay the fascist resonance by referring to Taoism as the inspiration for the Force, we point out that the Tao — famously symbolized by its interpenetrating yin and yang components — speaks of maintaining the balance between opposing forces. The Force, if Taoist, is a very deviant version.

42. Cohen, *Communism,* p. 300.

43. William Siska, "A Breath of Fresh Fantasy," *Christian Century* (July 20-27, 1977), pp. 66, 68.

44. Robert E. A. Lee, "Movies," *The Lutheran* (July 13, 1977), p. 30.

45. *The Journey of Luke Skywalker: An Analysis of Modern Myth and Symbol* (Chicago: Open Court, 2001), p. 82.

46. Ibid., p. 123. The discussion between Luke and Yoda occurs in *The Empire Strikes Back.*

47. Allnutt, *The Force of Star Wars,* p. 7.

48. Robert G. Collins, "*Star Wars:* The Pastiche of Myth and the Yearning for a Past Future," *The Journal of Popular Culture,* Vol. 11, No. 1 (Summer, 1977), pp. 8-9.

Chapter 14: Monomythic Credotainment

1. "The Emerging Faith Communities of Cyberspace," *CMC Magazine* (March 1997) <http://www.december.com/cmc/mag/1997/mar/hend.html), viewed July 15, 2001.

2. The confession was later archived at Ahrens' own First Church of Simba/Corpus Mufasa Chapel <http://www.lionking.org/~kovu> and linked by numerous other Lion King Web sites.

3. Revelation 1:16; 19:11-21.

4. Neil Postman, *Amusing Ourselves to Death: Public Discourse in the Age of Show Business* (New York: Viking/Penguin Books, 1986), pp. 116-17.

5. *Encarta World English Dictionary* (New York: St. Martin's Press, 1999) defines 'infotainment' as "television programs that deal with serious issues or current affairs in an entertaining way" and 'edutainment' as "media content designed to entertain and educate the user at the same time."

6. The mixture of entertaining performance with evangelism and broadcast media was nothing new. The career of Aimee Semple McPherson, who performed showy revivals at her Angelus Temple, also created a radio station for evangelical broadcasts.

7. The Bakkers quickly fell from grace after a period of financial and sexual scandal that carried Jim Bakker to prison for several years.

8. John Strausbaugh, *E: Reflections on the Birth of the Elvis Faith* (New York: Blast Books, 1995), p. 13, italics in original.

9. *Experience and Education* (New York: Macmillan, 1938), p. 18.

10. See for example Garth Jowett, *Film: The Democratic Art* (Boston: Little, Brown, 1976), for an account of several different moral campaigns against motion pictures; James Gilbert, *A Cycle of Outrage: America's Reaction to the Juvenile in the 1950s* (New York: Oxford University Press, 1986), describes post-WWII campaigns against comic books, television, and films — all widely believed to be causes of youth crime in that period.

11. Bibleman action figures seen at Family Christian Stores Web site <http://www.familychristian.com/shop/product.asp?ProdID=4665>, viewed July 15, 2001.

12. Don Munsch, "Actor-now-Bibleman visits Amarillo," *Amarillo (TX) Globe-News* (May 9, 2000), <http://amarillonet.com>.

13. Tom Beaudoin, *Virtual Faith* (San Francisco: Jossey-Bass, 1998), p. 89.

14. Orville Schell, *Virtual Tibet: The Search for Shangri-La from the Himalayas to Hollywood* (New York: Metropolitan Books, 2000), p. 72. The detail regarding reincarnation comes from Tim McGirk, "Asia: Just Right for the Part," <http://www.time.com/time/magazine/1997/int/970908/asia.lama.html>.

15. "Steven Seagal Speaks: an interview with screenwriter Stanley Weiser," *Shambhala Sun Magazine*, November 1997, available at <http://www.shambhalasun.com/Archives/Features/1997/Nov97/Seagal.htm>, viewed July 5, 2001.

16. Schell, *Virtual Tibet*, pp. 68-69.

17. A presentation offered in Minneapolis, June 4-6, 2001, reported in *The Edge* (Summer 2001) <http://www.edgenews.com>, viewed July 2001.

18. An early interview-based account of his life — qualified by contradictory evidence culled by the journalist — appeared in Mary H. J. Farrell, "Sure, he's making a box office killing, but who is Stephen Seagal?" *People Weekly* (Nov. 19, 1990), p. 163 (4).

19. "The Buddha from another planet: action star Steven Seagal has been officially anointed an action lama," *Esquire* (Oct. 1997), p. 60 (2).

20. Ibid.

21. The legend about his nickname "Glimmer Man" is that "you see a flash of movement in the jungle and then you're dead."

22. Stanley Weiser, *Shambhala Sun Magazine.*

23. This category is focused on the spiritual teachings.

24. Posting by Anal Scurvy [sic] to Aikido Message Board, July 4, 2001. There is no way to know whether any real situation was actually depicted.

25. The film received the 1999 Academy Award for Best Visual Effects. "Bullet time" as a form of freeze frame photography is characterized at the Warner Brothers Web site <http://whatisthematrix.warnerbros.com/cmp/sfx-bullet_text.html>, viewed July 17, 2001.

26. *The Matrix* was released during the Easter weekend of 1999.

27. "*The Matrix* or Malebranche in Hollywood," *Philosophy Today* 11:26 (1999), pp. 11-26. This source and many others in this section were called to my attention by the excellent presentation and paper of Kelly J. Triezenberg and Annalee R. Ward, "*The Matrix:* A Sci-Fi Sermon," delivered at the American Culture/Popular Culture Associations, Annual Conference, Apr. 11-14, 2001, Philadelphia, Section 116.

28. "Chat with The Wachowski Brothers," <http://whatisthematrix.warnerbrothers .com>, viewed July 17, 2001.

29. "303" appears as a room number in several scenes.

30. Bob Harvey, "Spiritualism turns Matrix into cult fare," *The Ottawa Citizen* (Apr. 17, 1999).

31. "Youth Ministry: *The Matrix* Discussion and Bible Study," <http://www. mbnconf.ca/ideabank/0003/youth-1.html?view=p>, viewed July 18, 2001.

32. "*The Matrix:* there can be a redeeming message in the midst of violence," *The Collegian,* Mar 30, 2000. <http://collegian.asbury.edu/archives/2000/mar30_00/opinion.htm>, July 17, 2001.

33. Paul Fontana, "Generation Exile and Neo-restoration: a study of messianic hope in *The Matrix,*" a PDF file at <http://www.awesomehouse.com>, viewed Apr. 15, 2000.

34. Ibid., p. 28.

35. Triezenberg, "*The Matrix:* A Sci-Fi Sermon," p. 5. James L. Ford, "Buddhism, Christianity, and *The Matrix:* The Dialectic of Contemporary Mythmaking in the Cinema," *The Journal of Religion and Film* 4.2 (2000) <http://www.unomaha.edu/~wwwjrf/>, viewed July 10, 2001, has developed parallels between Yogacara Buddhism, which emphasizes the unreality of the experienced world, and *The Matrix.*

36. W. T. Jones, *The Medieval Mind,* 2nd ed. (New York: Harcourt, Brace and World, 1969), p. 61.

37. Jake Horsley, *The Blood Poets.* "Gnosticism Reborn: *The Matrix* as Shamanic Journey." <http://www.wynd.org/matrix.htm>, July 17, 2001.

38. Betsey Watson, "'It Is from Understanding That the Power Comes; and the Power in the Ceremony Was in Understanding What It Means': The Power and Importance of Malleability in the 1890 Ghost Dance," Fall 2000 Seminar Essay for the Newberry Library of Chicago. <www.albion.edu/English/Diedrich/Newberry2000/bwatson.htm>, viewed July 18, 2001.

39. Michael Hittman, *Wovoka and the Ghost Dance* (Carson City, Nev.: Grace Dangberg Foundation/Yerington Paiute Tribe, 1990), p. 84.

40. Cited by Watson from James R. Walker, *Lakotah Belief and Ritual*, ed. Raymond J. Demallie and Elaine A. Jahner (Lincoln: University of Nebraska Press, 1980), p. 143.

41. John G. Neihardt, *Black Elk Speaks: Being the Life Story of a Holy Man of the Oglalah Sioux* (Lincoln: University of Nebraska Press, 1961).

42. On July 22, 2001, Amazon.com listed 2437 books with 'angel' in the title and 979 with 'angel' as subject. Frank Peretti's *Piercing the Darkness* (1989) was reported with 1.4 million sales by 1995. Alissa Rubin, "Power Angels," *The New Republic* (Nov. 20, 1995), p. 21(2).

43. "Sign of a Dove," *Touched by an Angel* Episode 720 (Apr. 22, 2001), CBS.

44. Joanna Powell, *Good Housekeeping*, "The TV show that works miracles" (Apr. 1997), pp. 108ff.

45. The e-mail address is fanmail@touched.com; the Web site www.touched.com.

46. Abbreviated word for fan fiction.

47. A Web site where fan fiction is published.

48. Posted Feb. 10, 2001 at the unofficial "TBA Angel" Web site <http://www.cl.ais.net/ finbair/tbaangel.html>, which maintains the discussion list with the e-mail address <TBAAngel@onellist.com>. Fan fiction activities embrace the TBAA-Fanfic list and the TBAA Creative Connection <http://groups.yahoo.com/group/tbaa-fanfic>, both viewed July 20, 2001.

49. Ezines is a recent term combining electronic and fanzine.

50. In its seventh season, *Touched* earned a Prime-Time Nielsen Rating of 6.8 million homes in a week when the National Basketball Association finals were being played. Source: "Prime-Time Nielsen Ratings," Associated Press, June 11-17, 2001.

51. "Upchurch" is the short form of this name, which appears in the Web address, www.upchurch.org.

52. <http://www.upchurch.org>, viewed July 23, 2001; Reese discusses her own angel experiences and the work of her church in *Angels Along the Way: My Life with Help from Above* (New York: G. P. Putnam, 1997).

53. Burnham quoted in Trudy Bush, *The Christian Century* (Mar. 1, 1995), pp. 263ff.

54. Craig Wilson, "Hark and Hallelujah! The Angels Are Here," *San Jose Mercury News* (Oct. 28, 1992); quoted by Berit Kjos, "Touched by an Angel — But Which Kind?" <http:\\www.crossroad.to/text/articles/tbaa1297.html>, viewed June 26, 2001.

55. Timothy Jones and Andrew J. Bandstra, *Christianity Today* (Apr. 5, 1993), pp. 18ff.

56. "How I became an angel" (excerpt from *Angels Along the Way*), *Ladies' Home Journal* (Dec. 1, 1997), pp. 135f.

57. Berit Kjos, *A Twist of Faith* (Los Angeles: New Leaf Press, 1997).

58. Berit Kjos, "Touched by an Angel — But Which Kind?" <http://www.crossroad.to/ text/articles/tbaa1297.html>, viewed June 26, 2001.

59. "Is Being Touched by an Angel Enough?" Probe Ministries <http://www.probe.org/ docs/touched.html>, viewed July 23, 2001.

60. For the beliefs and the leader of the Heaven's Gate group, see "Inward Aum?" in Robert Jay Lifton, *Destroying the World to Save It: Aum Shinrikyo, Apocalyptic Violence and the New Global Terrorism* (New York: Metropolitan Books, 1999), pp. 303-325.

61. For details on the attack, see Lifton's chapter "Crossing the Threshold," pp. 202-13.

Chapter 15: The Discordant Music of Catastrophe

1. *The Macmillan Book of Proverbs, Maxims and Famous Phrases,* ed. B. Stevenson (New York: Macmillan, 1948), p. 2026.

2. Cited by Harry Zohn, *Karl Kraus* (New York: Twayne, 1971), p. 49.

3. Cited by Charles L. Sanford, *The Quest for Paradise: Europe and the American Moral Imagination* (Urbana: University of Illinois Press, 1961), p. 173.

4. So steady were the formulas of *Airport* that several parodies scored at the box office: *The Big Bus* (1976), *Airplane* (1980), and *Airplane II* (1982).

5. George Fox, *Earthquake: The Story of a Movie* (New York: Signet, 1974), p. 96.

6. Gustav Niebuhr, "U.S. 'Secular' Groups Set Tone for Terror Attacks, Falwell Says," *New York Times* (Sept. 14, 2001), p. A18. Falwell later apologized. Robertson had earlier predicted that a "Gay Days" event at Disney World in Orlando, Florida would likely provoke hurricanes.

7. Murray Schumach, *Face on the Cutting Room Floor* (New York: Da Capo Press, 1974), p. 45.

8. Hollis Alpert, *Saturday Review* (July 12, 1975), p. 51.

9. Carl Gottlieb, *Jaws Log* (New York: Dell, 1975), p. 69.

10. Stan Lee, *The Origin of Marvel Comics* (New York: Simon & Schuster, 1974), pp. 133-36.

11. "The Epic of Creation," *Larousse Encyclopedia of Mythology* (New York: Prometheus, 1959), p. 51.

12. Psalms 58:10-11, KJV.

13. 2 Kings 9:30 and 1 Kings 22:38, KJV.

14. *The Ante-Nicene Fathers: Translations of the Writings of the Fathers down to* A.D. *325,* ed. A. Roberts and J. Donaldson, Vol. III, *Latin Christianity: Its Founder, Tertullian,* tr. S. Thelwall (Grand Rapids: Eerdmans, 1957), p. 91.

15. Cited by William Ruehlmann in *Saint with a Gun* (New York: New York University Press, 1974), p. 97.

16. John Cawelti, "The Spillane Phenomenon," *Journal of Popular Culture* 3, no. 1 (1969): 16.

17. "*Desecration,* Left Behind Book #9, Hits Stores October 31, 2001," Press Release from Tyndale House, May 14, 2001; *Desecration* was scheduled for an advance printing of 3 million copies.

18. Jeffrey L. Sheler and Mike Tharp, "Dark Prophecies," *U.S. News and World Report* (Dec. 15, 1997), p. 62; Lindsey's book was the basis for a film narrated by Orson Welles — *The Late Great Planet Earth.* Dir. Robert Amram. Amram/RCR, 1976.

19. "Action Packed Bible film gets a push from faithful volunteers," *Knight-Ridder News Service* (Feb. 2, 2001), <http://www.krtdirect.com>, viewed July 11, 2001.

20. In identifying the UN as the agency of the Antichrist, *Left Behind* follows the plot of *A Thief in the Night.* Dir. Donald W. Thompson. Mark IV Pictures, 1972 (reissued in 2000 by Russ Doughten Films, Inc.).

21. Cf. Robert Jewett for critical examinations of the scriptural basis for rapture and the religious implications. *Jesus Against the Rapture: Seven Unexpected Prophecies* (Phila-

delphia: Westminster Press, 1979) and "Coming to Terms with the Doom Boom," *Quarterly Review* (Fall, 1984), pp. 9-22.

22. Zohn, *Kraus*, p. 46.

23. Karl Kraus, *Die Letzten Tage der Menschheit* (Munich: Deutscher Taschenbuch Verlag, 1964), Vol. II, p. 309. All translations from this work by the authors.

24. Zohn, *Karl Kraus*, p. 71.

Chapter 16: Deceptive Fugues, Democratic Dances

1. Cited by William V. Shannon, "Why Did Reagan Forsake His Men, His Policies and the Truth?" *Des Moines Register* (July 9, 1987).

2. Hearing of the Senate Foreign Relations Committee, Nomination of John Robert Bolton to be Undersecretary for Arms Control and International Security, Mar. 29, 2001, Federal News Service. Helms was Chair of the U.S. Senate Foreign Relations Committee.

3. See for example Robert Jewett's *The Captain America Complex: The Dilemma of Zealous Nationalism* (Philadelphia: The Westminster Press, 1973), especially Chapter 1, "A Rod of Iron or a Light to the Nations."

4. North's activities and political stances are enumerated at the Freedom Alliance Web site <http://www.freedomalliance.org>, viewed Aug. 5, 2001.

5. John Dean, "John Dean on Ollie: The Ugly Road Ahead," *Newsweek* (July 20, 1987), p. 29.

6. Jonathan Alter, "Ollie Enters Folklore," *Newsweek* (July 20, 1987), p. 19.

7. Maureen Dowd, "For the 'Can Do' colonel, admissions, no apology," *New York Times* (July 8, 1987), p. A1.

8. Cf. Tom Brokaw, "If Only He'd Known What He Knows Now When He Met North in 1985," *Des Moines Register* (July 7, 1987): on the basis of an interview in 1985, Brokaw reported North saying, "Not so long ago, I fought in a far-off war we were not allowed to win. I vowed it would never happen again."

9. Cheryl Lavin, "Ollie's War Captivates a Nation," *Chicago Tribune* (July 12, 1987), p. A1.

10. Ibid.

11. North explains the fakeries needed to execute his secret missions in the memoir *Under Fire: An American Story* (New York: Harper Collins, 1991), pp. 293-94.

12. R. W. Apple, Jr., "Fighting the Good Fight; North's view is that of a band of patriots opposed by an unreliable world," *New York Times* (July 9, 1987), p. A1.

13. Jonathan Alter, "Ollie Enters Folklore," *Newsweek* (July 20, 1987), p. 19.

14. Cheryl Lavin, "Ollie's War Captivates a Nation," p. A1.

15. One recalls in this connection that Rambo's being recruited for his mission occurred while he was in prison, where he was serving a sentence for having shot up a small town in Oregon.

16. David Broder, "King in This Land of the Blind," *Chicago Tribune* (July 15, 1987), p. 15.

17. "The Committee's Turn: Some Speeches to North," *New York Times* (July 14, 1987), p. A8; punctuation and quotes around the word "Enough!" are added.

18. R. W. Apple, Jr., "Legislators seize Iran spotlight, eclipsing North; a shared love of nation; with political stakes high, members lecture Colonel on their philosophies," *New York Times* (July 14, 1987), p. A1.

19. "Panel's case: bullets and the rule of law," *The New York Times* (July 15, 1987), p. A5.

20. Ibid., punctuation corrected.

21. North was still fuming about the Nuremberg comparison in his memoir *Under Fire*, complaining that "Those defendants had been ordered to kill people. I had been ordered to protect them" (375). He omits the circumstance of promoting secret warfare in Nicaragua, providing weapons to Iran — officially labeled as "unfriendly" at the time, and the fact of his military obligation to obey only lawful orders.

22. *Close Encounters of the Third Kind*. Dir. Steven Spielberg. Columbia Pictures, 1977. The film dominated the Academy Awards for the films of 1977 and subsequently earned more than $300 million in worldwide theatrical revenue. See the International Movie Database, <http://www.imdb.com>.

23. Steven Spielberg, *Close Encounters of the Third Kind* (New York: Dell, 1977), pp. 127-29. Spielberg issued an accurate novelization of the script in the same year as the film's release.

24. Thomas Jefferson, letter to William C. Jarvis (September 28, 1820), cited in Carl Cohen, *Communism, Fascism and Democracy: The Theoretical Foundations*, 2nd ed. (New York: Random House, 1972), p. 441.

25. *The Perfect Candidate*. Director-producers R. J. Cutler and David Van Taylor. Arpie Films, 1996.

26. President George H. W. Bush, who served from 1988 to 1992; Goodin was the deputy secretary of the Bush-Quayle campaign in 1987.

27. Stanley Kaufmann, "Epiphany," *The New Republic* (Dec. 10, 1977), p. 21; Martin Gardner, "The Third Coming," *The New York Review* (Jan. 26, 1978), p. 22.

28. Spielberg, *Close Encounters*, p. 249.

29. From Jefferson's letter to Jarvis, note 24 above.

30. Spielberg, *Close Encounters*, pp. 249f.

31. Quotation from "The Aliens Are Coming," *Time* (Nov. 7, 1977), p. 105.

32. Mary Early, "Review," *Today's Student* (Jan. 16, 1978).

33. Robert D. Putnam, *Bowling Alone: The Collapse and Revival of American Community* (New York: Simon and Schuster, 2000), p. 22.

34. Ibid., p. 242, using the words of political scientist Alan McBride.

35. This 1915 film is discussed in Chapter 2.

36. *Star Trek's* crew members in the later series are treated more equally and consulted by their captain, but they do serve at all times under military command — hardly a democratic model for civilian citizens.

37. See "Robert Gould Shaw," *The Columbia Encyclopedia*, Fifth Edition.

38. James M. McPherson, "Glory," in *Past Imperfect: History According to the Movies*, ed. Mark C. Carnes (New York: Henry Holt and Company, 1995), p. 128.

39. *The Straight Story*. Dir. David Lynch. Walt Disney Pictures, 1999.

40. The facts about Straight's journey were told in "Brotherly love powers a lawn mower trek," *New York Times* (Aug. 24, 1994) p. A12; and "Lawn day's journey: a 325-mile trek by mower reunites two brothers," *People Weekly* (Sept. 12, 1994), p. 108.

41. "*Straight Story* Wins Spiritual Quest Award," *The Christian Century* (Nov. 22, 2000), p. 1211. Richard Farnsworth, who played Alvin Straight, received a "Best Actor" Academy Award Nomination. The film also received many other nominations from other organizations, including several in Europe. See International Movie Database <http://www.imdb.org> for a listing of awards.

42. See Thomas May, "'Dead Man' is execution extraordinaire; Savvy writing, vivid music lift S.F. opera," *USA Today* (Oct. 9, 2000), p. D5.

43. Marc Bruno, "Sympathy for the Devil" (Interview), *Salon Magazine* <http://www.salon.mag.com/06/reviews/dead3.html>, viewed Oct. 7, 2000.

44. Sister Helen Prejean, "Address at Annual Public Gathering — November 6, 1999," American Friends Service Committee <http://www.afsc.org/crimjust/apgprejn.htm>, viewed Oct. 7, 2000.

45. This is the film name for a composite character derived from several in the book. In our exposition, we include details from both book and film, which truncates the scope of the book significantly.

46. This is the name of the real prisoner who corresponds in part to the film's Poncelet.

47. Helen Prejean, *Dead Man Walking* (New York: Random House, 1993), p. 64.

48. Marc Bruno, "Sympathy for the Devil."

49. These forms of behavior, which also entail the delivery of massive amounts of social services, lie behind President George W. Bush's emphasis on "faith-based initiatives" within government. The constitutionality of such relationships is another question entirely.

50. Rollo May, *Love and Will* (New York: W. W. Norton, 1969), p. 74.

51. Vincent Bugliosi, *Helter Skelter: True Story of the Manson Murders*, pp. 634, 561.

52. May, *Love and Will*, p. 110.

53. We refer readers here to a project on the Clinton presidency in which we both participated: Gabriel Fackre, ed., *Judgment Day at the White House: A Critical Declaration Exploring Moral Issues and the Political Use and Abuse of Religion* (Grand Rapids: Wm. B. Eerdmans Publishing Co., 1998).

54. Reinhold Niebuhr, *The Children of Light and the Children of Darkness: A Vindication of Democracy and a Critique of Its Traditional Defense* (New York: Charles Scribner's Sons, New Foreword edition, 1960), p. 118.

55. John McDermott, "Nature Nostalgia and the City: An American Dilemma," in *The Family: Communes and Utopian Societies*, ed. S. Teselle (New York: Harper & Row, 1971), pp. 11-12.

56. Frederick Wertham, *Seduction of the Innocent* (New York: Rinehart, 1954).

57. Friedrich Hacker, *Aggression: Die Brutalisierung der modernen Welt* (Hamburg: Rohwohlt, 1973), p. 21, our translation.

58. Hacker's study, *Terror: Mythos-Realität-Analyse* (Vienna: Molden Verlag, 1973), provides a provocative analysis of terrorism in the late 60s and early 70s; cf. especially Chap. V, "Macht und Ohnmacht des Schreckens."

59. Alfred North Whitehead, *Symbolism: Its Meaning and Effect* (New York: Macmillan, 1927), p. 88.

60. See Charles Lane, Don Phillips, and David Snyder, "A Sky Filled with Chaos, Uncertainty and True Heroism," *Washington Post* (Sept. 17, 2001), p. A3.

61. Jack Rakove, "From Pompeii to Flight 93," *San Francisco Chronicle* (Sept. 23, 2001), p. D1.

62. Plato, *Republic, The Collected Dialogues of Plato,* ed. E. Hamilton and H. Cairns, tr. P. Shorey (Princeton: Princeton University Press, 1961), p. 666.

Afterword

This book extends a long evolutionary project that began in the mid-1970s with a time-slice of American popular culture in *The American Monomyth* (Anchor Press/Doubleday, 1977). Some chapters from that book remain in altered form along with fragments of a second edition published by the University Press of America (1988). This book both updates and rearranges earlier material while adding seven new chapters. For this book, John Shelton Lawrence was the principal researcher and writer, but Robert Jewett has reviewed and edited the entire manuscript in shaping it for publication.

Our journey of interpretation has exorbitantly consumed the resources, time, and valued opinions of students, friends, family, colleagues and conference hosts. For this book, valued insights have come to us from Charles Ess, Jerry Israel, John Knepper, Eric D. Lawrence, Nancy Lawrence, Mark McDermott, Tim Orwig, Clara Sneed, Paul Somerville, and Anthony W. Thompson. Marty Knepper must be singled out as a generous friend who added perspective and precise detail to every chapter.

We take inspiration from these scholars who have made creative applications of our mythic paradigm in their own work: Robert Alan Brookey and Robert Westfelterhaus, James Combs, William G. Doty, Bruce D. Forbes, Douglas Kellner, George Lewis, Elizabeth and Jay Mechling, Jeffrey Schrank, Harold Schechter and Jonna Gormely Semeiks, David Sutton and J. Emmet Winn, and Bernard Timberg.

Library staffs that steadily assisted our research include Garrett-Evangelical Seminary of Northwestern University, the Graduate Theological Union Library at Berkeley, Morningside College, the University of California-Berkeley, and the

University of Texas-Austin. The collections of books and videos at the home of Rhonda Hammer and Douglas Kellner in Austin were an unsurpassable resource in 1998-1999. Anthony W. Thompson was very helpful in the scanning process for the images.

Finally, we must thank Reinder Van Til, our editor at Eerdmans Publishing, who had the vision of extending our previous work into the 21st century. His perspective, patience, and firmness provided the guidance that this book needed.

November 2001

JOHN SHELTON LAWRENCE
Berkeley, California
ROBERT JEWETT
Heidelberg, Germany

Index